DOGMATIC THEOLOGY

By

William G.T. Shedd
Roosevelt Professor of Systematic Theology
Union Theological Seminary
1874–1890

Second Edition

VOLUME III

SUPPLEMENT

 Thomas Nelson Publishers
Nashville

Library of Congress Catalog Card Number 80-19709
ISBN 0-8407-5223-7 hardbound
    0-8407-5743-3 paperbound

Printed in the United States of America

PREFACE

THE two volumes of Dogmatic Theology published in 1888 aimed to state and defend the Augustinian and Elder-Calvinistic theology. The great difference between this system and the several schools of Modern Calvinism, and also the Arminian theology, consists in the doctrine of the self-determined and responsible fall of mankind as a species in Adam. This makes original sin to be really and literally guilty and condemning in every individual who is propagated out of the species, instead of only nominally and fictitiously so. It also makes the origin of sin, and the consequent ruin of the race of mankind, to occur at the beginning of human history. The destiny of man was decided *wholly* in Adam, and not at all in the subsequent generations of individuals propagated from him. Individual life and individual transgression, which in modern theological systems are largely employed to explain the problem of original sin, become of no consequence. They are only the necessary effect of the real cause—the voluntary determination of the race in the primitive apostasy, of which St. Paul in the fifth chapter of Romans gives a full account. Schleiermacher presents an example of this tendency to explain generic sin by individual transgression. In the seventy-first section of his Glaubenslehre he argues elaborately to convert the original sin propagated from Adam into the individual transgressions committed by the posterity. The former, he contends, is guilt only as it is subsequently *adopted* by each man in separate and conscious acts. "It is impossible," he says, "that innate and inherited corruption should be guilty and condemning, if it be torn from its connection with the personal transgressions of the individual."

The purpose of this Supplementary Volume is to elaborate more carefully some of the difficult points in specific unity, partly by original explanations by the author, and partly by extracts from that class of theologians who have advocated it. The volume contains an amount of carefully selected citations from works in the Ancient, Mediæval, and Reformation periods, and also from the English and Continental divines of the 16th and 17th centuries, that are not easily accessible, and are an equivalent for a large library of treatises beyond the power of most clergymen and students to possess or have access to. The original matter connected with this endeavors to clear up the obscure features of an actual existence in Adam and a responsible agency in him.

The divisions of the Supplement are the same as those of the Dogmatic Theology, and the heads under them indicate the pages in the Dogmatics which find an explanation or a citation in the supplement. The author believes that the value of the two volumes of Dogmatic Theology will be substantially increased by the Supplementary Volume.

NEW YORK, September, 1894.

CONTENTS

THEOLOGICAL INTRODUCTION

VOL. I., p. 5. Twesten (Dogmatik I., 214) represents Melanchthon's method in the Loci Communes as Christological. "Passing over the doctrines of God, creation, providence, and even the person of Christ which Melanchthon subsequently supplied, he begins with the sinful and corrupt state of man, then proceeds to the Divine provision for the suppression and removal of this corruption, to the doctrines of the law and the gospel, of grace and its conditions and effects, and concludes with the ultimate result, the final decision of human destiny." There is a prevailing Christological tendency in the Lutheran dogmatics generally, compared with the Calvinistic. The Heidelberg Catechism shows this influence in treating of man's misery and man's redemption before discussing the Trinity.

VOL. I., p. 17. One great difference between Christian and pagan ethics consists in the more searching and truthful estimate of human character made by the former. The sense of sin which is elicited by the decalogue, as explained by the Sermon on the Mount, is far deeper than that produced by an ethics which omits the relations of man to God, and is confined to those between man and man. A comparison of the two will demonstrate this. St. Paul (Rom. 7: 14–24) says, "The law is spiritual; but I am carnal, sold under sin. I know that in me (that is, in my flesh) dwelleth no good thing; for to will is present with me, but how to perform that which is good I find not.

1

I see a law in my members warring against the law of my mind, and bringing me into captivity to the law of sin which is in my members. O wretched man that I am! who shall deliver me from the body of this death?" Says Augustine (Confessions, ix. 1; x. 2, 36), "Who am I, and what man am I? Rather what evil have I not been, either in my deeds, or if not in my deeds in my words, or if not in my words in my will? But thou, O Lord, art good and merciful, and thy right hand had respect unto the depth of my death, and from the bottom of my heart emptied that abyss of corruption. From thee, O Lord, unto whose eyes the abyss of man's conscience is naked, what could be hidden in me even though I would not confess it? I might hide thee from me, not me from thee. By these temptations we are assailed daily, O Lord; without ceasing, we are assailed. And in this way, thou commandest us self-denial. Give what thou enjoinest, and enjoin what thou wilt. Thou knowest on this matter the groans of my heart, and the floods of mine eyes. For I cannot learn how far I am cleansed from this plague, and I much fear my secret sins, which thine eyes know, mine do not." Says Richard Baxter (Dying Thoughts), "O thou that freely gavest me thy grace, maintain it to the last against its enemies, and make it finally victorious. O let it not fail and be conquered by blind and base carnality, or by the temptations of a hellish enemy; without it I had lived as a beast, and without it I should die more miserably than a beast. My God, I have often sinned against thee; but yet thou knowest I would fain be thine. I have not served thee with the resolution, fidelity, and delight as such a master should have been served, but yet I would not forsake thy service, nor change my master, or my work. I have not loved thee as infinite goodness, and love itself and fatherly bounty should have been loved, but yet I would not forsake thy family. Forsake not, then, a sinner that would not forsake thee, that looketh every hour toward thee, that feeleth it as a piece of hell to be so dark and strange unto thee." Says Leighton (On Ps. cxxx.) : "'If thou, Lord, shouldest mark iniquity, O Lord, who could stand?' An uninstructed and incautious reader might perhaps imagine that the Psalmist was here seeking for refuge in a crowd, and desirous of sheltering himself under the common lot of human nature; at least, that he would endeavor to find some low excuse for himself in the mention of its universal degeneracy. But the design of the sacred writer is far different from this. He confesses that whatever he or any other person, on a transient and inattentive glance, may imagine of his innocency, yet when the eye of the mind is directed inward in a serious and fixed manner, then he sees the sum and bulk of his sins to be so immensely great that he is even struck with astonishment by it; so that he finds himself beset as it were on every side with armed troops which cut off all possibility of escape otherwise than by flying to the Divine mercy, and to the freedom of pardoning grace. He perceives himself unable to bear the examination of an awakened conscience exercising itself in impartial self-reflection; and arguing from thence how much less he would be able to endure the penetrating eye and strict scrutiny of the Divine justice, he cries out as it were, in horror and trembling, under an apprehension of it, 'If thou, Lord, shouldest mark iniquity, O Lord, who could stand?' It cannot be doubted that they who daily and accurately survey themselves and their own hearts, though they may indeed escape many of those evils which the generality of mankind who live as it were by chance fall into, yet in consequence of that very care and study see so much the more clearly their own impurity, and contract a greater abhorrence of themselves, and a more reverent dread of the Divine judgments. It is certain that the holier and more spiritual any one is, the viler he is in his own eyes."

The Pagan estimate of human character is found in the

ethical writings of Plato and Aristotle, neither of whom
expresses any sense of personal guilt and corruption like
that contained in the above extracts from Christian writers,
though they acknowledge their own failure to attain the
philosopher's ideal, and condemn the crimes of the openly
vicious, and denounce the judgments of the gods upon
them. They describe man as ideal, rather than actual.
Aristotle defines the virtuous man as self-sufficient (αὐταρ-
κες), having resources within himself for right action and
happiness. " We attribute self-sufficiency to him who
lives for his parents, and children, and wife, and for his
friends and fellow-citizens. The proper work of man is
an energy of the soul according to reason. The goodness
which we are in search of will exist in the happy man, for
he will live in the practice of virtuous actions, will bear the
accidents of fortune nobly, and in every case as a man
truly good, a faultless cube. The virtues are produced in
us neither by nature nor contrary to nature, but we are
naturally adapted to attain them, and this natural capacity
is perfected by habit. By performing good actions in our
intercourse with men we become just " (Ethics, I., vii. ;
II., i.).

Plato (Republic, I., 330, 331) distinguishes between the
vicious who fear the punishments of the future world and
the virtuous who do not. " When a man thinks himself
to be near death, he has fears which never entered his
mind before ; the tales of a life below, and the punishment
which is exacted there for deeds done here, were a laugh-
ing matter to him once, but now he is haunted with the
thought that they may be true. Either because of the
feebleness of age, or from the nearness of the prospect, he
seems to have a clearer view of the other world; suspicions
and alarms crowd upon him, and he begins to reckon up
in his own mind what wrongs he has done to others, and
when he finds that the sum of his transgressions is great,
he is filled with dark forebodings. But he who is con-

scious of no sin has in old age a sweet hope which, as Pindar says, is a kind of nurse to him. 'Hope cherishes the soul of him who lives in holiness and righteousness, and is the nurse of his age and the companion of his journey.'" Plutarch (Pyrrhus and Marius) borrows and endorses the sentiments of Plato : "The avenging Fury began to punish Marius in this life, and call him to a severe account for all the blood he had spilt. So true is what Plato says, that the impious and wicked at the approach of death begin to fear everything of which they had made a mock before. Then does dread and distrust seize them, remorse torments them, and their only companion is despair. Whereas that person who can reproach himself for nothing, and who has spent his life in innocency, is always full of hope, which Pindar calls the tender nurse of old men. 'They,' saith he, 'who have walked in the ways of purity and justice are always possessed of that comfortable hope which is the tender nurse of age.' For it is an incontestable truth that a happy old age is a crown of glory, and is nowhere to be found but in the paths of justice."

The moral treatises of Cicero are remarkably devoid of the sense of personal sin and demerit, and are equally remarkable for their comparatively good ethics. Though subject to the doubts incident to natural religion, yet, in the main, Cicero defends with an eloquence and positiveness not exceeded by any pagan writer, the doctrines of the divine existence, the immortality and spirituality of the soul, the freedom of the will, of providence as against fate, and of future reward and punishment ; and his denunciation of vice and wickedness is earnest and vehement. But the virtuous man, he teaches, has nothing to fear in this life or the next from the divine tribunal. At the close of his treatise on Old Age he gives glowing expression to his feelings at the prospect of death. "I am not disposed to lament the loss of life, as many men, and those learned men, too, have done ; neither do I regret that I have lived, since I have lived in such a way that I conceive I was not born in vain; and from this life I depart as from a temporary home. For nature has assigned it to us as an inn to sojourn in, not a place of habitation. Oh, glorious day! when I shall depart to that divine company and assemblage of spirits, and quit this troubled and polluted scene. For I shall go not only to those great men of whom I have spoken before, but also to my son Cato, than whom never was better man born, nor more distinguished for pious affection. If I am wrong in this, that I believe the souls of men to be immortal, I willingly delude myself; nor do I desire this mistake in which I take pleasure should be wrested from me as long as I live; but if I when dead shall have no consciousness, as some narrow-minded philosophers imagine, I do not fear lest dead philosophers should ridicule this my delusion. Even if we are not destined to be immortal, yet it is a desirable thing for a man to expire at his fit time. For as nature prescribes a boundary to all other things, so does she also to life. Now old age is the consummation of life, just as of a play, from the fatigue of which we ought to escape, especially when satiety is superadded." Two thousand years later, from the plane of deism and natural religion, Hume (Essays, I., xvi.) presents the same general view of human virtue and the future state. "Glory is the portion of virtue, the sweet reward of honorable toils, the triumphant crown which covers the thoughtful head of the disinterested patriot, or the dusty brow of the victorious warrior. Elevated by so sublime a prize the man of virtue looks down with contempt on all the allurements of pleasure and all the menaces of danger. Death itself loses its terrors when he considers that its dominion extends only over a part of him, and that in spite of death and time he is assured of an immortal fame among all the sons of men. There surely is a Being who presides over the universe, and who with infinite wisdom and power has reduced the jarring elements into just order and proportion. Let speculative reasoners dispute how far this beneficent Being extends his care, and whether he prolongs our existence beyond the grave in order to bestow on virtue its just reward, and render it fully triumphant. The man of morals, without deciding anything on so dubious a subject, is satisfied with the portion marked out to him by the supreme Disposer of all things. Gratefully he accepts that further reward prepared for him; but, if disappointed, he thinks not virtue an empty name, but justly esteeming it its own reward he gratefully acknowledges the bounty of his Creator, who by calling him into existence has thereby afforded him an opportunity of once acquiring so invaluable a possession."

The Meditations of Marcus Aurelius contain this view of human self-sufficiency and virtue in an extreme form. Though often represented as teaching an excellent morality, they are defective in the highest degree: First, because the Stoic doctrine of fate is the foundation of the ethics; and second, because of the egotism and pride which pervade them. These two characteristics place the ethics of Antoninus upon a lower level than that of Plato, Aristotle, and Cicero, who combat the doctrine of fate and assert free-will; and do not claim for human nature such an exorbitant grade of moral excellence. The following extracts from Casaubon's translation evince this: 1. The doctrine of fate is taught in these terms: " The nature of the universe hath prescribed unto this man sickness, or blindness, or some loss or damage, or some such thing. Whatsoever doth happen to any is ordained unto him as a thing subordinate unto the fates. Nothing shall happen unto thee which is not according to the nature of the universe. All that I consist of is either form or matter. No corruption can reduce either of these to nothing; for neither did I of nothing become a subsistent creature. Every part of me, then, will by mutation be disposed into a certain part of the whole world ; and that in time into another part; and so in infinitum ; by which kind of mutation I also became what I am, and so did they that begot me, and they before them, and so upward in infinitum. Consider how swiftly all things that subsist, and all things that are done in the world are carried away and conveyed out of sight. For both the substances themselves as a flood are in continual flux, and all actions in a perpetual change ; and the causes themselves subject to a thousand alterations; neither is there anything that may be said to be settled and constant. Next unto this, and which follows upon it, consider both the infiniteness of the time already passed, and the immense vastness of that which is to come wherein all things are to be resolved and annihilated. Art thou not then a very fool who for these things art either puffed up with pride, or distracted with cares, or canst find in thy heart to make such moans as for a thing that would trouble thee for a very long time? Consider the whole universe whereof thou art but a very little part, and the whole age of the world together, whereof but a short and momentary portion is allotted unto thee and all the fates and destinies together. All substances come soon to their change, and either they shall be resolved by way of exhalation, if so be that all things shall be reunited into one substance, or shall be scattered and dispersed. As for that rational essence by which all things are governed, it best understandeth itself both its own disposition and what it doeth, and what matter it hath to do with. Let this be thy only comfort from one action to pass into another, God [*i.e.*, nature] being ever in thy mind. All things come to pass according to the nature and general condition of the universe, and within a very little while all things will be at an end ; no man will be remembered " (V., viii., x., xiii., xix.; VI. ; iv.–vi. ; VIII., iv.).

2. That man's duty and virtue consist in submitting his

will to the nature of the universe and to fate, is taught in these terms : " The matter itself of which the universe doth consist is very tractable and pliable. That rational essence that doth govern it hath in itself no cause to do anything that is evil ; neither can anything be hurt by it ; And all things are done and determined according to its will and command. Be it all one to thee, therefore, whether half frozen or well warm, whether only slumbering or after a full sleep, whether discommended or commended for doing thy duty, or whether dying or doing something else : for dying must be reckoned as one of the duties and actions of our lives. Even then also must it suffice thee that thou dost well acquit thyself of that duty of dying. Let not things future trouble thee. For if necessity so require that they come to pass, thou shalt be prepared for them by the same reason by which whatsoever is now present is made both tolerable and acceptable unto thee. All things are linked and knit together, and the knot is sacred, neither is there anything in the world that is not kind and natural in regard to any other thing. For all things are ranked together, and by that decency of its due place and order that each particular doth observe, they all concur together to the making of one and the same cosmos, or orderly composition. Through all things there is one and the same God, the same substance, the same law. There is one common reason, and one common truth that belong unto all reasonable creatures ; for neither is there more than one perfection of all creatures that are homogeneous and partakers of the same reason. To a reasonable creature the same action is both according to nature and according to reason. As several members in our body are united, so are reasonable creatures in one body divided and dispersed, all made and prepared for one common operation. And this thou shalt apprehend the better if thou use thyself often to say to thyself : I am a member (μέλος) of the mass and body of reasonable substance.

Through this substance of the universe, as through a torrent, pass all particular bodies, being all of the same nature and all joint-workers with the universe itself; as in one of our bodies so many members co-work among themselves. How many such as Chrysippus, how many such as Socrates, how many such as Epictetus hath the age of the world long since swallowed up and devoured. Let this come into thy mind upon every occasion, be it either of men or business, that thou hast to do work. Of all my thoughts and cares one only shall be the object: that I myself do nothing which is contrary to the constitution of man. The time when I shall have forgotten all things is at hand; and the time also is at hand when I myself shall be forgotten. Upon every action that thou art about put this question to thyself: How will this, when it is done, agree with me? Shall I have no occasion to repent of it? Yet a very little while, and I am dead and gone, and all things are at an end. What then do I care for more than this, that my present action may be the proper action of one that is reasonable; whose end is the common good; who in all things is ruled and governed by the same law by which God himself is?" (VI. i., ii.; VII., vi., viii., x., xvi.; VIII., ii.).

3. The self-sufficiency of man is taught in these terms: "The time of a man's life is as a point; the substance of it is ever flowing, and the whole composition of the body tending to corruption. His soul is restless, fortune uncertain, and fame doubtful; in brief, as a stream so are all things belonging to the body; as a dream or a smoke so are all things that belong unto the soul. Fame after life is no better than oblivion. What is it, then, that will remain and support? Only one thing, philosophy. And philosophy consists in this: For a man to preserve that spirit which is within him from all manner of contumelies and injuries, and above all, pains and pleasures; never to do anything either rashly, or feignedly, or hypocritically;

wholly to depend upon himself and his own proper actions; to embrace contentedly all things that happen unto him, as coming from him from whom he himself also came; and above all things, with meekness and a calm cheerfulness to expect death, as being nothing but the resolution of those elements of which every creature is composed. And if the elements themselves suffer nothing by this their perpetual conversion of one into another, why should that dissolution, which is common to all, be feared by any? Is it not thus according to nature? But nothing that is according to nature can be evil. He liveth with the gods who at all times affords unto them the spectacle of a soul both contented and well-pleased with whatsoever is allotted unto her, and performing whatsoever is pleasing to that spirit whom, being part of himself, love hath appointed to every man as his overseer and governor: which is, every man's intellect and reason. Let not this chief commanding part of thy soul be ever subject to any variation through any corporal pain or pleasure, but let it both circumscribe itself and confine those affections to their own proper parts and members. But if at any time they do reflect and rebound upon the mind and understanding, as in an united and compacted body it must needs be, then must thou not go about to resist sense and feeling, it being natural and necessary. How ridiculous and strange is he that wonders at anything that happens in this life in the ordinary course of nature! Either there is Fate and an absolute necessity and an unavoidable decree; or a placable and flexible Providence; or a universe of mere casual confusion, void of all order and government. If an absolute and unavoidable necessity, why dost thou resist? If a placable and exorable providence, make thyself worthy of divine help and assistance. If all be a mere confusion without any governor, then hast thou reason to congratulate thyself that in such a flood of confusion thou thyself hast obtained a reasonable faculty whereby thou mayest govern thine own life and actions" (II., xv.; V., xx., xxi.; XII., x., xi.).

The difference between these two estimates of human character, as has been remarked, is owing to the difference between the two standards. Christian ethics places the relation of man to God in the forefront, and tests him by his feelings and actions toward the Supreme Being. "Thou shalt love the Lord thy God with all thy heart," is the first and great commandment. It then passes to the relations of man to his fellow-men : "Thou shalt love thy neighbor as thyself." Tried by these two commandments human nature finds itself to be deeply defective and corrupt. Pagan ethics omits the first test. Its virtue does not consist in the love and service of God, but in outward fidelity to the family, society, and the state. If a man is free from vice, and reputably discharges his domestic, social, and civil duties, he is free from fault and entitled to the rewards of loyal obedience.

The Stoic philosophy was the source and support of this view of human nature and human virtue, and Milton (Paradise Regained, iv., 300–321) puts the following description of it into the mouth of Christ, in his reply to the suggestions of Satan :

> " The Stoic last in philosophic pride,
>   By him called virtue ; and his virtuous man,
>   Wise, perfect in himself, and all possessing
>   Equal to God, oft shames not to prefer,
>   As fearing God nor man, contemning all
>   Wealth, pleasure, pain, or torment, death and life,
>   Which when he lists, he leaves ; or boasts he can,
>   For all his tedious talk is but vain boast,
>   Or subtle shifts conviction to evade.
>   Alas, what can they teach, and not mislead !
>   Ignorant of themselves, of God much more,
>   And how the world began, and how man fell
>   Degraded by himself, on grace depending ?
>   Much of the soul they talk, but all awry,

And in themselves seek virtue, and to themselves
All glory arrogate, to God give none ;
Rather accuse him under usual names,
Fortune and fate, as one regardless quite
Of mortal things. Who therefore seeks in these
True wisdom, finds her not ; or by delusion
Far worse, her false resemblance only meets,
An empty cloud."

VOL. I., p. 28. Respecting the inferiority and unimportance of knowledge in physics compared with knowledge in morals and religion, Johnson (Life of Milton) remarks as follows : " The knowledge of external nature and of the sciences which that knowledge requires or includes is not the great or the frequent business of the human mind. Whether we provide for action or conversation, whether we wish to be useful or pleasing, the first requisite is the religious and moral knowledge of right and wrong ; the next is an acquaintance with the history of mankind, and with those examples which may be said to embody truth, and prove by events the reasonableness of opinions. Prudence and justice are virtues and excellences of all times and of all places ; we are perpetually moralists, but we are geometricians by chance. Our intercourse with intellectual nature is necessary ; our speculations upon matter are voluntary and at leisure. Physical learning is of such rare emergence that one may know another half his life without being able to estimate his skill in hydrostatics or astronomy ; but his moral and prudential character immediately appears."

Augustine (Enchiridion, ix.) notices the same fact. " When the question is asked what we are to believe in regard to religion, it is not necessary to probe into the nature of material things, as was done by those whom the Greeks call *physici ;* nor need we be in alarm lest the Christian should be ignorant of the force and number of the elements ; the motion and order and eclipses of the heavenly bodies; the form of the heavens; the species and natures of animals, plants, stones, fountains, rivers, mountains; about chronology and distances; the signs of coming storms, and a thousand other things which those philosophers either have found out, or think they have found out. For even these men themselves, endowed though they are with so much genius, burning with zeal, abounding in leisure, tracking some things by the aid of human conjecture, searching into others with the aids of history and experience, have not found out all things; and even their boasted discoveries are oftener mere guesses than certain knowledge. It is enough for the Christian to believe that the only cause of all created things, whether heavenly or earthly, whether visible or invisible, is the goodness of the Creator, the one true God; and that nothing exists that does not derive its existence from him; and that he is the Trinity; to wit, the Father, and the Son begotten of the Father, and the Holy Spirit proceeding from the same Father, but one and the same Spirit of Father and Son."

In the same vein Guizot (History of Civilization, Lecture iv.) remarks: "Moral sciences nowadays are accused of a want of exactitude, of perspicuity, of certainty; they are reproached as not being sciences. They should, they may be sciences, just the same as physical sciences; for they also are occupied with facts. Moral facts are not less real than others; man has not invented them; he discovered and named them; he takes note of them every moment of his life; he studies them as he studies all that surrounds him, all that comes to his intelligence by the senses. Moral sciences have, if the expression be allowed, the same matter of fact as other sciences; they are, then, not by any means condemned by their nature to be less precise or less certain. It is more difficult, I grant, for them to arrive at exactitude, perspicuity, precision. Moral facts are, on the one hand, more extended and more exact, and on the other, more profoundly concealed than physical facts ; they are at once more complex in their development and more simple in their origin. Hence arises a much greater difficulty of observing them, classifying them, and reducing them to a science. This is the true source of the reproaches of which the moral sciences have often been the subject. Mark their singular fate : they are evidently the first upon which the human race occupied itself ; when we go back to the cradle of societies we everywhere encounter moral facts, which, under the cloak of religion, or of poetry, attracted the attention and excited the thought of men. And yet in order to succeed in thoroughly knowing them, scientifically knowing them, all the skill, all the penetration, and all the prudence of the most practised reason is necessary. Such, therefore, is the nature of the moral sciences that they are at once the first and the last in the chronological order ; the first, the necessity of which works upon the human mind ; the last, that it succeeds in elevating to the precision, clearness, and certainty, which is the scientific characteristic."

Plato (Phaedo, 96–99) represents Socrates as asserting the inferiority of physical to moral science. "When I was young, Cebes, I had a prodigious desire to know that department of philosophy which is called natural science ($\phi\acute{v}\sigma\epsilon\omega\varsigma$ $\acute{\iota}\sigma\tau o\rho\acute{\iota}av$) ; this appeared to me to have lofty aims, as being the science which has to do with the causes of things, and which teaches why a thing is, and is created and destroyed ; and I was always agitating myself with the consideration of such questions as these : Is the growth of animals the result of some decay which the hot and cold principle contract, as some have said ? Is the blood the element with which we think, or the air, or the fire ? or perhaps nothing of this sort, but the brain may be the originating power of the perceptions of hearing and sight and smell, and memory and opinion may come from them [thought is cerebration], and science may be based on memory and opinion when no longer in motion but at rest. And then I went on to examine the decay of them, and then to the things of heaven and earth, and at last I concluded that I was wholly incapable of these inquiries. For I was fascinated by them to such a degree that my eyes grew blind to things that I had seemed to myself, and also to others, to know quite well; and I forgot what I had before thought to be self-evident. Then I heard some one who had a book of Anaxagoras, as he said, out of which he read that mind was the disposer and cause of all, and I was quite delighted at the notion of this which appeared admirable. I seized the book and read it as fast as I could. But, as I proceeded, I found my philosopher altogether forsaking mind, or any other principle of order, and having recourse to air, and ether, and water, and other eccentricities. I might compare him to a person who began by maintaining generally that mind is the cause of the actions of Socrates, but who, when he endeavored to explain the causes of my several actions in detail, went on to show that I sit here because my body is made up of bones and muscles; and the bones, as he would say, are hard and have ligaments which unite them, and the muscles are elastic, and they cover the bones, which have also a covering or environment of flesh and skin which contains them; and as the bones are lifted at their joints by the contraction or relaxation of the muscles, I am able to bend my limbs, and this is why I am sitting here in a curved posture; and he would have a similar explanation of my talking to you, which he would attribute to sound, and air, and hearing, and he would assign a multitude of causes of the same sort, forgetting to mention the true cause, which is, that the Athenians have thought fit to condemn me, and accordingly I have thought it better and more right to remain here and undergo my sentence; for I am inclined to think that these muscles and bones of mine would have gone off to Megara or Bœotia—by the dog of Egypt they would, if they had been guided only by their own idea of what is best, and if I had not chosen as the better and nobler part, instead of playing truant and running away, to undergo any punishment which the state inflicts. There is surely a strange confusion of causes and conditions in all this. It may be said, indeed, that without bones and muscles and the other parts of the body, I cannot execute my purposes. But to say that I do as I do because of them, and that this is the way in which mind acts, and not from the choice of the best, is a very careless and idle mode of speaking. I wonder that they cannot distinguish the cause from the condition."

Varro, in Cicero's Academical Questions (I., iv.), declares that "Socrates called philosophy away from the obscure subjects with which previous philosophers had been occupied, and brought it down to practical common life, namely, to the consideration of virtue and vice, good and evil; being of the opinion that questions in physics (cælestia) are difficult to be known, and if known contribute nothing to right living."

In periods noted for excessive attention to physical science the higher and finer products of literature decline. Originality and creative power in these provinces disappear, owing to the materializing influence of physical studies and observations, and only ephemeral composition is produced. The last decades of the nineteenth century, when standard treatises are displaced by periodicals and fiction, are an example.

Vol. I., p. 30. The necessity of postulating the agency of a personal Will in the origination and control of the impersonal forces of matter is shown by a writer in the Foreign Quarterly Review (Vol. III.), on Laplace's Celestial Mechanics. After remarking that the mathematical investigations of Newton, Clairaut, d'Alembert, Euler, Lagrange, and Laplace demonstrate the stability of the solar system, he says: "The conditions which assure its stability, and exclude all access to confusion are the three following : First, that the excentricities of the orbits are inconsiderable, and their variations confined to very narrow limits.   Second, that all the planets, primary and second-ary, move in the same direction.   Third, that the inclina-tions of their orbits to the plane of the ecliptic are very small.   These conditions *are not necessary consequences of gravitation or of mechanical motion ;* of their prime causes, however, we are entirely ignorant, and probably will ever remain so : some barrier will always be interposed between the curiosity of man and Omniscience.   They cannot for a moment be admitted to result from *chance ;* for on com-paring, by means of the calculus of probabilities, the unique combination on which they depend with all the other combinations possible, it is found that there is almost infinity to wager against one, that the arrangement of the system is *the effect of a special cause.*"

The origination of curvilinear motion requires the agency of a Power higher than that of matter, because it cannot be produced by the forces inherent in matter.   The cur-vilinear motion of a planet around its central sun requires *two* motions in order to account for it ; namely, a cen-tripetal motion and a tangential.   If the earth obtains a tangential motion which causes it to move away into space, while at the same time it has a pull toward its solar cen-tre, the result will be a circular movement.   The force of gravitation will give the latter, but not the former.   None of the forces of attraction inherent in matter are tangential. They are all centripetal.   There must, therefore, be a tan-gential *impulse* given ab extra, if there is to be the move-ment of a body in an orbit.   And this tangential impulse can come only from the Creator of matter, by an exertion of will similar to that by which a man gives a tangential, or lateral, impulse to a stone that is falling in a perpendic-ular line by the force of gravity.   Were there only the centripetal force of attraction, every planetary mass would merely be pulled into its sun and remain there. The orbital motion cannot therefore be explained by the force of attraction between particles of matter. The writer of the article " Mechanics," in the Penny Cyclopædia, describes Newton as postulating a tangential impulse along with the centripetal attraction, in his Principia. " The Principia commences with the three well-known laws of motion. Assuming, then, as an hypothesis, that all the bodies of the universe and all the particles of every body exert on each other mutual attractions ; *assuming also* that the planetary bodies were originally *put in motion* [tangentially] *by impulsive forces ;* the rotations of these bodies on their axes, their revolutions in their orbits, and all the perturbations by which these movements are varied, are explained by means of the elementary theorem for the composition and resolution of motions." According to this, the rotary motion of the earth on its axis is the resultant of two motions, only one of which can be explained by the attraction of gravitation ; and so also is its orbital motion. There are two " assumptions," namely, that of the inherent attraction of matter, and that of an " impulsive force." But inherent attraction has no " impulse," and cannot impart one.

And this is not all. For the tangential force requisite to curvilinear motion that proceeds from a personal Will, requires to be perpetuated by the same Will that originated it, because of the resistance and impeding by the ether in which the planet moves. If not continually reinforced by the prime Mover, it will cease. Not only, therefore, must the first tangential " impulse " be imparted, but it must be perpetuated by the author of it.

" The doctrine of a resisting medium," says Whewell (Astronomy and General Physics, II., viii.), " leads us toward a point which the nebular hypothesis assumes : a *beginning* of the present order of things. There must have been a commencement of the motions now going on in the solar system.   Since these motions, when once begun, would be deranged and destroyed in a period which, however large, is yet finite, it is obvious we cannot carry their origin indefinitely backward in the range of past duration. There is a period in which these revolutions, whenever they had begun, would have brought the revolving bodies into contact with the central mass ; and this period has in our system not yet elapsed.   The watch is still going, and therefore, it must have been wound up within a limited time.   The solar system, at this its beginning, must have been arranged and put in motion by some cause.   If we suppose this cause to operate by means of the configurations and the properties of previously existing matter, these configurations must have resulted from some still previous cause, these properties must have produced some previous effects.   We are thus led to a condition still earlier than the assumed beginning—to an origin of the original state of the universe ; and in this manner we are carried perpetually further and further back, through a labyrinth of mechanical causation, without any possibility of finding anything in which the mind can acquiesce or rest, till we admit a First Cause which is not mechanical [but voluntary]."

Whewell (Astronomy and General Physics, I., xviii.) continues his argument as follows : " It has been shown in the preceding chapters that a great number of quantities and laws appear to have been *selected*, in the construction of the universe ; and that by the adjustment to each other of the magnitudes and laws thus selected, the constitution of the world is what we find it, and is fitted for the support of vegetables and animals in a manner in which it could not have been if the properties and quantities of the elements had been different from what they now are.   We shall here recapitulate the principal of the laws and magnitudes to which this conclusion has been shown to apply."

" 1. The length of the year, which depends on the force

of the attraction of the sun, and its distance from the earth. 2. The length of the day. 3. The mass of the earth, which depends on its magnitude and density. 4. The magnitude of the ocean. 5. The magnitude of the atmosphere. 6. The law and rate of the conducting power of the earth. 7. The law and rate of the radiating power of the earth. 8. The law and rate of the expansion of water by heat. 9. The law and rate of the expansion of water by cold below forty degrees. 10. The law and quantity of the expansion of water in freezing. 11. The quantity of latent heat absorbed in thawing. 12. The quantity of latent heat absorbed in evaporation. 13. The law and rate of evaporation with regard to heat. 14. The law and rate of the expansion of air by heat. 15. The quantity of heat absorbed in the expansion of air. 16. The law and rate of the passage of aqueous vapor through air. 17. The laws of electricity; its relations to air and moisture. 18. The fluidity, density, and elasticity of the air, by means of which its vibrations produce sound. 19. The fluidity, density, and elasticity of the ether, by means of which its vibrations produce light."

"These are the *data*, the *elements*, as astronomers call the quantities which determine a planet's orbit, on which the mere *inorganic* part of the universe is constructed. To these the constitution of the organic world is adapted in innumerable points by laws of which we can trace the results though we cannot analyze their machinery. Thus the vital functions of vegetables have periods which correspond to the length of the year and of the day; their vital powers have forces which correspond to the force of gravity; the sentient faculties of man are such that the vibrations of air, within certain limits, are perceived as sound, those of ether as light. And while we are enumerating these correspondences we perceive that there are thousands of others, and that we can only select but a very small number of those where the relation happens to be most clearly made out, or most easily explained."

"Now, in the list of the mathematical *elements* of the universe which has just been given, *why have we such laws and such quantities as occur, and no other ?* For the most part the data there enumerated are *independent of each other*, and might be *altered separately,* so far as the mechanical conditions of the case are concerned. Some of these data probably depend on each other. Thus the latent heat of aqueous vapor is perhaps connected with the difference of the rate of expansion of water and of steam. But all natural philosophers will probably agree that there must be in this list a great number of things entirely without mutual dependence—such as the year and the day, the expansion of air and the expansion of steam. There are, therefore, it appears, a number of things which in the structure of the world might have been otherwise, and which are what they are in consequence of choice, or else of chance. We have already seen, in many of the cases separately, how unlike chance everything looks—that substances which might have existed anyhow, so far as they themselves alone are concerned, exist exactly in such a manner and measure as they should, to secure the welfare of other things ; that the laws are tempered and fitted together in the only way in which the world could have gone on, according to all that we can conceive of it. This must, therefore, be the work of *choice ;* and if so, it cannot be doubted, of a most wise and benevolent Chooser."

"The appearance of choice is still further illustrated by the variety, as well as the number, of the laws selected. The laws are unlike one another. Steam certainly expands at a very different *rate* from air by the application of heat, and probably according to a different *law ;* water expands in freezing, but mercury contracts ; heat travels in a manner quite different through solids and through fluids. Every separate substance has its own density, gravity, cohesion, elasticity, its relations to heat, to electricity, to magnetism, besides all its chemical affinities, which form an endless throng of laws connecting every one substance in creation with every other, and different for each pair, however taken. Nothing can look less like a world formed of atoms operating upon each other, according to some universal and inevitable laws, than this does; if such a system of things be conceivable, it cannot be our system. We have, it may be, fifty simple substances in the world; each of which is invested with properties, and both chemical and mechanical action, altogether different from those of any other substance. Each portion, however minute, of any of these, possesses all the properties of the substance. Of each of these substances there is a certain definite and fixed quantity in the universe; when combined their compounds exhibit new chemical affinities, new mechanical laws. Who gave these different properties to the different simple substances? Who proportioned the quantity of each? But suppose this done. Suppose these simple primary substances in existence; in contact; in due proportion to each other. Is *this* a world, or at least our world? No more than the mine and the forest are the ship of war or the factory. These elements, with their constitution perfect, are still a mere chaos. They must be put in their places. They must not be where their own properties would place them. They must be made to assume a particular arrangement, or we can have no regular and permanent course of nature. This arrangement must again have additional peculiarities, or we can have no *organic* portion of the world. The millions of millions of particles which the world contains must be finished up in as complete a manner, and fitted into their places with as much nicety, as the most delicate wheel or spring in a piece of human machinery. What are the habits of thought to which it can appear possible that this could take place without design, intention, intelligence, purpose, knowledge? "

" In what has thus far been said we have spoken only

of the constitution of the *inorganic* part of the universe. The mechanism, if we may so call it, of vegetable and animal life is so far beyond our comprehension that, although some of the same observations might be applied to it, we do not dwell upon the subject. We know that in these processes, also, the mechanical and chemical properties of matter are necessary; but we know, too, that these alone will not account for the phenomena of life. There is something more than these. The lowest stage of vitality and irritability appears to carry us beyond mechanism, beyond chemical affinity. All that has been said with regard to the exactness of the adjustments, the combination of the various means, the tendency to continuance, to preservation, is applicable with additional force to the *organic* creation, so far as we can perceive the means employed."

VOL. I., p. 38. Sensible objects may be differently conceived of at the same moment; but moral and spiritual objects cannot be. A man may have simultaneously two diverse ideas of the sun; one from the senses and one from the mind. The first makes the sun a small body—as large as a cart-wheel. The last makes it an immense body—800,000 miles in diameter. The first is the idea of the savage; the last is that of the astronomer. But a man cannot have two such diverse ideas of God simultaneously. If he conceives that God is a wooden idol, he must renounce this idea in order to conceive of God as a spirit. He cannot conceive of God as related both to the senses and the mind; as being both an idol and a spirit. But if he conceives of the sun as being as large as a cart-wheel for the senses, it is not necessary that he should renounce the idea that it is 800,000 miles in diameter for the mind.

VOL. I., p. 44. The following are some of the great discoveries in physics which have been made by believers in Christianity: The heliocentric theory, by Copernicus; the laws of planetary motion, by Kepler; the law of gravitation, by Newton ; the sexual system in botany and the classification of the vegetable and animal systems, by Linnæus ; the circulation of the blood, by Harvey ; the identity of fixed alkalies and metallic oxides, by Davy ; magneto-electric induction and electro-chemical decomposition, by Faraday ; and the distinction between the nerves of motion and sensation, by Bell.

BIBLIOLOGY

Vol. I., p. 62. Under the general form of inspiration must be placed that of Bezaleel. His inventive skill and knowledge is attributed to God as its source. "I have filled him with the spirit of God to devise cunning works" (Ex. 31 : 3, 4). But more than such knowledge, coming through the natural and acquired qualities of the mind, is involved in the particular directions which Moses received in the mount respecting the general form of the tabernacle and its furniture : "Look that thou make them after their pattern which was shewed thee in the mount" (Ex. 25 : 40). This direction is referred to again in Exodus 26 : 30; 27 : 8 ; Num. 8 : 4 ; Acts 7 : 44 ; Heb. 8 : 5. This ocular vision of the form and figure of the tabernacle and its utensils would fall under the head of special revelation, like the visions of Ezekiel and St. John.

Vol. I., p. 72. Plenary inspiration is opposed to partial inspiration. It means that all the divisions of Scripture—history, chronology, geography, and physics, as well as doctrine—were composed under the infallible guidance of the Holy Spirit. The inspiration is full (plenus). Partial inspiration limits the operation of the Holy Spirit to the doctrinal part of the Bible, leaving the other parts to the possibility of error. Verbal inspiration may be associated with either view, or dissociated from either. He who asserts plenary inspiration may affirm that the language is inspired, or deny that it is; and so may he who asserts

partial inspiration. The assertion or denial depends upon
the view taken of the nature of language, and its relation
to thought. He who regards the relation as natural and
necessary, and holds that thoughts inevitably suggest
words, will hold that inspired thought is expressed in
inspired language. He who regards the relation as arbitrary and artificial, will hold that only the thought is
inspired. The elder theologians universally, like Turrettin
and Quenstedt, held both plenary and verbal inspiration.
And those who adopt the dynamical theory of language
should, logically, hold both.

VOL. I., p. 74. Augustine teaches the inerrancy of
Scripture in explicit terms. " It seems to me that most
disastrous consequences must follow upon our believing
that anything false is found in the sacred books ; that is
to say, that the men by whom the Scriptures have been
given to us, and committed to writing, did put down in
these books anything false. It is one question whether it
may be at any time the duty of a good man to deceive;
but it is another question whether it can have been the
duty of a writer of Holy Scripture to deceive—nay, it is
no question at all. For if you once admit into such a
high sanctuary of authority one false statement as officially
made, there will not be left a single sentence of those
books which, if appearing to any one difficult in practice
or hard to believe, may not by the same fatal rule be explained away, as a statement in which, intentionally, and
under a sense of duty, the author declared what was not
true " (Letter xxviii., 3. To Jerome, A.D. 394). " I have
learned to yield such [absolute] respect and honor only to
the canonical books of Scripture ; of these alone do I most
firmly believe that the authors were completely free from
error. And if in these writings I am perplexed by anything which appears to me opposed to truth, I do not
hesitate to suppose that either the manuscript is faulty, or
the translator has not caught the meaning of what was

said, or I myself have failed to understand it. As to all other writings, in reading them, however great the superiority of the authors to myself in sanctity and learning, I do not accept their teaching as true on the mere ground of the opinion being held by them ; but only because they have succeeded in convincing my judgment of its truth either by means of these canonical writings themselves, or by arguments addressed to my reason " (Letter lxxxii., 3. To Jerome, A.D. 405). "The Manichæans maintain that the greater part of the New Testament, by which their wicked error is confuted in the most explicit terms, is not worthy of credit, because they cannot pervert its language so as to support their opinions. Yet they lay the blame of the alleged mistake not upon the apostles who originally wrote the words, but upon some unknown corruptors of the manuscripts. Forasmuch, however, as they have never succeeded in proving this by *earlier manuscripts*, or by appealing to the *original language* from which the Latin translations have been made, they retire from the debate vanquished by truth which is well known to all" (Letter lxxxii., 6). "If you recall to memory the opinion of our Ambrose and Cyprian on the point in question, you will find that I have had some in whose footsteps I have followed in what I have maintained. At the same time, as I said already, it is to the canonical Scriptures alone that I am bound to yield such implicit subjection as to follow their teaching without admitting the slightest suspicion that in them any mistake, or any statement intended to mislead, would find a place " (Letter lxxxii., 24).

VOL. I., p. 82. Two general answers have been given to the question respecting the origin of the four Gospels. 1. The oldest and most universal is, that they had an *apostolical* origin, being composed by the four authors whose names they bear, who derived their information, two of them immediately and two of them mediately, from personal intercourse with Jesus Christ during his ministry

upon earth. Two of them, Matthew and John, belonged
to that company of "Twelve Apostles" who were specially
called and supernaturally endowed by Christ to be the
founders of the Christian Church (Matt. 10 : 1–16 ; Eph. 2 :
20) ; and two of them, Mark and Luke, were secretaries
under the superintendence of Peter and Paul, who also belonged to the apostolic college. That Paul was one of
"The Twelve" is proved by Rom. 1 : 1 ; 1 Cor. 1 : 1 ; 9 : 1 ;
15 : 3 ; Gal. 1 : 1, et alia. According to this traditional
view, each of the four Gospels has an individual origin like
secular writings generally. As Plato was the author of the
Phædo, and Thucydides of the History of the Peloponnesian
War, so Matthew was the author of the first Gospel, Peter-
Mark of the second, Paul-Luke of the third, and John of
the fourth. 2. The second and latest answer is, that the
four Gospels had an *ecclesiastical* origin. They sprang
from oral traditions concerning Christ that were current in
the first Christian brotherhood, and were gradually collected and combined by persons whose names are unknown.
This view has been invented by the rationalistic and pseudo-
critical schools, in opposition to the historical and catholic,
and has done more than anything else to destroy confidence
in the inspiration and infallibility of the life of Jesus Christ
as recorded by the four Evangelists. The unproven assumptions and innumerable hypotheses which have characterized the rationalistic schools of Biblical criticism in
Germany since the time of Semler are due to the substitution of the ecclesiastical origin of the Gospels for the
apostolic. So long as the life of Christ is referred to four
known and authorized persons, who from Justin Martyr
down are quoted by all the Fathers as the inspired writers
of the Gospels, there is no room for fancy and conjecture
respecting its origin. The testimony of the whole patristic
literature can be cited to substantiate this view. But the
moment it is surrendered and the Gospels are ascribed to
unknown and unauthorized persons who glean from the

legends of the Church, the way is opened for capricious conjectures and assumptions for which no proof can be furnished from the original manuscripts of the Gospels, or from the writings of the primitive Fathers and the history of the first centuries of the Christian Church, and which have to be accepted upon the mere assertion and assurance of their inventors. Of late years, and particularly at the present moment, the rationalistic theory has worked itself considerably into the Church, and is adopted by some otherwise evangelical scholars. There is, indeed, a difference in spirit and intention between the rationalistic and the "evangelical" critics who adopt the theory of a legendary origin of the Gospels; between Baur and Strauss, and Bleek and Weiss; but the fatal error of deriving the life of Christ from unauthorized, uninspired, and unknown sources cleaves to both alike. And the actual influence of the "evangelical" critic of this class is more unsettling upon the belief of the Church than that of the rationalist and skeptic, because error in a believer has more influence within the Church than error in an unbeliever has. There will be no improvement in this "evangelical" class of exegetes until there is a return to the apostolical origin of the Gospels. We present the following objections to the ecclesiastical origin of the Gospels:

1. It was not the view adopted by the Ancient Church, which was nearest in time to the composition of the Gospels. In classical philology, the consensus of the earliest ages weighs more than the hypothesis of a late critic or school respecting the authorship of the Iliad and Æneid, and the Greek and Latin literature generally. Philologists of all ages have accepted these works as the productions of the individual authors whose names have from the beginning been associated with them, and not of unknown collectors and editors, because of historical traditions that are as ancient as those which ascribe the Gospels to Matthew, Mark, Luke, and John. An attempt to set aside the

traditional testimony and to substitute for it the unproven
conjecture of a modern philologist, that the Platonic writings are not the work of the individual Plato, but of a circle
of unknown editors of oral traditions about the teachings
of Socrates, would meet with no credit.   The answer would
be, that the ancient opinion is far more probable than the
modern, because coming from centuries that had better
facilities than the nineteenth for determining the authorship of poems and histories composed two thousand years
ago.

The Ancient Church, with a unanimity even greater, perhaps, than upon any of the purely dogmatic questions that
arose among them, believed that the Gospels had an *apostolical* origin, not an ecclesiastical; that they were narratives of the life of Christ prepared by those persons who
" companied together all the time that the Lord Jesus went
in and out, beginning from the baptism of John unto that
same day that he was taken up," and who were " ordained
to be witnesses of his resurrection " (Acts 1 : 21, 22).   The
details of the proof of this cannot be given here.   It was
first collected and combined by Eusebius, and since the
Reformation has often and again been collected and re-
stated by a multitude of learned scholars like Lardner and
Michaelis.   The Apostolic Fathers, Justin Martyr, Irenæus,
Tertullian, Cyprian, Origen, Eusebius, Jerome, and Augustine, represent the opinion of the Ancient Church, and they
uniformly ascribe the four Gospels to the four biographers
whose names then as now were connected with them in the
Church generally.   These Fathers knew nothing of a canonical and commonly accepted life of Christ composed by unknown persons out of ecclesiastical legends.   The apoc-
ryphal Gospels, which were constructed in this way, they
carefully distinguished from the canonical, and rejected as
not authoritative for the Church.   Some of the Fathers, like
Origen and Jerome, were trained philologists, and others,
like Irenæus and Augustine, were men of strong and clear

minds and competent to weigh testimony, and none of them adopts such a theory as the one in question. If there had been such editors and authors they would have been contemporary with some of these Fathers, and would have been both mentioned and combated in their writings.

The testimony of Irenæus, whose Adversus Hæreses was written A.D. 182–188, to the apostolical authorship of the Gospels is as follows: "The Lord of All gave to his *apostles* the power of the gospel, through whom we have known the truth, that is the doctrine of the Son of God; to whom also did the Lord declare, 'He that heareth you heareth me, and he that despiseth you despiseth me and him that sent me'" (Preface). "We have learned from none others the plan of our salvation than from *those through whom the Gospel has come down to us*, which *they did at one time proclaim in public*, and at a later period, by the will of God, *handed down in the Scriptures* to be the pillar and ground of our faith. For after our Lord rose from the dead the apostles were invested with power from on high when the Holy Spirit came down upon them, were filled with his gifts, and had perfect knowledge [of the life and doctrine of Christ]. Matthew also issued a written Gospel among the Hebrews in their own dialect [in addition to his original Greek Gospel] while Peter and Paul were preaching at Rome and laying the foundations of the Church. After their decease, Mark, the disciple and interpreter of Peter, did also hand down to us in writing what had been preached by Peter. Luke also, the companion of Paul, recorded in a book the Gospel preached by him. Afterwards, John, the disciple of the Lord, who also had leaned upon his breast, did himself publish a Gospel during his residence at Ephesus in Asia" (Adv. Hæreses, III. i.). The writer of this evidently knew nothing of a gradual origin of the Gospels from ecclesiastical traditions and by unknown authors. And his view, declared within a century from the death of the last of the apostles, is without

3

an exception that of all the Christian Fathers and of the Patristic Church.

Says Thompson, "The quotations of Justin Martyr from the Gospels are about 110 from Matthew, 14 from Mark, 57 from Luke, and 29 from John—in all, more than 200. They are of every class: exact verbal quotation, verbal quotation with some variation, and allusion with little or no verbal agreement. The predominant mode is somewhat inexact, as though the quotations were from memory" (Introduction to the Gospels, in the Speaker's Commentary). For a thorough refutation of the legendary origin of the Gospels, see this Introduction, §§ 4–15, 32, 39, 43, 46, 52–57.

Neither do the Skeptical and Heretical writers of the first four centuries take any different view of the origin of the Gospels. They, too, refer them to individual authors, and to the same that the Church referred them. Gnostics like Basilides, Valentinus, and Marcion, and skeptics like Lucian, Celsus, and Porphyry, agree with the Christian Fathers in ascribing them to the four evangelists. The two brief quotations from John's Gospel (1 : 9 ; 2 : 4), contained in a fragment from Basilides (A.D. 110–120), found in the lately discovered treatise of Hippolytus, have done as much as any one thing to refute the conjecture of Baur and his school, that the Gospels were the gradual production of two or three centuries, instead of being the immediate product of the apostolic college. Strenuous attempts have been made to invalidate this consensus of all classes of writers of the first four centuries by modern theorists, among whom the author of Supernatural Religion is as ingenious as any. The garbled treatment to which he subjects the early patristic literature, to serve the end he has in view, has been conclusively exposed by the late Bishop of Durham. That this attempt is a desperate effort on the part of this class of critics, because the testimony of the Ancient Church is wholly against it, is evinced

by the great number of their hypotheses, the wearisome in-
genuity of their conjecturing, their continual correction and
contradiction of each other, and their transiency. There
is no consensus among them, and no permanence. They
are born and die one after another. The traditional view
of the origin of the Gospels, on the contrary, is one and the
same, harmonious and unchanging. From Eusebius down
to the latest apologist there is a single strong current of
opinion which is not diminished by any of the new facts
arising from time to time, but is increased by them.

2. The Gospels do not wear the appearance of having
been composed of legendary materials, put together by
a number of collectors and editors. They read like the
productions of individual authors. Each Gospel has its
own marked and striking characteristics, indicative of an
individual mind. These have been abundantly analyzed
and described by experts of all classes. A body of collectors and editors, especially if their work ran through
two or three centuries, could not have so fused their materials and blended their mental peculiarities as to make such
a single and homogeneous impression.

3. The Gospels are represented by their authors as
remembered by themselves, not as collected and received
from others. The matter is described as ἀνάμνησις. John
2 : 22 : " His disciples remembered that Jesus had said
this unto them." John 14 : 26 : " The Holy Ghost shall
teach you all things, and bring all things to your remembrance, whatsoever I have said unto you." Compare also
John 12 : 16 ; 15 : 20 ; 16 : 4 ; Luke 24 : 6 ; Acts 11 : 16.
This is not the gathering up of traditions current among
the Christian brotherhood, but the careful narration of
what the writers had themselves seen and heard during
their three years of daily intercourse with their divine Lord,
who had called and separated them from all other men to
lay the foundations of his Church, by composing for it the
inspired writings which must be its foundation, and by

overseeing its first organization. The Apostle Peter tersely states the case. "We have not followed cunningly devised myths, when we made known unto you the power and coming of the Lord Jesus Christ, but were eye-witnesses of his majesty" (2 Pet. 1 : 16). St. Paul represents his knowledge of Jesus Christ as independent even of the other apostles, and of course of the Christian brotherhood. He claims to be "an apostle, not of men, neither by man, but by Jesus Christ" (Gal. 1 : 1); distinctly says : "The gospel which was preached by me is not after man, for I neither received it of man, neither was I taught it but by the revelation of Jesus Christ" (Gal. 1 : 11, 12); declares that immediately after his conversion he did not go "up to Jerusalem to them which were apostles before him, but went into Arabia, and returned again to Damascus," and that three years after he "went up to Jerusalem to see Peter, but other of the apostles saw he none, save James the Lord's brother," and that, "fourteen years after he went up again to Jerusalem by revelation, and communicated unto them which were of reputation that gospel which he had preached among the Gentiles," and that in the "conference" which he had with the other apostles, they "added nothing" to his knowledge of Jesus Christ or his gospel (Gal. 1 : 17; 2 : 16). And, lastly, he boldly puts the question, challenging all denials, "Am I not an apostle? Have I not seen Jesus Christ our Lord?" (1 Cor. 9 : 1). When, therefore, St. Paul speaks of a tradition which he "received" (1 Cor. 15 : 3), he does not mean an ecclesiastical or even an apostolical tradition, but that body of knowledge concerning Christ and Christianity which was supernaturally "delivered" to him, and "received" by him, in those "visions and revelations of the Lord" to which he alludes in 2 Cor. 12 : 1, and which he has recorded for the Church in the Gospel according to Luke and his Epistles.

This "recollection" by the "Twelve Apostles" of what

Christ did and said during his public ministry did not
include all things, for the account would have been too
voluminous for the use of the Church (John 21 : 25). It
included only (a) the events that were cardinal points in
the Redeemer's life and career, namely, his conception,
birth, baptism, temptation, crucifixion, etc. ; (b) those
miracles that were connected with these events and with
the more remarkable of his discourses ; and (c) the most
important of his discourses. Luke (1 : 1) calls a Gospel
narrative a " digest " (διήγησις), and this term well describes
them all, as does the term " Memorabilia " employed by
Justin Martyr. In selecting, digesting, and arranging the
materials, the four Evangelists who acted for " The Twelve "
were under the inspiration of the same Holy Spirit who
had been promised to the apostles collectively by their
divine Lord, " to teach them all things, and bring all things
to their remembrance whatsoever he had said unto them "
(John 14 : 26). This Spirit does not make fac-similes.
Hence, one Evangelist selects some discourses and miracles which another omits, and arranges them differently.
Miracles and parables are grouped together because of
didactic resemblance (Luke 9 : 12 sq.; Matt. 13 : 3 sq.).
The Synoptists dwell upon Christ's existence in time, not
his preëxistence in eternity. John reverses this. The
Synoptists speak of Christ as having come, and to come
again at the end of the world. John does not enlarge
upon these points, though mentioning them, but upon
his divine nature as the Logos, and as this is manifested
in the profound discourses of his last days. The Synoptists are full upon the Galilean ministry and John upon the
Judean. The Synoptists particularly describe the miraculous conception and birth of Christ from a virgin. John,
though clearly affirming the incarnation of the Logos, omits
the details which had been given to the Church by the
other evangelists some forty years previously, and expends
the main force of his inspiration upon that infinite fulness

of being and knowledge which fitted Jesus Christ to be the
Way, the Truth, and the Life for fallen men.

It is important, in this connection, to remember that the
phrase "Twelve Apostles" is employed technically in the
New Testament to denote the Apostolic College. In two
instances, the "Twelve" are respectively thirteen and
eleven. In Rev. 21 : 14, it is said that the foundations of
the New Jerusalem had "in them the names of the twelve
apostles of the Lamb." It is not supposable that the name
of St. Paul, who was second to no apostle in founding the
Christian Church, was omitted. Here the Apostolic College is meant, which contained thirteen persons called and
set apart by Christ. Again, in 1 Cor. 15 : 5, St. Paul calls
eleven apostles "The Twelve." Compare Matt. 28 : 16.
If "The Twelve" may be thirteen or eleven, they may also
be four. Any part of the college, acting *officially* for the
body may be denominated "The Twelve." The four Gospels, composed by or under the superintendence of the
four to whom they have been ascribed from the very first,
are thus the Gospels of "The Twelve," and have the authority of the whole circle.

4. The origin of the Gospels is not to be explained
by the Church, but the origin of the Church by the
Gospels. The preaching of the apostles made the first
Christian brotherhood ; they could not, therefore, have
obtained the matter of their preaching from the brotherhood. The twelve apostles on the day of Pentecost began
to proclaim what they knew concerning Jesus Christ and
his mediatorial work. This knowledge they did not derive
from traditions that were current among the Jews, and
still less in the Christian Church, for as yet there was
none, but from their own memory, supernaturally strengthened and guided by the Holy Ghost, of what they had
themselves seen and heard during the public ministry of
their Lord and Master. This body of knowledge was the
same as that which makes the contents of the four Gospels.

Possibly it remained in an oral form for a time, but from the nature of the case it must soon have been committed to writing. The apostles well knew that their own lives were liable to be cut short by the persecutions and martyrdom which their Lord had foretold; that an accurate account of his ministry and teachings depended upon them as his only inspired and authorized agents; and that they had been positively commanded to give this account to the world. They began to give it orally, by public preaching, and private instruction of their converts and disciples; and ended by putting it into a written form. This is the natural method of authorship generally. An extemporaneous preacher, if he deems his thoughts to be important and valuable, always desires to reduce them, as soon as possible, to a form that will preserve them permanently. It is in the highest degree improbable that those twelve divinely inspired and authorized apostles, upon whose accurate account of Jesus of Nazareth the founding, progress, and perpetuity of the Christian religion, and the eternal salvation of vast multitudes of human beings, absolutely depended, would have left that account to be prepared at haphazard by their converts, who not only had no inspiration or authority for the work, but who had not " companied " with Christ in the days of his flesh, and could not therefore draw from their own recollections, and who as imperfectly sanctified Christians were full of ignorance, and liable to misconception both of Christ and Christianity. What kind of a life of Christ would have been produced among a brotherhood like that to which St. Paul addresses his two Epistles to the Corinthians?

According to the pseudo-critical theory, all this is reversed. This assumes that the twelve apostles composed no careful biography of their divine Lord; made no attempt to put it into a fixed form that precluded the introduction of legendary matter; continued while they lived to tell the story of the cross in a loose oral way, in company with a multitude of other preachers from among their converts and disciples, who must inevitably have mixed fancy with truth in their narrations; and, dying, left the whole subsequent preparation of the life of Christ to unknown persons who were to make it up gradually, in the lapse of perhaps a century or more, out of the accretion of truth and fiction which is sure to gather around a central figure. Such a dereliction of duty, and such a piece of unwisdom as this, on the part of such a divinely called, inspired, and miraculously endowed company as the twelve apostles of Jesus Christ, is incredible.

5. The narrative of the life of Christ required *inspiration* in order to its preparation, and *inspiration was confined to the Apostolic College.* The ministry of Christ extended over three years and a half. It was crowded with action and suffering, with discourses and miracles. To reproduce these, each in its environment, with sufficient fulness and accuracy, from memory, would be difficult even for exceptional mnemonic power directly after their occurrence, and still more after ten or twenty years. The last discourses of Christ, recorded by John, occurred more than fifty years previous to the date which is commonly accepted for his Gospel. If during all this time they had existed only in the oral discourse of the apostle, and his memory had not been helped by written memoranda, how could he have reported them with such fulness after the lapse of a half century, without the aid of that Spirit who had been promised to the apostles for such a purpose? And what would have been the fate of those mysterious and fathomless utterances of the God-man in that upper chamber, and down the slope to Gethsemane, if their preservation had been left to the random repetition and recital of the Christian fraternities from A.D. 33 to A.D. 80 or 90?

There is, furthermore, a kind of information in the Gospels which the apostles must have obtained from Christ by word of mouth before his ascension, or else by revelation after it, because it was not witnessed by them. Baxter (Dying Thoughts) refers to it. " When the disciples awaked from sleep on the Mount of Transfiguration, they saw Christ, Moses, and Elijah in converse. Did they hear what they said, or did Christ afterwards tell them? The latter is most probable. Doubtless, as Moses tells us how God made the world, which none could tell him but by God's telling them first, so the apostles have written many things of Christ which they neither saw nor heard but from Christ who told them by word, or inspiration. How else knew they what Satan said and did to him in his temptations in the wilderness, and on the pinnacle of the temple? How knew they what his prayer was in his agony? And so in this instance also. Christ's own testimony to them, either immediately on the Mount, or subsequently, was needed in order that they might know that the conversation with Moses and Elijah related to Christ's 'decease which he should accomplish at Jerusalem.' "

And not only the memory, but the judgment of the biographers of Jesus Christ required supernatural influence and direction. The selection from the great abundance of materials in that crowded and infinite life, so that each and all of the doctrines of the Christian religion should get its basis and illustration in that life, demanded an illumination from above. That very variety and diversity in the choice and arrangement, which sometimes makes it difficult to harmonize the four narratives, is really one of the signs that a higher Mind than that of any of the evangelists was seeing the end from the beginning, and swaying them by its afflatus.

The apostles were inspired both as biographers of Christ and as teachers of Christianity. Not only the narrative of the life of incarnate God upon earth, but the authentic and complete statement of his doctrine, was intrusted to

them *exclusively*. No authorship can be compared with
this in importance. The Gospels are an infallible biography, and the Epistles are an infallible theology. The
Epistles of St. Paul are declared to be contradictory to the
Gospels by rationalistic theologians, who contend that true
Christianity must be sought in the latter only. But the
writings of the apostle to the Gentiles, which have contributed as much as the Gospels themselves to the most
universal form of Christianity, both practical and theoret-
ical, are only the full systematic statement of the teachings of Christ himself. Those " visions " and " abundance
of revelations " from Christ which St. Paul asserts that he
received, are what gave him the analytical knowledge of
the cardinal truths of Christianity contained in his Epistles,
and his apostolical authority in the Church universal.
Without them, Saul of Tarsus of the year 30 could no
more have become Paul the apostle of the year 50 than
Confucius in twenty years could have become John Calvin
by natural evolution.

The relation of the New Testament Epistles to the
four Gospels is stated by Owen with his usual discrimination (Justification by Faith, Sec. vii.). " What the Lord
Christ revealed afterward by his Spirit unto the apostles
was no less immediately from himself than was the truth
which he spoke unto them with his own mouth in the days
of his flesh. The Epistles of the apostles are no less
Christ's sermons than that which he delivered on the
Mount. The things written in the Epistles proceed from
the same wisdom, the same grace, the same love, with the
things which he spake with his own mouth in the days of
his flesh, and are of the same divine veracity, authority,
and efficacy. The revelation which he made to the apostles
by his Spirit is no less divine and immediately from himself than what he spoke unto them on the earth."

" The writings of the evangelists do not contain the whole
of all the instructions which the Lord Christ gave unto his

disciples personally on the earth. 'For he was seen of them after his resurrection forty days, and spoke with them of the things pertaining to the kingdom of God' (Acts 1 : 3). And yet nothing hereof is recorded in their writings, except only some few occasional speeches. Nor had he given before unto them a clear and distinct understanding of those things which were delivered concerning his death and resurrection in the Old Testament, as is plainly declared in Luke 24 : 25–27. For it was not necessary for them in that state wherein they were. Wherefore, as to the extent of divine revelations objectively, those which he granted by his Spirit unto his apostles after his ascension were beyond those which he personally taught them, so far as they are recorded in the writings of the evangelists. For he told them plainly not long before his death that he had many things to say unto them which 'then they could not bear' (John 16 : 12). And for the knowledge of those things he refers them to the coming of the Spirit to make revelation of them from himself. 'When he the Spirit of truth is come, he will guide you into all truth ; for he shall not speak of himself, but whatsoever he shall hear that shall he speak ; and he will show you things to come. He shall glorify me ; for he shall receive of mine and show it unto you' (John 16 : 13, 14). And on this account he had told them before, that it was expedient for them that he should go away, that the Holy Spirit might come unto them, whom he would send from the Father (John 16 : 7). Hereunto he referred the full and clear manifestation of the mysteries of the gospel."

"The writings of the evangelists are full unto their proper ends and purposes. These were to record the genealogy, conception, birth, acts, miracles, and teachings of our Saviour, so far as to evince him to be the true, only promised Messiah. So he testifieth who wrote the last of them. 'Many other signs truly did Jesus which are not written in this book ; but these are written that ye might believe that Jesus is the Christ, the Son of God' (John 20 : 30, 31). Unto this end everything is recorded by them that is needful unto the ingenerating and establishing of faith. Upon this confirmation all things declared in the Old Testament concerning him, all that was taught in types and sacrifices, became the object of faith in that sense wherein they were interpreted in the accomplishment. It is therefore no wonder if some things, and those of the highest importance, should be declared more fully in other writings of the New Testament than they are in those of the evangelists."

That this inspiration of the Apostolic College, which fitted them to join on upon the teachings of their Lord and Master, and produce a body of doctrine intended to constitute an integral and necessary part of the Christian religion, was *confined* to them, and was not shared by the first Christian brotherhood any more than by the Church to-day, our limits compel us to be content with a brief proof ; and the burden of proof is upon him who widens the circle beyond this. To the " Twelve Apostles " alone does Christ promise the Holy Spirit as the Spirit of revelation and inspiration (John 14 : 26 ; 16 : 13). Them only does he command "not to depart from Jerusalem, but to wait for the promise of the Father " (Acts 1 : 4). To them alone does he say, " I will send unto you from the Father the Spirit of truth ; he shall teach you all things and *bring all things to your remembrance, whatsoever I have said unto you ;* he shall testify of me, and *ye also shall bear witness because ye have been with me from the beginning* " [of my ministry] (John 14 : 26 ; 15 : 26, 27). Such promises as these have no kind of connection with the alleged unknown collectors and editors of legends concerning Christ that were accumulating in the Early Church during two or three centuries after his death. They apply solely to the Apostolic College, and to no other persons. No such promise or command was given to the " seventy " disciples who were sent out to preach the gospel, and who were endowed with miraculous power. Stephen and Barnabas were "full of the Holy Ghost," but there is no evidence that they were authorized or inspired to prepare writings that were to make a part of the New Testament revelation. The "Twelve Apostles" alone, together with the "Prophets" of the Old Testament, constituted the "foundation" of the Christian Church, Christ their Lord being "the chief corner-stone" (Eph. 2 : 20). Only the names of the "twelve apostles of the Lamb" were cut into the jasper foundations of the New Jerusalem (Rev. 21 : 14). To the "Twelve Apostles" alone did the head of the Church say, "Ye are they which have continued with me in my temptations. And I appoint unto you a kingdom, as my Father hath appointed unto me ; that ye may eat and drink at my table in my kingdom, and sit on thrones judging the twelve tribes of Israel" (Luke 22 : 28–30).

The Apostolic writings, consequently, stand in a wholly different relation to the Christian Church from all others, secular or religious. The Church grew out of them, and rests upon them. This cannot be said of any or all of the immense body of Christian literature which has sprung from them. It has been asserted that "the gospel may exist without the Bible." It may exist temporarily without the printed volume, as when a missionary, prior to reducing the heathen language to writing preaches the Gospel orally ; but this supposes that the written Bible is in existence, and that from it the missionary has derived it. It is said, also, that the first Christian brotherhood had not the New Testament in a written form. Supposing this assertion can be proved, it certainly had the New Testament in an oral form from the lips of the Apostles, and their oral account of Christ and his teaching was the same thing with their written record.

6. The composition of the Gospels would naturally have been prior to that of the Epistles, because they were

more needed in founding and extending the Christian
Church among the nations. The common assumption of
the rationalistic critics that the Epistles were early and
the Gospels late, dating even into the second century, is
contrary to probability, as well as to patristic testimony.
From the nature of the case the narrative parts of the
New Testament would have been required in evangelistic
work sooner than the doctrinal. The first Christian
brotherhood would have needed the Synoptist account of
the life of Christ more than it would St. Paul's abstruse
and logical enunciation of the Christian system in his
Epistle to the Romans. But the date of this latter is very
generally acknowledged to be about A.D. 58. The Tü-
bingen school, with the caprice characteristic of conjectural
criticism, while asserting the spuriousness of Ephesians,
Philippians, and Colossians, concede the genuineness of
Romans, excepting the last two chapters, and also of the
Epistles to the Corinthians. But if within twenty-five
years after the crucifixion the Church required such a
written statement of the doctrine of predestination as St.
Paul gives in Rom. 8: 28—11: 36, and of the resurrection
in 1 Cor. 15: 12-58, it would surely require within the
same period such a written narrative of Christ's birth, life,
death, resurrection, and ascension as the Synoptists give
in their Gospels. If oral instruction upon predestination
and the resurrection body ceased to be sufficient for the
spread of Christianity, and a written statement upon these
subjects became necessary, much more would this have
been the case with all that historical matter connected
with the life of Christ which has always been regarded in
all missionary work as of prime importance. When a
modern missionary prepares for the founding of a Christian church in a heathen tribe, he does not first translate
the Pauline Epistles into their language, but the Gospels
of the evangelists.

We have already referred to another reason for the

probability that the first three Gospels had an earlier
origin than the Pauline Epistles; namely, the importance of their being composed before the death of the
apostles should make it impossible. So long as "The
Twelve" were alive and actively at work in the fulness of
their powers, a written record of the acts and discourses of
Christ might temporarily be dispensed with. The personal presence and teaching of those whom the Saviour
had chosen and inspired to be the organs of his religion
made a manuscript account less necessary. Moreover, for
the first twenty-five years after the death of Christ the
circle of believers was comparatively small, and the limits
of the Church confined. Oral instruction from the apostles and their assistants might perhaps suffice. But when
the circle was enlarged, and the apostles were departing
from earth, the necessity for the written Gospel became
urgent and imperative.

The apostles themselves would naturally provide for
this emergency in good season, before the close of their
career, and while they were in possession of their vigor.
Even if they had felt themselves to be at liberty to do so,
they would not have devolved the important work of laying the literary foundation of the Christian religion and
Church upon well-meaning but unqualified members of
the brotherhood. The manner in which Luke (1 : 1–4)
speaks of "many" who had attempted a biography of
Christ from the data furnished by "eye-witnesses and
ministers of the Word," but who were not members of the
Apostolic College, shows that it was an independent and
unauthorized, though well-intentioned procedure. Had
it been satisfactory in all respects, why should Luke have
prepared his Gospel, not from these same data, but from
the "perfect understanding of all things from the very
first," which he says he had, and why should not these
"many" narrations have acquired canonical authority and
been received by the Church as such?

Eusebius so understood Luke's remark respecting the "many who had taken in hand" the writing of the Life of Christ. "Luke, in the beginning of his narrative premises the cause which led him to write, namely, that many others had *rashly* undertaken to compose a narrative of matters which he had already completely ascertained. In order to free us from their uncertain suppositions, he delivered in his own Gospel the certain account of these things which he himself had fully received from his intimacy with Paul, and also his intercourse with the other apostles" (Eccl. History, iii., 24).

For these reasons it is both natural and probable that the Apostolic College, by the instrumentality of a part of their number, prepared that threefold synoptical account of the life of our Lord which for nearly twenty centuries has been ascribed to Matthew, Peter-Mark, and Paul-Luke. These three were virtually a committee of "The Twelve," to perform that important service which the Head of the Church had solemnly committed to them alone. The historical data furnished by all classes of writers of the first three centuries justify the belief that the Epistles of the New Testament were composed between A.D. 55 and A.D. 70. We have given the reasons for believing that the Synoptical Gospels were prior to the Epistles, speaking generally. Matthew's Gospel, especially if written first in Aramæan, probably had a much earlier date than that of the Epistle to the Romans, namely, A.D. 58. Eusebius carries it back to A.D. 41.

After the first three Gospels had made the Church familiar with the biography of its divine Founder in its principal features, a fourth supplementary Gospel was added by that one of the Twelve who, by natural gifts and intimate relationship to his Master, was best qualified to portray those pre-existent and eternal characteristics which were not so fully presented by the Synoptists, and to supply an account of the Judean ministry and other particulars omitted by them. This was composed near the close of the first century, after the destruction of Jerusalem, and the overthrow of the Jewish economy and temple service.

Respecting the early origin of the Gospels, Ewald contends for it in part, but as the work of unknown editors not of the Apostolic College. "It is," he says (History of Israel, VI., 143), "according to the results of my inquiries, pure and simple prejudice which leads many modern scholars to the conclusion that the evangelical literature generally did not take rise until quite late. On the contrary, all closer inquiries prove that it began quite early, and was developed down to the destruction of Jerusalem in the most various forms ; but was then, certainly, *continued for a considerable time* after that event." Ewald imagines the following " documents to have been worked up into the present Synoptic Gospels : 1. The earliest Gospel. 2. The collected sayings (τὰ λόγια) of Papias. 3. The same work re-edited. 4. Mark's Gospel in its first shape. 5. Mark's Gospel re-edited with the use of 1 and 2. 6. The book of Higher History. 7. The present Gospel of Matthew. 8. A sixth work. 9. A seventh work. 10. An eighth work. 11. The Gospel of Luke. 12. Mark's Gospel in its final shape." It is evident that such a long series of compositions and recompositions, of editing and re-editing of materials, must have been a process requiring far more time than between A.D. 40 and A.D. 70, and that in saying that " the evangelical literature began quite early," Ewald means that the first ecclesiastical materials so began. But the process of collecting and combining them " continued," he says, " for a considerable time after the destruction of Jerusalem." Let any one seriously try to find any evidence in the Christian fathers of the first three centuries, and in the general history of the Patristic Church, for the existence of most of the twelve documents Ewald here speaks of, and for such an origin for the four Gospels, and he will know how much value to ascribe to the scheme.

4

Vol. I., p. 85. The fact that inspiration is distinct from sanctification, as is also the power to work miracles, is of the first importance, and many of the objections to the divinity of the Old Testament revelation arise from overlooking it. Graves (Pentateuch III., ii.) thus remarks upon it: " Let me warn my readers against adopting a preconception very injurious with unthinking minds, namely, that all the individuals whom God used as instruments for the deliverance of his people are brought to our notice in Scripture as worthy of divine favor, and fit models for our imitation in the *entire* tenor of their lives. They generally, indeed, possessed the important and praiseworthy qualities of zeal and intrepidity in defence of their national religion and constitution, and were active and effective instruments in restoring the worship of Jehovah, and thus in the main forwarding the interests of virtue and religion. Hence, God frequently assisted their efforts with miraculous aid, or is said to have raised them up, or been with them as judges or kings of Israel. But we must by no means conceive that this implies that the divine approbation attended *all* their conduct. The excesses of Samson, the rash vow of Jephthah, the ephod of Gideon which proved a snare unto him and all his house, involving them in the guilt of idolatry ; the easy indulgence of Eli to his profligate sons ; the manner in which the sons of Samuel himself abused their pious father's authority; the crimes even of David and Solomon : all these facts supply abundant proofs that as in the people, so in their rulers, there was a mixture of weakness and unsteadiness, an immaturity of intellect, and dulness of sentiment as to morality and religion, which, though controlled and overruled by Providence, so as to prevent them from defeating the great objects of the divine dispensations which these individuals were otherwise qualified to promote, yet should always prevent us from considering them as held up by Scripture, as in every instance of their conduct favored of God and to be imitated by man. In general, indeed, this fact is expressly noted in the Scripture itself, and an immediate punishment declared to be inflicted for their offences."

" It is said to be utterly incredible that persons raised up, aided, inspired, endowed with miraculous power at times, directed and assisted by God, should have been guilty of such crimes as David, such idolatries as Solomon, such weaknesses as Samson, such apostasies and cruelties as the Jews. To this it may be answered that it is perfectly credible that they should be raised up for a particular purpose ; aided in effecting a particular object ; inspired with a certain degree of knowledge; miraculously assisted at particular periods, and in a special manner ; and yet, that *beyond* this their natural character, their external temptations, their acquired habits, may have produced all the irregularities and crimes which gave so much offence. To ask why God did not prevent this, is to ask why he did not exercise a greater degree of supernatural control than the purposes of Providence required. On this subject I transcribe the observations of Butler (Analogy, II., iii.), which appear to me decisive. Having illustrated by a variety of examples that the system of nature is liable to objections a priori analogous to those advanced against the scheme of revelation ; and that as the former are admitted to be inconclusive objections to natural religion, the latter are equally so with regard to revelation, he proceeds : ' By applying these general observations to a particular objection, it will be more distinctly seen how they are applicable to others of the like kind ; and indeed to almost all objections against Christianity, as distinguished from objections against its evidence. It appears from Scripture that as it was not unusual in the apostolic age for persons upon their conversion to Christianity to be endued with miraculous gifts, so some of those persons exercised these gifts in a strange-

ly irregular and disorderly manner; and this is made an
objection against their being really miraculous. Now the
foregoing observations quite remove this objection, how
considerable soever it may appear at first sight. For
consider a person endued with any of these gifts; for instance, that of tongues : it is to be supposed that he had
the same power over this miraculous gift that he would
have had over it had it been the effect of habit, of study,
and use, as it ordinarily is; or the same power over it
that he had over any other natural endowment. Consequently, he would use it in the same manner he did any
other; either regularly and upon proper occasions only,
or irregularly and upon improper ones, according to his
sense of decency and his prudence. Where, then, is the
objection ? Why, if this miraculous power was indeed
given to the world to propagate Christianity and attest
the truth of it, we might, it seems, have expected that another sort of persons should have been chosen to be invested with it; or that these should at the same time have
been endued with prudence ; or that they should have
been continually restrained and directed in the exercise
of it ; that is, that God should have miraculously interposed, if at all, in a different manner or higher degree.
But from the observations made above, it is undeniably
evident that *we are not judges* in what *degrees* and *manners*
it were to have been expected he should miraculously
interpose, upon the supposition of his doing it in some
degree and manner. Nor in the natural course of Providence are superior gifts of memory, eloquence, knowledge,
and other talents of great influence, conferred only on persons of prudence and decency, or such as are disposed to
make the properest use of them.' Such are the observations of Butler ; and they seem to show most clearly the
unreasonableness of disbelieving the reality of the divine
interpositions in the Jewish scheme, merely from the
crimes and idolatries of the nation at large, or of some of

the most remarkable persons employed in these interpositions."

In addition to the examples given in Vol. I., p. 85, of inspiration without sanctification, the case of the "old prophet," mentioned in 1 Kings 13: 11 is another instance, "He lied to the man of God," and yet "the word of the Lord came unto him" (ver. 20), and he foretold the truth respecting the death of "the man of God."

Vol. I., p. 86. It is an error to represent the Church as prior, either in the order of time or of nature, to the Scriptures. Though the Gospels, for example, were not put into writing before the Church at Pentecost was established, yet they were put into preaching before this. The preaching of the Gospel on the day of Pentecost applied by the Spirit made the Christian Church. The Gospels in the memory and oral discourse of the Apostles were the very same Divine revelation that was subsequently written down by them. The oral truth is identical with the written truth. The ten commandments spoken by God were the same ten commandments that were cut by him in the tables of stone. The Mosaic narrative respecting the patriarchs was not written until the fifteenth century B.C., but the facts, both miraculous and natural, and the truths relating to God and the "Seed of the Woman," recorded by Moses, exerted their influence from Adam down, making the course of events what it was in the line of Seth, and constructing the antediluvian and patriarchal churches long before the time of Moses. If revelation had not thus preceded, partly in an oral and perhaps partly in a written form, there would have been no patriarchal church. If Adam, Seth, and Noah had had no inspired teaching, but only the ethnic theology and mythological doctrine of God which Renan and others attribute to them, instead of the spiritual monotheism which the Pentateuch ascribes to them, the history of these patriarchs would have been like that of the mythological heroes generally. There would have been no "sons of God," like

Seth and Enoch and their descendants, walking with God in reverence and humility, and no antediluvian church free from idolatry and worshipping a spiritual Jehovah. Moses put into an orderly form a body of truth that had been gradually revealed from heaven centuries before, and had been preserved in the memory of the patriarchs, and perhaps also in some written documents, and added to it a body of truth partly supernaturally revealed to him, and partly the result of his own observation and connected with his own mission and history.

Modern rationalism reverses the places of cause and effect when composing its own "History of Israel." Ewald, for example, represents the Messianic idea and consciousness in the Israelites as producing the Old and New Testament Scriptures; whereas it was these Scriptures that produced this idea and consciousness. For if this race had been like the other contemporaneous races, destitute of a supernatural revelation through inspired prophets, it would no more have had a Messianic idea and consciousness than they had. The Bible made the Hebrews a peculiar people, with a peculiar idea and consciousness of redemption; and not the Hebrews the Bible a peculiar book, with its peculiar doctrines of a Saviour and salvation.

A similar misplacement of cause and effect is seen also in the rationalistic argument for the natural improvement of humanity by reason of its innate resources. The influence of Christianity for two thousand years in changing the moral and religious condition of the world is ignored, and the great process of Christian civilization during this time is ascribed to the workings of the human reason and will. Divine causation is thus transmuted into human causation, and human nature struts in borrowed plumes. The moral and spiritual products of the Gospel are attributed to ethnic religion and the evolution of man's religious sentiment. But none of the natural religions of the globe, and still less the meagre religion of a deist like Hume, could

have originated the England and United States of to-day.
Why did not Greece and Rome produce modern Christian
civilization?

VOL. I., p. 86. The ethics of the Old Testament is not
vitiated by such deeds as the slaying of Agag by Samuel
(2 Kings 10 : 30), and of the Canaanites by Israel, if the circumstances of the cases are considered. Such acts as these
would be obligatory and right at the present time, and in
all time, under the same circumstances. Should Almighty
God command a particular person in the United States in
the nineteenth century to slay a particular person, he
would be morally bound to do so. If the fact of a Divine
command is *certainly established*, this constitutes an obligation ; because God is the creator from nothing of every
man, and has the right to dispose of the life and being of
every one of his creatures as he pleases, on the principle
recognized by the common law, that absolute ownership
entitles to the use of the thing owned. It is on this
same ground that the destruction of mankind by the
deluge and Lisbon earthquakes is explained and justified.
When so commanded by God, the father and mother of a
false prophet are to thrust through the very son whom they
have begotten (Zech. 13 : 3).

VOL. I., p. 87. Revelation may be without error so far
as it professes to state truth, and yet it may not profess to
state all the truth belonging to the subject. The disclosure of the future Messiah to Adam and Eve in the first
promise was inerrant, but the time when he would appear
was not revealed to them to the degree it was to Daniel.
Similarly, the fact of the second advent of Christ was infallibly revealed to the Apostles, but the time when it was
to occur was concealed from them (Mark 13 : 32). If they
had gone beyond the teaching of the Holy Ghost that there
is to be a second advent of the Redeemer, and attempted
by the action of their own mind to fix the date of it, as
Premillenarians do, they would have made a fallible state-

ment. Some of the Thessalonian church did this, and St. Paul in the Second Epistle to this church, by inspiration informs them that the second advent will not occur until after a certain apostasy ; but when *this* will occur was not revealed to him, and he did not give a date for it. At the same time the apostles, in their ignorance of the exact date of Christ's second advent, together with their infallible knowledge that it would occur, represent it as an event that will come unexpectedly and suddenly whenever it does come, and exhort believers to be prepared for it. This explains Paul's " The Lord is at hand" (Phil. 4 : 5.) ; "Yet a little while, and he that shall come will come, and will not tarry" (Heb. 10 : 37) ; James's, "The coming of the Lord draweth nigh " (James 5 : 8) ; and Peter's " The end of all things is at hand " (1 Pet. 4 : 7).

VOL. I., p. 90. The homogeneity of thought and language is evinced by the fact that the vocal sound is the product of physical organs which are started into action and directed in their motion by the soul itself. Even the inarticulate tones of an animal are suited to the inward feeling by the particular play of muscles and organs of sound. The feeling of pleasure could not, so long as nature is herself, twist these muscles and organs into the emission of the sharp scream of physical agony, any more than it could light up the eye with the glare and flash of rage. Now, if this is true in the low sphere of animal existence, it is still more so in that of intellectual and moral existence. When full of earnest thought and feeling, the mind uses the body at will, and the latter naturally and spontaneously subserves the former. As thought becomes more and more earnest, and feeling more and more glowing, the body bends and yields with increasing pliancy, down to its minutest fibres and most delicate tissues, to the working of the engaged mind; the organs of speech become one with the soul, and are swayed and wielded by it. The word is as it were put into the mouth by the vehement and excited spirit. And the language inevitably follows the cast of the thought. The movements of the mouth, the positions of the vocal organs and tension of the vocal chords, in the utterance of such words as *shock*, *smite, writhe, slake, quench*, are produced by the energy and character of the conceptions which these words convey, just as the prolonged relaxation of the organs and muscles in the pronunciation of *soothe, breathe, dream, calm*, and the like, results necessarily from the nature of the thought of which they are not the mere arbitary unmeaning signs, like the algebraic symbols plus and minus, but the spontaneous significant embodiment. Even when the word is not only not pronounced, but not even whispered, it is sought to be expressed by dumb movements of the lips. "Hannah spoke in her heart; only her lips moved, but her voice was not heard: therefore Eli thought she had been drunken" (1 Sam. 1 : 13).

Carpenter (Physiology, § 542) describes the physiological connection between the conception and the word, as follows : "In the production of vocal sounds that nice adjustment of the muscles of the larynx which is requisite to the giving forth of determinate tones is ordinarily directed by the auditory sense : being learned in the first instance [in the case of the child] under the guidance of sounds actually produced [by its teachers] ; but being subsequently effected voluntarily in accordance with the *mental conception* (a sort of inward sensation) of the tone to be uttered, which conception cannot be formed unless the sense of hearing has previously brought similar tones to the mind. Hence it is that persons who are *deaf* are also *dumb*. They may have no malformation of the organs of speech ; but they are incapable of uttering distinct vocal sounds or musical tones, because they have not the guiding *conception*, or recalled sensation, of the nature of these."

It is objected that children have to learn to speak, and that consequently thought does not prompt language. The objection overlooks the difference between learning one's mother-tongue and a foreign language. The latter is learned artificially by a dictionary, and every word is taught separately by itself, but the former is learned naturally without such helps. As the child learns to think, he learns to talk. The latter is as spontaneous as the former. He is taught to spell every word, but not to utter every word. Children grow into speaking their native language as they grow into thinking. Technical terms, it is true, have to be taught. But even in this case the child often has an untechnical word for the thing which is suggested by his *idea* of it.

VOL. I., p. 92. That inspiration affects the language as well as the thought, is proved by what is said in Scripture concerning the "utterance" of revealed truth. This utterance is represented to be a special gift of the Holy Ghost. 1 Cor. 1 : 4, 5, "I thank my God always on your behalf that ye are enriched by him in all utterance (λόγῳ), and in all knowledge." 2 Cor. 8 : 7, "Ye abound in utterance (λόγῳ) and knowledge." Eph. 6 : 19, "Praying for me, that utterance (λόγος) may be given unto me." Col. 4 : 3, "Praying that God would open unto us a door of utterance (λόγου)." A free, fluent, and precise use of language is meant, when St. Paul prays that he may "open his mouth boldly, to make known the mystery of the gospel." It will be observed that in these passages the term λόγος denotes the expression of thought, while in other places it denotes thought itself, or the faculty of thought, showing that reason and "discourse of reason" are two modes or phases of the same thing.

Owen speaks thus of inward or mental prayer: "In prayer, by meditation the things and matter of prayer are to be formed in the mind into that sense and those sentences which may be expressed outwardly and vocally. So of Hannah, when she prayed in her heart ' out of the abundance of her meditation' as she said (1 Sam. 1 : 16), it is said that 'her lips moved, though her voice was not heard.' She not only inwardly framed the sense of her supplications into petitions, but tacitly expressed them to herself. And the obligation of any person unto prescribed forms is destructive of prayer by inward meditation; for it takes away the liberty and prevents the ability of framing petitions in the mind according to the sense which the party praying hath of them " (Holy Spirit in Prayer, ch. viii.).

In his treatise " De Magistro," Augustine discusses at considerable length the connection between thought and language, maintaining that it is natural not arbitrary, vital not mechanical. One of his remarks is, that " we think the words themselves [as well as the thought itself], and thus speak internally and mentally : Quia ipsa verba cogitamus nos intus apud animam loqui." This will be evident if we watch the mental action both in remembering and in reflecting. When we recall and *mentally* repeat a passage of the Lord's Prayer, the words of the passage are merely thought, or conceived of. They are not uttered either aloud, or in a whisper. The language in this instance is entirely internal, and disconnected from sound and the movements of the vocal organs. But the same is true in the instance of original thinking, when there is no recalling to memory. In reflecting upon a subject the mind inwardly *phrases* its thoughts as it goes along, without either whispering or speaking the words in which they are phrased. The thinking itself is real and clear only in proportion as this mental expression and linguistic formation of the thought takes place. If this is not done, there is no true thinking, but only a vague and mystical mental action which does not reach the truth of the subject, and does not explain it in the least. Says Augustine : " When my capacities of expression prove inferior to my inner apprehensions, I grieve over the inability which my tongue has betrayed in answering to my heart. This arises from the circumstance that the intellectual apprehension diffuses itself through the mind with something like a rapid flash, whereas the utterance is slow and occupies time, so that while the latter is moving on, the intellectual apprehension has already withdrawn itself within its secret abodes. Yet in consequence of its having stamped certain impressions of itself upon the memory, these prints endure with the brief pauses of the syllables; and as the outcome of these same impressions, we form vocal signs which get the name of a certain language, either Latin, Greek, or Hebrew, or some other. And these vocal signs may themselves be the objects of thought merely, or they may also be actually uttered by the voice. On the other hand, the mental impressions themselves are neither Latin, nor Greek, nor Hebrew, nor peculiar to any race whatsoever, but are made effective in the mind just as looks are in the body. For anger is designated by one word in Latin, by another in Greek, and by different terms in other languages, according to their several diversities. But the look of the angry man is neither peculiarly Latin nor peculiarly Greek. Thus it is that when a person says, *Iratus sum*, he is not understood by every nation, but only by the Latins; whereas, if the mood of his mind when it is kindling to wrath comes forth upon the face and affects the look, all who have the individual within their view understand that he is angry " (Catechizing the Unlearned, ch. iii.).

Augustine here notices that the vocal signs, that is, the words, may be merely *objects of thought*, and not actually spoken; that is, they may be conceived in the mind, and not articulated. This is so. If one will observe the process, he will discover that before he utters a particular word he has a notion of the sound which he means to utter, and forms it mentally. He phrases his thought inwardly, and this *conceived* sound is suggested and prompted by the thought behind it, of which it is the symbol, and with which it is connatural. We think the word before we

speak it out audibly. Hence the following advice is sound :
" When we write in a foreign language, we should not
think in English ; if we do, our writings will be but translations at best. If one is to write in French, one must use
one's self to think in French ; and even then, for a great
while, our Anglicisms will get uppermost, and betray us in
writing, as our native accent does in speaking when we are
among them " (Dean Lockier, Spence's Anecdotes).

Plato (Theatetus, 190) describes thinking as inward
speaking. " Socrates. Do you mean by thinking the
same which I mean ? Theatetus. What is that ? Socrates. I mean the conversation which the soul holds with
herself in considering anything. The soul when thinking
appears to me to be just talking ; asking questions of herself and answering them, affirming and denying. And
when she has arrived at a decision, either gradually or by
a sudden impulse, and has at last agreed and does not
doubt, this is called her opinion. I say, then, that to form
an opinion is to speak, and opinion is a word spoken, I
mean to one's self and in silence, not aloud or to another."

VOL. I., p. 93. The conjectural critics make misstate-
ments to support their alleged contradictions of Scripture.
Harper (Hebraica, V., pp. 27–29) asserts that Gen. 2 : 5–7,
" distinctly states that when the first man was created, there
was no plant or shrub in existence." It states directly the
contrary. " God created every plant of the field before it
was in the earth, and every herb of the field before it
grew, and *there was not a man* to till the ground." That
is to say, when the vegetable kingdom was created man
was not in being. Harper asserts again that Gen. 2 : 7, 8,
teaches that " after man came vegetation, which man was
to maintain." This can be true only upon the assumption
that the " *planting of a garden* eastward in Eden," was the
same thing as the *creation of the vegetable kingdom !* "The
Lord God formed man of the dust of the ground. And

the Lord God planted a garden, and there he put the man
he had formed." The Bible here teaches that the planting
of the *garden* was subsequent to the creation of man, but
not that the fiat of the third day (Gen. 1 : 11), by which the
vegetable kingdom was originated, was subsequent to this.
Such interpretation of Scripture as this is either dense
ignorance or wilful deceit.

VOL. I., p. 95. Genuine and truthful accounts from two
or more eye-witnesses of an event must have a certain
amount of variation, because no two spectators see, or can
see, identically the same things in identically the same way.
For example, two spectators of the passage of the Red Sea
by the Israelites would not have exactly the same consciousness in relation to the *total* scene. This would make
them two machines, like two stereopticons, giving identically the same pictures of the passage. Eye-witnesses are
not stereopticons. One spectator sees more of one part of
a scene, and less of another part; and the converse. A
truthful and accurate report of what each has seen, consequently shows this difference and variation. But this is
not a conflict or contradiction between the two accounts.
This fact is clearly stated by Torrey, in an article on Inspiration, in the Bibliotheca Sacra for 1858. " Inspiration
secured the sufficiently exact report of the facts observed.
We say, sufficiently exact; for, from the nature of the case,
facts are relative to the observer. No two witnesses can
possibly look at them from [identically] the same point of
view. No two reports, from different sources, can possibly
be exactly [identically] the same. We cannot demand, in
the case of sacred facts, a different kind of exactness from
that which belongs to the true report of all historical facts.
Variation, to a certain extent, is here the test of truth.
Inspiration, therefore, cannot consist in such a miraculous
infusion of light as would lead each historian to report
facts differently seen, and differently related by different
witnesses, precisely alike. Each can draw up his own

report only from one point of view, and minor differences
are unavoidable."

Vol. I., p. 101.   When an inspired person intentionally
adapts a passage from the Old Testament as the best way
of expressing the inspired thought which he is commis-
sioned to utter, this is not the same thing as an error in
quotation.   A misquotation is not conscious y intended,
but is the result of ignorance or carelessness ; but an adaptation supposes a clear understanding of the whole passage in the Old Testament, and a deliberate alteration of
it to meet the case in hand.   Take, for illustration, our
Lord's quotation of Ps. 40 : 10, in John 13 : 18, "He that
eateth bread with me hath lifted up his heel against me."
He purposely omits the words, " in whom I trusted," not
because he did not know they made a part of the Old Testament passage, but because had he verbally cited the
whole of it it would have expressed an untruth.   He had
not put his trust in Judas, for he " knew what is in man,"
and therefore did not "commit himself " to man, even his
best friends (John 2 : 23, 24).   Another illustration is the
quotation of Ps. 16 : 10 by Peter and Paul respectively.
The former (Acts 2 : 27) quotes it, "Thou wilt not leave
my soul in hell, neither wilt thou suffer thine Holy One
to see corruption."   The latter (Acts 13 : 35) quotes it,
"Thou wilt not suffer thine Holy One to see corruption."
This is not misquotation on Paul's part.   He omits a clause
of the original, but does not alter its meaning as he understood it ; because he evidently understood that " to leave
the soul in hell " was the same thing as " to suffer the
Holy One to see corruption ; " " hell," in his view, meaning the grave, and " soul " signifying a " dead body," as in
Num. 6 : 6 ; Lev. 5 : 2 ; 19 : 28 ; 21 : 1, 11 ; 22 : 4 ; Num.
18 : 11, 13 ; Hag. 2 : 13.   Again, such quotations from the
Old Testament (Ex. 12 : 46) as John 19 : 36, " A bone of
him shall not be broken," are not a mistaken citation for a
purpose that was not intended by the Holy Spirit, the

original inspirer. The slaying of the paschal lamb was a *type* of Christ the Lamb of God, and not an ordinary historical event that had no typical meaning. When, therefore, God commanded Moses, saying, "Neither shall ye break a bone thereof," he had in view both the present reference and the future. Both references were in the mind of the Holy Ghost, under whose inspiration both Moses and John wrote. The paschal lamb being a type of the Lamb of God was a prophecy of him, as well as an emblem. All Scripture types or symbols are prophetic, and are consequently both history and prophecy, and may be cited as either. They have a double reference; one to the present, and the other to the future. Moses, in Ex. 12 : 46, gave the historical reference; John, in John 19 : 36, gave the prophetical. Common historical events are not typical of the future, and therefore have but one meaning or reference. But some of the historical events of the Old Testament dispensation, such as the exodus from Egypt (Matt. 2 : 15), the killing of the paschal lamb (1 Cor. 5 : 7; John 1 : 2), the lifting up of the brazen serpent (John 3 : 14), the Nazarite vow in the instances of Samson and Samuel (Matt. 2 : 23), the miracle of Jonah (Matt. 12 : 40), et alia, were types as well as history, and therefore are cited in the New Testament in proof of the truth of the claim of Jesus Christ to be the Messiah thus typefied. This explanation supposes that the Old and New Dispensations are one organic whole, and that the former prepares for the latter and is prophetic of it.

Vol. I., p. 102. The divine and the human element in Scripture are erroneously supposed, by those who deny the inerrancy of the latter, to be merely in *juxtaposition* instead of *blending* and *fusion*. Mere juxtaposition would leave the human factor in its ordinary fallible condition, unaffected by the divine. But the mind of the prophet or apostle is represented as θεόπνευστος, divinely inspired (2 Tim. 3 : 16). This imbreathing of the human mind by the

Holy Spirit lifts it above its common fallible condition, and frees it from the liability to error which attaches to the uninspired human. An inspired human mind is in an *extraordinary* state, by reason of the divine afflatus which sweeps it along (φερόμενοι, 2 Pet. 1 : 21). If the relation of the two factors were merely that of juxtaposition, the Scriptures would be a mixture of the infallible with the fallible, as the rationalist asserts they are. But when the two are blended so as to fill the human with the divine, the product has in it no mixture of error. Both elements are alike inerrant; the divine originally in and of itself, the human derivatively, because illumined by the divine. To suppose that the human side of the Bible contains error, is to suppose the mind of the prophet or apostle to have been left in its common uninspired state when he contributed to its production. The attempt of rationalistic criticism to inject error into Revelation by means of its human side, can succeed only by assuming that the inspired human is the ordinary human, and that the prophet or apostle writes like any common human author. This is merely the contiguity of the divine and human, not the interpenetration and inspiration of the human by the divine. On this theory the Bible is the product of the divine as infallible, and of the human as fallible; in which case the errancy of the latter nullifies the inerrancy of the former. If the inerrant truth, which comes directly from the Holy Spirit, on passing through the fallible mind of the prophet or apostle becomes vitiated by the passage and is converted into error, the result is worthless. But if, while the Holy Spirit reveals the truth, he at the same time illumines and informs the human mind which he is employing as his human organ for communicating it to human beings, and preserves it from error, thus making it the inspired-human in distinction from the common-human, then the product will be completely inerrant.

VOL. I., page 104. The argument in proof of a conflict

5

between revelation and science commonly closes with a reference to the persecution of Galileo, and his "Yet it does move." Whewell has narrated the facts of the case with carefulness and accuracy. He establishes the following particulars : 1. The heliocentric theory was known to the Ancients. It was ascribed to Pythagoras, and also to Philolaus, one of his disciples. Archimedes says that it was held by his contemporary, Aristarchus. Aristotle recognized the existence of the doctrine by arguing against it. Cicero appears to make Mercury and Venus revolve about the sun. Seneca says that it deserves considering whether the earth be at rest or in motion. The Hindoos had their heliocentric theorists. Aryabatta (B.C. 1322) is said to have advocated the doctrine of the earth's revolution on its axis —an opinion rejected by subsequent Hindoo philosophers. 2. Copernicus (A.D. 1507) was the first to reduce the theory, held hitherto in a vague way, to a scientific form. The preface to his epoch-making treatise, "De Revolutionibus Orbium Cœlestium," was addressed to the Pope. His views met no resistance from the Church. He delayed their publication because he feared the opposition of the established school of astronomers, not of divines. The latter he seemed to consider a less formidable danger. The doctrine of the earth's motion around the sun when it was promulgated by Copernicus, soon after 1500, excited no alarm among the theologians of his own time. Indeed it was received with favor by the most intelligent ecclesiastics, and lectures in support of the heliocentric doctrine were delivered in the ecclesiastical colleges. 3. The Copernican theory had both its advocates and its opponents for two centuries after its publication, but both classes were mathematicians and astronomers, not ecclesiastics as such. It was adopted by Leonardo da Vinci (1510), Giordano Bruno (1591), Kepler (1600), Galileo (1630), Leibnitz (1670), Newton (1680), and subsequently by the British and continental mathematicians generally. It was more or less opposed, or else doubted, even down to the close of the 17th century. Lord Bacon never gave full assent to it. His contemporary, Gilbert, was also in doubt concerning parts of it. Milton was not a mathematician, but reflects the opinions of his time, and he was undecided. So also was John Howe. 4. The martyrdom of Giordano Bruno and the persecution of Galileo arose not from their astronomical but their theological opinions. Bruno published a bitter satire on religion and the Papal government, a work having no connection with the Copernican theory, and for this he was condemned to the flames. He had previously published his treatise "De Universo," in which he adopts the views of his master, Copernicus, and had been unmolested. Galileo's persecution arose from several causes: (a) The difference in the degree of toleration accorded to Copernicus and Galileo, respectively, was due to the controversies that had arisen out of the Reformation, which made the Romish Church more jealous of innovations in received opinions than previously. Moreover, the discussion of religious doctrines was in the time of Galileo less freely tolerated in Italy than in other countries. (b) Galileo's own behavior appears to have provoked the interference of the ecclesiastical authorities. When arguments against the fixity of the sun and the motion of the earth were adduced from expressions in Scripture, he could not be satisfied without asserting that his opinions were conformable to Scripture as well as philosophy; and was very eager in his attempts to obtain from the ecclesiastical authorities a declaration to this effect. The authorities were averse to granting this, particularly since the literal phraseology of Scripture favored the Ptolemaic theory. When compelled by Galileo's urgency to express an opinion, they decided against him, and advised him to confine himself to the mathematical reasons for his system, and to abstain from meddling with Scripture. Galileo's zeal soon led him again to bring the question under the notice of the Pope, and the result was a declaration of the Inquisition that the doctrine of the earth's motion appeared to be contrary to the Scriptures. Galileo was then prohibited from teaching and defending this doctrine in any manner, and promised obedience to this injunction. His subsequent violation of his promise, together with his impatient and passionate temper, brought about his imprisonment. Had he maintained the Copernican theory on purely scientific grounds, as the Church had enjoined upon him, and as had commonly been done by its advocates, and not sought the authority of the Church in its support, and so had not fallen into collision with it when it refused its support, there is no reason for believing that Galileo would have met with any more persecution than his great predecessors Copernicus and Kepler. For the full account of the subject, see Whewell's Inductive Sciences, Book V., ch. i.–iii.

Vol. I., p. 114. It should be noticed that in having the explicit testimony of Christ to its genuineness and credibility, the Old Testament is superior to the New. He nowhere directly says of the New Testament, " Search the Scriptures, for in them ye have eternal life." It is only indirectly and by implication that he said this, in commissioning and inspiring the Twelve Apostles to compose it. This is an equivalent for the comparative lack of historical testimony, in the case of the Old Testament.

Vol. I., p. 116. " The Apostles," says Grotius (Christian Religion, II., v.), " affirmed that they were eye-witnesses of the resurrection of Christ, in that they saw him alive after his death and burial. They also appealed to five hundred witnesses who saw Jesus after he was risen from the dead. It is not usual for those who speak untruths to appeal to so many witnesses. Nor is it possible that so many men should agree to bear a false testimony. Furthermore, nobody has a bad design for nothing. The apostles and first Christians could not hope for any honor from saying what was not true, because all the honors were in the power of the heathen and Jews, by whom they were reproached and contemptuously treated; nor for riches, because, on the contrary, the Christian profession was often attended with the loss of property, if they had any ; and, if it had been otherwise, yet the Gospel could not have been preached by them but with the neglect of temporal good. Nor could any other advantages of this life move them to speak a falsity, since the preaching of the Gospel exposed them to hardship, to hunger and thirst, to stripes and imprisonment. Fame amongst themselves only, was not so great that for the sake thereof men of upright intentions, whose lives and tenets were free from pride and ambition, should undergo such evils. Nor had they any ground to hope that their religion, which was so repugnant to human nature, which is wholly bent upon its own interests, and to the civil authority which everywhere governed, could make any progress but from a Divine promise. Furthermore, they could not expect that fame of any kind would be lasting, because (God on purpose concealing his intention from them) they expected that the end of the whole world was just at hand, as is plain from their own writings, and those of the Christians that came after them. It remains, therefore, that they must be said to have uttered a falsity for the sake of defending their religion, which, if we consider aright, cannot be said of them ; for either they believed from their heart that their religion was true, or they did not believe it. If they had not believed it to have been the best, they never would have chosen it from all other religions, which were more safe and honorable. Nay, though they believed it to be true, they would not have made a public profession of it unless they had believed such a profession necessary ; especially when they could easily foresee, and they quickly learned it by experience, that such a profession would be attended with the death of a vast number ; and they would

have been guilty of the highest wickedness to have given
such occasion without a just reason. If they believed their
religion to be true, nay, the best of all, and ought to be
professed by all men, and this, too, after the death of their
Master, it was impossible that this belief should continue
if their Master's promise concerning his resurrection had
failed. The failure of Christ to rise from the dead would
have been sufficient to any man in his senses to have
overthrown the belief in him which he had previously entertained. Again, all religion, particularly the Christian,
forbids lying and false witness, especially in divine matters ; they could not therefore be moved to tell a lie out of
love to religion, especially such a religion. To all which
may be added, that they were men who led such a life as
was not blamed by their adversaries, and who had no objection made against them but only their simplicity, the
nature of which is the most distant that can be from forging a lie. And there was none of them who did not undergo even the most grievous things for testifying to the
resurrection of Jesus. Many of them endured the most
torturing death for this testimony. Now to suppose it
possible that any man in his wits could undergo such things
for an opinion he had entertained in his mind, and also for
an opinion which is known to be a falsehood; that not
only one man, but very many, should be willing to endure
such hardships for an untruth, is a thing plainly incredible. What has been said of these first twelve apostles
may also be said of Paul, who openly declared that he saw
Christ reigning in heaven. He had the best learning of
the Jews and great prospect of honor if he had trod the
paths of his fathers. But, on the contrary, he thought
it his duty, for this profession, to expose himself to the
hatred of his relations, and to undergo difficult and dangerous voyages all over the world, and at last to suffer an
ignominious death." Says Stillingfleet (Letter to a Deist) :
" If the Christian religion had been a mere design of the

Apostles to make themselves heads of a new sect, what had this been but to have set the cunning of twelve or thirteen men, of no weight or reputation, against the wisdom and power of the whole world? If their aim were only at reputation, they might have thought of thousands of ways more probable and more advantageous than this. Consider the case of St. Paul. Is it reasonable to believe that when he was in favor with the Sanhedrim, and was likely to advance himself by his opposition to Christianity, and had a fair prospect of ease and honor together, he should quit all this to join such an inconsiderable and hated company as the Christians were, only to be one of the heads of a very small number of men, and to purchase it at so dear a rate as the loss of his friends and interest, and running on continual troubles and persecutions to the hazard of his life? It is hardly possible to suppose that a man who is self-deceived and means honestly would do this. But it is impossible to suppose that a man in his senses, knowing and believing all this to be a cheat, should own and embrace it, to so great disadvantage to himself, when he could not make himself so considerable by it as he might have been without it. Men must love cheating the world at a strange rate that will let go fair hopes of preferment and ease, and lead a life of perpetual trouble, and expose themselves to the utmost hazard only for the sake of deluding others."

Vol. I., p. 117. A miracle may be performed by an evil being and for an evil purpose, but only as he is permitted and enabled to do so by God. In this case the miracle is a trial of faith. Our Lord so teaches. " There shall arise false Christs and false prophets, and shall shew great signs and wonders; insomuch that, if it were possible, they shall deceive the very elect " (Matt. 24 : 24). St. Paul says that the coming of Antichrist will be " with all power, and signs, and lying wonders " (2 Thess. 2 : 9). In such cases as these the nature of the *doctrine* taught in connection with the miracle must be considered. When the accompanying doctrine is contrary to that which has been *previously verified* by miracles, it is an evidence that the miracle is that of Satan, not of God. Such, perhaps, were some of the miracles of the Egyptian magicians. The directions which God gave by Moses to the Israelites for their conduct in such instances illustrate this. " If there arise among you a prophet or a dreamer of dreams, and giveth thee a sign or a wonder, and the sign or the wonder come to pass, whereof he spake unto thee, *Let us go after other gods*, which thou hast not known, and let us serve them, thou shalt not hearken unto the words of that prophet, or that dreamer of dreams ; for the Lord your God *proveth* you, to know whether ye love the Lord your God with all your heart and with all your soul. And that prophet, or that dreamer of dreams, shall be put to death ; because he hath spoken to turn you away from the Lord your God which brought you out of the land of Egypt " (Deut. 13 : 1–5). When miracles have already been wrought to prove the doctrines of monotheism, then either real or pretended miracles that are subsequently wrought to prove the contradictory doctrines of polytheism are not to be believed. For it is not supposable that God would himself employ his miraculous power, first to establish certain truths and then to overthrow them ; first to give authority to Moses, and then to the Egyptian priests. This is self-contradiction. But it is not self-contradiction when God first demonstrates the truth of his own revelations to Moses by the wonderful miracles of the exodus and the desert, and then permits and empowers Satan and his agents to work some wonders, not in order to prove their truthfulness, but to strengthen by trial the faith of his people. Such a trial of faith Stillingfleet compares to " a father that hath used great care to make his son understand true coin, and who may afterwards suffer false to be laid before him, to try whether he will be cheated or not." Even supposing, as this comparison does, that the

Satanic miracles are spurious, they are genuine for the spectator. "It is plain," continues Stillingfleet, "that, after the true doctrine is confirmed by Divine miracles, God may give the devil or false prophets power to work, if not real miracles, yet such as men cannot judge by the things themselves whether they be real or not; and this God may do for the trial of men's faith, whether they will forsake the true doctrine confirmed by greater miracles, for the sake of such doctrines which are contrary thereto, and are confirmed by false prophets by signs and wonders" (Origines Sacræ, Bk. II., ch. x.).

Belief in the reality of a miracle is not *necessarily* accompanied with faith in the author of it. There is no infallible connection between miracles and faith. They do not operate mechanically. The Pharisees saw with their own eyes our Lord's miracles, as his disciples did, and had no more doubt than they had that they were genuine, but they did not, like them, believe that he was the Messiah and Saviour of mankind. "Though he had done so many miracles before them, yet they believed not on him" (John 12 : 37). The dislike of the doctrine associated with the miracle, and the consequent unwillingness to believe it, while yet the reality of the miracle is not denied, shows that miracle and doctrine are reciprocally related and cannot be torn apart. For this reason the performance of a miracle was sometimes conditioned by Christ upon faith in him. "Believe ye that I am able to do this?" (Matt. 9 : 28; Mark 9 : 23, et alia). "He did not many mighty works there because of their unbelief" (Matt. 13 : 58).

Consequently, a miracle in and of itself merely is not the *sole* test of a genuine revelation from God. The nature and contents of the revelation must also be considered in connection with it. The chief use and necessity of a miracle is to establish the truth of a *new* religion; in other words, of *revealed* religion. No miracles are wrought to prove the doctrines of natural religion. These are written in the human constitution, and are as old as the human conscience. No supernatural proof has been given of this class of truths. But whenever, under the Old economy or the New, God introduced new doctrines by inspiring prophets and apostles to communicate them, he corroborated them by miracles. When God commanded Moses to reveal to the Hebrews the new religion of the Old Covenant and the theocracy, and to conduct them from Egypt to Canaan, and give them the Levitical institute, he assisted the faith of both Moses himself and the Israelites, by a great series of wonderful miracles. And, subsequently, whenever in the history of Israel Jehovah introduced a new prophecy, or a new movement connected with the progress of the Messianic kingdom, the miracle often came in to strengthen faith. When Jesus Christ appeared and taught the New Covenant, the final form of revelation, this new revelation was associated with, and corroborated by, that stupendous series of miracles which began with the miraculous conception and ended with the ascension. Speaking generally, miracles accompany the truths of revealed religion because this is something new, uncommon, and not issuing from the mind of man, and miracles do not accompany natural religion, because this is something old, common, and issuing from the human constitution. The words of Moses to Jehovah, and the answer of Jehovah to him, are the key to miracles. "Moses answered and said, *They will not believe me*, nor hearken to my voice; for they will say, The Lord hath not appeared unto thee. And the Lord said unto him, What is that in thine hand? And he said, A rod. And he said, Cast it on the ground. And he cast it on the ground, and it became a serpent; and Moses fled from before it. And the Lord said unto Moses, Put forth thine hand, and take it by the tail. And he put forth his hand, and caught it, and it became a rod in his hand, *That they may believe* that the Lord God of their fathers, the God of Abraham, the God of Isaac, and the

God of Jacob, hath appeared unto thee" (Ex. 4 : 1-5). The personal appearance of Almighty God "talking with Moses," and giving him a long series of instructions and directions, was something wholly new; not provided for in the ordinary course of nature, and wholly distinct from all the natural religions that were upon the earth. This made it necessary to accompany it with supernatural acts, some of them immediately from God himself, and some of them mediately from Moses, that demonstrated to the observers that God had verily broken through the veil of eternity, and had come down into time, and upon earth, and was "speaking with Moses face to face, as a man speaketh unto his friend" (Ex. 33 : 11).

VOL. I., p. 120. The people of Egypt in the time of Moses, like the Jews in the time of Christ, were also involuntary witnesses to the truth of the Mosaic miracles. The attempt of the magicians to imitate the plagues wrought by the hand of Moses was a testimony that the latter had wrought something wonderful. The failure to imitate all of them, while imitating some, was a testimony to the superhuman nature of the Mosaic acts. And, lastly, the fact that the Egyptian people were not persuaded into a disbelief of the Mosaic miracles by the jugglery and counterfeited miracles of the magicians testifies to the reality of the former. The proof of this latter fact is given by St. Paul, who repeats and thereby endorses a tradition reported in the Chaldee Paraphrase, to the effect that the futile attempts of Jannes and Jambres to imitate Moses were well understood by the Egyptian people : "Their folly was manifest unto all men" (2 Tim. 3 : 8).

VOL. I., p. 126. The originality of Christ is described by Ullmann (Sinlessness of Jesus, iv. 1, 2): "As a teacher, Jesus was fully as eminent as the unparalleled greatness and dignity of his person would have led us to expect. His teaching was not like that of one who had worked out and carefully put together a system of thought in his own

mind, and then brings it before others to be considered
and weighed. He taught as one who was in authority,
with the certain consciousness that he was in possession of
the truth, and with the full conviction that he could meet
with no contradiction ; all of which must be regarded as
boundless and intolerable presumption and arrogance, did
there not underlie it a direct and infallible intuition of that
which is eternally true, and if he had not a perfect right
to say of himself, ' We speak that which we do know, and
testify that we have seen.' The exaltedness of his spirit
manifested itself also in the inimitable form of his discourses. Here there is not a trace of anything which had
been gained by study, and yet all is in the purest sense
and in the highest degree perfect. Exuberant fulness and
unfathomable depth of meaning are combined with perfect
simplicity and intelligibleness of form; strength and love-
liness, a world-comprehensive breadth and intuitional di-
rectness, the most exalted ideality and the most lively
imagery, are united and blended in a way which has never
been equalled. He is at once the profoundest and the
most popular teacher the world has ever seen."

Vol. I., p. 131. "Doubting," says Butler (Analogy, II.
vi.), " necessarily implies some degree of evidence for that
of which we doubt. For no person would be in doubt concerning the truth of a number of facts which should acci-
dentally come into his thoughts, and of which he had no
evidence at all. And though, in the case of an even chance,
and where consequently we were in doubt, we should in
common language say that we had no evidence at all for
either side, yet that situation of things which renders it an
even chance, and no more, that such an event will happen,
renders this case equivalent to those in which there is such
evidence on both sides of a question as leaves the mind in
doubt concerning the truth. In all these cases, there is
indeed no more evidence on the one side than on the other,
yet there is much more evidence for either side than for the

truth of a number of facts which come into one's thoughts at random. And thus in all these cases doubt as much presupposes evidence, lower degrees of evidence, as belief presupposes higher, and certainly higher still. Anyone who will a little attend to the nature of evidence will easily carry this observation on, and see that between no evidence at all, and that degree of it which affords ground of doubt, there are as many intermediate degrees as there are between that degree which is the ground of doubt and that which is the ground of demonstration. And though we have not faculties to distinguish these degrees of evidence with any sort of exactness, yet in proportion as they are discerned they ought to influence our practice. For it is as real an imperfection in the moral character not to be influenced in practice by a lower degree of evidence when discerned, as it is in the understanding not to discern it. And as in all subjects which men consider, they discern the lower as well as the higher degrees of evidence, proportionably to their capacity of understanding, so in practical subjects they are influenced in practice by the lower as well as the higher degrees of it proportionably to their fairness and honesty. And as in proportion to defects in the understanding men are inapt to see lower degrees of evidence, and are in danger of overlooking evidence when it is not glaring, and are easily imposed upon in such cases, so in proportion to the corruption of the heart, they seem capable of satisfying themselves with having no regard in practice to evidence acknowledged to be real, even if it be not overwhelming. From these things it must follow that doubting concerning religion implies such a degree of evidence for it as, joined with the consideration of its importance, unquestionably lays men under the obligations before mentioned to have a dutiful regard to it in all their behavior. If then it is certain that doubting implies a degree of evidence for that of which we doubt, it follows that this degree of evidence as really lays us under obligations [to believe in proportion to the strength of the evidence] as demonstrative evidence does." Locke (Understanding, **IV.** xv.) presents a similar view of probability : " Probability is likeliness to be true ; the very notation of the word signifying such a proposition for which there be arguments or proofs to make it to be received for true. [Probability (probo) is proveability.] The entertainment which the mind gives this sort of propositions is called belief, assent, or opinion ; which is the receiving any proposition for true upon proofs that are found to persuade us to receive it as true without absolutely certain knowledge that it is so. And herein lies the difference between probability and certainty, belief and knowledge ; that in the instance of certainty and knowledge there is self-evident intuition, while in the instance of probability and belief there is not. The grounds of probability are two : 1. Conformity with our own knowledge, observation, and experience. 2. The testimony of others vouching their own observation and experience. Probability, consequently, is wanting in that intuitive and mathematical certainty which accompanies an axiom or any self-evident proposition, and which admits of no degrees of evidence. Probable propositions, consequently, are capable of a great variety of degrees of proof ; from that which is so slight as to be almost equivalent to no proof at all, to that which is so strong as to be almost equivalent to demonstration."

There is nothing obligatory, or of the nature of duty, in assent to intuitive truth ; but there is in assent to probable truth. We never say that a person is bound to assent that the whole is equal to the sum of the parts ; but we do say that he is bound to yield assent to a proposition for which the evidence for is greater than the evidence against. A jury is always charged by the judge to give the verdict in favor of the party whose proof is the stronger. They have no moral right to decide contrary to the preponderance of testimony, and the probability of truth founded upon it.

Respecting the force of probable evidence, the remark of Anselm is true: " We should not reject the smallest reason, if it be not opposed by a greater. Any reason, however small, if not overbalanced by a greater, has the force of necessity " (Cur Deus, I., 10). The assent of intuitive perception depends upon something intrinsic to the thing perceived; that of belief upon something extraneous to it. A person assents to the proposition that the three angles of a triangle are equal to two right angles from what he perceives to be the nature of a triangle, and what is necessarily implied in it; but he assents to the proposition that the second Person of the Trinity became incarnate, not from the intrinsic nature of this Person and its corollaries, but from the testimony of God in revelation. There is nothing in the nature of the second trinitarian Person, any more than in that of the first and third, that necessarily implies his incarnation.

VOL. I., p. 132. There is a certain amount of evidence that makes for theism, and a certain amount that makes for atheism. If a person is inclined to theism because of his reverence and love for a personal God, this will concur with the probative force of the argument for the being of God and increase its effect. If he is disinclined or averse to it because of his non-reverence and dislike of a personal God, this will concur with the probative force of the argument against the divine existence and strengthen it. In this way a man's inclination or disinclination toward a doctrine, constitutes a voluntary element in his belief or disbelief of it. Bias for or against a doctrine presupposes that the doctrine is known, and affects the judgment respecting the arguments and testimony for it, either favorably or unfavorably.

Paley (Sermon on John 7 : 17) shows the influence of the vicious bias of the will upon the judgment of the understanding concerning the truth of Christianity, in the following manner. His general position is, that " virtue produces belief, and vice unbelief." Remarking upon the latter part of the proposition, he says: "A great many persons before they proceed upon an act of known transgression expressly raise the question in their own mind whether religion be true or not, in order to get at the object of their desire; for the real matter to be determined is, whether they shall have their desire gratified or not. In order to get at the vicious pleasure in some cases, or in other cases the worldly gain upon which they have set their hearts, they choose to decide, and do in fact decide with themselves, that the truths of religion are not so certain as to be a reason for them to give up the pleasure which lies before them, or the advantage which is now in their power to compass and may never be again. This conclusion does actually take place, and must almost necessarily take place, in the minds of men of bad morals. And now remark the effect which it has upon their thoughts and belief afterward. When they come at another time to reflect upon religion, they reflect upon it as something which they had before adjudged to be unfounded, and too uncertain to be acted upon, or to be depended upon; and reflections accompanied with this adverse and unfavorable impression naturally lead to infidelity. Herein, therefore, is seen the fallacious operation of sin: first in the unfair circumstances under which men form their opinions and conclusions concerning religion; and, secondly, in the effect which conclusions and doubts so formed have upon their judgment afterward. First, what is the situation of the mind in which they decide concerning religion? And what may be expected from such a situation? Some magnified and alluring pleasure has stirred their desires and passions. It cannot be enjoyed without sin. Here is religion denouncing and forbidding it one side, there is opportunity drawing and pulling on the other. With this drag and bias upon their thoughts, they pronounce and decide concerning the most important of all subjects, and of all questions. If they should decide for the truth and reality of religion, they must sit down disappointed of a gratification upon which they had set their hearts, and of using an opportunity which may never come again. Nevertheless they must decide one way or the other. And this process, namely, a similar deliberation and a similar conclusion, is renewed and repeated as often as occasions of sin offer. The effect, at length, is a settled persuasion against religion; for what is it in persons who proceed in this manner that rests and dwells upon their memories? What is it which gives to their judgment its turn and bias? It is these occasional decisions often repeated; which decisions have the same power and influence over the man's after-opinion as if they had been made ever so impartially, or ever so correctly, whereas in fact they are made under circumstances which exclude, almost, the possibility of their being made with fairness and with sufficient inquiry. Men decide under the power and influence of sinful temptation; but, having decided, the decision is afterward remembered by them, and grows into a settled and habitual opinion, as much as if they had proceeded in it without any bias or prejudice whatever."

"But not only do vicious and sinful men *expressly* raise the question to themselves, when they desire to gratify their desires, whether religion be true or not, there is also a *tacit* and *unconscious* rejection of religion which has the same effect. Whenever a man deliberately ventures upon an action which he knows that religion prohibits, he tacitly rejects religion. There may not pass in his thoughts every step which we have described, nor may he come consciously to the conclusion; but he acts upon the conclusion, he practically adopts it. And the doing so will alienate his mind from religion as surely, almost, as if he had formally argued himself into an opinion of its untruth. The effect of sin is necessarily, and highly, and in all cases, adverse to the production and existence of religious faith. Real

6

difficulties are doubled and trebled when they fall in with vicious propensities, and imaginary difficulties are readily started. Vice is wonderfully acute in discovering reasons on its own side. This may be said of all kinds of vice; but I think it more particularly holds good of what are called licentious vices; for sins of debauchery have a tendency which other species of sin have not so directly, to unsettle and weaken the powers of the understanding, as well as to render the heart thoroughly corrupt. In a mind so wholly depraved, the impression of any argument relating to a moral or religious subject is faint, and slight, and transitory. To a vitiated palate, no meat has its right taste; with a debauched mind no reasoning has its proper influence."

Vol. I., p. 134. There is a false and a true subjectivity. The former is not corroborated by the object; the latter is. When the "Christian consciousness" is appealed to as the ultimate authority, separate and apart from Divine Revelation, this is an instance of spurious subjectivity. Those who would substitute ecclesiastical tradition and the voice of the Church as the ultimate authority, instead of the Scriptures, as well as those who would substitute Christian consciousness for them, commit the same error in common. The Romanist and the Mystic are really upon one and the same ground, and are equally exposed to that corruption of Christianity to which every human mind is liable which does not place the Scriptures above both the Church and the Christian consciousness, whenever the question concerns an ultimate and infallible source of religious knowledge. Consciousness cannot be an absolute and final norm for consciousness; subjectivity cannot preserve subjectivity from error. It is the *object* of consciousness by which the process of consciousness is to be judged and determined. As that subjective process of faith and feeling which is seen in the Christian experience or consciousness owes its very existence to the objective written Revelation, so it must be kept free from deviation and error by the same. To leave the process to test itself, and protect itself from corruption, is dangerous. An individual Christian who should trust to the feelings of even a regenerate heart, and the inward light of even a renewed mind, without continually comparing this subjective feeling and knowledge with the written Word, would be the victim of a deteriorating, and, in the end, an irrational and fanatical, experience. A genuine Christian subjectivity is the simple perception and acknowledgment of the truth as it actually reads in the Scriptures. For illustration, the truth that " the Word was God " may be accepted and believed in the Arian sense, that " God " is here used in the secondary signification instead of the primary. This is not the natural meaning of the term, taking the context into consideration, and has not been the common interpretation. This is not supporting and corroborating the person's belief and experience by the real and true object, but by a false modification of it. Multitudes, in the present generation, are putting false interpretations upon Scripture and adopting a false view of God and man, of sin and salvation, and then appeal to their personal experience, under the name of " Christian consciousness," in corroboration of their views. Neither the Scriptures nor the Creeds derived from them are the final authority for this class, but the feeling of the hour.

Vol. I., p. 139. Josephus (Cont. Apionem, I., 8) testifies to the fixedness of the Old Testament writings, so far as the Jews themselves were concerned. " During so many ages as have already passed, no one has been so bold as either to add anything to them, or take anything from them, or to make any change in them. It is natural to all Jews from their very birth to esteem those books to contain divine doctrines. It is not so with the writings of the Greeks, who take their histories to be written agreeably to the inclinations of their writers, and who sometimes write histories without having been in the places, or near them in time."

Vol. I., p. 141. In the instances in which a sacred book has no author mentioned, like the Epistle to the Hebrews, it is claimed to be apostolical, that is, composed under the superintendence of one of "The Twelve." Respecting Hebrews, Calvin remarks : " I include it without controversy among the apostolical epistles. As to the question, Who composed it, we need not trouble ourselves" (Speaker's Commentary, Hebrews, p. 3). Calvin here means that it is of no consequence who was the amanuensis, provided an inspired apostle superintended him. Bleek (Introduction to the New Testament, II., 115) remarks that it was " within the circle of Paul's friends and fellow-laborers that those early writers who did not admit Paul to be the [immediate] author looked for the authorship, their choice lying between Luke, Clemens Romanus, and Barnabas, to whom in modern times have been added Sylvanus and Apollos." The Oriental church, from the first, ascribed this epistle to St. Paul. The Churches of Jerusalem, Palestine, Syria, Asia, Alexandria, concurred in this opinion. The council of Nicæa received it as a genuine work of St. Paul. " Doubts existed in the Western Church," says Wordsworth, " concerning the Pauline origin of the Epistle to the Hebrews, yet we have little evidence of distinct assertions that it was *not* written by the Apostle. The doubts of the West were dispersed in the fourth century, and did not appear again until they were revived by one or two persons in the sixteenth." Wordsworth, in his Introduction to the Epistle to the Hebrews, gives a full account of the opinions that have prevailed respecting the authorship.

Respecting the anonymous books of the Old Testament, their inspiration depends upon their having been composed within the circle of the inspired prophets, the " holy men of God who spake as they were moved by the Holy

Ghost." And the principal voucher for this is Ezra, who revised and settled the Old Testament canon on the return from the Exile. "That one final author and collector edited the books of Judges, Ruth, Samuel, and Kings, as a whole, is to be concluded from many signs." Ezra stands in reference to the final form of the Old Testament, as a whole, very much as Moses does in reference to the Pentateuch. He was an inspired prophet, who examined the questions of authorship and inspiration, and whose judgment was accepted by the Jewish Church first, and by the Christian afterward, as final and authoritative.

VOL. I., p. 143. Belief in the canonicity of a sacred book being the result of historical evidence, comes under the head of *historical* faith, not of saving faith. This explains the phraseology of some of the Reformed creeds. The Belgic Confession (Art. V.) declares : " We receive all these books, and these only, as holy and canonical, for the regulation, foundation, and confirmation of our faith ; believing, without any doubt, all things contained in them, not so much because the Church receives and approves them as such, but more especially because the Holy Ghost witnesseth in our hearts that they are from God, whereof they carry the evidence in themselves." The Gallican Confession (Art. IV.) says : " We know these books to be canonical, and the sure rule of our faith, not so much by the common accord and consent of the Church as by the testimony and inward illumination of the Holy Ghost, which enables us to distinguish them from other ecclesiastical books, upon which, however useful, we cannot found any articles of faith." In these statements two forms and grades of belief of Divine revelation are mentioned ; one weaker and one stronger. The first results from " the common accord and consent of the Church ; " the second from " the inward illumination of the Holy Ghost." The former is " not so much " as the latter ; but it is something valid and of probative force, so far as it extends. Saving faith itself depends upon it in some measure, because it presupposes historical faith. The Holy Ghost does not work saving faith in an infidel. The infidelity must first be removed. The historical evidence and belief prepare the way for that illumination and teaching of the Spirit by which saving faith is produced. Locke (Understanding, IV., xvi., 10) states the rule for the value of historical testimony as follows : " Any testimony, the farther off it is from the alleged fact, the less force and proof it has. A credible man vouching his knowledge of it is a good proof ; but if another equally credible do witness it from his report, the testimony is weaker ; and a third that attests the hearsay of an hearsay is yet less considerable ; so that in traditional truths each remove weakens the force of the proof."

Channing (Evidences of Christianity, p. 202) answers the inquiry how we determine the genuineness of books in general, as follows : " It is not necessary that we should ourselves be eye-witnesses of the composition of a book. The ascription of a book to an individual during his life by those who are interested in him, and who have the best means of knowing the truth, removes all doubt as to its author. When the question arises whether an ancient book was written by the individual whose name it bears, we must inquire into the opinion of his contemporaries, or of those who succeeded his contemporaries so nearly as to have intimate communication with them. On this testimony we ascribe many ancient books to their authors with the firmest faith. There are many books of which no notice can be found for several ages after the time of their reputed authors. Still, the fact that as soon as they are named they are ascribed, undoubtingly and by general consent, to certain authors, is esteemed a sufficient reason for regarding them as their productions, unless some opposite proof can be adduced."

Historical faith is the contrary of scepticism. It is

merely belief in the authenticity and canonicity of Scripture, and results from historical testimony and external evidence in distinction from inward and experimental. A person may believe in the genuineness and apostolical origin of the four Gospels without the saving faith in their teachings which is effected by regeneration. Yet this historical faith precedes and is *necessary in order to saving faith*. A person who is sceptical, asserting that the Life of Christ is not the product of the Apostles, but of forgers and unknown persons, cannot receive Christ and his doctrines into his heart with saving faith. The Divine Spirit regenerates only those who stand upon the Christian position, not the infidel, in respect to the historical credibility of the Gospels. Tested by this, that class of Biblical critics who are infidel respecting historical Christianity and historical Judaism cannot be the subjects of regeneration nor have a spiritual comprehension of the Christian religion. What sympathy had Spinoza and Strauss with St. Paul and St. Augustine ? The schools of infidel and rationalistic criticism destroy all saving faith in Christendom, because they destroy all historical faith. In making men unbelieving or doubtful respecting the genuineness and historical credibility of the several books of Scripture, they preclude that inward agency of the Holy Spirit by which regeneration and saving faith are produced, because this is never exerted in the mind of a sceptic as such. As matter of fact, vital religion invariably dies out under such influence as that of Strauss, Kuenen, Wellhausen, and their followers. Materialism and atheism prevail extensively in those countries where this species of " Biblical Criticism " occupies the professor's chair and pulpit.

THEOLOGY (DOCTRINE OF GOD)

VOL. I., p. 154. Osiander maintained that "man was created in the image of God, because he was formed after the similitude of the future Messiah, in order that he might resemble him whom the Father had already decreed to clothe with flesh. Whence he concluded that if Adam had never fallen, Christ would nevertheless have become man." Calvin opposes this as follows: "The notion that Christ would have become man, even though the human race had needed no redemption, is a vague speculation. I grant, indeed, that at the original creation Christ was exalted as head over angels and men; for which reason Paul calls him 'the first-born of every creature;' but since the whole Scriptures proclaim that he was clothed with flesh in order to become a Redeemer, it is excessive temerity to imagine another cause for it. The end for which Christ was promised from the beginning is sufficiently known; it was to restore a fallen world. Therefore under the law his image was exhibited in sacrifices, to inspire the faithful with a hope that God would be propitious to them, after he should be reconciled by the expiation of their sins. The prophets proclaimed and foretold him as the future reconciler of God and men. When Christ himself appeared in the world, he declared the design of his advent to be, to appease God and restore us from death to life. The apostles testified the same. If any one object, that it is not evinced by these testimonies that the same Christ

who has redeemed men from condemnation could not have
testified his love to them by assuming their nature if they
had remained in a state of integrity, we briefly reply, that
since the Spirit declares these two things, Christ's becoming our Redeemer, and his participation of our nature, to
have been connected by the eternal decree of God, it is not
right to make any further inquiry. For he who feels a
desire to know something more, not being content with
the immutable appointment of God, shows himself not to
be contented with this Christ, who has been given to us
as the price of our redemption. I admit that Adam bore
the Divine image because he was united to God; yet I
contend that the similitude of God is to be sought only in
those characteristics of excellence with which God distinguished Adam above the other creatures. And that Christ
was even then the image of God is universally allowed;
and therefore whatever excellence was impressed on Adam
proceeded from the circumstance that he approached to
the glory of his Maker by means of his only-begotten Son.
But this Son was a common head to angels as well as men;
so that the same dignity which was conferred on man belonged to angels also. But if God designed his glory to
be represented in angels as well as in men, and to be
equally conspicuous in the angelic as in the human nature,
it would follow from Osiander's view that angels were inferior to men; because they certainly were not made in the
image of Christ " (Institutes, II., xii., 4–6).

VOL. I., p. 158. Newton, in the Scholium generale at the
end of the Principia, says that God, " by his universal existence, both in time and space, is the creator of time and
space " (Penny Cyclopædia, Art. Principia). There are two
objections to this. 1. It makes time and space to be substances or entities; for whatever is created by God is a
substance or entity, either material or mental. God does
not create nonentities. 2. In making God to exist in
space, it makes him to be matter, for this is the only

space-filling substance; and in making him to exist in time, it makes his consciousness to be a consecutive series undergoing continual change, in which case it is not the simultaneous, all-comprehending, and immutable consciousness of an eternal Being.

That space and time are neither entities nor substances, nor properties of entity or substance, is proved by the fact that whether we add them to, or subtract them from, an object, be it matter or mind, the body or the soul, makes no difference with the object itself. They are not given as properties in a chemical analysis of matter. A piece of gold, when subjected to analysis, will yield all of its constituent properties without any reference to the question, *where* it is, or, *when* it is : that is, to space and time. The only question for the chemist is, *what* it is. Space and time are wholly foreign to it considered as a substance or entity. They are merely the mental forms under which material substance is contemplated by a finite understanding; and there is no more reason for asserting their objective reality than that of the categories of Aristotle and Kant, quantity, quality, relation, etc. These latter are confessedly only subjective in their nature; the manner in which the human mind thinks of objects. They are not substantial properties of objects. The propensity to regard space as an entity is seen in Newton's remark in this same Scholium, that "any particle of space always is [exists]." A particle is an atom, or molecule; and space has no atoms.

Locke (King's Life of Locke, p. 66. Ed. Bohn) in his Journal denies the substantiality of space. "Imaginary space seems to me to be no more anything than an imaginary world. For space or extension, separated in our thoughts from matter or body, seems to have no more real existence than number has without anything to be numbered; and one may as well say the number of the sea-sand does really exist, and is something, the world being annihilated, as that the space or extension of the sea does

exist, or is anything, after such annihilation." Also, in his
"Miscellaneous Papers" (Life, 336, 339), he argues to the
same effect. "If it be possible to suppose nothing, or, in
our thoughts, to remove all manner of beings from any
place, then this imaginary space is just nothing, and signifies no more but a bare possibility that body may exist
where now there is none. Besides this, there seems to me
this great and essential difference between space and body,
that body is divisible into separable parts, but space is
not. If one take a piece of matter of an inch square and
divide it into two, the parts will be separated if set at
further distance one from another; and yet nobody, I
think, will say that the parts of space are or can be removed to a further distance one from another."

VOL. I., p. 159. The distinction in substance and kind
between matter and mind was made by Plato and Aristotle,
who represent the best Greek philosophy; by Cicero, who
represents the best Roman; by Plotinus and Proclus, who
represent the later-Platonism; by the Christian Fathers;
by the Schoolmen; by the great discoverers in modern
physics—Copernicus, Galileo, Kepler, Newton, and Linnæus; and by the leading modern philosophers—Bacon,
Descartes, Leibnitz, Locke, and Kant. The distinction
has also gone into the literatures of the world, and been
recognized by the creative minds: by Homer and Æschy-
lus, by Virgil, by Dante and Cervantes, by Pascal, by
Shakespeare and Milton. The denial of the distinction is
confined to the pantheistic and materialistic schools, to
which physical science is not indebted for any of its leading discoveries, and to which literature in its higher forms
is not at all indebted.

If this distinction is valid, all substance in the created
universe is either matter or mind; and if it is the one it
cannot be or become the other. A chasm lies between
the two realms that cannot be filled up. The limits between them are impassable. There is no transmutation

of matter into mind, or of mind into matter; no evolution of one into the other. The dualism of theism, not the monism of pantheism, is the truth. The Darwinian physics is monistic, in asserting the transmutation of matter into mind; of brute into man; of animal life into moral and spiritual. An examination of the phenomena of animal life evinces that it is a part of the realm of matter, not of mind. The distinctive characteristic that differences the mental, moral, and spiritual world from the material, physical, and non-moral; the human from the animal soul, is *reason*. "Brutes," says Aristotle (Ethics, vii., 3) "have no universal conceptions, but only an instinct of particulars, and memory." In the Epinomis attributed to Plato, the animal is distinguished from man by its ignorance of number. "The animal does not know two and three, even and odd, and is entirely ignorant of number." By reason is not meant any and all intelligence, but a particular species of it. Animal life is intelligent in a certain way, because even in its very lowest forms there is selection of means to an end, and this implies a kind of knowledge. We never think of vegetable life as intelligent in any manner whatever, but the action of instinct in the animal world manifests both perception and volition. The volitions by which "infusoria avoid each other as well as obstacles in their way," and by which "animalcules move by undulations, leaps, oscillations, or successive gyrations;" the intelligence by which the ichneumon-fly deposits its eggs on the species of caterpillar that furnishes the appropriate food for its young, and by which the young grubs themselves "gnaw the inside of the caterpillar, carefully avoiding all the vital parts," in order to preserve their food as long as possible—such intelligence as this, though remarkable, is not *reason*, or the intuitive power. And neither is that still more wonderful instinct by which the bee constructs its hexagonal cells, and the ant builds its galleries and corridors; nor is that "wis-

dom " by which the hawk flies (Job 39 : 26), and by which
he plunges with the unerring velocity of a cannon-ball
from his height in the clouds to the depths where he
grasps his prey ; nor is that foresight by which the migra-
tions of birds are directed; nor is the still higher intelligence of the dog, horse, and " half-reasoning elephant "—
nothing of all this merely *adaptive* skill and foresight in
the tribes of earth, air, and water reaches into the sphere
of *intuitive perception* in mathematics, æsthetics, ethics,
and religion. Though it is the highest grade of instinct,
yet it is no grade at all of reason; as the power of the
architect, however great of its own kind, cannot be or
become the power to create life. " A magnificent temple," says Gibbon (Ch. XL.), " is a laudable monument of
national taste and religion, and the enthusiast who entered
the dome of St. Sophia might be tempted to suppose that
it was the residence, or even the workmanship of the Deity.
Yet how dull is the artifice, how insignificant the labor, if
it be compared with the formation of the vilest insect that
crawls upon the surface of the temple !" As one of the
senses cannot do the work of another ; as the sense of
smell, however acute, cannot possibly see objects or hear
sounds, so the intelligence of the animal, however keen in
its own sphere, cannot possibly enlighten it with the
knowledge of things above that sphere. The whole range
of cognition in mathematics, æsthetics, ethics, and religion
is absolutely beyond its ken. No education whatever can
give to an animal the power of intuitively perceiving axiomatic and necessary truth, because education is gradual,
but intuition is *instantaneous*. If the truth of the axiom
that the whole equals the sum of the parts is not perceived
immediately it cannot be perceived at all. No amount of
teaching and argument in support of it will produce the
intuition. The attempt to introduce an intuition into the
mind gradually is like the attempt to exhibit a mathematical point by making a dot with a pen. The attempt

is suicidal, because the mathematical intuition of the point excludes all dimension in space. The animal, consequently, though having an intelligence that is superior to that of man within a certain sphere (for what man can move to a distant unseen point like the bee on a "bee-line," or the wild-goose in his annual migration), must ever be an irrational, non-intuitive creature. It is not so with mental and rational life in man. The most degraded savage, conceivably and actually, may become by the development of his created capacity even a Newton or Milton, because the kind of his intelligence is like theirs. He is not barred out of the higher regions of knowledge by the structure and constitution of his mind. The most imbruted tribes of men may become the most civilized and enlightened, the most moral and religious, as is seen in the modern Englishman compared with his progenitors; but no tribe of apes, no breed of dogs, can be lifted by training and education above their animal and material range and plane. To the instinctive, irrational intelligence of the brute, the Creator has said: "Thus far shalt thou go, and no further."

Reason, strictly defined, with Kant, as distinct from understanding, is the power of intuitively perceiving the ideas and truths of mathematics, of æsthetics, of ethics, and of religion, and distinguishes animal intelligence from human. The most sagacious dog does not perceive that the whole is equal to the sum of the parts, that there is beauty in the object which strikes his eye, that his anger or deception are wrong and damnable before the moral law, that God is his creator and that he is obligated to him. Neither can he be taught these truths. He can be taught a great variety of actions and tricks that stretch his animal intelligence to the utmost; but no action or trick that involves the perception of any of these higher ideas. He cannot be trained to perceive the truth of an axiom, the beauty of a form, the guilt of a feeling or act, the infinity and glory of God. How do we know this? it may be objected. Because there is no manifestation of such knowledge as there is of that other kind of intelligence which we have noticed. The only conclusive evidence of the existence of a power is its actual operation. The burden of proof, consequently, is upon him who affirms that instinctive intelligence is potentially rational intelligence, and by a natural evolution may be transmuted into it. He is bound to furnish the instances and examples.

By reason, then, of the absence of rational intuitive perception, the animal belongs only to the world of living organic *matter*, not of mind or spirit. His animal soul is not spiritual like mind, but non-spiritual like matter; is not moral like mind, but non-moral like matter; is not immortal like mind, but mortal like matter. The intelligence with which he is endowed is related only to the world of sense, and has no connection with the immaterial world of spirit. It is given to him by his Maker only to subserve the purposes of a brief, transitory existence here upon earth. The " be all and the end all " of the animal is " here, on this bank and shoal of time."

Having thus located the animal within the world of matter, and excluded him from that of spirit, we proceed to consider more particularly the nature of animal *life*. Life in all its forms is an invisible power or principle. No man has seen or can see it. Be it vegetable or animal, it is a power and principle that cannot be detected by the naked or the armed eye. The vitality that builds up the individual plant or animal eludes all observation. Yet it is an objective entity and not a mere conception or figment of the mind, like a mathematical point or line, because, unlike these latter, it produces effects that are both visible and tangible. This evinces its objectivity, and proves that it belongs to the world of real substance. But if animal life is of the nature of matter, there must be a mode or form of matter that is *invisible, intangible,* and *impon-*

derable. In common phraseology, however, matter and mind are differenced as the visible and invisible, the tangible and intangible, the ponderable and imponderable. Matter is popularly defined as extension in the three geometrical dimensions, and this is supposed to exhaust the subject. But there is another form of matter which the mind must recognize. This is its unextended and invisible mode or form. The ultimate of matter, on either the dynamic or atomic theory of it, is without extension and invisible. If we adopt Kant's theory, that extended and visible matter is the resultant of two invisible forces that meet in equilibrium and evince their balancing counteraction by a visible product that fills space with a certain degree of intensity and impenetrability; or if we adopt the theory that visible matter is composed of invisible atoms —in either case we assume an invisible mode of matter. Neither these primordial forces nor these primordial atoms are extended, visible, or ponderable. And yet they are assumed to be entities. Their advocates will not concede that they are mere fictions of the imagination, or mere notions of the mind, like the square root of two. These unextended, invisible forces, or molecules, are claimed to be as objectively real as the visible matter of which they are the underlying substance and ground.

The same reasoning applies to the invisible form of matter in the *inorganic* world as well as in the organic. The forces of attraction and repulsion, of cohesion, of gravitation and chemical affinity, are not, like space and time in the Kantian theory, mere forms of the understanding without objective existence, but real powers and entities. They are substance or being of some kind, because they are able to produce effects, which absolute nonentity cannot do. They constitute a part, and a most important part, of the material universe. Without them there would be no extended and visible matter whatever. But they are themselves unseen ; they are inorganic matter in its invis-

7

ible mode or form. They are the μὴ φαινομένα of Heb.
11 : 3, which were created *ex nihilo* in that " beginning "
spoken of in Gen. 1 : 1, when the chaotic matter of the
universe was created of which they are the constitutive
and regulative forces. Once they were not ; now they are.
This places them among entities. But if non-extension
and invisibility may be a characteristic of inorganic and
dead matter, it surely may be of organic and living matter. If we can believe with Kant that the ultimate form
of matter in the rock is an invisible, we certainly can that
the ultimate form of matter in the vegetable and animal
is ; that that unseen vitality which is the *substans* of the
visible tree or lion is a real somewhat, and makes a constituent part of the material universe of God, the creator
of " all things, visible and invisible " (Col. 1 : 16).

The answer, then, to the question, " What is animal
life ? " is, that it is an invisible *material* principle that is
able to vitalize, organize, and assimilate inorganic and
lifeless matter, and thereby build up a living animal.
Having reference only to the distinction between matter
and mind, animal life is matter, not mind, and in this respect is no higher in kind than the inorganic forces of
gravity and chemical affinity below it. Like them, it is an
invisible form of matter. It no more belongs to the mental, moral, and spiritual world than they do. It is no more
rational, moral, spiritual, immortal, free, and responsible,
than they are. But considered within its own sphere of
the material and physical, and compared with other varieties
of matter, animal life is higher than vegetable life, and
vegetable life is higher than gravity and chemical affinity.
Though animal and vegetable life and the inorganic forces
are all alike physical, material, and non-moral, yet they cannot be evolved from one another. Animal life is not produced by a natural process from vegetable life, and still
less from the inorganic mechanical forces. A distinct and
definite fiat of the Creator is requisite to its origination, as

well as in order to that of the vegetable and the non-vital forces. Such fiats are indicated in Gen. 1 : 3, 11, 20, 24. " God said, Let there be light ; let the earth bring forth grass ; let the waters bring forth the moving creature that hath life ; let the earth bring forth the living creature after his kind."

This view of animal life and the animal soul, as different in kind from rational life and the rational soul, is supported by Scripture. The vitalizing and organizing principle in the animal is denominated a " soul of life," or a "living soul" Gen. (1 : 20, 21, 24). When God created it he addressed the " waters " and the " earth," and made both body and soul together and simultaneously. He did not "breathe" the animal soul, as a distinct and separate thing, into the animal body which it vivified and inhabited, nor did he create it after "his own image and likeness." But when he created the " soul of life," or rational soul, in the first man, he addressed himself, not the waters or the earth, and imbreathed it into a distinct and separate body previously made of " the dust of the ground," and described it as made after his own image and likeness. This difference in the manner of the creation infers the higher grade of being. Again, Scripture describes death in the instance of man as the separation of the soul from the body, the continued existence of the former, and the dissolution of the latter. The animal is never represented as " giving up the ghost," nor is the animal soul described as leaving the body, as being "gathered to its fathers," and continuing to exist in happiness or misery. The death of the animal is the physical destruction of the total creature, body and soul. "The spirit of the beast goeth downward to the earth " (Eccl. 3 : 21); " the beasts perish " (Ps. 49 : 12, 20).

According to this view the entire animal world and animal life, in all its varieties, is of the earth, earthy. It is matter, not mind ; physical, not spiritual. It has no immortality, no everlasting permanency. The animal soul, al-

though it may exhibit a striking kind of intelligence that
allies it with man in some degree, yet is destitute of man's
distinguishing characteristic of reason and rational intuition. Having no moral ideas and sustaining no moral relations, it dies with the body which it has vitalized, organized, and used, in accordance with the design of the Creator,
within that narrow and transitory sphere of existence in
this world, to which alone it belongs.

The instinctive intelligence of the animal is incapable
of passing beyond a certain point. It cannot be trained
or educated to pass it. Up to that point it may be very
acute and sagacious, even exceeding that of man upon the
same subject. The instinct of the beaver is an illustration. If the current is weak, the beavers build their dam
straight across; if strong, they build it convexly. This
supposes an intelligence or knowledge on the part of the
beaver upon *this* point; but not upon cognate points. The
beaver knows that the current is weak or strong, as the
case may be; otherwise he would not build in two ways.
And he knows that building in one way in one case will
not do in the other. But he does not know the properties
of the *arch*, in which figure he builds his dam in a strong
current, and cannot make the conclusions of the mathematician concerning it. His knowledge has a limit beyond which he cannot go, any more than if he were a
piece of inorganic matter. Now, how does he come to have
this degree of intelligence? He must get it, not from the
unintelligent molecules of dead matter and of living proto-
plasm, but from the intelligent Being who made him. The
Creator's *instruction* explains that form of intelligence
called " instinct." " Doth the hawk fly by *thy* wisdom? "
asks Jehovah of Job (39 : 26). The implied answer is,
"No; by *my* wisdom." The whole of the thirty-ninth
chapter of Job attributes all the instinctive intelligence of
animals and birds to God as the author and cause of it.
This lower form of intelligence, like the higher form in

man, is an illumination of the animal by the Creator. This is taught by Paley (Natural Theology, xviii.), who thus explains the *design* which the animal shows in his instinctive action : " When a male and female sparrow come together, they do not meet to confer upon the expediency of perpetuating their species. As an abstract proposition, they care not whether the species be perpetuated or not ; they follow their sensations ; and all those consequences follow which the most solicitous care of futurity, which the most anxious concern for the sparrow world, could have produced. But how do these consequences ensue? The sensations, and the physical constitution upon which they depend, are as manifestly directed to the purpose which we see fulfilled by them, and the train of intermediate effects as manifestly laid and planned with a view to that purpose—that is to say, *design* is as completely evinced by the phenomena as it would be even if we suppose the operations to begin and be carried on from what some will allow to be alone properly called instincts, that is, from desires directed to a future end and having no accomplishment or gratification distinct from the attainment of that end. Now, be it so that those actions of animals which we refer to instinct are not performed with any view to their consequences, but that they are attended in the animal with a present gratification alone ; what does all this prove but that the *prospection*, which must be somewhere, is not in the animal, but in the Creator ? "

Vol. I., p. 161. Augustine holds that angels have bodies. " The question arises, whether angels have bodies adapted to their duties and their swift motions from place to place, or whether they are only spirits ? For, if we say that they have bodies, we are met by the passage, ' He maketh his angels spirits ;' and if we say that they have not bodies, a still greater difficulty meets us in explaining how, if they are without bodily form, it is written that they appeared to the bodily senses of men, accepted offers of hospitality, permitted their feet to be washed, and used the meat and drink that was provided for them. For it seems to involve us in less difficulty if we suppose that the angels are called 'spirits' in the same manner as men are called 'souls;' *e.g.*, in the statement that so many souls (not meaning that they had not bodies also) went down with Jacob into Egypt, than if we suppose that without bodily form all these things were done by angels. Again, a certain definite height is mentioned in the Apocalypse as the stature of an angel, in dimensions which can apply only to bodies, showing that that which appeared to the eyes of men is not to be explained as an illusion, but as resulting from the power which we have spoken of as easily excited by spiritual bodies. But whether angels have bodies or not, and whether or not any one be able to show how without bodies they could do all these things, it is nevertheless certain that in that city of the holy in which those of our race who have been redeemed by Christ shall be united forever with thousands of angels, voices proceeding from organs of speech shall give expression to the thoughts of minds in which nothing is hidden ; for in that divine fellowship it will not be possible for any thought in one to remain concealed from another, but there shall be complete harmony and oneness of heart in the praise of God, and this shall find utterance not only from the spirit, but through the spiritual body as its instrument. This, at least, is what I believe" (Letter XCV., 8. To Paulinus and Therasia, A.D. 408).

VOL. I., p. 162. Fichte supposed that theism can be maintained, and yet the essentiality of God be denied. He denied that God is spiritual substance, and asserted that he is only "the moral order of the universe." "It is an error," he says (Smith's Fichte, I., 104), "to say that it is doubtful whether or not there is a God. It is not doubtful, but the most certain of all certainties, nay, the foundation of all certainties, the one absolutely valid objective truth, that there is a moral order in the world; that to every rational being is assigned his particular place in that order, and the work he has to do ; that his destiny, in so far as it is not occasioned by his own conduct, is the result of this plan; that in no other way can even a hair fall from his head, nor a sparrow fall to the ground about him ; that every true and good action prospers, and every bad action fails ; and that all things must work together for good to those who truly love goodness. On the other hand, no one who reflects for a moment, and honestly avows the result of his reflection, can remain in doubt that the conception of God as a particular *substance* is impossible and contradictory ; and it is right to say this candidly, and to silence the babbling of the schools, in order that the true religion of cheerful virtue may be established in its room."

An analysis of this extract yields the following definition of God : God is not a substantial Being, but the assignment of a place and work to every rational being, the plan of every man's work, and the process whereby all things work for good. He is not a spiritual essence or entity, but an arrangement, a plan, and a process. Fichte believed that he was defending the doctrine of the Divine existence in a statement that annihilates his existence, if by existence he meant real objective being. The moral order is no more a substance having objective existence than the moral law is. No one would think of denominating the latter a being or essence having qualities and attributes.

Vol. I., p. 172. The doctrine that God and the universe constitute an organic unity accords with the monism of pantheism, but not with the dualism of theism. If God is infinite and the universe finite, as theism affirms, the latter is immanent in, and dependent on, the former, but not organically one with it. Yet this last is affirmed sometimes by writers who repudiate pantheism. Caird (Philosophy of Religion, 241, 243, 251) asserts that a " true solution of the higher problems of religion is impossible if we start from dualistic suppositions. A true solution can be reached only by apprehending the divine and the human, the infinite and the finite, as the moments, or members, of an *organic whole*, in which both exist at once in their distinction and their unity. The true infinite is not the mere negation of the finite, but that which is the *organic unity* of the infinite and finite." There are the following objections to this view: 1. The infinite excludes the finite, because, so far as finite elements and qualities are conceived as belonging to an infinite essence, it is not infinite, as water is not water so far as fire is supposed to be a component in it. The true infinite is, therefore, the negation, or the exclusion, of the finite. 2. An organic unity constituted of both the infinite and finite would be an Infinite-Finite, not the simple Infinite; as when, for illustration, the Logos unites with an individual human nature he is no longer simply Divine, but Divine-Human. 3. An organic unity composed of God and the universe would make them one sum and system of being. The Deity would become a part of a general system. But God is not a part of anything. The universe is a creation from nothing by His omnipotence, and is of a different substance from the Divine essence. It cannot, therefore, be put into a sum-total along with God, and constitute one common mass of being with Him. Once the universe was not. But God always was. The universe is contingent being; God is necessary being. To combine under the notion of an organic whole such totally different objects as God and the world, temporal being and eternal being, contingent being and necessary being, contradicts the nature of each. But this is attempted. "We are required to show," says Caird, "first, that finite spirit presupposes, or is intelligible only in the light of, the idea of, the Infinite Spirit; and, secondly, that the Infinite Spirit contains, in the very idea of its nature, organic relations to the finite." Here the difference in kind between the infinite and finite is overlooked. It is true that man supposes God, and is inexplicable without him. But the converse is not true. God does not suppose man, and man's existence does not explain that of God. It is true that we cannot think of man independently of God; but we can and must think of God independently of man. "Before the mountains were brought forth, or ever thou hadst formed the earth and the world, even from everlasting to everlasting, thou art God." The infinite cannot, therefore, be brought into the same class of being with the finite. But it is so brought when it is made a part of one and the same system. Nature may be an organic unity. Man as a species may be an organic unity. But God and nature together cannot be an organic unity; and neither can God and universal man be such. 4. In a true organism the parts are equally necessary and coeval. All of the organs of an organism have the same contemporaneous origin in the original germ, and develop simultaneously. This, of course, cannot be true of the infinite mind and the finite mind, and still less of the infinite mind and matter.

We have taken notice of the error of making God a part of "Being in general" (Vol. I., 192). The doctrine that God and the universe are an organic unity is essentially the same thing. The duality in essence, and the difference in kind between God and the universe, affirmed from the beginning by theistic philosophers, precludes it. God is from eternity; the finite universe, both of mind and matter, began in time by a creative fiat of God. The latter is immanent in, but not emanent from, the former. Acts 17:28. The "immanence of God in the universe" is often asserted. But, strictly speaking, the universe is immanent in God, rather than God in the universe. The greater contains the less, not the less the greater. Compare what is said respecting the Divine omnipresence in Vol. I., 340. Whenever, therefore, the Divine immanence is mentioned it should be guarded by the Divine transcendence. There is no such existence of God in his universe as precludes his existence out of and beyond it. Otherwise God is only the soul of the universe. Man "lives, and moves, and has his being in God," says St. Paul; but he does not say that "God lives, and moves, and has his being in man."

The inscription on the temple of Sais, in Egypt, contains the error of making God and the universe one system of being, or the All. "I am all that was, and is, and shall be." Rothe, as cited by Müller (Sin, I., 11), contends that "all right speculative knowledge must start from one primary datum, and from this develop by strict logic a system of thought consecutively evolved. This system must be an exact counterpart or image of the universe; using this word in the widest sense as *including God*." Müller, in criticising Rothe's general position, remarks that "we have no right to put God and the world together in our conception of the universe, for then the world must be regarded as the complement of God, and this contradicts the idea of the Absolute. God is a universe in himself, whether the world exists or not" (Sin, I., 14, Note). It is by such a remark as this that Müller evinces his consistent theism, and that he was not influenced by the monism of Schelling and Hegel, as were theologians like Rothe, Martensen, and Dorner.

VOL. I., p. 179. Hamilton (Bowen's Ed., p. 127) defines consciousness by "I know that I know." This is self-consciousness, not simple consciousness. The latter is expressed by "I know." In self-consciousness the person is conscious that he is conscious. In consciousness he is merely conscious. Consciousness is the sentiency or feeling, in the inner or outer sense, which occurs in the waking moments of every man without his taking cognizance of it by reflection upon it. A man may see without reflecting that he sees; think without thinking of his thinking; feel without scrutinizing his feeling; in other words, may be conscious without being self-conscious. Again, in mere consciousness the object is other than the ego and external to it, but in self-consciousness the object is the ego in one of its modifications or subjective states. To illustrate : A man is conscious of a mountain ; he receives various impressions and sensations from it. Up to this point he is conscious of an object other than ego, namely, of the mountain. Thus far he is not conscious of himself as the ego that is modified by the mountain, but only of the mountain. If now he takes the second step, and makes this consciousness itself, these sensations and impressions themselves, the object of cognition, he passes to self-consciousness. He becomes conscious of his consciousness ; that is, he becomes self-conscious. For the object now is, not the mountain, as in the former case, but *himself* as affected by the mountain. He is now examining and cognizing the ego in one of its states, and not the non-ego, or mountain, and is getting a knowledge of himself rather than of the mountain. He obtained all the knowledge of the mountain that is possible to him by his previous sensation or consciousness of it, but obtained no knowledge of himself in the process, because he did not contemplate himself as affected by the mountain. But afterwards he ceases to obtain any more knowledge of the mountain, and gets a knowledge of himself by examining and becoming self-conscious of his inward experience. In this way it appears that consciousness is the knowledge of the non-ego as an object ; and self-consciousness is the knowledge of the ego as an object. There is therefore the same difference between consciousness and self-consciousness as between knowledge and self-knowledge.

Hamilton (Ed. Bowen, p. 131) defines consciousness to be "the recognition by the thinking subject of its own acts or affections." This also is self-consciousness, not consciousness. It is cognizing something subjective and internal, namely, the mind's own action and state, not cognizing something objective and external. As Hamilton denominates it, it is *recognition*, or cognizing again a second time.   The mind first knows the object consciously, and then again knows this knowledge or consciousness by reflecting upon it, and thereby becomes *self*-conscious.

This analysis, whereby the difference between consciousness and self-consciousness is apparent, shows the error in Berkeley's theory of consciousness.   He asserts that the sensation and the accompanying idea in the mind constitute the *object* of consciousness, and the only object there is.   In this way there is nothing externally and really objective.   But the truth is, that neither the inward sensation nor the inward idea is the object of the consciousness, but is the consciousness itself.   For illustration, I am conscious of the sensation of heat.   Heat is my sensation, or consciouness.   If now, according to Berkeley, this sensation is itself the object of my sensation or consciousness, then I have a sensation of a sensation, or a consciousness of a consciousness.   This is making a sensation both its own object and its own subject, both the thing perceived and the percipient.   It is no answer to the question, *Why* am I conscious, and of *what* am I conscious ? to say, I am conscious because of my consciousness, and of my consciousness because of my sensation and of my sensation. The true answer is, I am conscious of an external object that is not myself, or any modification of myself, like a sensation, which causes my consciousness or sensation. Instead of saying, as Berkeley does, that sensations and ideas are the *object* of consciousness, we must say that sensations and ideas *are* consciousness.

Berkeley's reasoning would apply better, but not fully, to self-consciousness, in distinction from consciousness.   In this case the subject does constitute the object.   In self-consciousness the object is not a different substance from the subject, but is identical with it.   The external reality of the object in *this* instance, in the sense of its being a different and another substance from the ego, must be denied.   But even in this instance the *consciousness* of the self *is* not the self.   It is the soul, the ego, and not the self-consciousness, that is the real object of the self-consciousness.

I am conscious of the sensation of heat from a hot coal. This sensation is not the hot coal; that is to say, is not the object of the sensation.   It is true that the sensation includes all that I *know* about the coal, but this does not prove that this is all there *is* of the coal.   My sensation is the measure of my *knowledge* of the object, but not of the whole reality and nature of the object.   If it were, then it would follow that nothing exists but what I know of, and as I know it.   The presence of a sensation infers the reality of an external object as the cause of it; otherwise, there is an effect without a cause.   But the absence of a sensation does not infer the unreality or nonentity of an external object.   When I cease to be conscious of a landscape, the landscape does not cease to exist.   My sensation of it ceases, but the external object does not.   This is proved by the fact that I can *recover* and *renew* my sensation of the landscape by going to it and beholding it once more.

Vol. I., p. 181.   Schelling's explanation of all cognition by an assumed identity of substance between the knowing subject and the known object, of which a clear statement is given by Coleridge in his Biographia Literaria, ch. xii., gets no support from the fact that in self-consciousness the subject and object are identical in substance.   For this is not because the object, in order to be *known*, must be identical in substance with the knowing subject, that is, because mind cannot know anything but mind, or matter anything but matter, but because in order to know *self* the self must, of course, be posited as the object to be known.   The monistic assumption that if mind and matter are heterogeneous the former cannot cognize the latter, and that therefore the fundamental distinction between them must be given up, converts all consciousness into self-consciousness.

This is expressly said by the advocates of this theory. " The apparent contradiction that the existence of things without us, which from its nature cannot be immediately certain, should be received as blindly and as independently of all grounds as the existence of our own being, the Transcendental philosopher can solve only on the supposition that the former is unconsciously involved in the latter ; that it is not only coherent but identical, and one and the same thing with our own immediate self-consciousness. To demonstrate this identity is the office and object of his philosophy " (Coleridge, Works, III., 340 ; Shedd's Ed.). But when a person is conscious of a tree or the sky, he knows as certainly as he knows anything that this is not being conscious of himself. The self must, of course, be the object, if the cognition is to be *self*-cognition. But when the cognition is to be the cognition of the *not-self;* when consciousness and not self-consciousness is to occur ; identity of substance between the knowing subject and the known object is excluded, from the very nature of the case.

VOL. I., p. 190. It is an error in Spinoza to say that in order to self-consciousness a person " must distinguish himself from something that is not himself ; " that is, from the world. This would be the consciousness of another object than self, which, of course, would not be the consciousness of self. The non-ego would be cognized, but the ego would still be uncognized. The person would indeed know negatively that he is not the world, but would not know positively what he himself is. What the ego is cannot be told until the cognition settles upon the ego, and the instant this is done the non-ego, or the world, is no longer the object contemplated. So that the very reverse of Spinoza's proposition is the truth. A person must cease distinguishing himself from and cognizing the world, and begin to distinguish himself from and cognize himself, in order to the very first step in personal self-knowledge. He must by an act of reflection duplicate *himself* and obtain an object for the contemplating subject by making himself, and not the world, the object. So long as he takes the world for the object he cannot take himself for it. And until he does this he has no *self*-knowledge, though he has knowledge. He knows the world, but not himself. He has consciousness, but not self-consciousness.

VOL. I., p. 191. The Unlimited as well as the All is often put for the Infinite. This is erroneous. The Unlimited is the Indefinite. It may be greater or less. Unlimited space, conceivably, may be added to or subtracted from. The Infinite, on the contrary, is the definite and fixed; it is incapable of either increase or diminution. A Divine attribute like omnipotence cannot be conceived of as being more or less of power. Indefiniteness in quantity is excluded by its strict infinity. Says Cudworth (Syst., III., 131, Ed. Tegg): "There appeareth no sufficient ground for this positive infinity of space, we being certain of no more than this, that be the world or any figurative [formed] body never so great, it is not impossible but that it might be still greater and greater without end. Which indefinite increasableness of body and space seems to be mistaken for a positive infinity thereof. Whereas for this very reason, because it can never be so great but that more magnitude may still be added to it, therefore it can never be positively infinite." Des Cartes makes a similar statement and confines the term Infinite to God (Principles of Philosophy, Pt. I., 26, 27, Tr. Veitch, 125). "To those who demand whether the half of an infinite line is also infinite, and whether an infinite number is even or odd, and the like, we answer that in reference to such things as these, in which we discover no limits, we will not therefore affirm that they are strictly infinite, but regard them simply as indefinite. Thus, because we cannot imagine extension so great that we cannot still conceive

greater, we will say that the magnitude of possible things
is indefinite, and because a body cannot be divided into
parts so small that each of these may not be conceived as
again divided into others still smaller, let us regard quantity
as divisible into parts whose number is indefinite; and as
we cannot imagine so many stars that it would seem impossible for God to create more, let us suppose that their
number is indefinite, and so in other instances. We will
therefore call all such things indefinite rather than infinite,
with the view of reserving to God alone the appellation of
infinite; in the first place, not only because we discover in
him no limits on any side, but also because we positively
perceive that he admits of none; and in the second place,
because we do not in the same way positively perceive that
things like space and bodies are in every part unlimited,
but merely negatively admit that their limits cannot be discovered by us." Cudworth (System, II., 536, Ed. Tegg)
also defines the Infinite as the Perfect, and confines the
term to God. "Infinity is nothing else but perfection.
For infinite understanding and knowledge is nothing else
but perfect knowledge, that which hath no defect or mixture
of ignorance with it. So in like manner infinite power is
nothing else but perfect power, that which hath no defect or
mixture of impotency in it; a power of producing and doing
all whatsoever is possible, that is, whatsoever is conceivable.
Infinite power can do whatsoever infinite understanding can
conceive, and nothing else; conception being the measure
of power, and its extent, and whatsoever is in itself inconceivable being therefore impossible. Lastly, infinity of
duration, or eternity, is really nothing else but perfection,
as including necessary existence and immutability in it;
so that it is not only contradictious to such a Being to
cease to be, or exist, but also to have had a newness or
beginning of being, or to have any flux or change therein,
by dying to the present, and acquiring something new to
itself which was not before. Notwithstanding which, this

Being comprehends the differences of past, present, and future, or the successive priority and posteriority of all temporary things. And because infinity is perfection, therefore can nothing which includeth anything of imperfection in the very idea and essence of it be truly and properly infinite, such as number, corporeal magnitude, and successive duration. All which can only counterfeit and imitate infinity in their having more and more added to them indefinitely, whereby notwithstanding they never reach it or overtake it. There is nothing truly infinite, neither in knowledge, nor in power, nor in duration, but only one absolutely perfect Being, or the Holy Trinity." Howe (Oracles, Pt. II., Lecture ix.) takes the same view, though rejecting a certain use of the term "indefinite." "It hath been a question much agitated amongst philosophers whether the created universe have any created limits at all or not. It hath been agitated by some with a very ill design. With a mixture of fraud and folly, in discussing the question whether the created universe were infinite or not, they have told us they would not say it was infinite, but it was indefinite. When the terms are distinguished of infinite and indefinite, I would fain know what they mean by the latter. If by indefinite they mean that which hath *in itself* no certain limits, then they plainly say that the created universe is infinite, because it hath no fixed and certain limits. But if they mean by it only that it hath no *known* limits to us, that every one readily acknowledgeth; and so it is best to say it is finite, if they mean only so. Infinity is the proper predicate or attribute of Deity alone. To say that the universe is infinite is to say that it is not a creation; and this would be taking away all the foundations of religion by confounding God and the creature. If the creature were infinite, there could be no subject of religion [*i.e.*, no finite subject to worship the infinite object of religion]. And there can be no place for religion if there were no subject of it, any more than if there were no object of it."

8

VOL. I., p. 193. Coleridge commits the error of finding the personality of the Godhead or Trinity in one of the persons alone and not in the union of the three persons, and thus of confounding the personality of the Trinity with the hypostatical personality. " I cannot," he says (Works, V., 269), " meditate too deeply or too devotionally on the personeity of God and his personality in the Word." " O most unhappy mistranslation of hypostasis by person ! The Word is properly the only Person " (Works, V., 406). It is difficult to determine what Coleridge means by " personeity " in distinction from " personality," as he says little upon the point (Compare Works, V., 410). But it seems to be what he elsewhere denominates the "thesis," which looks like the Sabellian and the Pythagorean *ground* for the Trinity. In this case the personality evolves from the personeity, and appears in the Son or Logos. This is not the Nicene doctrine, as Coleridge indirectly acknowledges by his partial disagreement with writers like Waterland and Bull. " It would be no easy matter," he says, " to find a tolerably competent individual who more venerates the writings of Waterland than I do. But still, in how many pages do I not see reason to regret that the total idea of the $4 = 3 = 1$ of the adorable Tetractys, eternally manifested in the Triad, Father, Son, and Spirit, was never in its cloudless unity present to him. Hence both he and Bishop Bull too often treat it as a peculiarity of positive religion, which is to be cleared of all contradiction to reason, and then, thus negatively qualified, to be actually received by an act of mere will " (Works, V., 404). " It cannot be denied that in changing the formula of the Tetractys into the Trias by merging the Prothesis in the Thesis, the Identity in the Ipseity, the Christian Fathers subjected their exposition to many inconveniences " (Works, V., 416). For further criticism of this feature in Coleridge's Trinitarianism, see Shedd, Literary Essays, pp. 320, 321.

VOL. I., p. 205. That the human race began with monotheism, and that the earlier forms of the ethnic religions
were higher and more spiritual than the later, is maintained
tained by Curtius (Greece, II., ii.). "The Pelasgi, like
their equals among the branches of the Aryan family, the
Persians and Germans, worshipped the supreme God
without images or temples ; spiritual edification, also, was
provided for them by their natural high-altars, the lofty
mountain tops. Their supreme God was adored by them
even without a name ; for Zeus (Deus) merely means the
heavens, the æther, the luminous abode of the Invisible ;
and when they wished to imply a nearer relation between
him and mankind they called him, as the author of all
things living, Father - Zeus, Dipatyros (Jupiter). This
pure and chaste worship of the godlike Pelasgi is not only
preserved as a pious tradition of antiquity, but in the
midst of Greece, where it abounded with images and temples,
ples, there flamed as of old on the mountains the altars of
Him who dwelleth not in temples made with hands. It is
the element of primitive simplicity which has always preserved
served itself longest and safest in the religions of antiquity.
Thus through all the centuries of Greek history the Arcadian
dian Zeus, formless, unapproachable, dwelt in sacred light
over the oak tops of the Lycæan mountain ; and the
boundaries of his domain were marked by every shadow
within them growing pale. Long, too, the people retained
tained a pious dread of representing the Divine Being
under a fixed name or by symbols recognizable by the
senses. For, besides the altar of the ' Unknown,' whom
Paul acknowledged as the living God, there stood here
and there in the towns altars to the ' pure,' the ' great,' the
' merciful ' gods ; and by far the greater number of the
names of the Greek gods are originally mere epithets of
the unknown deity."

The opinion upon such a subject as the primitive intellectual
lectual and moral condition of mankind of a historian like

Curtius, whose life has been devoted to the study of the
ancient literatures, philosophies, and religions, is far more
trustworthy than that of mere physicists like Darwin and
Lubbock, whose knowledge in these provinces is comparatively scanty. It is noteworthy, in this connection, that
there is no mention in Genesis of formal idolatry until
after the deluge.

VOL. I., p. 206. Stillingfleet (Origenes, Unfinished Book
I., i.) observes that when the common consent of mankind
concerning the Divine existence is denied, it should be
noticed : 1. " That we must distinguish the more brutish
and savage peoples from the more intelligent and rational ;
because it is possible for mankind, by a neglect of all kind
of instruction to degenerate almost to the nature of
brutes. But surely such are not fit to be brought in for
the instances of what naturally belongs to mankind. 2.
That we must not judge by the light information of mere
strangers and persons who land upon savage islands with
vicious and bad designs." Stillingfleet mentions that
atheists in his day contended that there was no knowledge
of God nor religion among the inhabitants of South Africa,
Japan, New Guinea, West Indies, Brazil, and North America, and cites authorities to disprove this.

VOL. I., p. 220. Owen (On Forgiveness, Works, XIV.,
129–133, Ed. Russell) marks the difference between natural and revealed religion, with respect to the attributes of
justice and mercy, as follows : " The things that belong to
God are of two sorts. 1. Natural and necessary ; such as
his benevolence, holiness, righteousness, omnipotence, eternity, and the like. These are spoken of in Rom. 1 : 19 as
τὸ γνωστὸν τοῦ θεοῦ. There are two ways, the apostle declares, whereby this class of attributes may be known ;
first, by the common conceptions which men have of God,
and second, by the teachings of the works of God. 2. The
second sort are the free acts of God's will and power; or
his free eternal purpose of mercy, with the temporal dis-

pensations that flow from it. Of this sort is the forgiveness of sin. This is not a property of the nature of God, but an act of his will, and a work of his grace. Although it has its rise and spring in the infinite goodness of God's nature, yet it is not exercised but by an absolute free and sovereign act of his will. Hence there is nothing of God of this kind that can be known except by special revelation. For, first, there is no inbred notion in the heart of man of the acts of God's will. Forgiveness is not revealed by the light of nature. Flesh and blood, that is, human nature, does not declare it. 'No man hath seen God at any time,' that is, as a God of mercy and pardon such as the Son reveals him (John 1 : 8). Adam had an intimate knowledge of those natural and necessary attributes of God mentioned by St. Paul. It was implanted in his heart as necessary to that natural worship which by the law of his creation he was to render. But when he had sinned, it is evident from the narrative that he had not the least apprehension that there was forgiveness with God. Such a thought would have laid a foundation of some further treaty with God about his condition. But he had no further intention but of fleeing and hiding himself (Gen. 3 : 10), and so showing that he was utterly ignorant of any such thing as pardoning mercy. Such are all the first or purely natural conceptions of sinners ; namely, that it is 'the judgment of God' that sin is to be punished with death (Rom. 1 : 32). Secondly, the consideration of the works of God's creation will not help a man to the knowledge that there is forgiveness with God. The apostle tells us that God's works reveal the 'eternal power and Godhood,' or the essential properties of his nature, but no more ; not the purposes of his grace, nor any of the free acts of his will ; not pardon and forgiveness. Thirdly, the works of God's providence do not reveal the forgiveness of sin. God has indeed given proof in the works of his providence that he is a kind and benevolent being, 'in that he did good, and gave us rain from heaven and fruitful seasons, filling our hearts with food and gladness' (Acts 14 : 15–17), but yet these things did not discover pardon and forgiveness. For God still suffered men to go on in their own ways, and patiently endured their sinful ignorance of him and disregard of his law. St. Paul, at Athens, by arguments drawn from the works and acts of God proved his being and benevolent character (Acts 17 : 23–27). But of the discovery of pardon and forgiveness in God by these ways and means he speaks not; yea, he plainly shows that this was not done by them. For after saying that men sinned under and against these benevolent dealings of God's providence, he adds, 'But now,' that is, by the word of the Gospel, God 'commandeth all men everywhere to repent.' The revelation of mercy and forgiveness, he thus teaches belongs to revealed religion, not to natural. Lastly, the law of God makes no discovery of the forgiveness of sin. God implanted the moral law in the heart of man by creation; but there was not annexed unto this law, or revealed with it, the least intimation of pardon to be obtained, if transgression should ensue. And the moral law written in the human conscience, together with the idea of God, make the substance of natural religion."

VOL. I., p. 223. Grotius makes use of Anselm's and Descartes's ontological argument. "God exists necessarily, or is self-existent. Now that which is necessary, or self-existent, cannot be considered as of any common kind or species of being, but as actually existing, and therefore a single [solitary] being. For if you imagine many gods, you will see that necessary existence belongs to none of them; nor can there be any reason why two gods should rather be believed than three, or ten than five " (Christian Religion, I., iii.). Stillingfleet (Origines, B. III., ch. i.) maintains that necessity of being is implied in perfection of being. " We have a clear perception that necessity of existence doth belong to the nature of God. In all other beings nothing else can be implied in the nature of them beyond bare possibility of existence. But in our conception of a being absolutely perfect, bare possibility or. contingency of existence is directly contradictory to the idea of him. For how can we conceive that being to be absolutely perfect who may be a nonentity ? We attribute bare possibility of existence to all beings except the absolutely perfect, because we cannot attribute necessity of existence to them, since this is not implied in the idea of them and in their nature. They depend upon some other being for existence, upon whose will and power it rests whether they shall come into being. Now all these reasons which make us attribute bare possibility of existence to all beings who are not absolutely perfect, are taken away when we conceive of a being absolutely perfect, and therefore we must conclude that necessity of existence doth immutably belong to the nature and idea of God, and is not merely a mode only of our conception; because if we take away necessity of existence from God, we lose the notion of a being absolutely perfect. But if necessary existence belongs to the nature of God, actual existence follows as a necessary condition; for it is a contradiction for a being to exist necessarily, and yet it be questionable whether he doth exist or not."

Vol. I., p. 224. The "Perfect" is a better term than the "Absolute" to denote God. The latter may be employed by the pantheist, and is very extensively, but the former excludes pantheism. For a being who is perfect must have such predicates as personality, and such attributes as holiness and justice, benevolence and mercy—all of which are denied by Spinoza. Furthermore, a being may be absolute in some respects but not in others; but he cannot be perfect without being complete in perfection, without having all conceivable perfections. The subtle insight of Anselm is apparent in his selection of the term "Perfect" wherewith to define the Infinite Being, instead of the "Absolute," which is the favorite term of all the pantheistic schools.

The definition of God as the Perfect, Necessary, and Infinite Being, furnishes the answer to the question, Whether good and evil are such because God so wills, or whether he so wills because they are such. Is God relative to these, or are they to him? The latter, of course, if he is the Infinite and they are the Finite; if he is the Eternal and they the Temporal; if he is the Necessary and they the Contingent. Evil is temporal in its nature, for, though it never ends, it begins. It was not from all eternity. Nor is it marked by necessity. It need not have been. Good also is temporal in its nature apart from God. Aside from him it exists only in created and finite spirits, and these are not from eternity. Nor is good in man or angel a necessary quality. The predicates of infinity, necessity, eternity, and perfection which are applicable to God but not to good apart from God, make him the primary object, and the latter the secondary, in considering the question of relativity and dependence. If God wills the right because right already is apart from God and has a nature separate from him which moves him to will it, then he is not primary, but secondary; he is dependent, and not it. And the same is true if he is displeased with evil because evil exists from eternity independently of his government and control. The truth in the case is stated in Hooker's position (Polity, I., i.), that "the *being* of God is a kind of law to his working; for that perfection which God *is* giveth perfection to what he *doeth*." The Divine reason is one with the Divine will immutably and necessarily, so that God is not guided and controlled, as all creatures are, by a reason that is above and outside of himself, but by his own holy and perfect nature. Similarly, Milton (Samson Agonistes, 307–314) describes the relation of God to the laws which he has laid down for his creatures:

> " Yet more there be who doubt his ways not just,
> As to his own edicts found contradicting,

These give the reins to wandering thought,
Regardless of his glory's diminution ;
Till, by their own perplexities involved,
They ravel more, still less resolved,
But never find self-satisfying solution.
As if they would confine the Interminable,
And tie him to his own prescript
Who made our laws to bind us, not himself ;
And hath full right to exempt
Whom so it pleases him by choice
From national obstruction, without taint
Of sin, or legal debt ;
For with his own laws he can best dispense."

VOL. I., p. 225. The ontological argument is the most rigorously conclusive and mathematical of any, because it requires only the idea of God to construct it. The a posteriori arguments require both the idea of God and of the created universe. In this respect the ontological argument corresponds better with the absolute independence of God. God's existence does not depend upon that of the universe. He exists before it, and without it. Similarly, the ontological proof of God's existence does not depend upon the existence of a universe by which to prove it. The proof is found in the very idea of God apart from the idea of anything else. If the a posteriori argument should fail, or be impossible of construction because of the non-existence of a created effect from which to infer a first cause, the a priori argument still remains and holds good. In this respect the ontological argument is strictly geometrical in its force. A theorem in geometry is demonstrated out of its own terms and logical implications.

VOL. I., p. 227. In his reply to the argument of Anselm, in the Proslogium, Gaunilo wholly overlooks the characteristic of " necessity of existence," which belongs to Anselm's idea of the most perfect Being. He even compares the idea of " a being than whom a greater cannot be conceived " with the idea of " a false being, having no existence," as if the two were analogous ideas, having common characteristics! " May I not," he says, " in the same manner be said to have in my intelligence false things of any kind which can have in themselves no existence whatever; since should any one speak of these things I could understand whatever he might say? (Pro Insipiente, 2). Anselm notices Gaunilo's misstatement of the argument, in substituting " a being greater than all things else that exist " for "a being greater than all things else that can be conceived." " In order to prove that the being in question exists in reality, it does not amount to the same thing whether we speak of a being greater than all that exists, or of a being the greatest that can be conceived. For it is not so evident that that which can be conceived not to be [or exists contingently] is not greater than all things which exist, as it is that it is not the greatest thing conceivable " (Contra Gaunilonem, V.). A contingent being might be greater than all other existing contingent beings, but not greater than all conceivable beings ; for among these would be a necessary being.

The idea of God is unique and without a true analogue, not only in differing from the idea of every contingent object or being in that it is the idea of a necessary Being, but also in that it is the idea of a *present* Being. It is not given by the memory as the idea of something that existed in the past, but by the mental constitution as the idea of something that exists here and now. When, for illustration, we remember a past experience, say of physical pain, we remember it as past. It has no present existence. But when we "remember God and are troubled" (Ps. 77 : 3), this is not the recalling of something in the past which no longer exists, but the recognition of something that is now. The idea of a past physical pain is the idea of something once actual, but which is so no longer. The idea of the past pain does not imply the present existence of the pain. But the idea of God implies the present existence of God.

For the idea of God is not the idea of an object that existed at a particular moment in our past experience, but which exists no longer, as was the case with the physical pain, but of an object that exists simultaneously with the idea itself. In the case of physical pain, or of any remembered object of consciousness, the actual presence of the object is not requisite in order to account for it. But in case of the idea of God, the actual presence of the object is requisite. In this latter instance, the mind does not go back into the past for the matter of the idea, as it does in the instance of all remembered contingent objects, but finds the matter of it in the present instant. The mind is conscious, not that God *was*, but that God *is*. This shows that the relation of the idea of God to God as its correspondent object is wholly different from the relation of the idea of a remembered contingent object to its correspondent object. In the former instance the idea implies the object as present ; in the latter it does not. But what is present is existent.

VOL. I., p. 239. Spinoza (Theologico-Political Treatise, ch. xiii.) thus defines the name Jehovah : " Jehovah is the only word found in Scripture with the meaning of the absolute essence of God, without reference to created things. The Jews maintain, for this reason, that this is, strictly speaking, the only name of God ; that the rest of the words used are merely titles ; and in truth the other names of God, whether they be substantives or adjectives, are merely attributive, and belong to him in so far as he is conceived of in relation to created things, or manifested through them. Thus El, or Eloah, signifies powerful, as is well known, and only applies to God in respect to his supremacy, as when we call Paul an apostle ; the faculties of his power are set forth in an accompanying adjective, as El, great, awful, just, merciful, etc., or else all are understood at once by the use of El in the plural number with a singular signification —an expression frequently adopted in Scripture."

VOL. I., p. 242. The finite rational implies the infinite rational. This is maintained by scientific physiologists. " There is," says Carpenter (Physiology, § 116), " no part of man's physical nature which does not speak of the Divine Being. The very perception of finite existence, whether in time or space, leads to the idea of the Infinite. The perception of dependent existence leads to the idea of the Self-existent. The perception of change in the external world leads to the idea of an Absolute Power as its source. The perception of the order and constancy underlying all these diversities which the surface of Nature presents, leads to the idea of the Unity of that power. The recognition of Intelligent Will as the source of the power we ourselves exert, leads to the idea of a like Will as operating in the Universe. And our own capacity for reasoning, which we know not to have been obtained by our individual exertions, is a direct testimony to the Intelligence of the Being who implanted it. Also, we are led from the existence of our Moral Feelings to the conception of the existence of attributes the same in kind, however exalted in degree, in the Divine Being. The sense of Truth implies its actual existence in a Being who is its source and centre. The perception of Right, in like manner, leads us to the Absolute Lawgiver who implanted it in our constitution. The aspirations of man's moral nature after Holiness and Purity meet their appropriate object only in the Divine Ideal. The sentiment of Beauty soars into the region of the Unseen, where the imagination contemplates such Beauty as no artistic representation can embody. By thus combining, so far as our capacity will admit, the ideas which we derive from our own consciousness, we are led to conceive of the Divine Being as Absolute, Unchangeable, Self-existent; Infinite in duration, Illimitable in space, the highest Ideal of Truth, Right, and Beauty ; the All-Powerful source of the agency we see in the phenomena of Nature, the All-Wise designer of its wondrous plan,

and the All-Just disposer of events in the Moral World.
And in proportion to the elevation of our own spiritual
nature, and more particularly as we succeed in raising ourselves towards that ideal of perfection which has been
graciously presented to us in the 'well-beloved Son of
God,' are the relations of the Divine Nature to our own
felt to be more intimate. It is from the consciousness of
our relation to God as his children that all those ideas
and sentiments arise which are designated as Religious,
and which constitute that most exalted portion of our nature, of whose endless existence we have the fullest assurance, both in the depths of our own consciousness and in
the promises of Revelation." It is striking to compare
this reasoning of Carpenter with that of Darwin and
Haeckel upon such subjects. There are, certainly, conflicting "scientists;" and also what St. Paul denominates
"oppositions of science falsely so called" (1 Tim., 6:
20).

VOL. I., p. 243. In the creation of entity from nonentity the cause must necessarily exist prior to the effect;
but not in the *emanation* of entity from entity. "It is
agreeable to reason," says Leighton (Theological Lectures,
xi.), "and for aught we know it is absolutely necessary,
that in all external productions (opera ad extra) by a free
agent the cause should be, even in time, prior to the
effect; that is, that there must have been some point of
time wherein the being producing did, but the thing produced did not, exist. As to the eternal generation which
we believe, it is within God himself (opus ad intra), nor
does it constitute anything external to him, or different
from his nature and essence. The external production
(opus ad extra) of a created being of a nature vastly different from the agent that is supposed to originate it, and
who acts freely in its origination, implies in its formal conception, as the schools express it, a translation from nonentity into being; whence it seems necessarily to follow

that there must have been some point of time wherein that created being did not exist."

Vol. I., p. 247. The etymology of "Nature" implies that it is not self-caused, but is originated by something other than itself. "Nascor" signifies to be born. "The very name of Nature," says Milton (Christian Doctrine, in initio), "implies that it must owe its birth to some prior agent." "A law of nature," says Dymond (Essay I., ch. ii.), " is a very imposing phrase; and it might be supposed from the language of some persons that nature is an independent legislator who had passed laws for the government of mankind. Nature is nothing self-originating and self-sustaining; yet some men imagine that a 'law of nature' possesses proper and independent authority, and set it up without reference to the will of God, and even in opposition to it. A law of any kind possesses no intrinsic authority; the authority rests only in the legislator, and is derived from him to the law he lays down. As nature makes no laws, a law of nature involves no obligation but that which is imposed by the Divine Will." To this it may be also added, that as nature makes no laws the energy with which natural laws operate does not come from the laws, but from their Author.

Vol. I., p. 261. Rationalistic critics endeavor to empty the Old Testament of its doctrinal contents, in order to establish their position that the religion of Israel is merely one of the ethnic religions which arise from the natural evolution of the religious sentiment in man. They deny that the germs of the Christian religion are found in the Jewish, and eliminate as far as possible from the Old Testament the doctrines of the trinity and incarnation, of apostasy and redemption. The historical criticism of the Church from the beginning has contended, on the contrary, that all of the truths of the New Testament are contained in an inchoate form in the Old Testament. The doctrine of the trinity is no exception. The consensus of ecclesiastical opinion is as great on this point as on any other. The Fathers, the Schoolmen, and the Reformation divines are unanimous upon it. The common view is expressed in the Belgic Confession, Art. ix.: "The testimonies of Holy Scripture which teach us to believe the Holy Trinity are written in many passages of the Old Testament, which do not so much need to be enumerated as to be selected with discretion. In Genesis 1 : 26, God says, 'Let us make man in our image, after our likeness.' From this saying, 'Let us make man in our image,' it appears that there are more persons in the Godhead than one; and when he says, 'God created,' this shows the unity of the Godhead. It is true that it is not said, here, how many persons there are, but that which is obscure in the Old Testament is plain in the New." Both the Elder-Lutheran and Reformed divines, in their systems, cite texts from the Old Testament to prove the doctrine of the Trinity. The Later-Lutherans, many of whom have departed from the Elder-Lutheranism on some points, yet retain the historical opinion on this. For example, Dorner remarks that "The Old Testament, which in opposition to polytheism strongly maintains the Divine unity, yet shows traces of a plurality in God. The plural Elohim, Adonai, Shaddai, show divine powers, potentialities, which are nevertheless referred to unity" (Christian Doctrine, § 19). Dorner, however, does not find so full a trinitarianism in the Old Testament as the Elder-Lutherans do. "If the living idea of God must be conceived as trinitarian, traces of the Trinity cannot be wanting in the Old Covenant. If traces of the Trinity are found in the heathen religions, especially those of India, how could they be wholly absent from the Hebrew religion? If Jehovah does not merely say, 'I am that I am' (Ex. 13 : 14), but also says, 'I am he' (Deut. 32 : 39), he contrasts himself with himself, and an internal distinction is thereby made in God. When he says, in Isaiah 43 : 25, 'I blot out thy

transgressions for mine own sake,' he represents himself
to be his own end when he works.   But there is wanting
in such statements the third element; and although there
is frequent mention in the Old Testament of the 'Spirit of
God,' and of the 'Holy Spirit' (Gen. 1 : 3 ; 6 : 3 ; Ps. 51 :
11, 12), nevertheless that Spirit is only the Spirit of life
given by God (Ps. 104 : 29 ; Job 27 : 3 ; 34 : 14), or the
immanent basis of all created life.   The Spirit of God is
only thought of as a gift or power, or he denotes the
Divine Essence as working and dwelling in the world
(Is. 32 : 15 ; Ezek. 36 : 27 ; Joel 2 : 28) ; or as the living
basis of the theocracy, animating artists, poets, heroes,
judges, kings, and prophets (Num. 11 : 17, 25 ; Deut. 34 :
9 ; Is. 63 : 10).   In the Old Testament the Spirit of God
has not an immediate trinitarian relation ; it does not
occupy there the position of the third member of the
Trinity.   The distinctions in the Old Testament are not
thought of so much ontologically as economically " (Christian Doctrine, § 28).

VOL. I., p. 262.   Augustine (City of God, xi., 26) thus
speaks of man as the image of the Trinity : " We recognize in ourselves the image of God, that is, of the supreme
Trinity, an image which though it be not equal to God, or
rather though it be very far removed from him, being
neither coeternal, nor, to say all in a word, consubstantial
with him, is yet nearer to him in nature than any other of
his works, and is destined to be yet restored, that it may
bear a still closer resemblance."

VOL. I., p. 268.   "It is very true," says Stillingfleet
(Trinity and Transubstantiation Compared), " that according to arithmetic three cannot be one nor one three ; but
we must distinguish between bare numeration and the
things numbered.   The repetition of three units certainly
makes three distinct numbers ; but it doth not make three
persons to be three natures.   And, therefore, as to the
things themselves, we must go from the bare numbers to

consider their nature. Wherever there is a real distinction we may multiply the number, though the subject be but one. As, suppose we say, the soul hath three faculties—understanding, will, and memory; we may, without the least absurdity, say these are three and one ; and these three not confounded with each other, and yet there is but one soul."

VOL. I., p. 270. Owen (Person of Christ, Preface) thus speaks of the confusion arising from the loose use of οὐσία and ὑπόστασις. " The Grecians themselves could not for a long season agree among themselves whether οὐσία and ὑπόστασις were of the same. signification or no, both of them denoting essence and substance ; or whether they differed in their signification, and if they did, wherein that difference lay. Athanasius at first affirmed them to be the same. Basil denied them so to be, or that they were used unto the same purpose (Epist. 78). The like difference immediately fell out between the Grecians and Latins about ' hypostasis ' and ' persona.' For the Latins rendered ' hypostasis ' by ' substantia,' and ' persona ' by πρόσωπον. Hereof Jerome complains, in his Epistle to Damasus, that they required of him in the East to confess ' tres hypostases,' and he would only acknowledge ' tres personas ' (Epist. 71). And Austin gives an account of the same difference in De Trinitate, v., 8, 9. Athanasius endeavored the composing of this difference, and in a good measure effected it, as Gregory of Nazianzen affirms in his oration concerning his praise. It was done by him in a synod of Alexandria, in the first year of Julian's reign."

VOL. I., p. 280. The will of a trinitarian person is the will that belongs to the one Divine Essence, and the understanding of a trinitarian person is also that of the one Divine Essence. There are not three wills and three understandings in the Trinity, but one only. When the essence is modified by eternal generation, or eternal spiration, both the Divine will and the Divine understanding

9

which belong to the essence are modified along with it, and this modification has its own corresponding hypostatical consciousness. In this way the three modifications of the one essence, with its one will and one understanding, yield three consciousnesses that are so distinct from each other that the Father knows that he is not the Son, and the Son that he is not the Father, and the Spirit that he is neither the Father nor the Son. The varieties in these three consciousnesses do not spring from three essences or beings each having a will and understanding, but from one numerical being or essence having one will and understanding in three varieties of subsistence.

VOL. I., p. 292. It is true that the phrase "Spirit of the Father" is not found in the New Testament, but its equivalent is in Rom. 8 : 11, "If the Spirit of him that raised up Jesus from the dead dwell in you," etc. Here the Holy Spirit is denominated the Spirit of the Father, since it is the Father who is said to have raised up Christ. By virtue of the eternal communication of the Divine essence to the Son, his words in John 17 : 10, "All mine are thine, and thine are mine," may be applied to the essential relation between the Father and the Son; so that if the third Person is the "Spirit of the Son," he is likewise the "Spirit of the Father." Furthermore, the fact that the spiration of the third Person is the joint act of the Father and Son, makes him to be the Spirit of both alike.

VOL. I., p. 294. One of the briefest and clearest defences of the doctrine of eternal generation is contained in the treatise on "Eternal Sonship" by the Scotch divine, Kidd. In it he quotes the following from Monboddo, as illustrating how the Son may be from the Father and yet be equally eternal with him: "There is another mystery in the Christian religion which is as incomprehensible to those who are not philosophers as the doctrine of the Trinity is. I mean the eternal generation of the Son of God. The Son, or second Person of the Trinity, is, ac-

cording to the Church doctrine, eternal as well as the
Father, from whom he is produced. Now to a man who
is not a philosopher, it must appear inconceivable that one
being should be produced by another, and yet be co-ex-
istent with him from all eternity. It is not therefore, I
think, to be wondered that there should be such a heresy
in the Church as Arianism. Now the doctrine of Arius was,
that as the Son was produced, or *begotten*, as it is expressed
in Scripture, by the Father, he must have been in existence
posterior to him; and then he must have existed in time,
and not from all eternity, as the Father existed; and accordingly Arius maintained that there was a time when he
was not. His expression was, ἦν πότε ὀτὲ οὐκ ἦν. But
ancient learning will explain that one thing may proceed
from another as its cause [source] and yet be coeval with
it. This may be explained by an example which every
man who has learned the elements of geometry will readily
understand. It is this: That every corollary of a proposition is a truth eternal as well as the proposition itself;
and yet it is derived from the proposition as its cause
[source], and could not have existed if the proposition
had not been an eternal truth. What has led Arius and
his followers into the error of supposing that the Son,
being produced [or begotten] by the Father, could not be
coeternal with him, but must have existed in time, is what
we observe of the production of things on this earth, where
the product is always posterior to the cause producing it.
But this is true only of material things, which have no
permanent existence but are constantly changing, being
never the same thing for two moments together. Yet there
is one material thing which will illustrate this matter very
much, and make it intelligible even to those who are not
versed in philosophical distinctions. The thing I mean
is the sun, which produces rays that are coeval with the
cause producing them; as we cannot suppose the sun to
exist without rays. And this example, together with the

other I have given from geometry, proves this general proposition, that whenever anything *by the necessity of its own nature* produces another thing, both the thing produced and the producer must be coexistent. So that if the latter is eternal, the former must be. Now this is the case with the generation of the Son of God; for as production [generation] is essential to the Supreme Being, and as the first production [generation], according to the order of nature, must have been the principle of intelligence, or the eternal Word or Reason, who is the second Person of the Trinity, it was necessary that this production should be coeval with the first Person from whom it is derived, and therefore coeternal with him. In this way, I think, the eternal generation is clearly explained, as it is shown that the first Person of the Trinity himself cannot exist without producing [generating] the second" (Kidd, Eternal Sonship, p. 340).

Vol. I., p. 299. It may be asked why "a Divine attribute cannot belong to a fraction of the Divine essence," as well as a human attribute may belong to a fraction of the human nature? Rationality and immortality as properties, and wisdom and power as attributes, belong to every individual man, and he is only a part of the human species. The answer is that the *infinitude* of the attribute or property in one case, and the finiteness in the other, accounts for the difference. There may be a multitude of degrees of *finite* power, wisdom, rationality, and immortality, but there are no degrees of infinite power, wisdom, rationality, and immortality. In these latter instances there must therefore either be the whole or none of the attribute or quality. It is not so in the former instances. Division is possible, consequently, in the former case, but not in the latter. Infinite wisdom must be possessed as a whole, or not at all. But finite wisdom is a part only of wisdom, and there may be an unlimited number of parts, each of which may belong to an unlimited number of individuals.

Vol. I., p. 305.   The unity of the Divine essence in connection with the trinality and distinctness of the Divine persons is carefully asserted by Christ whenever he speaks either of himself or of the Father and the Spirit.   In respect to the Father and the Son he says, " All things that the Father hath are mine " (John 16 : 15).   " The Son can do nothing of himself (ἀφ᾽ ἑαυτοῦ), but what he seeth the Father do; for what things soever he doeth, these also doeth the Son likewise " (John 5 : 19).   " I do nothing of myself (ἀπ᾽ ἐμαυτοῦ); but as the Father hath taught me I speak these things " (John 8 : 28; 12 : 49; 14 : 10).   In respect to the Spirit and the Son he says, " The Spirit of truth shall not speak of himself (ἀφ᾽ ἑαυτοῦ), but whatsoever he shall hear, that shall he speak; he shall glorify me, for he shall receive of mine and shall show it unto you " (John 16 : 13, 14).   In these passages the doctrine is taught that while each person is so distinct from the others that he can speak of himself as doing acts that are peculiar to himself and not to the others, yet the distinctness is not so great as to make him another Being who does the acts ἀφ᾽ ἑαυτοῦ exclusively and apart from the others.   There is a common ground of being, a common nature or essence, which unifies the Three.

Vol. I., p. 307.   To the quotations from Witsius and Augustine, asserting that the term Father, in the providential and universal sense, is applicable to the Trinity, may, be added the following from Ursinus (Christian Religion, Q. 20): " The name Father, as also the name God, when it is opposed to all creatures, is taken essentially, not personally; but when it is put with another person of the Godhead it is taken personally."   An example of the former is Luke 12 : 30, " Your Father knoweth that ye have need of these things."   The " Father " here is the same as " God who clothes the grass in the field " (Luke 12 : 28), and whose " kingdom " the disciples are commanded to " seek " (Luke 12 : 31).   This is the Trinity.   An example of the latter is Matt. 12 : 50 : "Whosoever shall do the will of my Father which is in heaven, the same is my brother, and sister, and mother." This is the first person in the Trinity. Pearson, also (Creed, Art. I.), teaches that the Trinity is both the providential and redeeming Father. "As I am assured that there is an infinite and independent Being which we call a God, and that it is impossible there should be more infinities than one, so I assure myself that this one God is the Father of all things, especially of all men and angels, so far as the mere act of creation may be styled generation; and that he is further yet, and in a more peculiar manner the Father of all those whom he regenerateth by his Spirit, whom he adopteth in his Son as heirs and coheirs with him in the heavens. But beyond and far above all this, besides his general offspring, and peculiar people, I believe him to be the Father in a more eminent and transcendent manner of one singular and proper Son, his own, his beloved, his only-begotten Son. Hence, the Father is to be considered both personally and essentially; personally as the first in the glorious Trinity, with relation and opposition to the Son; essentially, as comprehending the whole Trinity, Father, Son, and Holy Ghost."

Vol. I., p. 309. The fact that the first person does not issue from any person, but is ingenerate and has the essence "originally," was cited by the ancient Trinitarians in proof of the *unity* of God. Were there two Divine persons that are "of none," there would be two Gods. They would not be two modes of one essence, but two essences. Pearson (Creed, I.) directs attention to this, and gives quotations from the Fathers, who use it in argument with the Arians. "That the Father is neither generated nor proceeds," he says, "is most true, and so fit to be believed, and also a most necessary truth, and therefore to be acknowledged for the avoiding the multiplication and plurality of gods. For if there were more than one which

were from none, it could not be denied but there were
more gods than one. Wherefore, this origination in the
divine *paternity* hath anciently been looked upon as the
assertion of the unity; and therefore the Son and Holy
Ghost have been believed to be but one God with the
Father, because both are from the Father, who is one, and
so the *union* of them. Says Fulgentius, ' In two ingenerate
persons a diverse divinity is found; but in one generate
from one ingenerate a natural unity is demonstrated.' Says
the Sirmium Council : ' If any one shall say that the Son
is ingenerate and without emanation [from the Father],
and saying that there are two ingenerates and two without
origination makes two gods, let him be anathema.' Says
Novatian : ' If the Son had not been generate of the
Father, there would be two persons neither of whom is
from the other, and both of whom are God unoriginate.
This would be two Gods. The Son, like the Father, would
not be God *of* God, but God *beside* God.' " Pearson also
cites Basil, Athanasius, and Gregory of Nazianzen, to the
same effect.

VOL. I., p. 315.   A close examination shows that the selection of prepositions in the Gospels and Epistles is carefully made, in order to mark the reality of the trinitarian
distinction in the Divine essence.   In John 16 : 28, ἐγὼ
παρὰ τοῦ πατρὸς ἐξῆλθον, denotes leaving a position by the
Father's side.   In John 15 : 26, παρά signifies the same
thing in reference to the Holy Spirit.

VOL. I., p. 340.   Augustine (Letter 166) thus explains
that peculiarity of spirit which consists in being present,
not partitively, but as an entire whole, wherever it is
present.   " If matter be used as a term denoting everything
which in any form has a distinct and separate existence of
its own, whether it be called an essence, or a substance, or
by another name, then the soul is ' material ' [*i. e.*, substan-
tial].   Again, if you choose to apply the epithet immaterial only to that [divine] nature which is supremely im-

mutable and is everywhere present in its entirety, the soul is material, for it is not at all endowed with such [supremely immutable] qualities. But if matter be used to designate nothing but that which, whether at rest or in motion, has some length, breadth, and height, so that with a greater part of itself it occupies a greater part of space, and with a smaller part a smaller space, and is in every part of it less than the whole, then the soul is not material. For it pervades the whole body which it animates, not by a local distribution of parts, but by a certain vital influence, being at the same moment present in its entirety in all parts of the body, and not less in smaller parts and greater in larger parts, but here with more energy and there with less energy, it is in its entirety present in the whole body and in every part of it. For even that which the mind perceives in only a part of the body is nevertheless not otherwise perceived than by the whole soul; for when any part of the living flesh is touched by a needle, although the place affected is not only not the whole body, but scarcely discernible on its surface, the contact does not escape the entire mind, and yet the contact is not felt over the whole body, but only at the one point where it takes place. How comes it, then, that what takes place in only a part of the body is immediately known to the whole mind, unless the whole mind is present at that part, and at the same time not deserting all the other parts of the body in order to be present in its entirety at this one? For all the other parts of the body in which no such contact takes place are still living by the soul being present with them. And if a similar contact occur in the other parts, and the contact occur in both parts simultaneously, it would in both cases alike be known at the same moment to the whole mind. Now, this presence of the mind in all parts of the body at the same moment would be impossible if it were distributed over these parts in the same way as we see matter distributed in space, occupying less space with a smaller portion of itself, and greater space with a greater portion. For all things composed of matter are larger in larger places, or smaller in smaller places, and no one of them is in its entirety present at any part of itself, but the dimensions of material substances are according to the dimensions of the space occupied."

Vol. I., p. 344. The Platonist, John Smith (Discourses, 126), defines time like Berkeley. "That which first begets the notion of time in us is nothing else but that succession and multiplicity which we find in our own thoughts, which move from one thing to another, as the sun in the firmament is said to walk from one planetary house to another, and to have his several stages to pass by. And therefore where there is no such vicissitude or variety, as there can be no sense of time, so there can be nothing of the thing."

Vol. I., p. 346. That the effect of the Divine energizing in creation is temporal while the causative energizing itself is eternal, must be postulated in order to the Divine immutability. We cannot say that the Divine energizing produces its effect simultaneously with itself, because in this case the created universe would be eternal, as in Origen's doctrine of eternal creation. Assuming the correctness of Usher's chronology, we cannot affirm that God's creative power in originating man from nothing was not exerted until B.C. 4004, and that up to this date he had been inactive in this respect, and then acted. This would imply a change and passage in the Divine essence from an inactive to an active state, like that of man and angel. Neither can we say that man existed prior to B.C. 4004. God's causative action cannot be successive, because the ideas of beginning and ending inhere in that of succession. The beginning is before the ending, and there is an interval between the two. But God "sees the end from the beginning," not from the end, without an interval between.

The remark on p. 396, that "the Divine thought or idea, unlike the thought or idea of a finite mind, is not in any particular *inferior* to the actual thing," is perhaps the best explanation possible of the eternity of the cause and the temporality of the effect, in regard to creation ex nihilo. Although the effect (say the planet earth) is not actually existent, but held in suspense after the creative act until the point of time arrives when it is to be made real in space and time, yet the Divine *knowledge* of it, which is involved in the Divine idea or thought of it, is complete and exhaustive. This absolutely perfect knowledge is equivalent to actual existence for God.

The divine purpose is like the human, in that there may be an interval between the formation of it and the execution. A man decides to-day to commit murder, but he does not do the deed until to-morrow, or a month later. The difference between the two is, that execution of the purpose in the case of man may fail or be changed, but not in the case of God. The human purpose is uncertain, but the divine is absolutely certain, because all the causes and events in the interval of time between the formation and execution are not under the control of the human agent, while they are of the divine agent. Something therefore may occur in the former instance to defeat the purpose, but not in the latter. Man, also, alters his mind and retracts what he has once determined to do, but God does not. The language of Peter (1 Pet. 1 : 20), "Who verily was foreordained before the foundation of the world, but was manifest in these last times," may be applied to the creation of the world. The world was decreed from eternity before the foundation of the world, but was created in time.

VOL. I., p. 355. Owen (Saints' Perseverance, ch. iii.) defines scientia simplicis intelligentiæ. "All things originally owe their futurition [actuality] to a free act of the will of God. Their relation thereunto translates them out of the state of possibility, and of being objects of God's absolute omnipotency and infinite simple intelligence or understanding, whereby he intuitively beholdeth all things that might be produced by the exertion of infinite power, into a state of futurition [actuality], making them objects of God's foreknowledge, or science of vision."

Vol. I., p. 358. It is objected that the selfish ethics which makes happiness man's ultimate end finds a support in the Scripture doctrine of a "recompense of reward" in the next life. This is erroneous, because the reward promised and looked for is the Divine approval and love. It is not any form of earthly and finite good. The Christian does not obey God because he desires or expects in return for his obedience, wealth, health, earthly pleasure, fame, or any of that good which self-love desires, but simply and only the " Well done, good and faithful servant." Without this Divine approbation all other good would be worthless to him; and with it, all other good is nothing in comparison. The rewards of eternity are a payment in kind: "grace for grace." The reward of loving and serving God is more and more love and service; of holiness, is more and more holiness, etc. God himself is represented as the believer's reward. "The word of the Lord came unto Abram in a vision, saying, Fear not, Abram; I am thy shield and thy exceeding great reward " (Gen. 15 : 1). "The Lord is the portion of mine inheritance and of my cup " (Ps. 16 : 5).

Anselm (De Præscientiæ, xiii.) observes that happiness depends upon the attainment of an object different from itself, but holiness does not because it is its own reward. "Voluntas quidem justitiæ est ipsa justitia; voluntas vero beatitudinis non est beatitudo; quia non omnis habet beatitudinem qui habet ejus voluntatem."

Vol. I., p. 360. Anselm (Proslogium, vii.) takes the same view with Augustine respecting the meaning of power when ascribed to God. " To be able to lie, to make

that which is true to be false, and the like, is not power
but weakness.   He that can do these things can do what
is wrong and injurious to himself; and the greater his
ability to do these things, the greater will be the power of
evil and adversity over him, and the less will he be able to
resist them.   Whoever therefore has such ability, has it
not from his power but from his weakness."

VOL. I., p. 375.   If the validity of the distinction between the agent and the agency, the substance of the soul
and its activity or self-determination, is not conceded, the
view of Flacius is inevitable, namely, that sin is the substance of the soul.

VOL. I., p. 382.   The justice of punishment really cannot
be separated from its utility and expediency, as is done by
those who assert the latter and deny the former.   If judicial suffering is not just, it will not prove to be useful or expedient.   There will be no reformation of the criminal, nor
protection of society, if the criminal does not first perceive
and acknowledge that his act is *guilt*, and ought to be punished as such.   So long as he denies the criminality and ill
desert of his act, he will say that his suffering is the unjust
infliction of a tyrannical power.   This will exasperate and
harden him, and lead him to commit the crime again, if he
has the opportunity.   No personal moral improvement will
result from the infliction, and no security to society against
the repetition of the crime.   In this way, it is evident that
the expediency of penalty depends upon the justice of it.
He who denies the latter must deny the former.   If the infliction is not first of all just, it cannot be expedient and useful.   It will fail of accomplishing the two things desired, the
protection of the community from crime and the reformation of the criminal.   Faber in his hymn combines the two:

> " There is a wideness in God's mercy
> Like the wideness of the sea;
> There is a kindness in his justice
> Which is more than liberty."

The first two lines are often quoted, and the last two omitted.

Vol. I., p. 388. The suffering of animals decreases as we go down the scale. The following statement respecting this point is made in Kirby and Spence's Entomology (Letter ii.). " It is well known that in proportion as we descend the scale of being the sensibility of objects diminishes. The tortoise walks about after losing its head; and the polypus, so far from being injured by the application of the knife, thereby acquires an extension of existence. Insensibility almost equally great may be found in the insect world. This, indeed, might be inferred a priori, since Providence seems to have been more prodigal of insect life than of any order of creatures, animalcula perhaps alone excepted. Can it be believed that the beneficent Creator, whose tender mercies are over all his works, would expose these helpless beings to such innumerable enemies and injuries were they endued with the same irritability of nerve with the higher orders of animals? But this inference is reduced to a certainty when we attend to the facts which insects every day present to us, proving that the very converse of our great poet's conclusion,

> " ' The poor beetle that we tread upon,
>   In corporal sufferance finds a pang as great
>   As when a giant dies,'

must be regarded as nearer the truth. Not to mention the peculiar organization of insects which strongly favors the position we are taking, their sang froid upon the loss of their limbs, even those that we account most necessary to life, proves that the pain they suffer cannot be very acute. A tipula will leave half of its legs in the hands of a boy who has endeavored to catch it, and will fly here and there with as much agility and unconcern as if nothing had happened to it; and an insect impaled upon a pin will often devour its prey with as much avidity as when at liberty. We have seen the common cockchafer walk about with apparent indifference after some bird had nearly emptied its body of its viscera ; a humble-bee will eat honey with greediness though deprived of its abdomen ; and we have seen an ant which had been brought out of its nest by its comrades walk when deprived of its head. The head of a wasp will attempt to bite after it is separated from the body ; and the abdomen under similar circumstances, if the finger is moved to it, will attempt to sting. These facts, out of hundreds that might be adduced, are sufficient to prove that insects do not experience the same acute sensations of pain with the higher orders of animals. Had a giant lost an arm or a leg, or were a sword or spear run through his body, he would feel no great inclination for running about, dancing, or eating."

The statement in the text is erroneous, that " if the majority of a species did not survive the species would diminish and become extinct." The immense number of eggs which a single cod deposits, or a single insect lays, makes the destruction of vast numbers necessary in order to prevent such a multiplication of the species as would overrun the sea and the land. " Wasps," say Kirby and Spence (Entomology, Letter xi.), " at the beginning of winter drag out of the cells all the grubs and unrelentingly destroy them. They have no stock of provisions ; the young must linger on a short period, and at length die of hunger. A sudden death by their own hands is comparatively a merciful stroke. We do not mean to say that this train of reasoning actually passes through the mind of the wasps. It is more correct to regard it as having actuated the benevolent Author of the instinct so singularly and wisely created in them. Were a nest of wasps to survive the winter, they would increase so rapidly that not only would all the bees, flies, and other insects on which they prey be extirpated, but man himself would find them a grievous pest. It is necessary, therefore, that the great mass should annually perish."

Vol. I., p. 389. The inexactness and freedom of mercy contrasted with the exactitude and necessity of justice explains St. Paul's declaration : " Where sin abounded grace did much more abound." Justice is rigorously exact. It cannot inflict any more than is due, or any less. It is confined to strict limits. But mercy is inexact because boundless. It may give more than is due, though never less than is due. As Shakspeare says, " The quality of mercy is not strained," that is, confined to immutable bounds. In Christ's redeeming work the Divine mercy is infinite upon infinite, and exceeds all computation. Justice " abounds," but within its limits ; mercy " superabounds " beyond all limits. Pascal (Thoughts, 163), remarks that " the justice of God must be immense as well as his compassion ; yet is the justice of God toward the condemned less immense and less overwhelming to the thought than his grace toward the elect." The exactness and rigor of justice as an attribute are thus expressed by Dorner (Christian Doctrine, I., 291): " In one aspect, justice is logic and mathematics applied to the sphere of the will, and in this very fact lies the proof of its no mere subjective nature. Its demands contain a logical and mathematical necessity, that is, the necessity that the will as well as the understanding must act according to the logic of things, and direct itself according to the measure placed upon everything."

Vol. I., p. 391. The relation of Christ's satisfaction to the non-elect is thus stated by Charnocke : " The power of God is more manifest in his patience toward a multitude of sinners than it would be in creating millions of worlds out of nothing ; for this is the exertion of a power over himself. The exercise of this patience is founded in the death of Christ. Without the consideration of this we can give no reason why divine patience should extend itself to us

and not to the fallen angels. The threatening extends itself to us as well as to the fallen angels, and must necessarily have sunk man, as well as those glorious creatures,
had not Christ stepped in to our relief. Had not Christ
interposed to satisfy the justice of God, man upon his sinning had been actually bound over to punishment as well
as the fallen angels were upon theirs, and been fettered in
chains as strong as those spirits feel. The reason why
man was not hurled into the same deplorable condition as
they were is Christ's promise of taking our nature and not
theirs. Had God designed Christ's taking their nature the
same patience had been exercised toward them, and the
same offers would have been made to them as are made to
us. In regard to these fruits of this patience Christ is said
to buy the wickedest apostates : 'Denying the Lord that
bought them' (1 Pet. 2 : 1). Such were bought by him as
'bring upon themselves just destruction, and whose damnation slumbers not' (1 Pet. 2 : 3) ; he purchased the continuance of their lives and the stay of their execution that
offers of grace might be made to them. This patience must
be either upon the account of the law or the gospel ; for
there are no other rules whereby God governs the world.
A fruit of the law it was not that spake nothing but curses
after disobedience ; not a letter of mercy was written upon
that, and therefore nothing of patience ; death and wrath
were denounced ; no slowness of anger intimated. It must
be, therefore, upon the account of the gospel, and a fruit of
the covenant of grace, whereof Christ was the mediator "
(God's Patience, 720, Ed. Bohn).

VOL. I., p. 394. Owen (Saints' Perseverance, ch. iii.) observes that the Divine decree relates only to what may
or may not be, not to what must be ; to what depends
upon the optional will of God, not to what depends upon his
intrinsic being and nature. "God's purposes are not concerning anything that is in itself absolutely necessary. He
doth not purpose that he will be wise, holy, good, just."

VOL. I., p. 402. " It does not follow that though there is for God a certain order of all causes, there must therefore be nothing depending on the free exercise of our own wills; for our wills themselves are included in that order of causes which is certain to God, and is embraced by his foreknowledge, for human wills are also causes of human actions; and he who foreknew all the causes of things would certainly among those causes not have been ignorant of our wills " (Augustine, City of God, v., 9). Augustine here uses "foreknow" in the common classical signification of simply knowing beforehand, and not in the uncommon Hebrew signification of " choosing," as in Rom. 8 : 29 ; 11 : 2. There is nothing in simply foreknowing, or foreseeing, that interferes with free agency, any more than the simple on-looking of a spectator interferes with the action of a thief or murderer. The difficulty arises when the reconciliation of free agency with foreknowledge, in the sense of *foreordination* or *predestination*, is attempted. In this latter instance God does not merely look on like a spectator, but he does something like an actor. And the problem is how to make his action consistent with the creature's action. The clew to the reconciliation is in the distinction between God's efficient and permissive action. But this does not clear up the mystery in the instance of the origination of sin by a holy being like unfallen Adam, though it does in the instance of the continuation of sin in a sinful being like fallen Adam.

VOL. I., p. 403. Schleiermacher directs attention to the fact that while God's decree makes all events certain, it does not make them so by the same kind of power. He says (Glaubenslehre, § 80) that " it leads to Manichæism [the doctrine of two eternal principles of good and evil] if sin is denied to have its ground in God in any sense whatever, and it leads to Pelagianism if this is asserted and no distinction is made in the *manner* of the Divine causality."

10

Here he evidently has in mind the permissive as distinguished from the efficient decree.

VOL. I., p. 404.   Augustine teaches as distinctly as Calvin that sinners are elected to faith, not because of faith. "God elected us in Christ before the foundation of the world, predestinating us to the adoption of children, not because we were going to be of ourselves holy and immaculate, but he elected and predestinated that we might be so" (Predestination, ch. 37).   "The elect are not those who are elected because they have believed, but that they might believe.   For the Lord himself explains this election when he says: 'Ye have not chosen me, but I have chosen you.'   If they had been elected because they first believed, they themselves would have first chosen him by believing in him, so that they should deserve to be elected" (Predestination, ch. 34).   "Let us look into the words of the apostle and see whether God elected us before the foundation of the world because we were going to be holy, or in order that we might be so.   'Blessed,' says he, 'be the God and Father of our Lord Jesus Christ, who hath blessed us with all spiritual blessing in the heavens in Christ; even as he hath chosen us in himself before the foundation of the world that we should be holy and unspotted.'   Not, then, because we were to be so, but that we might be so" (Predestination, ch. 36).

Vol. I., p. 405.   Charnocke (Immutability of God, p. 222, Ed. Bohn) thus remarks upon the relation of prayer to the Divine immutability: "Prayer doth not desire any change in God, but is offered to God that he would confer those things which he hath immutably willed and purposed to communicate; but he willed them not without prayer as *the means of bestowing them.*   The light of the sun is ordered for our discovery of visible things; but withal it is required that we use our faculty of seeing.   If a man shuts his eyes and complains that the sun is changed into darkness, it would be ridiculous; the sun is not changed, but we alter ourselves. Nor is God changed in his giving us the blessings he hath promised, because he hath promised in the way of a due address to him, and opening our souls to receive his influence, and to this his immutability is the greatest encouragement."

VOL. I., p. 406. In endeavoring to explain how God decrees sin, some theologians make the Divine concursus to be identically the same thing in relation to both holiness and sin, namely, that of internal and positive actuation, or inclining of the human will. In both cases God works in the finite will "to will and to do." This destroys the distinction between the efficient and the permissive decree. Howe (Postscript to Letter on God's Prescience) discusses this point in his answer to the criticism of Theophilus Gale, who charged him with denying the Divine concursus altogether, because he refused to make "the concurrence of God to the sins of men" identical with that to the holiness of men. The substance of his answer is, that there is both an "immediate," and a "determinative," that is, *causative* concourse of God to the will of man in *good* action, but only an "immediate," not "determinative" or causative concourse in *evil* action. In the first instance God both upholds and inwardly inclines or actuates the will of man; in the second instance he upholds but does not inwardly incline it. "The divine concourse or influence (for I here affect not the curiosity to distinguish these terms, as some do), which I deny not to be immediate to any actions, I only deny to be determinative as to those that are wicked. It is only God's determinative concurrence to *all* actions, even those that are most malignantly wicked, which is the thing I speak of; as what I cannot reconcile with the wisdom and sincerity of his councils and exhortations against such actions." Howe sums up his view in the following declarations: "1. That God exerciseth a universal providence about all his creatures, both in sustaining and governing them. 2. That, more

particularly, he exerciseth such a providence about man.
3. That this providence about man extends to all the
actions of all men. 4. That it consists not alone in beholding the actions of men, as if he were only a mere
spectator of them, but is positively active about them. 5.
That this active providence of God about all the actions
of men consists not merely in giving them the natural
powers whereby they can work of themselves, but in a real
influence upon those powers. 6. That this influence is, in
reference to holy and spiritual actions (whereto, since the
apostasy, the nature of man is become viciously disinclined), necessary to be efficaciously determinative; that
is, such as shall overcome that disinclination and reduce
those powers into act. 7. That the ordinary way for the
communication of this determinative influence is by the
inducements which God presents in his Word, namely, the
precepts, promises, and threatenings, which are the moral
instruments of his government. [This is common grace,
which Howe elsewhere describes as failing to overcome
the sinner's opposition.] No doubt but he may extraordinarily actuate men by inward impulse, but he hath left
them destitute of any encouragement to expect his influences in the neglect of his ordinary methods. 8. That,
in reference to all other actions which are not sinful,
though there be not a sinful disinclination to them, yet
because there may be a sluggishness and ineptitude to
some purposes God intends to serve by them, this influence is always determinative [causative] thereunto. [Howe
here refers to the struggle with indwelling sin in the regenerate which is assisted by God.] 9. That, in reference
to sinful actions, by this influence God doth not only sustain men who do them, and continue to them their natural
faculties and powers whereby they are done, but also, as
the first mover, so far excite and actuate those powers as
that they are apt and habile for any congenerous action
to which they have a natural [created] designation; and

whereto they are not so sinfully disinclined. 10. That, if men do then employ them to the doing of any sinful action; by that same influence he doth, as to him seems meet, limit, moderate, and, against the inclination and design of the sinful agent, overrule and dispose it to good. But now if, besides all this, they will also assert: That God doth by an *efficacious* influence *move* and *determine* men to wicked actions; this is that which I most resolvedly deny. That is, in this I shall differ with them; that I do not suppose God to have, by internal influence, as far a hand in the worst and wickedest actions as in the best. I assert more [internal influence] to be necessary to actions to which men are wickedly disinclined; but that less will suffice for their doing of actions to which they have inclination more than enough."

Neander (History, I., 374) remarks that "the Gnostics would not allow of any distinction between permission and causation on the part of God. Τὸ μὴ κωλοῦον αἴτιόν ἐστιν, is their usual motto in opposing the doctrine of the church."

Milton (Par. Lost, x., 40 sq.) states the permissive decree as follows:

> " I told ye then he should prevail, and speed
> On his bad errand ; man should be seduced,
> And flattered out of all, believing lies
> Against his Maker ; no decree of mine
> Concurring to *necessitate* his fall,
> Or touch with lightest moment of *impulse*
> His free-will, to her own inclining left
> In even scale."

Here the certainty of the fall is announced by God, but not the necessity in the sense of compulsion. There is no inward "impulse" and actuation of the will by God, when it inclines and falls from holiness to sin. This mode of internal and causative actuation is confined to the inclining of man's will to holiness; to "working in him to will that which is pleasing to God," and accompanies the efficient decree, not the permissive.

The permissive decree is executed in part by the withdrawal of restraints, as a punitive act of God which St. Paul speaks of in Rom. 1 : 24, 28. This is a punishment for sin previously committed. " When God 'gives up' the sinner to sin, he does not himself cause the sin. To withdraw a restraint is not the same as to impart an impulse. The two principal restraints of sin are the fear of punishment before its commission, and remorse after it. These are an effect of the Divine operation in the conscience ; the revelation of the Divine ὀργή in human consciousness. When God 'gives over' an individual he ceases, temporarily, to awaken these feelings. The consequence is utter moral apathy and recklessness in sin " (Shedd, On Romans, 1 : 24). The view of Augustine is expressed in the following extracts, and is the same as Calvin's. " When you hear the Lord say, ' I the Lord have deceived that prophet' (Ezek. 14 : 9), and likewise what the apostle says, ' He hath mercy on whom he will have mercy, and whom he will he hardeneth ' (Rom. 9 : 18), believe that in the case of him whom he permits to be deceived and hardened his evil deeds have deserved the judgment. Nor should you take away from Pharaoh free-will, because in several passages God says, ' I have hardened Pharaoh,' or, ' I have hardened, or will harden, Pharaoh's heart ; ' for it does not by any means follow that Pharaoh did not, on this account, harden his own heart " (Grace and Free Will, ch. 45). "From these statements of the inspired word (Ps. 105 : 25 ; Prov. 21 : 1 ; 1 Kings 12 : 15 ; 2 Chron. 21 : 16, 17), and from similar passages, it is, I think, sufficiently clear that God works in the hearts of men to incline their wills (ad inclinandas eorum voluntates) whithersoever he wills, whether to good deeds according to his mercy, or to evil after their own deserts ; his own judgment being sometimes manifest, sometimes secret, but always righteous.

This ought to be the fixed and immovable conviction of
your heart, that there is no unrighteousness with God.
Therefore, whenever you read in the Scriptures that men
are led aside, or that their hearts are blunted and hardened
by God, never doubt that some ill deserts of their own
have first occurred so that they shall justly suffer these
things " (Grace and Free-Will, ch. 43). " There are some
sins which are also the punishment of sins " (Predestination of the Saints, ch. 19). The permission to sin, according to these extracts, is punitive. The sinner is left to
his own will without restraint from God, as a punishment for his obstinacy in sin. When God, after striving
with the sinner in common grace which is resisted and
nullified, decides to desist from further striving with him,
this is retribution. It is the manifestation of justice.
The process is described in Rom. 1 : 21-24. The heathen
" changed the glory of the incorruptible God into an
image made like to corruptible man. Wherefore God
gave them up to uncleanness, through the lusts of their
own hearts, to dishonor their own bodies between themselves." Man's active commission of sin, St. Paul teaches,
is punished by God's subsequent passive permission of it.
It will be noticed that Augustine says that " God works
(operari) in the hearts of men, to *incline* their wills to evil
deeds." To incline the will, strictly speaking, is to " work
in it to will " (Phil. 2 : 13) ; is to originate an inclination
or disposition in the voluntary faculty. Scripture everywhere asserts that God exerts such action whenever the
human will wills holiness, but never when it wills sin.
Respecting sin, it declares that God " suffered (εἴασε)
all nations to walk in their own ways " (Acts 14 : 16) ;
" the times of this ignorance God overlooked " (Acts 17 :
30) ; God " gave them their own desire " (Ps. 78 : 29) ;
God " gave them their own request " (Ps. 106 : 15). That
Augustine did not intend to use the term " incline " in the
strict sense of causation, or inward actuation, is proved by

his caution: "Nor should you take away from Pharaoh free-will, because in several passages God says, 'I have hard-ened Pharaoh's heart; for it does not by any means follow that Pharaoh did not on this account harden his own heart." The following extracts from Grace and Free-Will, ch. 41, puts this beyond all doubt. "Was it not of their own will that the enemies of the children of Israel fought against the people of God, as led by Joshua the son of Nun? And yet the Scripture says, 'It was of the Lord to harden their hearts, that they should come against Israel in battle, that he might destroy them utterly' (Josh. 11 : 20). And was it not likewise of his own will that Shimei, the wicked son of Gera, cursed King David? And yet what says David, full of true, and deep, and pious wisdom? 'Let him alone, and let him curse, because the Lord hath said unto him, Curse David' (2 Sam. 16 : 9, 10). Now what prudent reader will fail to understand in what way the Lord bade this profane man to curse David? It was not by literal command that he bade him, in which case his obedience would be praiseworthy; but he inclined (inclinavit) the man's will, which had [already] become debased by his own perverseness, to commit this sin. Therefore it is said, 'The Lord said unto him.'" The "inclining," here, in Augustine's use of the term, is not the origination by God of an evil inclination in Shimei's will, for this already existed, but the permitting of it to continue and the using of it to accomplish his own pur-poses. "See, then," concludes Augustine, "what proof we have here that God *uses the hearts* of even wicked men for the praise and assistance of the good. Thus did he make use of Judas when betraying Christ; thus did he make use of the Jews when they crucified Christ." To "incline" the will of a wicked man in this qualified use of the term, is to permit instead of restraining and stopping its sinful inclining, as in Ps. 119 : 36, "Incline my heart unto thy testimonies and not to covetousness;" and to "make use " of it for a wise and benevolent purpose. But the term is liable to be understood to denote more than merely permissive divine agency, and it would have prevented some misapprehension and misrepresentation of the doctrine of predestination if it had always been strictly confined to the efficient agency of God in the origin of holiness. The author of sin is necessarily a sinner, and he who inclines a will to sin, in the strict sense of " incline," is the author of sin. God is indisputably the author of holiness, when by regeneration he inclines the unregenerate to will holily. But Augustine invariably denies that God is the author of sin, while he invariably affirms that he is the author of holiness. " If any one suffers some hurt through another's wickedness or error, the man indeed sins whose ignorance or injustice does the harm ; but God, who by his just though hidden judgment, *permits* it to be done, sins not " (City of God, xxi., 13).

For a fuller account of the double predestination to both holiness and sin, see Shedd, Calvinism; Pure and Mixed, pp. 88-95.

Vol. I., p. 409.   Möhler, in his Symbolics, contends that the doctrine of the absolute dependence of man upon God, held by both Luther and Calvin, makes God the author of sin. Baur (Gegensatz, 145 sq.) replies as follows: " If man is absolutely dependent upon God, it seems, certainly, that with the same right and reason that all goodness is to be carried back to the divine agency, all evil also has God for its efficient and working cause. Nevertheless the Reformers do not concede this inference, and as decidedly as they derive all goodness from God only, so decidedly do they also assert that man alone bears the guilt of evil. Often as Calvin speaks of the fall of man as a fall foreordained of God, he at the same time designates it as a fall self-incurred and culpable. ' Lapsus est primus homo,' so reads the leading passage on this point (Inst., III., xxiii., 8, 9), ' quia Dominus ita expedire cen-

suerat; cur censuerit nos latet. Certum tamen est non
aliter censuisse, nisi quia videbat nominis sui gloriam inde
merito illustrari. Ubi mentionem gloriæ Dei audis, illic
justitiam cogita. Justum enim oportet quod laudem mer-
etur. Cadit igitur homo, Dei providentia sic ordinante :
sed *suo vitio cadit.* [In a note Baur adds, "It is remarkable that Möhler repeatedly cites this passage from Calvin,
but in every instance omits the clause upon which everything depends : 'sed suo vitio cadit.' His bold assertion
in his Neue Untersuchungen, § 125, that the 'vitio suo
cadere' is not omitted, is refuted by ocular demonstration
(Augenschein)."] Pronuntiaverat paulo ante Dominus omnia quæ fecerat esse valde bona. Unde ergo illa homini
pravitas ut a Deo deficiat? Ne ex creatione putaretur,
elogio suo approbaverat Deus quod profectum erat a se
ipso. *Propria ergo malitia,* quam acceperat a Domino
puram naturam corrupit; sua ruina totam posteritatem in
exitium suum attraxit. Quare in corrupta potius humani
generis natura evidentem damnationis causam, quæ nobis
propinquior est, contemplemur, quam absconditam ac peni-
tus incomprehensibilem inquiramus in Dei prædestina-
tione. Tametsi æterna Dei providentia in eam cui sub-
jacet calamitatem conditus est homo, *a se ipso tamen ejus
materiam,* non a Deo, sumpsit; quando nulla alia ratione
sic perditus est, nisi quia a pura Dei creatione in vitiosam
et impuram perversitatem degeneravit.' Can it be said
any more plainly than it is here by Calvin, that man is
fallen by his own fault alone ? "

While, however, Baur accurately states the view of
Luther and Calvin in correction of the misconception of
Möhler, he follows it with an explanation which ascribes
to them his own theory of the origin of sin as the necessary evolution of the Divine idea, instead, as the Reformers
held, of the origination of sin by an act of man's free-will
in Adam. In this, as in other instances, the remarkable
power which this dogmatic historian possessed of perceiv-

ing and stating the contents of a theological system, is vitiated by an obtuseness in expounding it which leads him to suppose that his own pantheistic explanation of it is what its author really meant. After the above-given analysis of Calvin's doctrine he thus proceeds: "Is not this view, however, a logical inconsistency, whereby what is affirmed on one side of the proposition is denied on the other? How can man have fallen by free-will, and culpably, if he fell only because God so willed and ordained? Does not the all-determining and ordaining agency of God necessarily exclude all freedom of will? So indeed it looks; but everything depends upon the view taken of the nature of the evil which man received into his nature by the fall. If the fall can be conceived of only as a deterioration of the originally pure and holy nature of man as created by God, then the fall, or the evil coming into this nature by the fall, is related to this nature only as the negative is to the positive. Hence we must distinguish a positive and a negative side of human nature; all that belongs to the positive side is the nature as it was created by God, but what is negative in the positive cannot be carried back, like the positive, to the same Divine activity, since it is to be regarded as only *the negation and limitation of the creative activity of God* in respect to man. Accordingly, what can the Calvinistic proposition, 'cadit homo Deo sic ordinante, sed suo vitio,' mean but merely this: Man, so far as he is created by God, is originally pure and good, but he has also a side of his being (Wesen) which is averse from God and finite, and therefore perverse and evil? As upon the one side [of his being] he bears the image of God in himself, so on the other side he has a fallen nature, and for this very reason the fall is his own fault, since if he is to be man he cannot be conceived of without this negativity and finiteness of being which places him wholly in the antithesis (Gegensatz) [point of indifference] between Infinite and Finite, Perfect and Imperfect, Positive and

Negative, Good and Evil.   He *is* therefore the original sin itself that is imputable to him, so far as this negativity and finiteness which is the source of all evil in him so belongs to the *conception* of his being that it cannot be separated from it; on which account the fall, at least ideally, must be eternally attributed to the nature of man.   But since all that the fall potentially includes for human nature can be conceived only as something to be developed consequentially and additionally; inasmuch as the Evil is ever only in the Good, and is antithetic to it as the Negative is to the Positive; therefore Calvin represents the fall not merely as an absolutely necessary consequence, but also as a contingent and arbitrary one.   'In his perfect condition,' says Calvin (Inst., I., xv., 8), 'man was endowed with free-will, by which if he had so inclined he might have obtained eternal life.   Adam could have stood if he would, since he fell merely by his own will; but because his will was flexible to either side, and he was not endowed with constancy to persevere in holiness, therefore he fell so easily.   He had, indeed, received the power to persevere in holiness if he chose to exert it; but he had not the will to use that power, for perseverance would have been the consequence of this will.'"

This explanation of Calvin's meaning in these extracts from the Institutes is as far as possible from the truth. Calvin teaches that human nature as created was positive only; Baur, that it was positive and negative together. Calvin teaches that it was good only; Baur, that it was good and evil together.   Calvin teaches that God is unconditioned in the creative act; Baur, that there is "a negation and limitation of the creative activity of God."   Calvin teaches that sin is an origination de nihilo by the self-determination of the human will; Baur, that it is a development of the positive and negative sides of human nature.   Calvin makes original sin to be culpable because it is the *product* of man; Baur destroys its culpability (while at the same time asserting it) by making it to *be* the man himself in the necessary evolution of his being. Baur asserts that evil belongs necessarily and eternally to the idea of man, and that he cannot be conceived of as man without it; Calvin denies this. Baur holds that "the idea of human nature can be realized only through the medium of the fall and of sin;" Calvin holds that sin is not only not necessary to the ideal and perfect condition of human nature, but is the absolute ruin of it. Baur declares that man is culpable for sin because while "on one side of his being he bears the image of God, on the other side of it he has a fallen nature which is averse from God and is evil because it is finite;" Calvin would deny that man is culpable for sin, if sin were one of two sides of his being, and if finiteness is intrinsically evil. In brief, the difference between Calvin's and Baur's theories of sin is as wide as between the theistic and pantheistic views of God, man, and the universe, from which each theory takes its start, and in which each has its basis.

There are some passages both in Calvin and Augustine which on the face of them seem to teach that God's agency in relation to sin is efficient, and not permissive. They are passages in which the term "incline" is used. Augustine (Grace and Free Will, Ch. 41), after citing David's words to Abishai respecting Shimei, "Let him curse, for the Lord hath bidden him" (2 Sam. 16 : 11), remarks : "It was not by a command that he bade him, in which case his obedience would be praiseworthy; but by his own just and secret judgment. He inclined (inclinavit) the man's will, which had become debased by his own perverseness, to commit this sin." That "incline" does not here mean inward actuation, or "working in the will to will and to do," is evident from the following considerations : 1. Augustine denies that God *commanded* Shimei to curse David; for in this case, says he, "he would have deserved to be praised rather than punished, as we know he was afterwards punished for this sin." But God works efficiently in the human will to do what he commands, or to do duty. 2. Augustine, in the context, explains " incline " by " using the heart of a wicked man." " See what proof we have here that God uses the hearts of even wicked men for the praise and assistance of the good." 3. He describes Shimei's will, which God " inclined," as a will already wickedly inclined. " He inclined the man's will, which had become debased by *his own* perverseness, to commit this sin." These explanations show that Augustine employs the term "incline " in the Biblical and Oriental sense of giving the will up to its own inclining. When David prays to God : " Incline not my heart to any evil thing, to practise wicked works with men that work iniquity " (Ps. 141 : 4) ; "Incline not my heart to covetousness" (Ps. 119 : 36) ; he prays that God would not leave his heart, or will, to its wilful propensity to sin. This is not a prayer that God would work inwardly upon his will to make it wicked and covetous. It was already so. As in the Biblical and Oriental idiom, God is said to harden when he does not soften (Rom. 9 : 18), and to blind when he does not enlighten (Rom. 11 : 8, 10 ; John 12 : 40 ; Isa. 6 : 10), so he is said to incline when he does not disincline. In all these instances of "inclining," " hardening," and " blinding," the existence and presence of sin is supposed in the person of whom they are predicated. As Augustine (Grace and Free Will, Ch. 43) says : " Whenever you read in the Scriptures of truth that men are led aside, or that their hearts are blunted and hardened by God, never doubt that some ill-deserts of their own have first occurred, so that they justly suffer these things. Then you will not run against that proverb of Solomon : ' The foolishness of a man perverteth his ways, yet he blameth God in his heart ' (Prov. 19 : 3)."

The phraseology of Calvin upon this subject is like that of Augustine. In Inst. II., iv., 4, he remarks : " Moses expressly declared to the people of Israel that it was the Lord who had made the heart of their enemies obstinate (Deut. 2 : 30). The Psalmist, reciting the same history, says : ' He turned their heart to hate his people ' (Ps. 105 : 25). Now, it cannot be said that they stumbled (impegisse) [merely] because they were destitute of the counsel of God. For if they are ' made obstinate,' and are ' turned,' they are designedly inclined (destinato flectuntur) to this very thing. Besides, whenever it has pleased God to punish the transgressions of his people, how has he accomplished his work by means of the reprobate ? In such a manner that any one may see that the power of acting (efficaciam agendi) proceeded from him, and that they were the ministers of his will." Again, he says (Inst. I., xviii., 2) : " Nothing can be more explicit than God's frequent declarations that he blinds the minds of men, strikes them with giddiness, inebriates them with the spirit of slumber, fills them with infatuation, and hardens their hearts. These passages many persons refer to permission, as though, in abandoning the reprobate, God only permitted them to be blinded by Satan. But this solution is frivolous, since the Holy Spirit expressly declares that their blindness and infatuation are inflicted by the righteous judgment of God." That this phraseology is not intended to teach that God works in the human will " to will and to do " evil, is evident for the following reason : Calvin teaches that the agency of God in relation to sin is different from that of man. He says (Inst. I., xviii., 2) : " Some elude the force of these expressions [concerning God's hardening, etc.] with a foolish cavil; that since Pharaoh himself is said to have hardened his own heart his own will is the [only] cause of his obduracy ; as if these two things did not agree well together, *although in different modes* (licet diversis modis): namely, that when man is made to act by God, he nevertheless is active himself (ubi agitur a deo, simul tamen agere)." The mode, according to Calvin, in which God acts when he " hardens " the human heart is: 1. By *voluntary* permission, not involuntary or "bare" permission. God *decides* to permit the sinful will to sin, though he could prevent it. " It is nugatory to substitute for the [active] providence of God a bare [passive] permission ; as though God were sitting in a watch-tower awaiting fortuitous events, and so his decisions were dependent on the will of man " (Inst. I., xviii., 1). 2. By positively withdrawing the restraints of conscience and the common influences of the Spirit, after they have been resisted and made ineffectual, as taught by St. Paul in Rom. 1 : 24, 28. 3. By using the agency of Satan, as described in John 13 : 2, 27. " I grant, indeed, that God often actuates (agere) the reprobate by the interposition of Satan ; but in such a manner that Satan himself acts his part by the Divine impulse, and proceeds only so far as God appoints " (Inst., I., xviii., 2). " According to one view of the subject, it is said : ' If the prophet be deceived when he hath spoken a thing, I the Lord have deceived that prophet ' (Ezek. 14 : 9). But according to another, God is said himself to give men over to a reprobate mind (Rom. 1 : 28), and to the vilest lusts ; because he is the principal author of his own righteous retribution, and Satan is only the dispenser of it " (Inst., I., xviii., 1). " The whole," says Calvin (Inst., I., xviii., 1), " may be summed up thus : that as the will of God is said to be the cause of all things, his providence is established as the governor in all the counsels and works of man, so that it not only exerts its power in the elect, who are influenced by the Holy Spirit, but also compels the compliance of the reprobate." The term " compel " here, like the term " necessitate," is employed in the sense of " making certain." See Supplement, Anthropology, II., 230.

Finally, while the inward actuation of the human will " to will and to do " right is invariably represented by Calvin as the agency of the Holy Spirit, there is nothing in his harshest and most unguarded teachings concerning God's predestination of the non-elect to sin, that can be construed to mean that the Holy Spirit in the same manner, by inward actuation, works in the sinner "to will and to do" wrong. Calvin drew up the Gallican Confession of 1559. Article viii. says : " We believe that God not only created all things, but that he governs and directs them, disposing and ordaining by his sovereign will all that happens in the world ; not that he is the author of evil, or that the guilt of it can be imputed to him, seeing that his will is the sovereign and infallible rule of all right and justice ; but he hath wonderful means of so making use of devils and sinners that he can turn to good the evil which they do, and of which they are guilty." Again, in his articles on Predestination (Opera, IX., 713), he says : " Although the will of God is the first and highest cause of all things, and God has the devil and all the wicked subject to his decree (arbitrio), yet he cannot be called the cause of sin, nor the author of evil, nor is he obnoxious to any blame. Although the devil and the reprobated are the servants and instruments of God, and execute his secret judgments, yet God so operates in an incomprehensible manner in and by them, that he contracts no corruption from their fault, because he uses their wickeness rightly and justly for a good end, although the mode and manner is often hidden from us. They act ignorantly and calumniously who say that God is the author of sin, if all things occur according to his will and ordination ; because they do not distinguish between the manifested depravity of man and the secret decrees of God."

Vol. I., p. 413. "What I will is fate," says God, according to Milton ; by which he means that what God wills is certain to occur. This statement does not imply that the action of the human will is necessitated because it is willed by God. For God wills this species of action as the action of mind, not of matter ; *self*-action, or *self*-

11

motion; and therefore it is free action. If he willed it as physical action ab extra, like the fall of a stone by the action of gravity which is extraneous to the stone, it would be involuntary and compulsory action. When God wills physical action in the material world, his "will is fate" in the sense of necessity, because he wills the action of impersonal and involuntary agents. But when he wills personal and voluntary action in the moral world, his "will is fate" in the sense of certainty, because he wills the action of self-determining agents. There is nothing in the idea of certainty that implies compulsion. It is certain that some men will steal to-morrow, but this does not make their theft involuntary and necessitated.

The pagan conception of fate, as something to which God is subject, is expressed by Aeschylus (Prom. Vinctus, 524–527):

"CHOR. Who then is it that manages the helm of necessity?
PROM. The triform Fates and the unforgetful Furies.
CHOR. Is Jupiter less powerful than these?
PROM. Most certainly he cannot in any way escape his doom."

Cicero asserted human freedom, but denied Divine foreknowledge as incompatible with it. Augustine (City of God, V., ix.) combats his view. Anselm (Cur Deus, II., xviii.) makes a distinction between "antecedent" and "subsequent" necessity which is valuable in explaining the self-motion and responsibility of the enslaved will. "There is an antecedent necessity which is the cause of a thing, and there is also a subsequent necessity arising from the thing itself. Thus when the heavens are said to revolve, it is an antecedent and efficient necessity, for they must revolve. But when I say that you speak of necessity because you are speaking, this is nothing but a subsequent and inoperative necessity. For I only mean that it is impossible for you to speak and not to speak at the same time, and not that some one compels you to speak. This subsequent necessity pertains to everything, so that we say: Whatever has been necessarily has been. Whatever is must be. Whatever is to be of necessity will be. Wherever there is an antecedent necessity, there is also a subsequent one; but not vice versa. For we can say that the heaven revolves of necessity, because it revolves; but it is not likewise true, that because you speak, you do it of necessity." In the instance of "subsequent" necessity within the voluntary or moral sphere, the necessity is made by a foregoing free act of the will. Says Anselm (Cur Deus, II., v.): "When one does a benefit from a necessity to which he is unwillingly subjected, less thanks are due to him, or none at all. But when he freely *places* himself under the necessity of benefiting another, and sustains that necessity without reluctance, then he certainly deserves greater thanks for the favor. For this should not be called necessity but grace, inasmuch as he undertook it not with any constraint, but freely. For what you promise to-day of your own accord that you will give to-morrow, you give to-morrow with the same willingness that you promised it, though it be 'necessary' for you to redeem your promise or make yourself a liar."

Applying this distinction to the fall of mankind in Adam: There was no "antecedent" necessity that this fall from holiness should occur. It was left to the self-determination of the human will whether it should occur. But having occurred, then there was a "subsequent" necessity of two kinds. 1. It was necessary that what is should be. 2. It was necessary that sin having freely originated should continue to be, because of its enslaving effect upon the will that originated it.

Voluntary action, be it inclination or volition, is *certain* to occur, whether the certainty be ascribed to chance or to the divine decree. If it can be made certain by chance, this would not prove that it was necessitated in the sense of compelled. For the very object which the opponent

of decrees has in view in asserting that voluntary actions
are fortuitous is to evince thereby that they are free.   If,
again, a voluntary act can be made certain by leaving the
will to itself and exerting no divine influence of any kind
upon it, this would not prove that it was necessitated in
the sense of compelled.   This shows that certainty and
necessity are not synonyms.   In English usage the term
"necessity" sometimes denotes compulsion, and sometimes only certainty.   Consider the two following propositions: It is "certain and necessary" that a stone will fall
by gravitation.   It is "certain and necessary" that man
will incline and exert volitions.   In the first of these propositions the certainty is also strict necessity, because it
is brought about by a force of nature; in the last, the
certainty is not strict necessity, because it is brought about
by the self-motion of the human will.

VOL. I., p. 418.   Augustine teaches that the number of
the elect is definite and fixed.   "I speak of those who
are predestinated to the kingdom of God, whose number
is so certain that a single one can neither be added to
tnem nor taken from them.   For that the number of elect
is certain, and neither to be increased nor diminished, is
signified by John the Baptist when he says, 'Bring forth,
therefore, fruits meet for repentance, and think not to say
within yourselves we have Abraham to our father; for
God is able of these stones to raise up children to Abraham.'   This shows that those who do not produce the
fruits of true repentance will be cast off and others put in
their places, so that the complete number of the spiritual
seed promised to Abraham should not be wanting.   The
certain number of the elect is yet more plainly declared in
the Apocalypse: 'Hold fast that which thou hast, lest another take thy crown' (Rev. 3:11).   For if another is not
to receive unless one has lost, the number is fixed" (Rebuke
and Grace, ch. 39).

VOL. I., p. 419.   Milton (Par. Lost, iii., 129) assigns as

the reason for the preterition of the fallen angels and the election of fallen man, the fact that the fall of the former was a more wilful act than that of the latter, because it occurred without external temptation.

> " The first sort by their own suggestion fell,
> Self-tempted, self-depraved ; man falls deceived
> By the other first : man therefore shall find grace,
> The others none."

But this is contrary to St. Paul's doctrine of election and preterition, according to which neither of the two is explicable by the fact of more or less sin in the parties, and the reason for the discrimination is wholly secret (Rom. 9 : 11, 12). The difference in the treatment of individuals, both in regard to the gifts of providence and the gifts of grace, is like the difference in the world of material nature. If we ask, Why ten blades of grass rather than nine grow up in a particular spot, the answer is, That it is the will of the Creator. But if we ask, Why the Creator so willed, the reply must be, as in the instance of election and preterition, that the reason is unknown.

Augustine (Rebuke and Grace, ch. 27) thus describes the elect and non-elect angels, " We believe that the God and Lord of all things, who created all things very good, and foreknew that evil things would arise out of good, and knew that it belonged to his omnipotent goodness even to educe good out of evil things rather than not to *allow* evil things to be at all, so *ordained* the life of angels and men that in it he might first of all show what their free-will was capable of, and then what the compassion of his grace and the righteousness of his justice was capable of. In brief, certain angels, of whom the chief is he who is called the devil, became by free-will outcasts from the Lord God. Yet although they fled from his goodness wherein they had been blessed, they could not flee from his judgment by which they were made most wretched. Others, however, by the same free-will stood fast in the truth, and obtained the knowledge of that most certain truth that they should never fall." Augustine omits to mention the *reason* why the free-will of these latter persevered in holiness, namely, the bestowment of a higher grade of grace than that given in creation to both classes of angels alike. The grace given by creation to all angels was sufficient to enable them all to persevere in holiness, but not *to prevent their apostasy.* But the grace given to those who did not fall was sufficient to "keep them from falling." This constituted them "elect angels," the others being non-elect. Angelic election and non-election have reference to perseverance or continuance in holiness; human election and non-election, to perseverance or continuance in sin. A holy angel if kept in holiness is an elect angel; if not kept, but left to decide the event of apostasy for himself, is a non-elect angel. A sinful man, if delivered from sin by regenerating grace, is an elect man; if left in sin, is a non-elect man. Angelic election and non-election relate to the perpetuity of holiness; human election and non-election to the perpetuity of sin.

Vol. I., p. 420. The following is the view of Socrates concerning God and evil: "We must not listen to Homer or any other poet who is guilty of the folly of saying that, 'At the threshold of Zeus lie two casks full of lots, one of good, the other of evil' (Iliad, xxiv., 527), and again, 'Zeus is the dispenser of good and evil to us.' And if any one asserts that the violation of oaths and treaties of which Pandarus was the real author (Iliad, ii., 69), was brought about by Athene and Zeus, he shall not have our approval; neither will we allow our young men to hear the words of Aeschylus, when he says that 'God plants guilt among men when he desires utterly to destroy a house.' The poet may say that the wicked are miserable because they require to be punished, and are benefited by receiving punishment from God; but that God, being good, is the author of evil to any one, is to be strenuously denied, and not allowed to be sung or said in any well-ordered commonwealth by old or young. Such a fiction is suicidal, ruinous, impious. Let this then be one of the rules of recitation and invention—that God is not the author of evil, but of good only." The "good" and "evil" spoken of in the first two extracts from Homer are physical good and evil, but that spoken of in the third extract from Homer, and in the extract from Aeschylus, is moral good and evil. God may be the author of the first without dishonor to his nature, but not of the second.

VOL. I., p. 422. While revelation teaches that the majority of the human race are saved by Christ's redemption, it also teaches that the lost minority are a large multitude; but much less than those of the saved, and infinitely less than the immense number of the holy and blessed in the whole universe of God. The fact of sin looks very differently when confined to the small sphere of earth, from what it does when viewed from the immense range of the universe. Even if there had been no redemption of man, and the whole family of mankind had been left like the fallen angels in their voluntary and self-originated ruin, the proportion of moral evil in the wide creation of God would still have been small. The kingdom of God is infinitely greater than that of Satan. Holy angels and redeemed men vastly outnumber lost angels and lost men. The human race has had an existence of only six or eight thousand years, but the " heavenly host " has existed ages upon ages. The supplication, " Thy will be done on earth as it is in heaven," implies that heaven is the rule in the universe of God, and hell the exception. God " inhabits the praises of eternity " and of infinity. This means that praises have been ascending to him from the hosts of holy intelligences during a past eternity, compared with which the short duration of man's existence on earth is nothing. While, therefore, earth appears gloomy and dark because of apostasy, the illimitable universe looks bright and glorious because of obedience and holiness. This is often forgotten, and explains the exaggerated statements of both infidels and Christians concerning the extent of moral evil, making the problem of sin more difficult of explanation with reference to the benevolence and power of God. For if sin had been permitted throughout all of God's dominions in the same proportion that it has been in the little province called earth, it would have required a greater faith in God's unsearchable wisdom than it does now. When, therefore, the theologian is depressed, and tempted to " charge God foolishly " because of the reign of sin and death among the generations of men, let him look up and out into the immense universe of God and remember that through this vast range of being there is innocence, and purity, and the love and worship of God.

Leibnitz (Theodicée, i., 19, Ed. Erdmann, p. 509), who with Augustine assumed that the majority of mankind are lost, relieves this opinion by the observation that this is an insignificant number compared with that of the holy and happy in the remainder of the universe. In this way he makes out that the existing universe is the best possible, notwithstanding that there is so much sin and misery in this planet on which man is placed. Howe, also (Christian's Triumph, sub fine), says : " Consider how minute a part of the creation of God this globe of earth is, where death has reigned. For aught we know, death never reaches higher than this earth of ours ; and therefore there are vast and ample regions, incomparably beyond the range of our thought, where no death ever comes. We are told (Eph. 1 : 20, 21) that God hath set the Mediator in the heavenly places, far above all principality, and power, and dominion ; angels, authorities, and powers being made subject to him. Though we cannot form distinct thoughts what these dominions are, yet we cannot but suppose those inconceivably vast regions peopled with immortal inhabitants that live and reign in holy life and blessedness. Furthermore, death is to be confined, and go no further. In the future state of things all death is to be gathered into death, and hell into hell (Rev. 20 : 14). It shall be contracted, gathered into itself. Whereas formerly it ranged to and fro uncontrolled, it now is confined to its own narrow circle, and can get no new subjects ; and shall therefore give no further trouble or disturbance to the rest of God's universe."

Similarly, Baxter (Dying Thoughts) remarks that " God's infinite kingdom is not to be judged of by his jail or gibbets. And what though God give not to all men an overcoming measure of grace, nor to the best of men so much as they desire, yet the earth is but a spot or point of God's creation ; not so much as an anthillock to a kingdom, or perhaps to all the earth. And who is scandalized because the earth hath an heap of ants in it, yea, or a nest of snakes that are not men ? The vast, unmeasurable worlds of light which are above us are possessed by inhabitants suitable to their glory."

Such a broad and lofty view of holiness compared with sin as this should be introduced into eschatology, and mitigate the dark subject of moral evil, not by the unscriptural doctrine of future redemption and the denial of endless punishment, but by the Biblical teaching of the infinitude of holiness and blessedness, and the finiteness of sin and misery.

If it is proper to attempt to compute the number of lost men, perhaps the statement is measurably correct that most of them belong to early manhood, middle age, and old age. All infants who die in infancy are saved by infant regeneration. This constitutes one-half of the human family. Of the other half, there is reason to hope that the majority of those who die in childhood and youth are regenerated. Original sin, in their case, has not been intensified by actual transgression to the degree that it is in early manhood, middle life, and old age. Consequently, the influence of religious instruction in the family, the Sabbath-school, and the sanctuary, is more effective in them than upon adults generally. The total population of school age in the United States is 22,447,392. Of these, 9,718,422 are Sabbath-school scholars. The majority of conversions are between the ages of six and twenty years. This leaves adults from twenty to seventy years; and looking abroad over the world as it now appears, the millennium not being considered, there is melancholy reason to fear that the majority of these do not turn from sin to God. This part of mankind is more inclined and self-determined to this world, more absorbed in its business and pleasures, more sunk in hardened vice and besotted luxury, and less susceptible to the influence of Divine truth. Few of them are in the Bible class, and a very large number of them never enter the sanctuary for religious instruction. The greater part of the lost, consequently, come from this class. Few of this class, to human view, have the broken and contrite spirit of the publican respecting their personal sinfulness, and any son of Adam who goes into the Divine Presence unable, because unwilling, to pray, "God be merciful to me, a sinner," is a lost spirit.

That more of mankind are lost than are saved was, on the whole, the patristic and mediæval opinion. The doctrine that baptism by the Church is necessary to salvation, which prevailed universally in those periods, contributed to this. Augustine teaches that the elect are the minority of mankind. "St. Paul says, 'Not as the offence so also is the free gift. For if through the offence of one many be dead, much more the grace of God, and the gift by grace, which is by one man, Jesus Christ, hath abounded unto many.' Not *many more*, that is, many more men, for there are not more persons justified than condemned; but it runs, *much more hath abounded;* since, while Adam produced sinners from his one sin, Christ has by his grace procured free forgiveness even for the sins which men have of their own accord added by actual transgression to the original sin in which they were born" (Forgiveness and Baptism, i., 14). "As many of the human race as are delivered by God's grace, are delivered from the condemnation in which they are held bound by the sin in Adam. Hence, even if none should be delivered, no one can justly blame the judgment of God. That, therefore, in comparison with those that perish, *few*, but in their absolute number *many*, are delivered from this condemnation, is effected by grace (gratia); is effected gratuitously (gratis); and thanks must be given because it is effected so that no one may be lifted up as of his own deservings, but that every mouth may be stopped, and he that glorieth may glory in the Lord" (Rebuke and Grace, ch. 28). "It is a matter of fact that not all, nor even a majority of mankind are saved" (Euchiridion, ch. 97).

VOL. I., p. 426. The following texts are sometimes erroneously explained to teach that election is mutable: John 6 : 70, "Have I not chosen you twelve, and one of you is a devil." The election meant here is not election to salvation, but to the apostolate. "He called unto him his disciples ; and of them he chose twelve whom he also named apostles" (Luke 6 : 13). John 17 : 12, "Those whom thou gavest me I have kept, and none of them is lost, but the son of perdition : that the Scripture might be fulfilled." The particles ϵi $\mu \dot{\eta}$, qualifying $\dot{o}$ $\upsilon \dot{\iota} o s$ $\tau \hat{\eta} s$ $\dot{a} \pi o \lambda \epsilon i a s$, are adversative, making two propositions, not exceptive, making only one. None of those whom the Father had given to Christ, and whom Christ had kept, were lost, is the first proposition. But the son of perdition is lost, that the Scripture might be fulfilled, is the second. The son of perdition in the second proposition is not one of those whom Christ kept in the first proposition. Luke 4 : 27 (comp. Luke 4 : 25, 26) illustrates. "Many lepers were in Israel in the time of Eliseus the prophet; and none of them was cleansed saving Naaman the Syrian." The particles εἰ μή, qualifying Νεεμὰν ὁ Σύρος, are not exceptive here, as the word "saving" implies, but adversative. Naaman was not one of the lepers of Israel, and so was not an exception, belonging to them. The true rendering, therefore, of John 17 : 12 is as follows: "Those whom thou gavest me I have kept, and none of them [whom thou gavest me] is lost; but the son of perdition [is lost] that the Scripture might be fulfilled." This is Turrettin's explanation (Inst., IV., xii., 24).

VOL. I., p. 432.   Bunyan (Reprobation Asserted, ch. x.) clearly states the difference between common grace and saving grace as follows: "There is a great difference between the grace of election and the grace in the general tenders of the Gospel: a difference as to its timing, latituding, and working.   1. Touching its timing; it is before, yea, long before there was either tender of the grace in the general offer of the Gospel to any, or any need of such a tender.   [The grace of election is from eternity; that of the general offer is at a particular time.]   2. Touching the latitude or extent; the tenders of grace in the Gospel are common and universal to all, but the extension of that of election is special and peculiar to some.   'There is a remnant according to the election of grace.'   3. Touching the working of the grace of election, it differs from the working of grace in the general offers of the Gospel in the following particulars: (a) The grace that is offered in the general tenders of the Gospel calleth for faith to lay hold upon and accept thereof; but the special grace of election worketh that faith which doth lay hold thereof.   (b) The grace that is offered in the general tenders of the Gospel calleth for faith as a condition to be performed by us, without which there is no life; but the special grace of election worketh faith in us without any such condition. [It imparts the life which produces the faith.]   (c) The grace that is offered in the general tenders of the Gospel promoteth happiness upon the condition of persevering in the faith; but the special grace of election causeth this perseverance. (*d*) The grace offered in the general tenders of the Gospel, when it sparkleth most, leaveth the greatest part of men behind it; but the special grace of election, when it shineth least, doth infallibly bring every soul therein concerned to everlasting life. (*e*) A man may overcome and put out all the light that is begotten in him by the general tenders of the Gospel; but none shall overcome, or make void, or frustrate the grace of election. (*f*) The general tenders of the Gospel, apart from the concurrence with them of the grace of election, are insufficient to save the elect himself, as well as the non-elect."

Vol. I., p. 433. Augustine teaches preterition in the following places: "Faith, as well in its beginning as in its completion, is God's gift. But why it is not given to all, ought not to disturb the believer who believes that from one all have gone into a condemnation which undoubtedly is most righteous; so that even if none were delivered therefrom there would be no just cause for finding fault with God. Whence it is plain that it is a great grace for many to be delivered, and that those who are not delivered should acknowledge what is due to themselves. But why God delivers one rather than another—his judgments are unsearchable, and his ways past finding out" (Predestination, ch. 16). "So far as concerns justice and mercy, it may be truly said to the guilty who is condemned, and also concerning the guilty who is saved, 'Take what thine is, and go thy way; I will give unto this one that which is not due. Is it not lawful for me to do what I will with mine own? Is thine eye evil [envious] because I am good?' And if he shall say, 'Why not to me also?' he will hear, and with reason, 'Who art thou, O man, that repliest against God?' And although in the one case you see a most benignant benefactor, and in the other a most righteous exactor, in neither case do you behold an *unjust*

God.   For although God would be righteous if he were to
punish both, yet he who is saved has good ground for
thankfulness, and he who is condemned has no ground for
finding fault" (Perseverance, ch. 16).   " I do not know the
reason why one or another is more or less helped or not
helped by that grace which restrains sinful self-will and
changes it; this only I know, that God does this with perfect justice, and for reasons which to himself are known as
sufficient" (Letter xcv., 6.   To Paulinus, A.D. 408).

Augustine teaches that preterition does not apply to baptized infants.   " Persons, whether parents or others, who attempt to place those who have been baptized under idolatry and heathen worship, are guilty of spiritual homicide.
True, they do not actually kill the children's souls, but
they go as far toward killing them as is in their power.
The warning, ' Do not kill your little ones,' may with
all propriety be addressed to them ; for the apostle says,
' Quench not the Spirit;' not that he can be quenched [in
baptized infants], but that those who so act as if they
wished to have him quenched, are deservedly spoken of
as quenchers of the Spirit.   In this sense the words of
Cyprian are to be understood respecting the ' lapsed ' who
in times of persecution had sacrificed to idols : ' And that
nothing might be wanting to fill up the measure of their
crime, their infant children lost, while yet in their infancy,
that which they had received [in baptism] as soon as life
began.'   They lost it, he meant, so far as pertained to the
guilt of those by whom they were compelled to incur
the loss ; that is to say, they lost it in the purpose and
wish of those who perpetrated on them such a wrong [as
to bring them up in idolatry].   For had they actually in
their own persons lost it, they must have remained under
the divine sentence of condemnation.   But shall not these
infants say, when the judgment-day has come : ' We have
done nothing ; we have not of our own accord hastened to
participate in profane rites, forsaking the bread and the

cup of our Lord; the apostasy of others caused our destruction.' Hence, in the just dispensation of judgment by God, those shall not be doomed to perish whose souls their parents did, so far as concerns their own guilt in the transaction, bring to ruin" (Letter xcviii., 3. To Boniface, A.D. 408). "You must refer it to the hidden determination of God, when you see in one and the same condition, such as all infants unquestionably have who derive their hereditary sin from Adam, that one is assisted so as to be baptized, and another is not assisted, so that he dies in bondage" (Grace and Free-Will, ch. 45).

VOL. I., p. 434. It is impossible to make sense out of Rom. 11 : 7, without supposing two kinds of election and preterition, namely national and individual, and two corresponding grades of grace, namely, common and special. St. Paul says that "Israel hath not obtained that which he seeketh for, but the election hath obtained it, and the rest were blinded." The "rest" of whom ? The rest of Israel, of course. Whom does he mean by "Israel ? " All of the descendants of Abraham. These were all without exception nationally elected. They were all without exception "Israelites, to whom pertaineth the adoption, and the glory, and the covenants, and the giving of the law, and the promises ; whose are the fathers, and of whom as concerning the flesh Christ came, who is over all, God blessed forever " (Rom. 9 : 4, 5). This national election entitled the subjects of it to all the blessings of the theocracy, on *condition* of observing the Mosaic ordinances and keeping the theocratic covenant, of which circumcision was the sign and seal. Ishmael as well as Isaac, Esau as well as Jacob, were sealed with the sign of circumcision, and were entitled, together with their offspring, to the blessings of the theocracy, if faithful in this relation. By birth they all belonged to the chosen people and the national church. "By faith Isaac blessed Jacob and Esau concerning things to come" (Heb. 11 : 20 ; Gen. 27 : 27, 39). But Ishmael,

and Esau, and their descendants separated from the theocracy and renounced the Messianic covenant, and for this
reason, though born of Abraham, failed to obtain the Messianic salvation. "Was not Esau Jacob's brother? saith
the Lord; yet I loved Jacob and I hated Esau" (Mal. 1:
2, 3).   Jacob I effectually called, and Esau I left to his own
will.   Ishmael, Esau, and their descendants, together with
a part of the descendants of Isaac and Jacob were the
"rest that were blinded" (Rom. 11 : 7); who "were Jews
outwardly, but not inwardly" (Rom. 2: 28, 29); who
"were of Israel, but were not Israel" (Rom. 9: 6); who
"were the seed of Abraham, but were not children"
(Rom. 9: 7); who were nationally, but not individually
and spiritually elected.   If there is but one election,
namely, the national and universal, there can be no discrimination like this; no "rest that were blinded."   But
in one case, according to the apostle, the "election" includes *all* of the descendants of Abraham ; in the other,
only a *part* of them.   The entire Hebrew nation were outwardly called by the ministry of the law, moral and cere-
monial.   Many of them rejected this call, and did not
obtain salvation.   A part of them were individually and
effectually called, and were saved.

Calvin thus distinguishes between national and individual election: "Predestination we call the eternal decree
of God, by which he has determined in himself what he
would have to become of every individual of mankind.
For they are not all created with a similar destiny; but
eternal life is foreordained for some, and eternal damnation for others.   Every man, therefore, being created for
one or other of these ends, we say, he is predestinated
either to life or to death.   This, God has not only testified
in particular persons, but has given a specimen of it in
the *whole posterity* of Abraham, which should evidently
show the future condition of every *nation* to depend upon
his decision.   'When the Most High divided the nations,

when he separated the sons of Adam, the Lord's portion was his people; Jacob was the lot of his inheritance' (Deut. 32 : 8, 9). The separation is before the eyes of all; in the person of Abraham, as in the dry trunk of a tree, one people is peculiarly chosen to the rejection of others: no reason for this appears, except that Moses, to deprive their posterity of all occasion of glorying, teaches them that their exaltation is wholly from God's gratuitous love (Deut. 7 : 7, 8; 10 : 14, 15). There is a *second degree* of election, still more restricted, or that in which the Divine grace was displayed in a more special manner, when of the same race of Abraham God rejected some, and by nourishing others in the Church, proved that he retained them among his children. Ishmael at first obtained the same station [of national election] as his brother Isaac, for the spiritual covenant was equally sealed in him by the symbol of circumcision. He is cut off [in individual election]; afterward Esau is, and lastly an innumerable multitude, and almost all Israel, are. In Isaac the seed was called; the same calling continued in Jacob. God exhibited a similar example in the rejection of Saul, which is celebrated by the Psalmist: 'He refused the tabernacle of Joseph, and chose not the tribe of Ephraim, but chose the tribe of Judah' (Ps. 78 : 67, 68). I grant that it was by their own crime and guilt that Ishmael, Esau, and persons of similar character, fell from [national] adoption; because the condition annexed was, that they should faithfully keep the covenant of God, which they perfidiously violated. Malachi thus aggravates the ingratitude of Israel, because though not only nationally elected out of the whole race of mankind, but also separated from a sacred family to be a peculiar people, they despised God, their most beneficent Father. ' Was not Esau Jacob's brother? saith the Lord; yet I loved Jacob, and I hated Esau' " (Mal. 1 : 2, 3).

"Though it is sufficiently clear that God in his secret

12

counsel freely chooses whom he will and rejects others, his gratuitous election is but half displayed till we come to *particular individuals*, to whom God not only *offers salvation*, but assigns it in such a manner that the *certainty* of the effect is liable to no suspense or doubt. That the general election of a *people* is not invariably effectual and permanent, a reason readily presents itself, because when God covenants with them he does not also give them the spirit of *regeneration* to enable them to persevere in the covenant to the end; but the *external call*, without the internal efficacy of grace, which would be sufficient for their preservation, is a kind of medium between the rejection of all mankind and the election of the small number of believers" (Inst., III., xxi., 5–7).

VOL. I., p. 435. Calvin, in his comment on Rom. 9 : 8, thus describes the difference between common and special grace : "Two things are to be considered, in reference to the selection by God of the posterity of Abraham as a peculiar people. The first is, that the promise of blessing through the Messiah has a relation to all who can trace their natural descent from him. It is offered to all, without exception, and for this reason they are all denominated the heirs of the covenant made with Abraham, and the children of promise. It was God's will that his covenant with Abraham should be sealed by the rite of circumcision with Ishmael and Esau, as well as with Isaac and Jacob, which shows that the former were not wholly excluded from him. Accordingly, all the lineal descendants of Abraham are denominated by St. Peter (Acts 3 : 25) the 'children of the covenant,' though they were unbelieving; and St. Paul, in this chapter (verse 4), says of unbelieving Jews : 'Whose are the covenants.' The second point to be considered is, that this covenant, though thus offered, was rejected by great numbers of the lineal descendants of Abraham. Such Jews, though they are of Israel,' they are not the 'children of the promise.' When, therefore, the whole Jewish people are indiscriminately denominated the heritage and peculiar people of God, it is meant that they have been selected from other nations, the offer of salvation through the Messiah has been made to them, and confirmed by the symbol of circumcision. But inasmuch as many reject this outward adoption, and thus enjoy none of its benefits, there arises another difference with regard to the fulfilment of the promise. The *general* and *national* election of the people of Israel not resulting in faith and salvation, is no hindrance that God should not choose from among them those whom he pleases to make the subjects of his *special* grace. This is a second election, which is confined to a part, only, of the nation."

VOL. I., p. 441. The preterition of a part of mankind in the bestowment of regenerating grace presupposes the fall, according to Calvin. This places him among the sublapsarians. The following extracts from his Institutes show this : " If any one attack us with such an inquiry as this, ' Why God has from the beginning predestinated some men to death, who not yet being brought into existence could not yet deserve the sentence of death ' [This is the objector's, not Calvin's phraseology. In his reply, Calvin says, "previously to *birth* adjudged to endless misery," not previously to creation], we will reply by asking them in return, What they suppose God owes to man if He chooses to judge of him from his own [sinful] nature. As we are all *corrupted by sin*, we must necessarily be odious to God, and that not from tyrannical cruelty, but in the most equitable estimation of justice. If all whom the Lord predestinates to death are *in their natural condition* liable to the sentence of death, what injustice do they complain of receiving from him ? Let all the sons of Adam come forward ; let them all contend and dispute with their Creator, because by his eternal providence they were previously to their *birth* [not previously to their creation and fall in Adam, as the objector states it] adjudged to endless

misery.   What murmur will they be able to raise against
this vindication when God, on the other hand, shall call
them to *a review of themselves*.   If they have all been
taken from a corrupt mass, it is no wonder that they are
subject to condemnation.   Let them not, therefore, accuse
God of injustice, if his eternal decree has destined them to
death, to which they feel themselves, whatever be their
desire or aversion, spontaneously led forward by their own
[sinful] nature.   Hence appears the perverseness of their
disposition to murmur, because they intentionally suppress
the *cause* of condemnation which they are constrained to
acknowledge in themselves, hoping to excuse themselves
by charging it upon God.   But though I ever so often admit God to be the author of it [*i.e.*, the condemnation],
which is perfectly correct, yet this does not abolish the
guilt impressed upon their consciences, and from time to
time recurring to their view" (Inst., III., xxiii., 3).   "They
further object, 'Were they not by the decree of God antecedently *predestinated* to that corruption which is now
stated as the cause of condemnation?   When they perish
in their corruption, therefore, they only suffer the punishment of that misery into which, in consequence of God's
predestination, Adam fell and precipitated his posterity
with him.   Is not God unjust, therefore, in treating his
creatures with such cruel mockery?   I confess, indeed,
that all the descendants of Adam fell *by the divine will*
into that miserable condition in which they are now involved; and this is what I asserted from the beginning,
that we must always return at last to the sovereign determination of God's will, the cause of which is hidden in
himself.   But it follows not, therefore, that God is liable
to this reproach [of injustice]" (Inst., III., xxiii., 4).   Calvin then gives two replies to the allegation that the fall of
Adam, by being decreed by God, was necessitated by him.
The first reply is that of St. Paul, "O man, who art thou
that repliest against God?"   "What stronger reason,"

says Calvin, " can be presented than when we are directed
to consider who God is ? How could any injustice be
committed by him who is the judge of the world? If it is
the peculiar property of the nature of God to do justice,
then he naturally loves righteousness and hates iniquity.
The apostle, therefore, has not resorted to sophistry, as if
he were in danger of confutation, but has shown that the
reason of the divine justice is too high to be measured by
a human standard, or comprehended by the littleness of
the human mind " (Inst., III., xxiii., 4). The second reply
is, that sin is decreed *in such a manner* as not to interfere
with the free agency and responsibility of Adam and his
posterity in the fall. Before proceeding to this important
particular, Calvin first objects to that statement of the
permissive decree which makes God a mere passive spectator of the fall without a positive act of will concerning
it; and asserts, with Augustine, that " the permission is
not involuntary, but voluntary " (Inst., I., xviii., 3). "Here
they recur to the distinction between will and permission,
and insist that God permits the destruction of the wicked,
but does not *will* it. But what reason shall we assign for
his permitting it, but because it is his *will?* It is not
probable that man procured his own destruction by the
mere permission without any appointment (ordinatione) of
God ; as though God had not determined what he would
choose to be the condition of the principal of his creatures.
I shall not hesitate, therefore, to confess plainly with Augustine, 'that the will of God is the certainty (necessitatem) of things, and that what he has willed will certainly
(necessario) come to pass ; as those things are surely
about to happen which he has foreseen '" (Inst., III., xxiii.,
8). Having given what he regards as the true view of
God's permission of sin by a voluntary decree to permit it,
Calvin then affirms that the fall of Adam thus actively-
permissively decreed was free and guilty. " Now, if either
Pelagians, or Manichæans, or Anabaptists, or Epicureans

(for we are concerned with these four sects in this argument), in excuse for themselves, and the impious, plead the certainty (necessitatem) with which they are bound by God's predestination, they allege nothing applicable to the case. For if predestination [to death] *is no other than a dispensation of divine justice*, mysterious, indeed, but liable to no blame, since it is certain that *they were not unworthy of being predestinated to that fate*, it is equally certain that the destination they incur by predestination is consistent with the strictest justice. Moreover, their perdition depends on the divine predestination *in such a manner* that *the cause and matter of it are found in themselves*. For the first man fell because the Lord had determined it was so expedient. The reason of this determination is unknown to us. Man falls, therefore, according to the appointment of Divine Providence ; but he falls *by his own fault*. The Lord had a little before pronounced ' everything that he had made ' to be ' very good.' Whence, then, comes the depravity of man to revolt from his God? Lest it should be thought to come from creation, God had approved and commended what had proceeded from himself. *By his own wickedness*, therefore, Adam corrupted the nature he had received pure from the Lord, and by his fall he drew all his posterity with him into destruction. Wherefore let us rather contemplate the evident cause of condemnation, which is nearer to us in the corrupt nature of mankind, than search after a hidden and altogether incomprehensible one in the predestination of God " (Inst., III., xxiii., 8). Calvin quotes from Augustine to the same effect. " Wherefore there is the greatest propriety in the following observations of Augustine (Ep. 106; De Persev., ch. 12) : ' The whole mass of mankind having fallen into condemnation in the first man, the vessels that are formed from it to honor are not vessels of personal righteousness, but of Divine mercy ; and the formation of others to dishonor is to be attributed not to iniquity [*i.e.*, to a greater degree of iniquity], but to the Divine decree.' While God rewards those whom he rejects with deserved punishment, and to those whom he calls freely gives undeserved grace, he is liable to no accusation, but may be compared to a creditor who has power to release one and enforce his demands on another. The Lord, therefore, may give grace to whom he will, because he is merciful, and yet not give it to all, because he is a just judge ; may manifest his free grace by giving to some what they do not deserve, while by not giving to all he declares the demerits of all " (Inst., III., xxiii., 11).

Respecting the preterition of some by Christ in the days of his flesh, Calvin remarks as follows : " Christ testifies that he confined to his apostles the explanations of the parables in which he had addressed the multitude ; ' because to you it is given to know the mysteries of the kingdom of heaven, but to them it is not given ' (Matt. 13 : 11). What does the Lord mean, you will say, by teaching those by whom he takes care not to be understood? Consider *whence the fault arises*, and you will cease the inquiry ; for whatever obscurity there is in the word, yet *there is always light enough to convince the consciences of the wicked*. It remains now to be seen why the Lord does that which it is evident he does. If it be replied that this is done because men have deserved it by their impiety, wickedness, and ingratitude, it will be a just and true observation ; but as we have not yet discovered the reason of the *diversity*, why some persist in obduracy while others are inclined to obedience, the discussion of it will necessarily lead us to the same remark that Paul has quoted from Moses concerning Pharaoh : ' Even for this same purpose have I raised thee up, that I might show my power in thee, and that my name might be declared throughout all the earth ' (Rom. 9 : 17). That the reprobate obey not the word of God when made known to them, is justly imputed to the wickedness and depravity

of their hearts, provided it be at the same time stated
that they are *abandoned* to this depravity because they have
been raised up by a just but inscrutable judgment of
God to display his glory in their condemnation. So when
it is related of the sons of Eli that they listened not to his
salutary admonitions, ' because the Lord would slay them '
(1 Sam. 2 : 25), it is not denied that their obstinacy *proceeded from their own wickedness*, but it is also plainly implied that though the Lord was able to soften their hearts,
yet they were left in their obstinacy, because his immutable
decree had predestinated them to destruction " (Inst., III.,
xxiv., 13, 14). " Examples of reprobation present themselves every day. The same sermon is addressed to a
hundred persons ; twenty receive it with the obedience of
faith ; the others despise, or ridicule, or reject, or condemn it. If it be replied that the difference proceeds
from their wickedness and perverseness, this will afford no
satisfaction, because the minds of the *others* would have
been influenced by the same wickedness but for the correction of the divine goodness. And thus we shall always
be perplexed, unless we recur to Paul's question, ' Who
maketh thee to differ ? ' In which he signifies that the
excellence of some men beyond others is not from their
own virtue, but solely from divine grace. Why, then, in
bestowing [regenerating] grace upon some does he pass
over others ? Luke assigns a reason for the former, that
they ' were ordained to eternal life ' (Acts 13 : 48). What
conclusion, then, shall be drawn respecting the latter, but
that they are vessels of wrath to dishonor? Therefore let
us not hesitate to say with Augustine (De Genesi, xi., 10),
' God could convert the will of the wicked because he is
omnipotent. It is evident that he could. Why, then,
does he not ? Because he would not. Why he would not,
remains with himself.' For we ought not to aim at more
wisdom than becomes us [by assigning some other reason
for preterition than the sovereign will of God]. That

will be much better than adopting the evasion of Chrysostom, that 'God draws those that are willing, and who
stretch out their hands for his aid,' so that the difference
may not appear to consist in the decree of God, but wholly
in the will of man " (Inst., III., xxiv., 12, 13).

The doctrine that the sin of man was decreed, but in
such a manner as to leave the origination of sin to the free
agency of man was also held by Des Cartes. In his Principles of Philosophy, Pt. I., §§ 40, 41, he remarks as follows : " What we have already discovered of God gives us
assurance that his power is so immense that we would sin
in thinking ourselves capable of ever doing anything which
he had not ordained beforehand, and yet we should soon
be embarrassed in great difficulties if we undertook to *harmonize* the preordination of God with the freedom of our
will, and endeavored to comprehend both truths at once.
But in place of this we shall be free from these embar-
rassments if we recollect that our mind is limited, while
the power of God, by which he not only *knew* from all
eternity what is or can be, but also *willed* and *preordained*
it, is infinite. It thus happens that we possess sufficient
intelligence to know clearly and distinctly that this power
is in God, but not enough to comprehend *how* he leaves
the free actions of men indeterminate ; and, on the other
hand, we have such consciousness of the liberty which
exists in ourselves that there is nothing we more clearly
or perfectly comprehend, so that the omnipotence of God
ought not to keep us from believing it. For it would be
absurd to doubt of that of which we are fully conscious,
and which we experience as existing in ourselves, merely
because we do not comprehend another matter which from
its very nature we know to be incomprehensible." This
presents the subject in a practical and conclusive manner.
The *omnipotence* of God requires a decree by which all
things are ordained and come to pass, both good and evil,
holiness and sin. For unless all events are under the

control of his will he is not almighty. And the *justice* of God requires that in the execution of the decree that sin shall come into the world, the free self-determination of man and his responsibility for sin shall be intact.

The doctrine of the permissive decree, as explained by Calvin, must be associated with the following statement of his, which has often been misconceived and misrepresented. " I inquire, again, how it came to pass that the fall of Adam, apart from any remedy (absque remedio), should involve so many nations with their infant children in eternal death, but *because it was the will of God*. It is an awe-exciting (horribile) decree I confess; but no one can deny that God foreknew the future final state of man before he created him, and that he foreknew it because it was appointed by his own decree. This subject is judiciously discussed by Augustine. ' We most wholesomely confess, what we most rightly believe, that the God and Lord of all things, who created everything very good, and foreknew that it was more suitable to his almighty goodness to bring good out of evil than not to suffer evil to exist, *ordained* the life of angels and men in such a manner as to exhibit in it, first, what *free-will was capable of doing*, and afterward, what could be effected by the blessings of his grace and the sentence of his justice ' " (Inst., III., xxiii., 7). These extracts show that both Augustine and Calvin assert the decreed origin of human sin only in connection with a free and responsible fall in Adam. All mankind, as a common mass and unity, sinned and fell in the first self-moved and uncompelled act of transgression. That act was permissively decreed; that is, foreordained in such a way as not to necessitate the act, but to leave it to the self-determination of Adam and his posterity in him. The election of some men from sin, and the leaving of others in sin, suppose this free but foreordained fall from the holiness in which Adam and his posterity were primarily created. If the facts and premises upon which both Augustine and

Calvin reason are granted, there is no ground for charging the doctrine of predestination to sin with either compulsion or fatalism.

The Biblical proof of a permissive decree that brings about the event without working efficiently in the human will " to will and to do " is abundant. Take the following as an example : God decrees that Magog shall invade Israel. " Son of man prophesy and say unto Gog, Thus saith the Lord God, In that day when my people of Israel dwelleth safely, shalt thou not know it ? And thou shalt come from thy place out of the north parts, thou, and many people with thee, all of them riding upon horses, a great company, and a mighty army ; and thou shalt come up against my people of Israel as a cloud to cover the land ; it shall be in the latter days, and I will bring thee against my land, that the heathen may know me, when I shall be sanctified in thee, O Gog, before their eyes " (Ezek. 38 : 14–16). God also decrees that Gog shall fail in this invasion, and that he will punish him for the attempt. " It shall come to pass at the same time, when Gog shall come up against the land of Israel, saith the Lord God, that my fury shall come up in my face. For in my jealousy and in the fire of my wrath have I said, Surely in that day there shall be a great shaking in the land of Israel. Therefore thou son of man prophesy against Gog, and say, Thus saith the Lord God, Behold I am against thee, O Gog, and I will turn thee back, and leave but the sixth part of thee, and will cause thee to come up from the north parts, and will bring thee upon the mountains of Israel, and I will smite thy bow out of thy left hand, and will cause thine arrows to fall out of thy right hand. And thou shalt fall upon the mountains of Israel, thou, and all thy bands, and the people that is with thee ; I will give thee to the ravenous birds of every sort, and to the beasts of the field to be devoured. Thou shalt fall upon the open field ; for I have spoken it, saith the Lord God" (Ezek. 38 : 18, 19; 39 : 1–5). It is impossible to suppose that the holy and just God positively inclined and inwardly changed the heart of Magog and his hosts from friendship toward himself and his people to enmity against them, and then punished them for their hostility. And there is no need of so supposing. Gog and his hosts were a part of the human race which fell from holiness in Adam. They already had the carnal mind which is enmity against God. The permissive decree that they should invade Israel supposed this fallen condition. God decided not to counterwork against this evil heart, but to permit its free self-moved operation. An evil heart, if not restrained by Divine grace, is infallibly certain to act wrongly. In determining not to hinder and prevent Gog from following his own evil free-will, God made his invasion of Israel a certainty. At the same time this sure and certain agency of Gog was his own voluntary self-determination, and deserving of the retribution which it received. This same reasoning applies to the case of Pharaoh, and many others like it mentioned in Scripture. It will not apply, however, to the fall of man itself. The first *origin* of sin by the permissive decree presents a difficulty not found in the subsequent *continuance* of sin by it. The certainty that sin will *continue* to be, if God decides not to overcome it by regeneration and sanctification, is explicable; but the certainty that sin will *come* to be, if God decides not to originate it himself in the created will, but leaves the origination to the creature alone, is an insoluble problem, yet a revealed truth. It should be observed, however, that the first *origin* of sin, in the fall of Adam, has no connection with the doctrines of election and preterition. It is only the subsequent *continuance* of sin that is so connected. Some men are not elected to apostasy, and others passed by. The apostasy is universal, and there is no discrimination in this respect. But some men are elected to deliverance from apostasy, and some are not elected to deliverance and are left in sin. Comp. Shedd : Calvinism, Pure and Mixed, p. 93.

Vol. I., p. 446. One of the best defences of the doctrine of preterition is found in Charnock (Holiness of God, Prop. vii.). "That God withdraws his grace from men, and gives them up sometimes to the fury of their lusts, is as clear in Scripture as anything. 'The Lord hath not given you a heart to perceive, and eyes to see, and ears to hear' (Deut. 29 : 4). Judas was delivered to Satan after the sop, and put into his power for despising former admonitions. God often leaves the reins to the devil that he may use what efficacy he can in those that have offended the majesty of God ; and he withholds further influences of grace, or withdraws what before he had granted them. Thus he withheld that grace from the sons of Eli that might have made their father's pious admonitions effectual to them (1 Sam. 2 : 25) : 'They hearkened not to the voice of their father, because the Lord would slay them.' He gave grace to Eli to reprove them, and withheld that grace from them which might have enabled them, against their natural corruption and obstinacy, to receive that reproof. But the holiness of God is not blemished by withdrawing his grace from a sinful creature, whereby he falls into more sin. 1. Because the act of God in this is only negative. Thus God is said to 'harden' men, not by positive hardening, or working anything in the creature, but by not working, not softening, leaving a a man to the hardness of his own heart, whereby it is unavoidable by the depravation of man's nature, and the fury of his passions, but that he should be further hardened, and 'increase unto more ungodliness' (2 Tim. 2 : 19). As a man is said to give another his life, when he doth not take it away when it lay at his mercy, so God is said to 'harden' a man, when he doth not mollify him when it was in his power, and inwardly quicken him with that grace whereby he might infallibly avoid any further provoking him. God is said to harden man when he removes not from them the incentives to sin, curbs not those principles which are ready to comply with those incentives, withdraws the common assistance of his grace, concurs not with counsels and admonitions to make them effectual, and flasheth not in the convincing light which he darted upon them before. If hardness follows upon God's withholding his softening grace, it is not by a positive act of God, but from the natural hardness of man. If you put fire near to wax or rosin, both will melt; but when that fire is removed they return to their natural quality of hardness and brittleness; the positive act of the fire is to melt and soften, and the softness of the rosin is to be ascribed to that; but the hardness is from the rosin itself, wherein the fire hath no influence but only a negative act by a removal of it: so when God hardens a man he only leaves him to that stony heart which he derived from [and originated in] Adam, and brought with him into the world. 2. The whole positive cause of this hardness is from man's corruption. God infuseth not any sin into his creatures, but forbears to infuse his grace, and restrain their lusts, which upon the removal of his grace work impetuously. God only gives them up to that which he knows will work strongly in their hearts. And therefore the apostle wipes off from God any positive act [actuation] in that uncleanness the heathen were given up to: 'Wherefore God gave them up to uncleanness, through the lusts of their own hearts' (Rom. 1 : 24). God's giving them up was the logical [or occasional] cause [of the uncleanness]; their own lusts were the true and natural cause [of it]. Their own lusts they were before they were given up to them, and belonging to no one as their author but themselves after they were given up to them. 3. God is holy and righteous, because he doth not withdraw from man till man deserts him. To say that God withdrew that grace from Adam which he had afforded him in creation, or anything that was due to him, till he had abused the gifts of God and turned them to an end contrary to that of creation, would be a reflection upon the divine holiness. God was first deserted by man before man was deserted by God; and man doth first contemn and abuse the common grace of God, and those relics of natural light that 'enlighten every man that comes into the world' (John 1 : 9), before God leaves him to the hurry of his own passions. Ephraim was first joined to idols before God pronounced the fatal sentence, 'Let him alone' (Hos. 4 : 17). God discovers himself to man in the works of his hands; he hath left in him prints of natural reason; he doth attend him with the common motions of his Spirit; and corrects him for his faults with gentle chastisements. He is near to all men in some kind of moral instructions; he puts, many times, providential bars in the way of their sinning; but when they will rush into it as the horse into the battle, when they will rebel against the light, God doth often leave them to their own course, and sentence him that is 'filthy to be filthy still' (Rev. 22 : 11), which is a righteous act of God as the rector and governor of the world. It is so far from being repugnant to the holiness and righteousness of God that it is rather a commendable act of his holiness and righteousness, as the rector of the world, not to let those gifts continue in the hands of a man who abuses them. Who will blame a father that, after all the good counsels he hath given to his son to reclaim him, all the corrections he hath inflicted on him for his irregular practices, leaves him to his own courses, and withdraws those assistances which he scoffed at and turned a deaf ear to? Or who will blame the physician for deserting the patient who rejects his counsel, will not follow his prescriptions, but dasheth his physic against the wall? No man will blame him, no man will say that he is the cause of the patient's death; but the true cause is the fury of the distemper, and the obstinacy of the diseased person, to which the physician left him. And who can justly blame God in a similar case, who never yet denied supplies of grace to any that sincerely sought it at his hands? What unholiness is it to deprive men of the assistances of common grace because of their sinful resistance of them, and afterward to direct those sinful counsels and practices of theirs which he hath justly given them up unto, to serve the ends of his own glory in his own plan and methods? 4. God is not under obligation to continue the bestowment of grace to any sinner whatever. It was at his liberty whether he would give renewing grace to Adam after his fall, or to any of his posterity. He was at liberty either to withhold it or communicate it. But if the obligation were none just after the fall, there is none now since the multiplication of sin by man. But God is certainly less obliged to continue his grace after a repeated refusal, and resistance, and a peremptory abuse, than he was bound to proffer it after the first apostasy. God cannot be charged with unholiness in withdrawing his grace after we have received it, unless we can make it appear that his grace was a thing due to us, as we are his creatures, and as he is the governor of the world. If there be an obligation on God as a governor, it would lie rather on the side of justice to leave man to the power of the devil whom he courted, and the prevalency of those lusts he hath so often caressed, and to wrap up in a cloud all his common illuminations, and leave him destitute of all the common workings of his Spirit."

VOL. I., p. 447. Turrettin (XI., ii., 22) defines the Hebraistic "hate" as loving in a less degree. "Τὸ μισεῖν intelligendum est comparate pro amore minori et diminuto." The "hardening" of a part of the Israelites is described as not softening them, in Deut. 29 : 4. "Yet the Lord hath not given [all of you] an heart to perceive, and eyes to see, and ears to hear, unto this day." This identical process is described in Isa. 6 : 10, by, "*Make* the heart of this people fat, and *make* their eyes heavy, and *shut* their eyes;" and in Isa. 63:17, by, "O Lord, why hast thou *made* us to err from thy ways, and hardened our heart from thy fear?" And in John 12:40, Christ himself adopts the same phraseology, and teaches the doctrine of preterition in the words, "He hath blinded their eyes, and hardened their heart, that they should not see with their eyes, nor understand with their heart, and be converted."

Vol. I., p. 448. A common objection to the doctrine that God's final end in all that he does is his own glory is, that this is selfishness, and God is compared with man in proof. Should man do this, he would be actuated by egotism and self-love. But the argument from analogy between God and man cannot be carried beyond the *communicable* attributes. It stops at the incommunicable. We can argue from human justice to Divine justice, from human benevolence to Divine, etc., because man has these attributes by virtue of being made in the Divine image. But neither man nor angel has the attributes of infinity, eternity, immensity, and omnipotence. These are incapable of degrees, or of being bestowed upon a creature. There is no inferior degree of eternity, or infinity, etc. These make no part of the Divine image in which man was created. In such cases there must be the whole of the attribute, or none of it. Consequently, to reason from analogy in regard to the incommunicable attributes of God is false reasoning, because there *is* no analogy.

Now, in the instance of the "glory of God," the reasoning relates to a subject of this latter class. The Divine glory or excellence is an infinite, eternal, omnipotent, and omnipresent excellence. No creature can have such an excellence as this. The glory or excellence of man or angel is a finite, temporal, local, weak, and dependent excellence. The two differ in kind, not merely in degree, as in the case of the communicable attributes. Consequently the two "glories" cannot be used in an argument from

13

analogy. It does not follow that because the glory of a man, say Napoleon, does not permit him to make it the chief end of his action, the glory of God does not permit him to do so. There are properties in God's excellence that cannot possibly belong to man's excellence, so that what can be argued from the latter cannot be from the former, and the converse. If analogical reasoning should be pushed in reference to the subject of the worship of God, which has its ground in the glory of God, it would plainly be improper, because worship is incommunicable to the creature and is confined to the Infinite. God demands that all his rational creatures adore and praise him. No man or angel has the right to make such a demand upon his fellow-creatures.

VOL. I., p. 449. There is no logical intermediate between Calvinism and Arminianism that is capable of combining both systems. It is impossible to say: (a) That man is both totally and partially depraved. (b) That election is both unconditional and conditional. (c) That regenerating grace is both irresistible and resistible. (d) That redemption is both limited and unlimited. (e) That perseverance is both certain and uncertain. Nor can there be a modification of one by the other. One or the other of the above-mentioned points must overcome the other. It is impossible to *blend* the two, which is requisite in order to a modification. This is not a gloomy view of Christian theology because: (a) Both systems hold in common the saving doctrines of the Gospel. A sinner may be regenerated and sanctified under either. (b) The influence of each upon the other is best when each is pure and simple. Medicines of opposite properties produce their good effect when they are unmixed with foreign ingredients. If the Calvinistic churches hold their ancestral Calvinism with frank sincerity and logical consistency, and the Arminian churches hold their ancestral Arminianism in the same manner, they will have a better understanding with each other, and do a greater work in extending the common Gospel and destroying the common enemy, than they would by endeavoring to formulate a theology that should be neither Calvinistic nor Arminian. The endeavor of the Arminians in Holland, in the seventeenth century, to modify the Belgic Calvinistic creed, and of the Calvinists to suppress the Arminian creed by the civil power, resulted in one of the most bitter conflicts in church history, and filled both parties with an unchristian spirit. Had there been no union of Church and State at the time, and had all denominations of Christians then stood upon an independent position, unrestrained by the civil authority, as is now the case very generally in Europe and America, neither of these two theological divisions would have interfered, by civil and military power, with the doctrine and practice of the other, and mutual respect would have characterized both. Whenever the endeavor is made to mix the immiscible and to fuse two types of theology that exclude each other, each party strives to outwit the other, and this produces jealousy and animosity. Mutual confidence is impossible. Hypocrisy and the pretence of being what one is not, are liable to prevail. A Calvinist is a dishonest disorganizer if he poses as an Arminian, and so is an Arminian if he pretends to be a Calvinist. The recent attempt within the Northern Presbyterian Church in America to revise the Westminster Standards, which was initiated by a very small minority of the whole body who were dissatisfied with Calvinism, and who, under the claim of improving it by conforming it to popular opinion and the lax religious sentiment of the day, proposed changes that would utterly demolish it, was of the same general nature with that in Holland. But the rationalism and infidelity into which it developed under the leadership of the "higher critics" had nothing in common with the evangelical doctrines which were retained in their creed by Arminius and his followers.

Vol. I., p. 451. That the sincerity of God's desire that the sinner would repent and forsake sin is independent of the result, is evinced by the *temporary* preterition of his own church. "My people would not hearken to my voice, and Israel would none of me. So I gave them up unto their own hearts' lust: and they walked in their own counsels. Oh that my people had hearkened unto me, and Israel had walked in my ways! I should soon have subdued their enemies, and turned my hand against their adversaries" (Ps. 81 : 11–14). In this instance God bestowed a certain degree of grace upon his chosen people. It was frustrated and unsuccessful. God might have increased the degree of grace, and "made them willing in the day of his power." He did not immediately do this, though he did subsequently to a part of them, who were the individually called in distinction from the nationally called. Does this prove that Jehovah was insincere when he said, with reference to those who resisted and frustrated the lower grade of his grace, "Oh that my people had hearkened unto me, and Israel had walked in my ways?"

Howe (Redeemer's Tears) upon this text thus remarks : "We must take heed lest under the pretence that we cannot ascribe everything unto God that such expressions seem to import, we therefore ascribe nothing. We ascribe nothing if we do ascribe a real unwillingness that men should sin on and perish ; and consequently a real willingness that they should turn to him and live, as so many plain texts assert. And therefore it is unavoidably imposed upon us to believe that God is truly unwilling of some things which he doth not think fit to interpose his omnipotency to hinder, and is truly willing of some things which he doth not put forth his omnipotency to effect ; that he makes this the ordinary course of his dispensations toward men, to govern them by laws, and promises, and threatenings, to work upon their minds, their hope, and their fear ; affording them the ordinary assistances of supernatural light and influence, with which he requires them to comply, and which, upon their refusing to do so, he may most righteously withhold and give them the victory to their own ruin ; though oftentimes he doth, from a sovereignty of grace, put forth that greater power upon others, equally negligent and obstinate, not to enforce, but effectually to incline their wills and gain a victory over them to their salvation."

The question arises, whether when God offers salvation to all men without exception, but does not save all men without exception by overcoming their opposition, this is real compassion ? It is real but not so high a degree of compassion as actual salvation. There are degrees of compassion. To offer the sinner a full pardon of all his sins on condition of faith and repentance (which condition the sinner must fulfil), instead of making no such offer, but immediately punishing him for them, is certainly a grade of mercy. Because God manifests a yet higher grade in the case of those whose opposition he overcomes, it does not follow that the lower grade is not mercy. Charnock (God's Patience, p. 733, Ed. Bohn) argues that the patience of God in forbearing to inflict the penalty of sin immediately upon its commission is suggestive, even to the heathen, of mercy in remitting it, though not demonstrative of it. It is adopted to awaken hope, but cannot produce certainty. Only revelation does the latter. " The heathen could not but read in the benevolence of God, shown in his daily providences, favorable inclinations toward them ; and though they could not be ignorant that they deserved the inflictions of justice, yet seeing themselves supported by God they might draw from thence the natural conclusion that God was placable." St. Paul teaches the same truth in saying that the benevolence of God in his common providence is fitted to produce penitence for sin, and hope in his mercy. "The goodness of God in his forbearance and long-suffering leadeth thee to repentance" (Rom. 2: 4).

VOL. I., p. 455. Christ (Luke 10 : 13) declares that if the common grace granted to Chorazin and Bethsaida, which was ineffectual with them, had been granted to Tyre and Sidon, it would have been effectual with these. The miracles (δυνάμεις) together with the ordinary influences of the Holy Spirit which produced no repentance in the former case, he says, would have produced it in the latter. According to this statement of our Lord, the very same amount of Divine influence may succeed in overcoming a sinner's opposition in one instance, and not in another. When it succeeds, it is effectual and irresistible grace ; when it fails, it is ineffectual and resistible. This shows that grace is to be measured relatively by the *result*, and not absolutely by a stiff rule which states arithmetically the amount of power exerted. All grace that fails, be it greater or less, is common ; all that succeeds, be it greater or less, is special. In order to have effected repentance in the people of Chorazin, it would have been necessary to exert a higher degree of grace than was exerted upon them ; while in order to effect repentance in the people of Tyre, no higher degree would have been requisite than that exerted upon Chorazin. But it is to be carefully noticed that the failure in the instance of Chorazin was owing wholly to the sinful resistance made to the grace ; and the success affirmed in the instance of Tyre would be owing not to any *assistance* of the grace by the co-operation of the sinful will of Tyre, but wholly to the overcoming of Tyre's resistance by the grace exerted. The sinful will of the inhabitants of Tyre, in the supposed case, was a wholly resisting will like that of the inhabitants of Chorazin, and hence could not synergize with the Divine Spirit any more than theirs could, but the degree of resistance, according to our Lord's statement, was less.

VOL. I., p. 464. Creation ex nihilo more than any other metaphysical idea differences and separates the Bible from all human cosmogonies. All of these latter exclude this

idea by their postulate of an eternal, amorphous, and chaotic matter, which is formed by the operation of its own
intrinsic properties and forces into the universe. Scripture
refers all chaotic matter, with its properties and laws, to a
personal Deity who is other than it, and before it. The
creative power of God, according to the Biblical conception, is as much needed to account for the forces and laws
of material nature as the voluntary power of the watchmaker is needed to account for the watch. In the case of
an artificial product like a watch, both the working force
and the intelligent art by which it is made are in the artificer. In the case of a natural product like a tree, both
the working force and the formative art by which it is constructed are in the tree ; the watch is manufactured ; the
tree grows. But in both cases a Creator other than the
watchmaker and the informing vegetable life is requisite.
The watch cannot make the watchmaker; and the principle of vegetable life cannot make itself. Both artificial
and natural products must therefore ultimately be referred
to a First Cause, who from nothing, by an absolutely
originating act, creates the artificer who makes the watch,
and the vital principle which builds up the tree.

Augustine (Faith and Creed, ch. ii.) teaches the creation
of matter ex nihilo, and of matter in its visible and invisible
modes. "Thou didst make the world out of 'matter unseen,' or also 'without form,' as some copies give it ; yet
we are not to believe that this material of which the universe was made, although it might be 'without form' [cha-
otic], although it might be 'unseen,' whatever might be
the mode of its subsistence, could possibly have subsisted
of itself, as if it were coeternal and coeval with God.
For even although the world was made of some sort of
material, this self-same material itself was made of nothing."

Neander (History, I., 372) directs attention to the radical
difference between creation and evolution or emanation, as

constituting the difference in kind between the Christian cos-
mogony and the pagan or ethnic. " Christianity separated
entirely what belongs to the province of religion from what
belongs to speculation, and a merely speculative interest.
And just by so doing Christianity preserved religion from the
danger of confounding things divine with the things of this
world ; the idea of God with that of nature. It directed
the eye of the mind beyond that whole series of the phenomena of the world, where, in the chain of causes and effects, one thing ever evolves out of another, to that almighty
creative Word of God by which the worlds were framed ;
so that things which are seen were not made of things
which do appear (Heb. 11 : 3). The creation was here
apprehended as an incomprehensible fact by the upward
gaze of faith, which rose above the position of the understanding, the faculty which would derive all things from
one another, which would explain everything [sensuously],
and hence denies all immediate [or intuitive] truth. This
one practically important truth the Church was for holding fast in the doctrine of creation from nothing ; taking
her stand in opposition to the *ancient* view, which would
condition God's act of creation by a previously existing
matter ; and which, in an anthropopathic manner conceived of him, not as the free, self-sufficient author of all
existence, but as the fashioner of a material already extent. Gnosticism would not acknowledge any such limits
to speculation. It would explain, clear up to the mental
vision, *how* God is the source and ground of all existence. It was thus compelled to place in the essence of
God himself a process of development, through which God
is the source and ground of all existence. From overlooking the *negative* sense of the doctrine concerning creation
from nothing, it was led to oppose against it the old principle, ' nothing can come out of nothing.' It substituted in
place of this doctrine the sensuous imageable idea of an
efflux of all existence out of the supreme being of the

Deity. This idea of an emanation admits of being presented under a great variety of images; of an eradiation of light from an original light; of a development of spiritual powers or ideas acquiring self-subsistence; of an expression in a series of syllables and tones, dying away gradually to an echo."

The pagan cosmogonies postulate a germ or egg when they explain "creation." Absolute origination of entity from nonentity is not only denied, but asserted to be impossible. On this scheme there is nothing but second causes. The eternal germ is operated upon by secondary agents and agencies, and the so-called " creation " is merely the emanation and evolution of an existing substance. There is no First Cause originating substance itself. Charnock (Power of God, 419) thus notices the need of a Creator in order to such an evolution : " Nature, or the order of second causes, hath a vast power ; and the sun and the earth bring forth harvests of corn, but from seed first sown in the earth ; were there no seed in the earth, the power of the earth would be idle, and the influence of the sun insignificant. All the united strength of nature cannot produce the least thing out of nothing. It may multiply and increase things by the powerful blessing God gave it at the first erecting of the world, but it cannot create." The pagan cosmogonies which account for the universe by emanation reappear in the modern materialism which accounts for it by evolution.

VOL. I., p. 468. Spinoza, often and with emphasis, denies that substance can be created. In a letter to Oldenburg (Letter II.) he says : "In the universe there cannot exist two substances without their differing utterly in essence. Substance cannot be created. All substance must be infinite or supremely perfect." The assertion that " there cannot be two substances without their differing utterly in essence " is true. One must be infinite, and the other finite. But as Spinoza assumes that the postulate

upon which his whole system depends, namely, that
there is only one substance and that infinite, is axiomatic
and needs no proof, it follows from his assumption that
there cannot be two substances. Two infinites are impossible.

VOL. I., p. 472. Howe (Oracles, II., ix.) thus explains
the phrase "heaven and earth" in Gen. 1 : 1 : "The first
and most obvious distribution of the created universe is
into these two heads, matter and mind. This is the distribution in Col. 1 : 16 : 'By him were all things made
that are in heaven, or that are in earth, visible and invisible.' We may well enough suppose all matter to be, some
way or other, visible, though there be indeed a finer sort
of matter than is visible to us. [Howe refers here to the
invisible material forces—gravitation, electricity, attraction,
etc.—and the invisible physical principles, namely, vegetable and animal life. See Dogmatics, Vol. I., 159, note.]
But then there is the other head of things that are absolutely invisible ; as it is altogether impossible that any
sense can perceive a mind, or a thought, which is the immediate product of that mind. Some, indeed, will have
by 'heavens' all intellectual beings that are created to be
comprehended and meant ; and by 'earth,' all matter
whatsoever. We shall not dispute the propriety of that
conjecture, or what probability it hath or hath not ; but
take what is more obvious to ourselves. And so, by
'heaven' must be understood not only all the several superior orbs, but all their inhabitants, unto which our own
minds and spirits do originally appertain, as being nearer
of kin, and more allied to the world of spirits than they
are to this world of flesh and earth. And then, by 'earth'
is meant this lower orb, which is replenished with numerous sorts of creatures with one or another sort of lives ;
either that do live an intellectual life, or from an intelligent soul, as we live ; or else, that live a merely sensitive
life, as all the brutes do ; or else, that live a merely vege-

table life, as the plants do ; and then there are inanimate things, that have no proper life at all. Of such extent is this created universe ; it takes in all these several sorts of things." Pearson (Creed, Art. I.) explains similarly, " The two terms, ' heaven and earth,' taken together, signify the Universe, or that which is called the World, in which are contained all things material and immaterial, visible and invisible. Under the name of ' heaven and earth ' are comprehended all things contained in them, which are of two classes. Some were made immediately out of nothing, by a proper creation ; and some only mediately, as out of something formerly made out of nothing, by an improper kind of creation. By the first were made all immaterial substances, all the orders of angels, and the souls of men, the heavens, and the simple or elemental bodies, as the earth, the water, and the air. By the second were made all the ' hosts of the earth ' (Gen. 2 : 1), the grass and herb yielding seed, the fowls of the air, and the fishes of the sea. ' Let the earth bring forth grass ; let the waters bring forth the moving creature that hath life, and fowl that may fly above the earth.' As well may we grant these plants and animals to have their origination from such principles [namely, earth, water, and air] when we read, ' God formed man out of the dust of the ground,' and said unto him whom he created in his own image, ' Dust thou art.' " This statement needs qualification. Plants, and animals, and the body of man, did not " originate " from earth, water, and air, in the strict sense of the term ; for a vital principle was required to *vitalize* and *organize* these non-vital and inorganic elements. "Nothing is satisfactory," says Bell (Hand, ch. ii.), " until it is declared that it has been the will of God to create life ; and that it was he who gave the animating principle to produce organization." This animating principle was as much an immediate creation from nothing as the spirits of angels and men, or the simple elements of matter. When

it is said, " Let the earth bring forth grass ; let the waters
bring forth the moving creature," the meaning is, that the
earth and waters " furnish the non-vital material elements
that constitute the visibility of a plant or animal, which
are vivified and assimilated by an invisible principle of
vegetable or animal life created ex nihilo " (Dogmatics,
I., 482). So that the vegetable and animal kingdoms fall
into Pearson's first class.

Augustine (City of God, xi., 33) sums up as follows :
" Under these names, 'heaven and earth,' the whole creation is signified, either as divided into spiritual and material, which seems the more likely, or into the two great
parts of the world [universe] in which all created things
are contained, so that, first of all, the creation is presented
in sum, and then its parts are enumerated, according to the
mystic number of the days."

VOL. I., 476. Grabe, in his Spicilegium Patrum (II.,
195), gives a fragment from the Commentary of Anastasius
upon the Six Days' Work, in which the latter remarks that
" Justin Martyr says that all things which were made by
God are sextuply divided : Into immortal and intelligent
things such as angels ; into mortal things endowed with
reason, such as men ; into sentient things destitute of
reason, such as cattle, birds, and fishes; into insentient
things that move, such as winds, clouds, waters, and stars ;
into things that grow but do not move, such as trees ; and
into insentient things that do not move, such as mountains,
land, and the like. All the creatures of God fall into one
of these divisions, and are circumscribed by them." This
shows that the classification of the works of creation was a
familiar conception at a very early date. This would harmonize with the theory of long periods and creative days,
and would naturally suggest it.

VOL. I., p. 485. The tendency to explain the kingdoms of
vegetable and animal life by evolution the one from the
other, instead of by a Divine fiat creating them from noth-

ing, is seen in the following remark of Coleridge (Table-Talk, April 30, 1823): "There are only two acts of creation, properly so called, in the Mosaic account: the material universe and man. The intermediate acts [the origination of vegetables and animals] seem more as the results of secondary causes, or, at any rate, of a modification of prepared materials." Bacon (Natural History, Century V.), on the contrary, calls attention to the creation from nothing of life as the organizing principle and power which vivifies and assimilates the lifeless elements of earth, air, and water. "Plants or vegetables are the principal part of the third day's work. They are the first *producat*, which is the word of animation; for the other words [of the inorganic days] are but words of essence" [inorganic substance]. Agassiz, also, during the recent revival by Darwin of the pseudo-evolution of Lamarck and St. Hilaire, has maintained the historical physics of Linnæus, Blumenbach, Cuvier, and Hunter. "To Agassiz, as the leading opponent of the development or Darwinian theories, development meant development of plan as expressed in structure, not the change of one structure into another. To his apprehension this change was based upon intellectual not upon material causes" (Life of Agassiz, I., 244). Similarly, Davy (Consolations, Dialogue iv.) remarks: "I can never believe that any division, or refinement, or subtilization, or juxtaposition, or arrangement of the particles of matter can give them sensibility; or that intelligence can result from the combinations of insensate and brute atoms. I can as easily imagine that the planets are moving by their will or design round the sun, or that a cannon-ball is reasoning in making its parabolic curve." Sir Charles Bell (The Hand, ch. vi.) says, "Everything declares the diversity of species to have its origin in distinct creations; and not to be owing to a process of gradual transition from some original type. Any other hypothesis than that of new creations of animals, suited to the successive changes in the inorganic

matter of the globe ; the condition of the water, atmosphere, and temperature ; brings with it only an accumula-
tion of difficulties. Life preserves the materials of the body
free from the influence of those affinities which hold the
inorganic world together ; and it not only does that, but it
substitutes other laws. Of the wonders of the microscope
none exceed those presented on looking at the early rudi-
ments of an animal. This rudimentary structure will appear but an homogeneous, transparent, soft jelly ; there
will be visible in it only a single pulsating point ; yet this
mass possesses within it a principle of life ; and it is not
only ordered what this principle shall perform in attract-
ing matter, and building up the complex structure of the
body, but even the duration of the animal's existence is
from the beginning defined. The term may be limited to
a day, and the life be truly ephemeral ; or it may be prolonged to a hundred years ; but the period is adjusted according to the condition and enjoyment of the individual,
and to the continuance of its species, as perfectly as are
the mechanism and structure themselves. . . . There
is nothing like this in inanimate nature. It is beautiful to
see the shooting of a crystal ; to note the formation of the
integrant particles from their elements in solution, and
these, under the influence of attraction or crystalline polar-
ity, assuming a determinate shape ; but the form here is
permanent. In the different processes of elective attraction and in fermentation we perceive a commotion ; but
in a little time the products are formed, and the particles
are rigidly at rest. In these instances there is nothing like
the revolutions of the living animal substance, where the
material is alternately arranged, decomposed, and rear-
ranged. The changes in the embryo state are a remarkable example of the latter. The human brain in its earlier
stage of growth resembles that of a fish ; next, it bears a
resemblance to the cerebral mass of the reptile ; in its increase it is like that of a bird ; and slowly, and only after

birth, does it assume the proper form and consistence of the human brain." Such is the judgment of the eminent naturalist to whom " the honor is exclusively due of having demonstrated for the first time that the nerve of motion is distinct from the nerve of sensation, and that when a nerve, apparently simple, possesses both properties, it is a sign that it is really compound, and consists of fibrils derived from distinct divisions of the brain or spinal cord "—a discovery with which, in respect to originality and influence upon biology, nothing in the entire results of the recent materialistic physics can be compared for a moment.

Haeckel (Evolution of Man, I., 73 sq.) calls attention to the fact that the current pseudo-evolutionary theory is a revival of that of Lamarck and St. Hilaire, and until recently had no sway in biology. " As an instance how utterly biologists refrained from inquiries into the origin of organisms, and the creation of the animal and vegetable species during the period from 1830 to 1859, I mention from my own experience the fact that during the whole course of my studies at the university I never heard a single word on these most important and fundamental questions of biology. During the time from 1852 to 1857 I had the good fortune to listen to the most distinguished teachers in all branches of the science of organic nature ; but not one of them even once alluded to the question of the origin of the vegetable and animal species. It was never thought worth while to allude to Lamarck's valuable Philosophie Zoölogique, in which the attempt to answer it had been made in 1809. The enormous opposition which Darwin met with when he first took up this question again may therefore be understood. His attempt seemed at first to be unsubstantial and unsupported by previous labors. Even in 1859 the entire problem of creation, the whole question of the origin of organisms, was considered by biologists as supernatural and transcendental. The dualistic position taken by Kant, and the extraordinary importance attached during the whole of this century to this most influential of modern philosophers, probably offer the best explanation of this fact. For while this great genius, equally excellent as a naturalist and a philosopher, in the field of inorganic nature made a successful attempt in his theory of the heavens to treat the constitution and mechanical origin of the material universe according to Newtonian principles, in other words, to treat it mechanically and to conceive it monistically, he for the most part adopted the supernatural view of the origin of organisms. He maintained that 'the principle of the mechanism of [inorganic] nature, without which there could be no science of [inorganic] nature, was wholly inadequate to explain the origin of living organisms, and that it was necessary to assume supernatural causes effecting a design (causæ finales) for the origin of these.'" Haeckel then adds that Kant sometimes departed from this view, and "expressed himself in quite the opposite or monistic sense." But he gives no passages in proof and remarks that "these monistic utterences are but stray rays of light; as a rule Kant adhered in biology to those obscure dualistic notions according to which the powers which operate in organic nature are entirely different from those which prevail in the inorganic world." The assertion that Kant, in his theory of the heavens adopted monism, or Spinoza's doctrine of only one substance, is contradicted by Haeckel's own statement that Kant explained the material universe "according to Newtonian principles." Newton held with energy to the dualism of mind and matter, and to theism, and his Principia is the strongest of all demonstrations of the truth of this theory, because it is mathematical. Haeckel has confounded Newton's explanation of inorganic nature by the operation of inorganic and mechanical forces employed by the Creator with the very different theory which explains it by the operation of these inorganic forces of themselves and without a superintending mind. The fact that Kant accounted for the inorganic world by the operation of non-vital and mechanical forces, and of the organic world by the operation of vital and non-mechanical forces — the forces in both instances being created, upheld, and controlled by the Creator—by no means proves that in the former domain he adopted pantheistic monism and in the latter theistic dualism.

VOL. I., p. 490. Haeckel (Evolution of Man, II., 391) endows matter with the intelligent properties of mind, namely, self-motion and choice, in the most extreme form conceivable. Even the germ-cell, he maintains, decides for itself whether it will be male or female. "At first two united cells may have been entirely alike. Soon, however, by natural selection a contrast must [sic] have arisen between them. One cell became a female egg-cell, the other a male seed or sperm-cell."

VOL. I., p. 492. The discussions respecting the scientific value of the theory of pseudo-evolution which makes all the phenomena of the mineral, vegetable, animal, and rational kingdoms to be alike the mechanical motion of molecules of matter, have overlooked the fact that it has no foundation or support in *mathematics*. A really mechanical force and motion can be investigated and enunciated arithmetically and algebraically. Gravitation is expressed in the well-known formula, that its attraction is inversely as the square of the distance. The motion of light, in the refraction and dispersion of its rays, is governed by laws that have been demonstrated by the employment of the calculus. Mathematical optics is one of the most striking examples of the manner in which material nature operates mathematically. The motion of heat has been subjected to the tests of mathematics, and Clausius by this method has proved that when the heat-motion of ignited gunpowder is converted into the motion of the cannon-ball, and then is reconverted into heat-motion by impact upon an iron plate, there is an actual loss of heat,

14

and consequently of motion.   This is something which no observation of the senses, naked or armed, could have demonstrated.   Electricity and magnetism are likewise beginning to be measured by this method.   " Geometers," says a French journalist, " who are the continuators of Ampère, Fourier, Ohm, Gauss, Helmholz, Thompson, and Maxwell, and have helped so much in connecting electricity with the laws of mechanics, are preparing a great synthesis which will mark an epoch in the history of natural philosophy.   They are very near demonstrating that the electro-magnetic phenomena are subjected to the same elementary laws as the optical ; that they are two manifestations of a motion in the same element, namely, ether ; the problems of optics are solved by equations of electromagnetism ; and the speed of light, determined by optical methods, is measured also by purely electrical measures."

It is owing to the fact that whatsoever is really mechanical is also mathematical, that it has from the first been the aim of the natural philosopher to introduce as much as possible the calculations and methods of mathematical science into physics, because in this way a precision and certainty are secured such as the most careful observations by the senses, even when aided by instruments, cannot afford.   In some instances the algebraic process demonstrates irrefragably a result that contradicts the notices of the senses.   An eminent geometer has demonstrated that the centre of the shadow made by a circular plate of metal in a ray of light coming through an aperture is in fact no shadow, but an illumination as bright as if the metal plate were away.   The remark of Euler, after demonstrating certain properties of the arch, that " all experience is in contradiction to this, but that this is no reason for doubting its truth," paradoxical as it sounds, is scientific certainty.

Accordingly, the progress of genuine, in distinction from spurious, physics has invariably been accompanied with that of mathematics. Newton's theory of gravitation immediately resulted in the Principia—that wonderful treatise of which the full title is, The Mathematical Principles of Natural Philosophy—in which the calculus is employed by an intellect never excelled in the power of concentrated reflection, to demonstrate the truth of an hypothesis which without this method of proof would be open to doubt and denial. For subtract the evidence furnished by the theorems and calculations of the Principia, and leave the law of gravitation to be accepted merely on the ground of what can be observed and measured of its operations by the naked or the armed eye, and it would no longer have the certainty which it now has for the scientific mind.

Now if, as the materialist contends, the phenomena of the vegetable, animal, and rational kingdoms are really and truly *mechanical*, like those of gravitation, cohesion, chemical affinity, light, heat, electricity, and magnetism, they should like these latter be capable of mathematical expression and demonstration. If it indeed be true, as Haeckel (Creation, I., 21) asserts, that " when a stone falls by certain laws to the ground, or a solution of salt forms a crystal, the result is no less a mechanical manifestation of *life* than the flowering of a plant, the generation or sensibility of animals, or the feelings or mental activity of man "—if it be indeed true, that all these phenomena are alike the effect of molecular motion, then the vitality of the plant, the sensibility of the animal, and the rationality of the man can be examined mathematically and the results expressed in mathematical formulæ. In this case treatises in biology and psychology should be as full of mathematical propositions and calculations as those in chemistry and mechanics. But the mere assertion of such a possibility is the refutation of the theory of pseudo-evolution. The law of vegetable life has nothing in common with that of gravitation, and to attempt to express it in mathematical terms is absurd. The same is true of the

law of animal life, and still more of rational. How would
a " scientist " set about describing the motion of the sap,
or the circulation of the blood, in terms of the calculus ?
How would he express the thinking of the human mind,
or the feeling of the human heart, by algebraic equations ?
No evolutionist has yet gone to the length of asserting
that one sense can evolve from another ; that smelling can
transmute itself into hearing, or seeing into tasting ; and
no one of this class has attempted to explain one sensation
by another ; but the task would not be greater than to explain vegetable life in the blooming of a rose, or animal
life in the crawling of a worm, or rational life in " the
thoughts that wander through eternity," and are " too deep
for tears," by the mechanical motion of atoms algebraically
formulated by some Newton or Laplace.

When one considers the great amount of publication by
materialistic physicists during the last twenty years upon
subjects in physics, and how little of mathematics there is
in it all, he is made suspicious respecting its credibility.
Former periods in the history of science that were distinguished, as the last two decades have not been, for real
discoveries and additions to the knowledge of nature, were
marked by the cultivation of mathematical analysis. But
the present is a time when the most novel and improbable
theories of matter and mind are broached without a particle of this highest order of proof. Let any one read the
History of the Physical Sciences, by Whewell, one of the
first mathematicians of the century, and a natural philosopher in the line of Newton and Leibnitz, and see how constantly and inextricably mathematical calculation is in-
woven with all that is really mechanical and inorganic in
them, and then let him turn to the physics of Haeckel,
Huxley, Maudsley, and Büchner, and see how destitute
their schematizing is of all support from the exact sciences,
and how contradictory it is to the demonstrated and established results of past investigation, and he will perceive

the immense difference between the historical and the provincial physics.

A striking instance of the error introduced into the physics of inorganic nature by theories that not merely lack corroboration by mathematics, but are refuted by it, is seen in Goethe's theory of colors. He contended, in opposition to Newton and physicists generally, that color is not a particular mode of light, but a mixture of light and darkness. He held that darkness is a positive quality, and not the mere negation of light, and that colors are composed of light and darkness—which, as his biographer, Lewis, remarks, is "like saying that tones are composed of sound and silence." He prosecuted his experiments and observations with great industry, but in a purely empirical way, without any knowledge or employment of mathematical optics. On the contrary, he rejected the aid of this science, and actually took credit to himself for so doing. "I raised," he said, "the whole school of mathematicians against me, and people were greatly amazed that one who had no insight into mathematics could venture to contradict Newton. For that physics could exist independently of mathematics, no one seemed to have the slightest suspicion." His biographer, who shared in the exaggerated estimate of Goethe common to all his devotees, was nevertheless too sound a physicist to fall in with this view of mathematics. Respecting Goethe's theory of color, and those sciences which are concerned with really mechanical forces, he remarks: "On Goethe's theory, the phenomena are not measurable; and whoever glances into a modern work on optics will see that the precision and extent to which calculation has been carried are themselves sufficient ground for preferring the theory which admits such calculation. No amount of observation will render observation precise, unless it can be measured. You may watch falling bodies for an eternity, but without mathematics mere watching will yield no law of gravitation. You may mix acids and alkalies together with prodigality, but no amount of experiment will yield the secret of their composition if you have flung away the balance. Goethe flung away the balance " (Lewis, Life of Goethe, V., ix.). It is worthy of particular notice that this error of the poet was endorsed by the philosophers Schelling and Hegel, both of whom, like Goethe, adopted the monism of Spinoza, which explains all the phenomena of the universe by the doctrine of one infinite substance. This accounts for the agreement between them.

Goethe was more successful in botany than in optics. His Metamorphoses of Plants, in which he developed a theory that had been suggested, but not adopted, by Linnæus, namely, that all the parts of a plant are varieties of the leaf, has met with favor among scientific botanists. But botany is within the domain of *life*, not of mechanics, if the historical physics is to be accepted rather than that of the materialistic schools. Because botany is concerned with a vital force, it cannot be constructed mathematically, and consequently Goethe's ignorance of the exact sciences did no great harm in this instance, as it did in that of optics.

The inability of the materialist to ground his theory that mind is matter, and thought, like heat, is a mode of molecular motion, in the mathematics that support all genuine mechanics, is proof that it will be short lived ; that the pseudo-evolution of Darwin at the close of the nineteenth century will share the fate of the pseudo-evolution of Lamarck at the beginning of it.

A writer in the Foreign Quarterly Review (Vol. III., 194, sq.) makes the following objections to the position that life is a property of inorganic matter, and the effect of the arrangement of its atoms. " 1. If the living principle is an essential property of inorganic matter, it would follow that this property would increase with the quantity of matter. This, however, is not the fact. Nature nowhere manifests more living energy than in its minutest productions. The insect, for example the spider, with its instincts performs more remarkable functions than many a larger animal; the dog more than the horse, and man more than the elephant, and this more than the whale. 2. The first rudiment of all living forms, whether animal or vegetable, is a fluid in which a few globules are found. If the arrangement of particles, or structural organization, were the cause of life, this cause would have little energy in a fluid in which *no organ* at all is to be detected; and yet the reverse is the fact, for in no state does the living principle act so energetically as in the first periods of existence. In the first month of conception the human embryo weighs only a few grains; at the ninth month it weighs eight pounds, and is twenty inches in length. In the first month it is as simple as a worm in its structure; at the ninth it has all the characteristic complication of the human species. In the early periods of our existence, therefore, the living principle operates with much greater intensity than in the later; being employed not so much in merely preserving as in the later periods, but in forming and building up from the beginning. Every minutest artery, nerve, or vein is then laid out with uniform skill; parts are planned and formed which had no previous existence; and it seems as unreasonable to assert from a contemplation of such facts that organization or structure is the cause of life, as that the house is the cause of the architect. If the arrangement of particles is the cause of life, then the consistent materialist must in physics give up the axiom that the effect is in proportion to the cause. The effects and changes are far greater in the embryo and uterine existence than they are in the body after birth; but the number of the particles of matter that are arranged is far smaller. 3. In the mechanical sciences, we say that certain substances are the conductors of electricity, but we do not say that they cause electricity; they develop its phenomena, and that is all. Now life, like electricity, or any other mechanical force, though it does not exist separate from matter, yet is *transferable* from one body to another. The plant, for example, collects from air, earth, and water that which it transforms into wood, sap, leaf, and fruit, thus *vivifying* these elements. The animal collects from the plant its material for nerve, blood, and muscle. Man converts bread and meat into blood, muscle, nerve, and bone, all of which are capable of vital motion. In all these instances a piece of inanimate matter has received the gift of life; it has *acquired* vital properties. Is it not a distinct transfer of something from one substance to another, which something cannot be a mere property of the substance to which it is transferred? Is the principle of life any more a property of the matter which is vitalized by it than the principle of heat is the property of the iron that is melted by it? If the two things are entirely diverse in the latter case, are they not also in the former? 4. Extension, figure, impenetrability, are properties of matter, and we never see them leave matter; but the dead nerve, although to all appearance the same as the living, loses sensation, and the dead muscle loses irritability. If it be replied that the dead muscle or nerve is not the same as the living, but that death has been accompanied by a cessation of motion in the fluids or atoms, this implies that the *motion* of the fluids or atoms produces life. But is there a single instance in nature of motion producing anything but motion of identically the same kind? Is there any proof from observed phenomena that mechanical motion sometimes does more than this, and produces sensation, thought, and volition?"

In agreement with this last remark, Quatrefages (Human Species, 13) remarks: "We do not find in the application of the laws of life, and in the results to which they lead, the mathematical precision of the laws of gravitation and ethero-dynamy [sound and light]. Crystals, when similar in composition, and when formed under similar circumstances, resemble each other perfectly ; but we never find two leaves exactly alike upon the same tree."

Regarding spontaneous generation, " Pasteur proves and Tyndal corroborates, that if all germs of life are excluded, inorganic matter never ferments, never of itself produces life, and remains inorganic " (Popular Science Monthly, December, 1876, p. 135).

VOL. I., p. 494. The effect of friction in diminishing force is seen even in the provinces of imponderable matter. Every reflection of a ray of light diminishes its intensity ; going in a direct line it is stronger, in a zigzag it is weaker. Moonlight is paler than sunlight. But reflection is resistance by friction. The deflection of a bullet diminishes its motion. When it glances from a rock its movement is less swift than before the glancing. The same is true of sound when deflected, and of heat when reflected.

VOL. I., p. 499. The fallacy in pseudo-evolution is the assumption that *variation* is identical with *transmutation ;* that the rise of new varieties is the same thing as the rise of new species. Quatrefages (Human Species, 37) notices this. " Lamarck, St. Hilaire, Darwin and his school consider the species not only as variable but as transmutable. The specific types are not merely modified, they are replaced by new types. Variation is, in their estimation, only a phase of the very different phenomena of transmutation." Consider, for illustration of this remark of Quatrefages, Darwin's explanation of the moral sense out of the gregarious instinct in animals, and this latter from animal instinct. Animals associate ; thence co-operation, as in the instance of beavers ; then the wishes of others of the same community are perceived ; then the idea of a common good ; then the notion of obligation to consult the common good. There are the following objections to this genesis of the moral sense. 1. This process stops with the animal, but moral obligation stops with God. Even if the improbable supposition be granted that a beaver may come to feel obliged and bound by a sense of duty to another beaver, this would not make him feel obliged and bound to a Supreme Being; if for no other reason, that there is nothing in Darwin's account of the matter by which the beaver can get the idea of such a being. The only idea the beaver has is the idea of another beaver. But a "moral sense" without a knowledge of a Supreme Being, and a sense of duty to him, is nonsense. 2. This process surreptitiously injects elements into succeeding parts of it that cannot be derived out of the preceding. This destroys the alleged "evolution." There is a leap from actual fact to mere imagination of a fact. An examination shows this. Animals "associate" from animal instinct, and "co-operate" from animal instinct. But they do not "perceive the wishes of others" from animal instinct; nor "have the idea of a common good" from animal instinct; nor "the notion of obligation to consult the common good" from animal instinct. Association and co-operation are *action;* but perception of others' wishes, the idea of a common good, and the notion of obligation to consult the common good are *reflection.* The former may be explained by animal instinct; but the latter require human reason to account for them. This pedigree of the moral sense is like Irving's derivation of mango from Jeremiah King: "Jerry King, gherkin, cucumber, mango."

This criticism applies also to Spencer's explanation of the moral sense by the idea of utility: "Experiences of utility organized and consolidated in generations by transmission become experiences of morality; of right and wrong." The mere "organization" and "consolidation" of a thing does not alter the nature and substance of it. It only changes its form. Utility condensed ad infinitum is only infinite utility.

VOL. I., p. 502. The materialist when pressed with the fact that there is no visible transmutation of species within the period of time that man has existed, replies that the asserted change requires vast ages. This implies that natural forces grow stronger as they grow older. But the inherent force of matter is no more augmented by the increase of time than by the increase of size. If a minute atom of matter cannot start itself into motion to-day, it cannot in three hundred and sixty-five days; and the same is true of a granite bowlder, or the planet Jupiter. Longer duration will add no new and additional force to either of these which it does not intrinsically have. So also with the increase of bulk. If a grain of sand cannot begin motion from a state of rest, neither can the entire globe of which it is a part. Size, greater or smaller, is of no account in such a case, and neither is time.

VOL. I., p. 504. Sir J. W. Dawson (Salient Points in the Science of the Earth, ch. vii.) presents the following view of the succession of Animal Forms, as the teaching of scientific Palæontology. " 1. The existence of life and organization on the earth is not eternal, or even coeval with the beginning of the physical universe, but may possibly date from Laurentinian or immediately pre-Laurentinian ages. 2. The introduction of new species of animals and plants has been a continuous process, not in the sense of derivation of one species from another, but in the higher sense of the continued operation of the cause or causes which introduced life at first. 3. Though thus continuous the process has not been uniform; but periods of rapid production of species have alternated with others in which many disappeared and few were introduced. This may have been an effect of physical cycles reacting on the progress of life. 4. Species, like individuals, have greater energy and vitality in their younger stages, and rapidly assume all their varietal forms, and extend themselves as widely as external circumstances will permit. Like individuals, also, they have their periods of old age and decay, though the life of some species has been of enormous duration in comparison with that of others; the difference appearing to be connected with degrees of adaptation to different conditions of life. 5. Many allied species, constituting groups of animals and plants, have made their appearance at once in various parts of the earth, and these groups have obeyed the same laws with the individual and the species in culminating rapidly, and then slowly diminishing, though a large group once introduced has rarely disappeared together. 6. Groups of species, as genera and orders, do not usually begin with their highest or lowest forms, but with intermediate and generalized types, and they show a capacity for both elevation and degradation in their subsequent history. 7. The history of life presents a progress from the lower to the higher, and from the simpler to the more complex, and from the more generalized to the more specialized. In this progress new types are introduced, and take the place of the older ones, which sink to a relatively subordinate place and thus become degraded. But the physical and organic changes have been so correlated and adjusted that life has been enabled to assume more complex forms, and thus older forms have been made to prepare the way for newer, so that there has been, on the whole, a steady elevation culminating in man. Elevation and specialization have, however, been secured at the expense of vital energy and range of adaptation, until the new element of a rational and spiritual nature was introduced in the case of man. 8. In regard to the larger and more distinct types, we cannot find evidence that they have in their introduction been preceded by similar forms connecting them with previous groups; but there is reason to believe that many supposed representative species in successive formations are really only races or varieties. 9. In so far as we can trace their history, specific types are permanent in their characters from their introduction to their extinction, and their earlier varietal forms are similar to their later ones. 10. Palæontology furnishes no direct evidence, perhaps never can furnish any, as to the actual transmutation of one species into another; but the drift of its testimony is to show that species come in per saltum, rather than by any slow and gradual process. 11. The origin and history of life cannot, any more than the origin and determination of matter, be explained on purely material grounds, but involve the consideration of power referable to the unseen and spiritual world. There is a *creative force* above and beyond them, to the threshold of which we shall inevitably be brought."

VOL. I., p. 511. Respecting Haeckel's assertion, that "natural selection, which acts without a plan, produces quite the same result as artificial selection, which the will of man makes according to a plan," Janet (Materialism of the Present: A Critique of Büchner, 174) remarks: "The true stumbling-block of Darwin's theory is the passage from artificial to natural selection; it is when he wishes to prove that a blind and designless nature has been able to obtain, by the fortuitous occurrence of circumstances, the same results which man obtains by well-calculated industry."

VOL. I., p. 512. A striking example of the punctilious carrying out of the plan of structure when there is no use for the organ is seen in the whale. The whale is not a fish, but a mammal. It has lungs, not gills; cannot live continually under water, but must come to the surface to breathe; is warm-blooded, having a bilocular heart, movable eyelids, ears opening externally, viviparous generation, and suckles its young. In all these respects it is like a quadruped, yet there are no external legs. "But," observes Roget (Physiology, I., 485), "although the bones of the legs do not exist, yet there are found in the hinder and lower part of the trunk, concealed in the flesh and quite detached from the spine, two small bones, apparently corresponding to pelvic bones, for the presence of which no more probable reason can be assigned than the tendency to preserve an analogy with the more developed structures of the same type. A similar adherence to the law of uniformity in the plan and construction of all the animals belonging to the same class is strikingly shown in the conformation of the bones of the anterior extremities of the cetacea; for although they present, externally, no resemblance to the leg and foot of a quadruped, being fashioned into fin-like members, with a flat oval surface for striking the water, yet when the bones are stripped of the thick integument which covers them and conceals their real form, we find them exhibiting the same divisions into carpal and metacarpal bones, and phalanges of fingers, as exist in the most highly developed organization, not merely of a quadruped, but also of a monkey, and even of a man."

Vol. I., p. 516. The Biblical Chronology, while forbidding the immense antiquity for the existence of man on the globe attributed to him by one class of geologists, does not require an exact mathematical definiteness, but allows an uncertain margin of one or two thousand years. This is due to the difference between the two texts from which the contents of Scripture are derived. The following account of the case is given by a learned writer in the London Quarterly Review (Vol. xliii., 120 sq.) : " We are accustomed to suppose that we possess an undoubted, precise canon of chronology in the Holy Scriptures ; but perhaps next to a clear acquaintance with what the sacred volume does undoubtedly contain, the most valuable knowledge is of what it does not. In the ' Universal History' above one hundred and twenty dates are given for the creation, most of them made out by persons who regard with sincere reverence, and derive their arguments from, the sacred writings. The first of these places that event B.C. 6984; the last, B.C. 3616; differing by the amount of more than 3,000 years. The period of the deluge is fixed with no greater uniformity. The Septuagint gives B.C. 3246; the Hebrew text, according to Usher, gives B.C. 2348. The extreme dates assigned to the exodus are those of Josephus, according to Hales, who agrees nearly with Des Vignolles, B.C. 1648; of the English Bible, according to Usher, B.C. 1491; and by the common Jewish chronology, B.C. 1312."

"Our object is to show that the longer of these chronologies is the best supported, and affords ample space for the highest antiquity which the great Egyptian kingdom can claim. For the period between the flood and the first connection of sacred history with Egypt we have four distinct authorities: the Septuagint version; the Samaritan text; Josephus, who professes to have adhered faithfully to the sacred volume; and the Hebrew chronology adopted in our Bibles. None of these, strictly speaking, agree, but the first three concur in assigning a much longer period between the deluge and the birth of Abraham; the Septuagint, 1,070 years; the Hebrew, only 292. If it should be urged that the translators of the Septuagint, environed on all sides by Egyptian antiquities, and standing in awe of Alexandrian learning, endeavored to conform their national annals to the more extended chronological system, and that Josephus, either influenced by their authority, or actuated by the same motives, may have adopted the same views, yet the ancient Samaritan text still remains an unexceptionable witness to the high antiquity of the longer period. In fact, we are perhaps wasting our time in contesting this point, as we may fairly consider the Hebrew chronology of *this period* between the deluge and the call of Abraham almost exploded. In our own country, most of those who have investigated the subject, men who certainly cannot be suspected of want of reverence for the sacred volume—Bryant, Faber, and Hales—concur in reverting to the system which generally prevailed in the early Christian Church; and, lastly, Russell, in an essay prefixed to his work on the connection of sacred and profane history, has shown, with great probability, not only the late construction of what may perhaps fairly be called the Rabbinical chronology, in the second century of Christianity, but also, following the steps of the ancient Christian writers on the subject, the peculiar object for which it was framed."

"It would be difficult, indeed, to conceive the vast extension and multiplication of the human race, the slow development of civilization, the revolutions in the forms of government, the rise of mighty empires, the splendor of great cities, within the narrow limits of two or three centuries; but in above a thousand years what changes might not be wrought. Compare the France and England, the Paris and London, of the days of William the Conqueror, with their present state; or the wild woods of America, inhabited by wandering tribes of savages, with her present populous cities. Nor must it be forgotten that from the visit of Abraham to Egypt, above two centuries more elapsed before the migration of his descendants; and of the state of Egypt in the days of the patriarch we know little more than that a king was ruling, with some degree of state, in some part of Lower Egypt—probably at Tanis or Zoan; and that the valley of the Nile had begun to make its rich return to the toil of the agricultural cultivator."

Vol. I., p. 518. In corroboration of the position that the population of the globe at the beginning of profane history was comparatively sparse, the following estimates are noteworthy. Cæsar states that the population of Helvetia, or Switzerland, in his time was 368,000. In 1880 it was 2,846,000. Gibbon (ch. ix.) asserts that the populousness of Northern Europe in the time of Cæsar has been much exaggerated. Robertson (Charles V., sect. i.) says the same; and so does Hume (Populousness of An-

cient Nations).   Burke, in 1756, says: " I think the numbers of men now upon earth are computed at five hundred
millions, at the most " (Vindication of Natural Society).
The Abbé Raynal (History, Book VI.) says concerning the
Mexican empire : "The Castilian historians tell us that
before the tenth century after Christ this vast space was
inhabited only by some wandering hordes that were entirely
savage.   They tell us that about this period some tribes
issuing from the north and northwest occupied parts of
the territories, and introduced milder manners.   They tell
us that three hundred years after, a people still more advanced in civilization and coming from the neighborhood
of California, settled on the borders of the lakes and built
Mexico there."

VOL. I., p. 520.   Whether some of the dynasties of
Manetho were contemporaneous, or all of them were successive, makes a great difference with the antiquity of
Egypt.   Eratosthenes (d. 194 B.C.), adopting the first view,
reduced Manetho's old empire from 2,900 years to 1,076.
Panadorus (?) reduced the 5,000 or more years of the
thirty dynasties to 3,555.   The total number of years
assigned by Manetho to his thirty dynasties is given in
the Eusebius of Syncellus (A.D. 800) as 4,728 ; in the Arme-
nian Eusebius, as 5,205 ; in the Africanus of Syncellus, as
5,374.   Eusebius (Chronicon, i., 20) says : "We are told
that there were, perhaps, at one and the same time several
kings of Egypt " (Rawlinson : Egypt, ii., 6–8).

VOL. I., p. 521.   Carpenter (Physiology, § 941–948) mentions the following facts in proof of the original unity of
the human species, and of the variations produced by
climate and manner of life : " The influence of habits of
life, continued from generation to generation, upon the form
of the head is remarkably evinced by the transition from
one type to another [namely, the prognathous, pyramidal,
and elliptical skulls], which may be observed in nations
that have undergone a change in their manners and cus-

15

toms, and have made an advance in civilization.   Thus, to
mention but one instance, the Turks at present inhabiting
the Ottoman and Persian empires are undoubtedly descended from the same stock with those nomadic races
which are still spread through Central Asia.   The former,
however, having conquered the countries which they now
inhabit, eight centuries since, have gradually settled down
to the fixed and regular habits of the Indo-European race,
and have made corresponding advances in civilization ;
whilst the latter have continued their wandering mode of
life, and can scarcely be said to have made any decided
advance during the same interval.   Now the long-since
civilized Turks have undergone a complete transformation
into the likeness of Europeans, whilst their nomadic rela-
tives retain the pyramidal configuration of the skull in a
very marked degree.   Some have attributed this change in
the physical structure of the Turkish race to the introduction of Circassian slaves into the harems of the Turks ; but
this could only affect the opulent and powerful amongst
the race ; and the great mass of the Turkish population
have always intermarried among themselves.   In like
manner, even the negro prognathous head and face may
become assimilated to the European by long subjection to
similar influences.   Thus, in some of our older West Indian colonies, it is not uncommon to meet with negroes,
the descendants of those first introduced there, who exhibit a very European physiognomy ; and it has even been
asserted that a negro belonging to the Dutch portion of
Guiana may be distinguished from another belonging to
the British settlements, by the similarity of the features and
expression of each to those which respectively characterize
his masters.   The effect could not be here produced by the
intermixture of bloods, since this would be made apparent
by alteration of color.   But not only may the pyramidal
and prognathous types be elevated toward the elliptical ;
the elliptical may be degraded toward either of these.

Want, squalor, and ignorance have a special tendency to induce that diminution of the cranial portion of the skull, and that increase of the facial, which characterizes the prognathous type, as cannot but be observed by any one who takes an accurate and candid survey of the condition of the most degraded part of the population of the great towns of Great Britain, and as it is seen to be pre-eminently the case with regard to the lowest class of Irish emigrants. A certain degree of retrogression to the pyramidal type is also to be noticed among the nomadic tribes which are to be found in every civilized community. Among these, as has been remarked by a very acute observer (Mayhew, in London Labor and the London Poor), according as they partake more or less of the purely vagabond nature, doing nothing whatsoever for their living, but moving from place to place, preying on the earnings of the more industrious portion of the community, so will the attributes of the nomadic races be found more or less marked in them; and they are all more or less distinguished for their high cheek-bones and protruding jaws, thus showing that kind of mixture of the pyramidal with the prognathous type, which is to be seen among the lowest of the Indian and Malayo-Polynesian race. Hence we are led to conclude that, so far as regards their anatomical structure, there is no such difference among the different races of mankind as would justify to the zoölogist the assertion of their distinct origin. The variations which they present in physical respects are not greater than those which we meet with between the individuals of any one race. Thus, we not only find the average duration of life to be the same, making allowance for the circumstances which induce disease, but the various epochs of life—such as the times of the first and second dentition, the period of puberty, the duration of pregnancy, the intervals of cata-menia and the time of their final cessation—present a marked general uniformity, such as does not exist among similar epochs in the lives of species allied but unquestionably distinct. Further, the different races of man are all subject to the same diseases—to the sporadic, endemic, and epidemic; the only exceptions being those in which the constitution of a race has *grown* to a certain set of influences (as that of the negro to the malaria which generates certain pernicious fevers in the Europeans) producing an hereditary immunity in the race, which is capable of being acquired by individuals of other races by acclimatization begun sufficiently early. Although the comparison of the structural characters of the human races does not furnish any positive evidence of their descent from a common stock, it yet justifies the assertion that even if their stocks *were* originally distinct, there could have been no essential difference between them—the descendants of any one stock being able to assume the characteristics of the other. The most important physiological test, however, of specific unity or diversity is that furnished by the generative process. It may be considered as a fundamental fact, alike in the vegetable and in the animal kingdom, that *hybrid* races originating in the sexual connection of individuals of two different *species*, do not tend to self-perpetuation; the hybrids being nearly sterile with each other, although they may propagate with either of their parent races, in which the hybrid race will soon merge; whilst, on the other hand, if the parents be themselves *varieties* of the same species, the hybrid constitutes but another variety, and its powers of reproduction are rather increased than diminished, so that it may continue to propagate its own race, or may be used for the production of other varieties almost ad infinitum. The application of this principle to the human races leaves no doubt with respect to their specific unity; for, as is well known, not only do all the races of men breed freely with each other, but the mixed race is generally superior in physical development, and in tendency to rapid multiplication, to either of the parent stocks. Finally, the question of *psychical* conformity or difference among the races of mankind, is one which has a most direct bearing upon the question of their specific unity or diversity; but it has an importance of its own, even greater than that which it derives from this source. For, as has been recently argued with great justice and power by Agassiz, the real unity of mankind does not lie in the consanguinity of a common descent, but has its basis in the participation of every race in the same moral nature, and in the community of moral rights which hence becomes the privilege of all. ' This is a bond,' says Agassiz, ' which every man feels more and more the further he advances in his intellectual and moral culture, and which in this development is continually placed upon higher and higher ground; so much so that the physical relation arising from a common descent is finally lost sight of in the consciousness of higher moral obligations. It is in these obligations that the moral rights of men have their foundation; and thus while Africans have the hearts and consciences of human beings, it could never be right to treat them as domestic cattle or as wild fowl, even if it were ever so abundantly demonstrated that their race was but an improved species of ape and ours a degenerate kind of god.' The psychical comparison of the various races of mankind is really, therefore, the most important part of the whole investigation; but it has been, nevertheless, the most imperfectly pursued until the inquiry was taken up by Dr. Prichard. The mass of evidence which he has accumulated on this subject leaves no reasonable doubt that no more ' impassable barrier ' really exists between the different races with respect to their psychical than in regard to their physical peculiarities; the variations in the development of their respective psychical powers and capacities not being greater, either in kind or degree, than those which present themselves between individuals of our own or of any other race, by some members of which a high intellectual and moral standard has been attained. The tests by which we recognize the claims of the outcast and degraded of our own or any other highly civilized community to a common humanity, are the same as those by which we should estimate the true relation of the negro, the Bushman, or the Australian to the cultivated European. If, on the one hand, we admit the influence of want, ignorance, and neglect in accounting for the debasement of the savages of our own great cities, and if we witness the same effects occurring under the same conditions among the Bushmen of Southern Africa, we can scarcely hesitate in admitting that the long-continued operation of the same agencies has had much to do with the psychical as well as the physical deterioration of the negro, Australian, and other degraded races."

VOL. I., p. 523. The following article upon the Antiquity of Man, by Rev. John A. Zahn, was published in the American Catholic Review: "Archæologists divide the first period of human history into three ages, called, in the order of succession, the Stone Age, the Bronze Age, and the Iron Age."

"If the evolution theory of the origin of man and the development of civilization be true, we should expect to find the archæological division universally true and applicable equally to all peoples in all parts of the world. There does not seem to be any doubt that in certain parts of Europe, perhaps throughout the greater portion of it, the Stone Age preceded the Ages of Bronze and Iron. It would be a mistake, however, to imagine that the Stone Age marks a fixed period in human history, and that it prevailed at the same time in all lands and among all peoples. Nothing could be farther from the truth. While one nation, or one tribe, was living in the Age of Stone, its next neighbors may have been enjoying the advantages of the Age of Bronze or of Iron."

"If there is no fixed period in time for the Stone Age,

neither is there a hard-and-fast line of demarcation between the Age of Stone and that of Bronze, or between the Age of Bronze and that of Iron. They frequently overlap one another, and are, in many instances, quite synchronous."

"Again, it would be equally wide of the truth to assert that all peoples passed through the three phases of civilization indicated by the Ages of Stone, Bronze, and Iron. This is so far from being the case that numerous instances are citable when there were but two Ages, and sometimes only one. Some of the more barbarous tribes of the earth are still in the Stone Age, and have never known any other. There are others, in Europe, that have never known a Bronze Age, but who passed directly from the Stone to the Iron Age. From the fact that stone, bronze, and iron implements are found together in the most ancient Chaldean tombs and Assyrian ruins, archæologists have inferred that neither Chaldea nor Assyria ever knew the Ages of Bronze and Iron as distinct from that of Stone. More remarkable still, we find that, in the case of the majority of the tribes of Africa, excluding the Egyptians, the only age that has ever existed is the Age of Iron. Stone has been used, but from the most remote period that archæology has been able to reach, iron has been in common use, while bronze has been entirely unknown."

"Yet more. According to the researches of Dr. Schliemann, there was neither a Stone Age nor a Metal Age in Greece and Asia Minor. In the finds at Troy, especially, there is the most striking evidence of devolution. Here, as well as at Mycenæ, the ornaments and implements discovered, even in the lowest strata, far from indicating a state of savagery and degradation, betoken one of high civilization. In the light of Schliemann's discoveries, not to speak of others pointing in the same direction, made in Egypt, and among the ruins of Assyria and Babylonia, bearing on the condition of primitive man in the Orient,

the conclusion seems to be inevitable that the modern evo-
lution-school is wrong—that the history of our race is not
one of development, but one of degeneration. Thus the
story of the Fall, as recorded in Holy Writ, is corroborated
by the declarations of the newest of sciences—prehistoric
archæology."

"The Age of Iron, even according to those who claim a
great antiquity for our race, was posterior to the alleged
Age of Bronze. But when, in European countries, was
the Age of Bronze ushered in, and when did it close?
The bronze used in Europe, in prehistoric times, and even
in historic times, was brought by the Phœnicians. The
period of commercial prosperity for Phœnicia, it is thought,
extended approximately from the Twelfth to the Fifth
Century before the Christian Era. And this is the epoch,
according to the latest and most reliable researches, during which the many objects of bronze, mostly of Phœni-
cian design and manufacture, were distributed over western, central, and northern Europe. This would place the
so-called Bronze Age in the neighborhoond of 1,000 years
B.C. But this, probably, is assigning it a maximum antiquity."

"As to the Iron Age in Scandinavia, it belonged, if we
are to credit the ablest authorities on the subject, to the
Fourth and Sixth Centuries after Christ. The Age of Iron
in Gaul dates back, probably, to the Fourth Century before
our Era. Judging from the finds in the necropolis of
Hallstatt, the Iron Age began in Austria one or two centuries earlier. The Stone Age terminated in Denmark
about 500 or 600 B.C."

"But the fact is, it is utterly impossible to arrive at
anything even approximating exact dates for any of the
three Ages. They are different for different peoples. For
this reason, therefore, to construct a system of chronology based on the implements of stone, bronze, and
iron that have been used by man in the prehistoric past,

is, at least in the present state of science, clearly impracticable."

"What has been said of the futility of all attempts to arrive at a system of chronology based on the various objects of human industry, obviously applies with equal force to the skulls and other bones of primitive man that have attracted so much attention during the past few decades. They can, no more than the implements of stone, and bronze, and iron so far discovered, be accepted as evidence of the great antiquity of the human race."

"We heartily endorse the words of Mr. W. H. Holmes, of the Smithsonian Institution, when he says : 'The whole discussion of early man has been so surcharged with misconception of facts and errors of interpretation that all is vitiated, as a stream with impurities about its source. Until an exhaustive scientific study of the origin, form, genesis, and meaning of all the handiwork of man, made use of in the discussion, is completed, the discussion of man and culture is worse than useless, and speculation can lead but to embarrassment and disaster.'"

"When examining some of the evidence presented by geologists in favor of the antiquity of man, one cannot help saying with Goethe, 'The thing the most terrible to hear is the constantly reiterated assurance that geologists agree on a given point.' In 1857 the famous Neanderthal skull was discovered near Düsseldorf. Professor Schaaffhausen adjudged it to be 'the most ancient memorial of the early inhabitants of Europe.' Professor Fuhrott wrote a book on it, in which he declared the age of the relic to be from 200,000 to 300,000 years, but Dr. Mayer, of Bonn, after a critical examination of the 'fossil,' and the locality in which it was found, came to the conclusion that it was the skull of a Cossack killed in 1814!"

The conclusions that are drawn within the province of palæontology are of a very uncertain nature, because the data are largely conjecture, and are also exposed to mis-

representation and forgery. The following extract from
the public press illustrates this :

"In those parts of England and Europe where relics of
the Stone Age have been found, and where new discoveries
occasionally come to light, the manufacture of counterfeit
palæolithic implements has become a fine art. Forgeries
of prehistoric antiquities, both in stone and bronze, are
numerous. The chipping of the English imitations is said
to be superior to that of the French, but in each case the
lanceolate form is the favorite. The appearance of antiquity is usually given by a thin coating of fine clay, but at
Amiens a plan of whitening the flint by long boiling in the
family-kettle has been introduced. In some of the bone-
caves of the Reindeer period, both in France and Germany, ancient bones have had designs engraved upon them
by modern forgers, and ancient flint tools have been inserted in sockets of ancient bone so as together to form
a composite falsification. Something of the same kind
has been practised with regard to relics from the Swiss
lake dwellings, many of the bronze objects from which
have also been imitated by casting. Of neolithic implements forgeries are equally abundant, and in some
instances equally difficult to detect. Large perforated axe-
heads, when made of soft sandstone, which could not possibly be used for cutting purposes, of course betray themselves ; but the modern flint axes and arrowheads are not so
easily distinguishable from the ancient. To the experienced
eye there is, however, a difference both in the workmanship and the character of the surface, the ancient arrowheads having probably been worked into shape by pressure
with a tool of stag's horn, and not by blows of an iron
hammer. The grinding of the edges of modern imitations
has usually been effected on a revolving grindstone; in
ancient times a fixed stone was always used, on which the surface and edges of axes or hatchets were ground by friction."

VOL. I., p. 524. In some nations civilization is found

to be very ancient, and in others barbarism very modern.
Two thousand years before Christ, Egypt, Babylon, and
Assyria were far advanced in the knowledge of the mechanical arts and inventions. Two thousand years after
Christ the barbarous tribes of the islands of the sea, and
of portions of the continents, like Alaska and Greenland,
have little or no knowledge of them. "The tools of the
pyramid-builders," says Petrie, "show that the Egyptian
stone-workers of 4,000 years ago had a surprising acquaintance with what have been considered modern tools. Among
the many tools used by the pyramid-builders were both
solid and tubular drills and straight and circular saws.
The drills, like those of to-day, were set with jewels
(probably coriandrum, as the diamond was very scarce),
and even lathe-tools had such cutting edges. So remarkable was the quality of the tubular drills and the skill of the
workmen that the cutting-marks in hard granite give no
indication of wear of the tool, while a cut of a tenth of an
inch was made in the hardest rock at each revolution, and
a hole through both the hardest and softest material was
bored perfectly smooth and uniform throughout. Of the
material and method of making the tools nothing is
known." Even in semi-barbarous tribes a considerable
inventiveness is found. "We were shown," says Lady
Brassy (Last Voyage, 148), "one of the ingenious air-com-
pressing tubes which have been used by the natives of
Borneo for hundreds of years to produce fire. Professor
Faraday alluded in one of his lectures to the possibility of
producing fire by means of compressed air as a discovery
of comparatively modern science ; whereas the fact has
long been known, and put to use in these obscure regions
of the earth."

Respecting the high degree of civilization in Egypt and
Babylon at a very early date, corroborating the representa-
tions of the Pentateuch and Job, Sir J. W. Dawson (London Expositor) says : " We are only beginning to under-

stand the height of civilization to which Egypt and other ancient countries around the Mediterranean had attained even before the time of Moses. Maspero and Tomkins have illustrated the extent and accuracy of the geographical knowledge of the Egyptians of this period. The latter closes a paper on this subject with the following words : 'The Egyptians, dwelling in their green, warm river-course, and on the watered levels of their Fayoum and Delta, were yet a very enterprising people, full of curiosity, literary, scientific in method, admirable delineators of nature, skilled surveyors, makers of maps, trained and methodical administrators of domestic and foreign affairs, kept alert by the movements of their great river, and by the necessities of commerce, which forced them to the Syrian forests for their building timber, and to Kush and Pun for their precious furniture-woods and ivory, to say nothing of incense, aromatics, cosmetics, asphalt, exotic plants, and pet and strange animals, with a hundred other needful things.' The heads copied by Petrie, from Egyptian tombs, show that the physical features of all the people inhabiting the surrounding countries, as well as their manners, industries, and arts, were well known to the Egyptians. The papers of Lockyer have shown that long before the Mosaic age the dwellers by the Euphrates and the Nile had mapped out the heavens, ascertained the movements of the moon and planets, established the zodiacal signs, discriminated the poles of the ecliptic and the equator, ascertained the law of eclipses and the precession of the equinoxes, and, in fact, had worked out all the astronomical data which can be learned by observation, and had applied them to practical uses. Lockyer would even ask us to trace this knowledge as far back as 6,000 years B.C., or into the post-glacial or antediluvian period ; but, however this may be, astronomy was a very old science in the time of Moses, and it is quite unnecessary to postulate a late date for the references to the heavens in Genesis or Job. In geodesy and allied arts also, the Egyptians had long before this time attained to a perfection never since excelled, so that our best instruments can detect no errors in very old measurements and levellings. The arts of architecture, metallurgy, and weaving had attained to the highest development; civilization and irrigation, with their consequent agriculture and cattle-breeding, were old and well-understood arts; and how much of science and practical sagacity is needed for regulating the distribution of Nile water, anyone may learn who will refer to the reports of Sir Colin Scott Moncrieff and his assistants. Sculpture and painting in the age of Moses had attained their acme, and were falling into conventional styles. Law and the acts of government had become fixed and settled. Theology and morals, and the doctrine of rewards and punishments had been elaborated into complex systems. Ample material existed for history, not only in monuments and temple-inscriptions, but in detailed writings on papyrus. Egypt has left a wealth of records of this kind, unsurpassed by any nation, and very much of these belongs to the time before Moses; while, as Birch has truly said, the Egyptian historical texts are, 'in most instances, contemporaneous with the events they record, and written and executed under public control.' There was also abundance of poetical and imaginative literature, and treatises on medicine and other useful arts. At the court of Pharaoh correspondence was carried on with all parts of the civilized world, in many languages, and in various forms of writing, including that of Egypt itself, that of Chaldea, and probably also the alphabetical writing afterward used by the Hebrews, Phœnicians, and Greeks, but which seems to have originated at a very early period among the Mineans, or Punites, of South Arabia. Educations were carried on in institutions of various grades, from ordinary schools to universities. In the latter, we are told, were professors or 'mystery-teachers' of Astronomy, Geography, Mining, Theology, History, and Languages, as well as many of the higher technical arts."

According to a correspondent of the London Daily Chronicle, an exhibition of exceeding interest has just been opened at the Vienna Museum. "This consists of a collection of upward of 10,000 Egyptian papyrus documents, which were discovered at El Fayûm, and purchased by the Austrian Archduke Rainer several years ago. The collection is unique, and the documents, which are written in eleven different languages, have all been deciphered and arranged scientifically. They cover a period of 2,500 years, and furnish remarkable evidence as to the culture and public and private life of the ancient Egyptians and other nations. They are also said to contain evidence that printing from type was known to the Egyptians as far back as the tenth century B.C. Other documents show that a flourishing trade in the manufacture of paper from linen rags existed six centuries before the process was known in Europe. Another interesting feature in the collection is a number of commercial letters, contracts, tax-records, wills, novels, tailors' bills, and even love-letters, dating from 1,200 B.C."

"There are two documents in existence which sufficiently prove the wealth and civilization of Jerusalem in the time of Hezekiah (B.C. 726). The first contains evidence of wide commercial relations; the second gives indications of a considerable lapse of time since the first birth of Hebrew civilization. The first is the account given by Sennacherib of his unsuccessful siege of Jerusalem; the second is the celebrated Siloam inscription, the oldest monument of Hebrew literature still extant. In the face of these documents it is no longer possible to suppose that the Hebrews were merely rude tribes, which only attained to a knowledge of writing, and to a national literature, by adopting the civilization of their Assyrian and Babylonian captors. Hezekiah, we are told by Sennacherib, sent a tribute, including £15,000 of gold, 800 talents (£400,000) of silver, precious stones, a chain of ivory, elephants' hides and tusks, rare woods, etc. The mention of ivory is important. We know that Egyptian ivory objects have been found in Nineveh, and in the oldest remains of Troy. It appears, therefore, that during, or more probably before, the time of Hezekiah, a trade with Egypt existed. We learn that Sargon took 27,280 prisoners from the city of Samaria in 772 B. C. This would make Jerusalem, which was a city certainly as important as Samaria, cover about 200 acres of ground, representing a population of at least 20,000 souls. The Siloam inscription has been placed by Dr. Taylor as late as the time of Manasseh ; but if we accept the Old Testament account of the great water-works of Hezekiah (2 Chron. 32 : 30), it seems more probable that the date should be earlier than 703 B.C." (Conder, Syrian Stone Lore, 116, 117).

VOL. I., p. 527. Taylor (Physical Theory of Another Life, ch. xviii.) affirms that all material motion is the effect ultimately of mental volition. " Motion in the natural universe in all cases originates from mind ; or, in other words, is the effect of will, either the Supreme Will, or the will of created minds. Motion is either constant and uniform, obeying what we call a law, or it is incidental and intermittent. The visible and palpable world then, according to this theory, is *motion*, constant and uniform, emanating from infinite centres, and springing during every instant of its continuance from the creative energy. The instantaneous cessation of this energy, at any period, is therefore abstractly quite as easily conceived of as its continuance ; and whether in the next instant it shall continue or shall cease ; whether the material universe shall stand or vanish, is an alternative of which, irrespective of other reasons, the one member may be as easily taken as the other ; just as the moving of the hand, or the not moving it, in the next moment, depends upon nothing but our voli-

tion. The annihilation of the solid spheres, the planets
and the suns, that occupy the celestial spaces, would not,
on this supposition, be an act of irresistible force, crush-
ing that which resists compression, or dissipating and reducing to an ether that which firmly coheres ; but it would
simply be the non-exertion in the next instant of a power
which has been exerted in this instant ; it would be, not a
destruction, but a rest ; not a crash and ruin, but a pause."

VOL. I., p. 536. The following fatalistic definitions of
Spinoza follow logically from his postulate that God is impersonal and of one substance with the universe. They
also exhibit his abuse of the terms of theism and of Scripture.   God, decrees, election, and miracles are words
which he continually uses, but in a wholly different signification from the true one.   No writer so " palters with us
in a double sense."   " By *the help of God*, I mean the fixed
and unchangeable order of nature, or the chain of natural
events ; for I have said before, and shown elsewhere, that
the universal laws of nature, according to which all things
exist and are determined, are only another name for *the decrees of God*, which always involve eternal truth and necessity.   So that to say *that everything happens according to
natural law*, and to say *that everything is ordained by the decree and ordinance of God, is the same thing*.   Now, since the
power in nature is identical with the power of God, by which
alone all things happen and are determined, it follows that
whatsoever man, as a part of nature, provides himself with
to aid and preserve his existence, or whatsoever nature affords him without his help, is given him solely by the Divine
power, acting either through human nature or external circumstances.   So whatever human nature can furnish itself
with by its own efforts to preserve its existence may fitly
be called *the inward aid* of God, whereas, whatever else ac-
crues to man's profit from outward causes may be called *the
external aid* of God " (Theologico-Political Treatise, ch.
iii.).   " We can now easily understand what is meant by

the election of God. For since no one can do anything save by the predetermined order of nature, that is, by God's eternal ordinance and decree, it follows that no one can choose a plan of life for himself, or accomplish any work, save by God's vocation choosing him for the work, or the plan of life in question, rather than any other person " (Theologico-Political Treatise, ch. iii.). "By *fortune or chance* I mean the ordinance of God, in so far as it directs human life through external and unexpected means" (Theologico-Political Treatise, ch. iii.). " *Miracles* require causes, and follow not from some mysterious royal power which the masses attribute to God, but from the Divine rule and decree; that is, as we have shown from Scripture itself, from the laws and order of nature. Miracles were *natural occurrences,* and must therefore be so explained as to appear neither new (in the words of Solomon, Eccl. 1 : 9), nor contrary to nature, but as far as possible in complete agreement with ordinary events. We may be absolutely certain that every event which is truly described in Scripture necessarily happened, like everything else, *according to natural laws ;* and if anything is there set down which can be proved in set terms to contravene the order of nature, or not to be deducible therefrom, we must believe it to have been foisted into the sacred writings by irreligious hands. Scripture does not explain things by their secondary causes, but only narrates them in the order and the style which has most power to move men, and especially uneducated men, to devotion, and therefore it speaks inaccurately of God and of events, seeing that its object is not to convince the reason, but to attract and lay hold of the imagination. If the Bible were to describe the destruction of an empire in the style of political historians, the masses would remain unstirred, whereas the contrary is the case when it adopts the method of poetic description, and refers all things immediately to God " (Theologico-Political Treatise, ch. vi.).

VOL. I., p. 538.   A miracle necessarily implies the difference in kind between mind and matter.   He who denies
this difference cannot believe in miracles.   For a miracle
is an effect of mind exerted upon matter with nothing
intervening; of a spiritual agent operating directly upon
a material object.   When matter operates upon matter in
accordance with material laws there is no miracle ; but
when will operates upon material and physical nature, not
in accordance with material and physical laws, but above
them, and without them, by pure self-decision, this is of
the essence of the miraculous.   The operation of a man's
will upon his own body furnishes an analogue to the
miracle.   When a volition of the will, which is spirit not
matter, moves a muscle and thereby a limb of the body,
this is finite mind moving matter *immediately*, without the
instrumentality of anything material or physical.   A person does not raise his hand by employing the law of gravitation, or any other material law, but by a pure volition.
This immediate action of the human will upon the muscles
of the body is so common that its supermaterial, and in
this sense supernatural, character is overlooked.   But if a
person by the exertion of a volition should move immediately without the use of any means the muscle of *another*
person, this would be considered miraculous.   Yet both
cases are alike, in regard to the point of the direct action
of mind upon matter without intervening media.

Locke (Understanding, Bk. IV., ch. x.) calls attention
to the inexplicableness and wonderful nature of the voluntary action of mind upon matter, and to the impossibility of explaining it by the operation of material and
physical properties.   "We cannot conceive how anything
but impulse of body can move body ; and yet that is not a
reason sufficient to make us deny it to be possible, against
the constant experience we have of it in ourselves in all our
voluntary motions, which are produced in us only by the
free action or thought of our own minds, and are not, nor

can be the effects of the impulse or determination of the motion of blind matter in or upon our bodies; for then it could not be in our power or choice to alter it. For example: My right hand writes, whilst my left hand is still. What causes rest in one, and motion in the other? Nothing but my will, a thought in my mind. If my thought changes, the right hand rests, and the left hand moves. This is matter of fact, which cannot be denied. Explain this and make it intelligible, and then the next step will be to understand creation [from nothing, which is likewise an effect of pure will without means or instruments]. For the giving a new determination to the motion of the animal spirits, which some make use of to explain voluntary motion [as the present materialism, for the same purpose, makes use of the motion of molecules], clears not the difficulty one jot; for to alter the determination of [material or physical] motion in this case is no easier, nor less, than to give motion itself; since the new determination given to the animal spirits must be either immediately by thought [will], or by some other body put in their way by thought [will] which was not in their way before, and so must owe its motion to thought [will]; either of which suppositions leaves voluntary motion as unintelligible [inexplicable] as it was before."

Coleridge (Works, V., 543) reasons in a similar manner. "A phenomenon in no connection with any other phenomenon as its immediate cause, is a miracle; and what is believed to have been such is miraculous for the person so believing. When it is strange or surprising, that is, without any analogy in our former experience, it is called a miracle. The kind defines the thing; the circumstances the word. To stretch out my arm is a miracle, unless the materialists should be more cunning than they have proved themselves hitherto [by explaining the movement by a purely physical or material cause]. To reanimate a dead man by an act of will, no intermediate agency being employed, not only is, but is called, a miracle. A Scripture miracle, therefore, must be so defined as to express not only its miraculous essence, but likewise the condition of its appearing miraculous; add therefore to the preceding, the words præter omnem priorem experientiam. A miracle might be defined, likewise, as an effect not having its cause in anything congenerous [homogeneous]. That thought calls up thought is no more miraculous than than that a billiard-ball moves a billiard-ball; but that a billiard ball should excite a thought, that is, be perceived [by the agency of the ball], is a miracle, and were it solitary and strange would be called such. For suppose the converse, that a thought should produce a billiard-ball! Yet where is the difference, but that the one is a common experience, the other never yet experienced? It is not strictly accurate to affirm that everything would appear a miracle if we were wholly uninfluenced by custom, and saw things as they are; for then the very ground of all miracles would probably vanish, namely, the heterogeneity of spirit and matter. As objective, the essence of a miracle consists in the heterogeneity of the consequent and its causative antecedent; as subjective, it consists in the assumption [recognition] of the heterogeneity. Add the wonder and surprise excited when the consequent is out of the course of experience, and we know the popular sense and ordinary use of the word."

Of the same tenor is the following from Carlyle (Sartor Resartus, B. III., ch. viii.): "Were it not miraculous could I stretch forth my hand and clutch the sun? Yet thou seest me daily stretch forth my hand and therewith clutch many a thing, and swing it hither and thither. Art thou a grown baby, then, to fancy that the miracle lies in miles of distance, or in pounds avoirdupois of weight; and not to see that the true inexplicable God-revealing miracle lies in this, that I can stretch forth my hand at all; that I have free force to clutch aught therewith?"

That the miracle is wrought by an exertion of personal will that is independent of the usual means or instruments that are employed in non-miraculous events, is taught by Shakespeare :

> " Miracles are ceased,
> And therefore we must admit the *means*
> How things are perfected."—(*Henry V.*, i., 1.)

The essence of the miracle is creation ex nihilo. Whoever holds this doctrine holds that of miracles generally ; for every miracle is an exercise of this kind of power. In every one of the Biblical miracles there is an element of creation from nonentity by pure will, without the use of existing materials or instruments. This element is greater in some miracles than in others, but it is in them all. When Christ multiplied the loaves, there was some existing material to begin with ; but the *addition* to them was origination of bread from nothing. The "five loaves" could not become a mass of bread sufficient for "five thousand men besides women and children," by mere evolution. But when Christ raised Lazarus from the dead, there was no existing life to which life was added by an act of will. Here there was no existing element upon which the miraculous power joined. This was a higher grade of miracle than the former. Christ teaches that the power to work a miracle originally, as he did, and not by delegated power, is proof conclusive of omnipotent deity, like the power to forgive sin (Mark, 2 : 6–11).

VOL. I., p. 541. To explain a miracle as the effect of a higher natural law is to make the miracle natural, not supernatural. A higher law of nature is as much within the sphere of nature as a lower law is. Says the writer of the Article on Miracles, in the Penny Cyclopædia : " If the raising of Lazarus from the dead was an event which took place by virtue of a pre-established law or course of events, in which this one event, to us an apparent exception, was in fact a necessary consequence of this pre-established law or course of events, such event is not a miracle, nor such an event as is generally understood by the word miracle. Those then who would bring miracles within what are called the laws of nature mistake the question. If the event of raising of Lazarus, and all the attendant circumstances, took place in the course of things agreeably to a law unknown by us, such an event is as much an event consistent with what are called the laws of nature as the event of any man's death; but in that case it is not the kind of event which the New Testament presents to us." The miracle of the woman with the issue of blood is a good illustration of this. Had the touch of Christ wrought the cure naturally and mechanically, apart from his *will* in the particular instance, and apart also from the faith of the person to be healed, which was also an act of will though not an efficient in producing the miracle like the will of Christ, every touch of Christ in a crowd would have healed a disease in a diseased person. The operation of the " virtue " in this case would have been like that of gravity and chemical affinity. But it was not. Our Lord evidently knew who the woman was, and only asked the question, " Who touched me ? " in order that she might avow her faith. The "virtue went out " of him, in this instance, because he so willed, and not by a uniform material law of operation. " A plain farmer who was teaching a Sabbath-school in a country school-house was asked to define a miracle. He was thoughtful for a moment, and then replied : ' A miracle is something which there is no law to produce, no law to govern, but is the direct act of God himself.' "

VOL. I., p. 543. Hume rests his argument very much upon the *improbability* of a miracle. But in a question that depends upon the testimony of eye-witnesses this feature is of secondary importance. A particular murder by a particular person may, on the face of it, seem highly improbable, but if actual witnesses testify to its commission by such a person, and there is no reason to doubt their veracity, the improbability in the case does not nullify the testimony. Witnesses in a court are believed or disbelieved, not because of the probability or improbability of the fact to which they testify, but because of the soundness of their senses and their honesty.

It is too generally forgotten, in discussing the argument for miracles, that there is no *rebutting* testimony against them to contradict or weaken the testimony of the Jewish and Christian eye-witnesses. Not a single person of the generation contemporary with the Apostles testifies that he was present when the alleged miracles were wrought, and that he did not see them. In a court trial, if the testimony is all in one way, and not a single witness appears to contradict, it is considered to make the case highly certain. The denial of miracles is not supported by any counter-testimony of persons living at the time. It is merely the verbal denial of persons living in later generations, who offer no testimony of eye-witnesses to support their denial. In the eighteenth century Hume asserts that no miracles were wrought in the first century, but brings forward no witnesses from the first century who were present at the crucifixion of Christ and testify that they saw no darkness over the whole land, that there was no earthquake, no resurrection of dead men, and no rending of the temple-vail. Such rebutting testimony as this from persons on the ground at the time of the crucifixion, would be a strong argument against miracles, compared with the weak argument from the inference that because miracles are not wrought now, and have not been for centuries, they never were—which is the substance of Hume's argument.

That there should not be much testimony to the truths and facts of the Old Testament from profane or secular history is to be expected. The history of Israel does not make a part of secular history, like that of Egypt,

Greece, and Rome. It is a lesser circle by itself within the great circle of universal history. Being founded upon a supernatural revelation, it is not in the common stream of merely natural events, and therefore is not known to the common historian, and is not noticed by him. It has its own special history, recorded by its own prophets, and contained in its own documents. The same remark holds true of Christianity and the life of its Founder. This is the reason why there are so few references to Christ in contemporary historians. At the same time it should be observed that there are many events and things in secular history that are not spoken of by secular writers. The magnificent temples at Pæstum, for example, which are among the most remarkable structures of antiquity, are not alluded to by any classical author.

ANTHROPOLOGY

Vol. II., p. 6. Augustine argues against the doctrine of pre-existence, in Forgiveness and Baptism, i., 31. "Perhaps, however, the now exploded and rejected opinion must be resumed, that souls which once sinned in their heavenly abode descend by stages and degrees to bodies suited to their deserts, and as a penalty for their previous life are more or less tormented by corporeal punishments. They who entertain such an opinion are unable to escape the perplexities of this question: Whence does it come to pass that a person shall from his earliest boyhood show greater moderation, mental excellence, and temperance, and shall to a great extent conquer lust, and yet live in such a place as to be unable to hear the grace of Christ preached; while another man, although addicted to lust, and covered with crime, shall be so directed as to hear, and believe, and be baptized? Where, I say, did they acquire such diverse deserts? If they had indeed passed any part of their life in heaven, so as to be thrust down, or to sink down to this world, and to tenant such bodily receptacles as are congruous to their own former life, then, of course, that man ought to be supposed to have led the better life previous to his present mortal body, who did not much deserve to be burdened with it, so as both to have a good disposition and to be importuned by milder desires, which he could easily overcome; and yet he did not deserve to have that grace preached to him whereby he could be delivered from the ruin of the second death. Whereas the other, who was hampered with a grosser body as a penalty, so they suppose, for worse deserts, and was accordingly possessed of obtuser affections, whilst he was in the ardor of his lust succumbing to the flesh and by his wicked life aggravating his former sins, which had brought him to such a pass, either heard upon the cross, ' To-day shalt thou be with me in Paradise,' or else joined himself to some apostle, by whose preaching he became a changed man. I am at a loss to know what answer they can give to this, who wish us to maintain God's righteousness by human conjectures, and, knowing nothing of the depths of grace, have woven webs of improbable fable." In Letter CLXVI., 27 (to Jerome), he says: "That souls sin in another earlier life, and that for their sins in that state of being they are cast down into bodies as prisons, I do not believe. I reject and protest against such an opinion. I do this, in the first place, because they affirm that this is accomplished by means of some incomprehensible revolutions, so that, after I know not how many cycles, the soul must return again to the same burden of corruptible flesh, and to the endurance of punishment—than which opinion, I do not know that anything more horrible can be conceived. In the next place, who is the righteous man gone from the earth, about whom we should not, if what they say be true, feel afraid, at least, lest sinning in Abraham's bosom he should be cast down into the flames which tormented the rich man in the parable? For why may not the soul sin after leaving the body, if it can sin before entering it? Finally, to have sinned in Adam, in whom the apostle says all have sinned, is one thing; but it is a wholly different thing to have sinned, I know not where, outside of Adam, and then, because of this, to be thrust into Adam, that is, into the body which is derived from Adam, as into a prison-house."

VOL. II., p. 7. The following series of extracts presents

Augustine's traducianism. Notwithstanding his refusal to declare positively for either theory, no such series in favor of creationism can be found in his works. "Those sins of infancy are not so said to be *another's*, as if they did not belong to the infants at all, inasmuch as all of them sinned in Adam when in his nature, and by virtue of that power whereby he was able to produce them, were all as yet the one Adam ; but they are called *another's* (aliena), because as yet they were not living their own [individual] lives, but the life of the one man contained whatsoever was in his future posterity " (Forgiveness and Baptism, iii., 14). " Now observe, I pray you, how the circumspect Pelagius felt the question about the soul to be a very difficult one, for he says, ' *If* the soul is not propagated, but the flesh alone, then the latter alone deserves punishment, and it is unjust that the soul, which is newly made, and that not out of Adam's substance, should bear the sin of another committed so long ago.' He does not say absolutely, ' *Because* the soul is not propagated.' Wherefore I, too, on my side, answer this question with no hasty assertion : If the soul is not propagated,where is the justice that what has been but recently created, and is quite free from the contagion of sin, should be compelled in infants to endure the passions and other torments of the flesh, and, what is more terrible still, even the attacks of evil spirits ? " (Forgiveness and Baptism, iii., 18).

" Let it not be said to me that the words of Zechariah, ' He formeth the spirit of man within him,' and of the Psalmist, ' He formeth their hearts severally' (Sept.), support the opinion that souls are created one by one. For to create means more than to form. It is written, nevertheless, ' Create in me a clean heart, O God ;' yet it cannot be supposed that a soul here desires to be made before it has begun to exist. [" Create," consequently, is used here in a secondary sense.] Nor is your [Jerome's] opinion, which [if proved from Scripture] I would willingly make my own, supported by that sentence in Ecclesiastes, ' Then shall the dust return to the earth as it was, and the spirit shall return to God who gave it.' Nay, it rather favors those who think that all souls are derived from one ; fcr they say that as the dust returns to the earth as it was, and yet the body of which this is said returns not to the first man from whom it was derived, but to the earth, from which the first man was made, the spirit, in like manner, though derived from the spirit of the first man, does not return to him, but to the Lord, by whom it was given to our first parent. Meanwhile, though I do not yet know which of these opinions is to be preferred, this one thing I profess as my deliberate conviction, that the opinion which is true does not conflict with that most firm and well-grounded article in the faith of the Church, that infant children, even when they are newly born, can be delivered from perdition in no other way than through the grace of Christ's name, which he has given in his sacraments" (Letter CLXVI., 26, 28, to Jerome, A.D. 415). " The words of the Scripture passage, ' The spirit returns to God who gave it,' are somewhat adverse to these two opinions : namely, the one which supposes each soul to be created in its own body, and the one which supposes each soul to introduce itself into its own body spontaneously. But there is no difficulty in showing that the words are consistent with either of the other two opinions, namely, that all souls are derived by propagation from the one first created, or that, having been created and kept in readiness with God, they are given to each body as required " (Letter cxliii., 9. To Marcellinus, A.D. 412). " Whether all souls are derived by propagation from the first [soul], or are in the case of each individual specially created, or, being created apart from the body, are sent into it, or introduce themselves into it of their own accord, without doubt this creature endowed with reason—namely, the human soul—after the entrance of sin does not govern its own body absolutely

according to its free-will. Whoever is disposed to maintain
any one of these four theories of the soul's origin, must
bring forward either from the Scriptures passages which
do not admit of any other interpretation, or reasonings
founded on premises so obviously true that to call them in
question would be madness " (Letter cxliii., 6, 11. To Marcellinus, A.D. 412). " There are four opinions as to the
manner of the soul's incarnation: (1) That all other souls
are derived from the one which was given to the first man;
(2) that for each individual a new soul is made; (3) that
souls already in existence somewhere are sent by divine
act into the bodies; or (4), glide into them of their own
accord " (Letter clxvi., 7. To Jerome, A.D. 410). " I know
that you [Jerome] are not one of those who have begun of
late to utter certain new and absurd opinions, alleging that
there is no guilt derived from Adam which is removed by
baptism in the case of infants. If I knew that you held
this view, I would certainly neither address this question
[namely, how the dying infant can have contracted guilt
requiring the sacrament of baptism] to you, nor think that
it ought to be put to you at all. Teach me, therefore, I
beseech you, what I may teach others, and tell me this: If
souls are from day to day made for each individual separately at birth, where, in the case of infant children, is sin
committed by these souls so that they require the remission of sin in the sacrament of Christ because of the sin
of Adam from whom the sinful flesh has been derived?
Or, if they do not sin, how is it compatible with the justice
of the Creator that, because of their being united to mortal bodies derived from another person, they are so brought
under the bond of the sin of that other that, unless they
be rescued by the Church, perdition overtakes them, although it is not in their own power to secure that they be
rescued by the grace of baptism? Where, therefore, is the
justice of the condemnation of so many thousands of souls,
which in the deaths of infant children leave this world

without the benefit of the Christian sacrament, if, being
newly created, they have no preceding sin [derived from
Adam]?   Seeing, therefore, that we may not say concerning God either that he compels them to become sinners,
or that he punishes innocent souls; and, seeing that on
the other hand, it is not lawful for us to deny that nothing
else than perdition is the doom of the souls even of little
children which have departed from the body without the
sacrament of Christ, tell me, I implore you, where anything can be found to support the opinion that souls are
not all derived from that one soul of the first man, but are
each created separately for each individual as Adam's soul
was made for him " (Letter clxvi., 6, 10.   To Jerome, A.D.
415).

Odo, at first Abbot of Tornay and afterward Bishop of
Cambray, adopted traducianism, but not as Augustine and
subsequent traducianists generally did, by postulating a
complex specific nature which is both psychical and physical, and furnishes the substance of which the individual
soul and body are constituted by division and derivation.
His specific nature is physical substance only, that is, material seed which is made psychical by the modifying influence and action upon it of the individual soul in the act
of propagation.   This feature is not an improvement, and
introduces difficulties that do not attach to the other view.
Odo died in 1113.   His treatise, De Peccato Originali, is
in the Bibliotheca Maxima Patrum, xxi., 221 sq., and in
Migne's Patrology, tom. clx., 1071 sq.   The following account is taken from it :

" The orthodox," he says (Liber ii.), " favor creationism
and declare that we were in Adam only according to
the flesh.   They deny that the soul is propagated.   There
are, nevertheless, many who derive the soul, like the body,
by traduction or propagation.   The reasons which they
assign are not to be despised, so that we shall discuss
both views, and first we examine those of the orthodox.

The orthodox view has this difficulty. If I have my body from Adam, and not my soul (anima) from Adam but from God alone, since sin is in the soul and not in the body, how can I be said to have sinned in Adam? Adam sinned, and sin was in his soul alone, not in his body; but my soul, in which my sin is, I do not have from him. How then am I said to have sinned in him? If sin were in the body, I might rightly be said to have sinned in him because my body was in him; but as sin is not in the body, I cannot properly be said to have sinned in Adam."

Odo then defines the relation of the individual to the species, and the difference between specific and individual transgression. "Dicitur duobus modis peccatum, personale et naturale. Et naturale est cum quo nascimur, et quod ab Adam trahimus in quo omnes peccavimus. In ipso enim erat anima mea, specie non persona, non individua sed communi natura. Nam omnis humanæ animæ natura erat in Adam obnoxia peccato. Et ideo omnis humana anima culpabilis est secundum suam naturam, etsi non secundum suam personam. Ita peccatum quo peccavimus in Adam, mihi quidem naturale est, in Adam vero personale. In Adam gravius, levius in me; nam peccavi in eo non qui sum, sed quod sum. Peccavi homo [quod sum], sed non Odo [qui sum]. Peccavi substantia, non persona; et quia substantia non est nisi in persona, peccatum substantiæ est etiam personæ, sed non personale. Peccatum vero personale est quod facio ego qui sum, non hoc quod sum; quo pecco Odo, non homo; quo pecco persona, non natura; sed quia persona non est sine natura, peccatum personæ est etiam naturæ, sed non naturale" (Liber ii.). "Sicut aliquid de universali dicitur pro individuo, sic aliquid dicitur pro parte de toto; ut propter animam solam dicatur peccator homo individuus, qui animam simul habet et corpus. Ad corpus peccatum non pertinet, et tamen peccator est qui corpus habet; non igitur anima sola peccase dicitur in Adam, sed et ipse per animam, scilicet totus ex pluribus partibus per unam. Dicitur ergo et Adam pecasse, quia peccavit anima quam habuit ipse. Et si peccavit Adam, peccavit homo; quia si peccavit ipse homo, peccavit humana natura quæ est homo. Sed humana natura tota tunc erat in ipso, nec usquam erat alibi specialis homo. Cum ergo peccavit persona, scilicet ipse homo, peccavit tota natura, scilicet communis homo. Et in peccato personæ, culpabilis factus est homo communis naturæ. Et qualem Adam fecit humanam naturam in se, talem posteris etiam post se. Et qualis facta est humana natura per insipientiam peccatoris, talis necesse est transfundatur in posteros per justitiam " (Liber iii.).

Odo would explain the propagation of the soul by the fact that the soul is the animating, energizing, and governing part of the man. The life and force of the body come from the mind or spirit behind it; for when the spirit leaves the body, this has neither life nor force. In man the material sensations of the five senses are spiritualized by the higher intellectual principle which penetrates them, and makes them to be human sensation instead of merely brutal and animal. The bodily sensations of a man are of a higher grade than those of a beast. And, generally, it is the mind in the human body, and using it, that makes it and its sensations to be what they are. Now this, says Odo, holds true of the bodily act of propagation, as well as of all other bodily acts. The merely material and physical semen is rationalized and spiritualized by the mental life which ejects it, so that the human embryo becomes both psychical and physical, animal and rational, while the brute embryo remains only physical and animal. The human embryo is the resultant of one solely physical ovum. It is not the resultant of an ovum which contains a rational principle and is a combination of both psychical and physical substance from which the individual soul and body issue. There is no such thing as this latter. But the merely physical ovum is animated and rationalized by the life of reason which is in the mind or spirit of the man, so that the human embryo in this way comes to have two principles, an animal and a rational, and is both body and soul. The brute embryo contains only one principle, the animal, because the ovum is not modified by the life of reason, of which the brute is destitute. This action of the rational soul in propagation is evinced in the mental and human pleasure connected with coition, which is higher than the wholly brutal and animal pleasure of the dog or hog in the same act. The following extracts give Odo's explanation :

"Tolle *animam*, non facit corpus semen ; facit semen, habet igitur animam. Habet ergo semen ab anima vim vegetabilem. Aut habet ab anima, aut a corpore. Si a corpore, tolle animam et funde semen, et dabimus palmam tibi victoriæ si videamus sequentem prolem. Si autem non potest fieri, confitere veritatem, et animæ concede vim vegetabilem. Et licet ipsa vis non sit anima, per eam tamen ab anima propagatur anima, et fit semen animæ propagantis animam. Dicunt seminatores animarum, quorum rationem post orthodoxos insumpsimus dicere, quod omnis anima venit de traduce, id est anima per semen de anima, sicut ejus corpus per semen propagatur de corpore, vel arbor de arbore, et sic esse vim seminariam in anima, quemadmodum in corpore. In animalibus enim nisi vim vegetabilem trahat semen parentis, non proficit ad creationem [*i.e.*, generationem] sequentis prolis, nam semen fusum in femina, quomodo pullulat nisi vim *ani-mæ* vegetabilem trahat ? Quomodo concrescit in viscera prægnantis seminatum, nisi utcunque fuerit animatum ? Infundantur urina de parente, vel sputum, vel aliud quidquam, non proficit in partum, vel in prolem ullam, nec unquam natum est animal tali infusione, quia talis infusio caret animatione. Nullam vim *animæ* talis infusio trahit,

17

ideo non prospicit in partum, nec inde pullulat aliquid. Trahit ergo secum semen corporis semen animæ, scilicet vim vegetationis quæ corporeum semen vegetet in humanam formam, ipse cum eo succrescens in rationalem animam, ut sicut particula quæ non est humanum corpus ab humano corpore fluit in sementem, sic particula quæ non est humana anima ab humana anima decurrat ut semen. Et sicut pruritus corporis non solet sine delectatione *animæ* fieri, sic pruritus a corpore non excutit seminarium liquorem nisi simul animæ delectatio producat ab anima seminariam vim, id est vegetabilitatem ut sit humanæ *animæ* vis vegetabilis, sicut seminarius liquor semen est corporis. Et sicut simul procedunt causæ, scilicet delectatio et pruritus, sic simul sequuntur effectus, id est vis vegetabilis et liquor seminarius simul etiam cum crescendo proficiunt, hoc usque ad humanam formam, illud ad rationalem *animam*, inde simul manent in una persona usque ad mortem. Causæ conjunctæ simul jungunt suos effectus in unum individuum ejus quod constat ex animæ et corpore " (Liber iii.).

Vol. II., p. 9. The Arminian Watson (Institutes, Vol. II., 82) favors traducianism. " Some contend," he says, " that the soul is extraduce ; others that it is by immediate creation. As to the metaphysical part of this question, we can come to no satisfactory conclusion. The Scriptures, however, appear to be more in favor of the doctrine of traduction. ' Adam begat a son in his own likeness.' ' That which is born of the flesh is flesh ;' which refers certainly to the soul as well as the body. The usual argument against the traduction of the human spirit is, that the doctrine of its generation tends to materialism. But this arises from a mistaken view of that in which the procreation of a human being lies ; which does not consist in the production out of nothing of either of the parts of which the compounded being, man, is constituted, but in uniting them substantially with one another. The matter of the body is not, then, first made, but disposed ; nor can it be supposed that the soul is by that act first produced. That belongs to a higher Power ; and then the only question is, whether all souls were created in Adam, and are transmitted by a law peculiar to themselves, which is always under the control of the will of that same watchful Providence of whose constant agency in the production and ordering of the kinds, sexes, and circumstances of the animal creation we have abundant proof ; or whether they are immediately created. The tenet of the soul's *descent* appears to have most countenance from the language of Scripture, and it is no small confirmation of it, that when God designed to incarnate his own Son, he stepped out of the ordinary course, and found a sinless human nature immediately by the power of the Holy Ghost."

Vol. II., p. 10. The difficulty which the creationist finds in retaining the Augustinian anthropology generally, and particularly the doctrine that original sin had a free origin and is damnable for every man, is seen in his disposition to emphasize the natural union of Adam and his posterity. For example, Aquinas, though formally rejecting traducianism, nevertheless often asserts the unity of nature between them. Says Neander (History, IV., 495), "Thomas Aquinas declares, it is true, against traducianism ; at the same time, however, he says all the descendants of Adam are to be considered as one man, by reason of the community of nature received from the father of the race." Aquinas's argument against traducianism is given in his Summa, I., cxviii.

Hagenbach (§ 248) says that " Luther taught traducianism, followed by most of the Lutheran divines, with the exception of Calixtus. Gerhard (ix., 8, § 118) left it to the philosophers to define the modus propagationis, but he himself taught (§ 116) that ' animas eorum qui Adamo et Eva progeniti fuissent non creatas, neque etiam generatas, sed propagatas fuisse.' Similar views were expressed by

Calovius (iii., 1081), and Hollaz (i., 5, q. 9). 'Anima humana non immediate creatur, sed mediante semine fœcundo a parentibus generatur et in liberos traducitur. Non generatur anima *ex* traduce sine semine fœcundo tanquam principio materiali, sed *per* traducem seu mediante semine prolifico tanquam vehiculo, propagatur.' The Consensus Repetitus, Fidei veræ Lutheranæ, Punct. 22 (in Henke, p. 18) declares: 'Profitemur et docemus, hominem generare hominem, idque non tantum quoad corpus sed etiam animam. Rejicimus eos qui docent in hominibus singulis animas singulas non ex propagine oriri sed ex nihilo tunc primum creari et infundi cum in uteris matrum fœtus concepti atque ad animationem præperati sunt."

VOL. II., p. 17. The prime importance of the doctrine of the original unity of Adam and his posterity appears from the fact, that it is only at this point in man's history that his self-determination in the origin of sin and responsibility for it can be found. At the instant when Adam and his posterity as an included specific nature were created ex nihilo, this unity was holy and self-determined in holiness; yet *mutably* be so, because it was not *infinitely* so. Self-determination to sin was possible, but not in the least necessary. At the instant when Adam and the included human nature inclined or self-determined to evil, he might have persisted in the holy self-determination which he was already exerting. At this point his destiny and that of his posterity is placed by his Maker in his free agency. But when he has acted, and a new self-determination to evil has occurred, he has lost his original freedom to good and become enslaved to evil. He can no longer self-determine or incline to holiness; and yet his self-determination or inclination to sin is, and continues to be, unforced self-motion. When a man commits suicide, it is in his power at the instant of the suicide, to continue to live; but after the suicide, to live is no longer in his power. At no point subsequent to Adam and Eve in Eden can man be found upon a position of holiness and innocency, with plenary power to remain in it, from which he falls by an act of free self-determination —a state of things necessary, in order justly to charge him with the guilt of both original sin and actual transgression, of both native depravity and sinful conduct, and justly to expose him to eternal death.

Vol. II., p. 19. The employment of the term "Adam" in the first chapter of Genesis to denote the species, and in the second chapter to denote only the individual Adam, might as well be cited by the rationalistic critic to prove his hypothesis of a non-Mosaic composite origin of the Pentateuch by several authors, as the fact that Elohim is employed in it, and subsequently Jehovah to denote the Divine Being. Moses in the Pentateuch presents subjects *comprehensively*, in their various parts and aspects. Consequently, in one place the Supreme Being is described in his abstract and universal character as the deity; and in another in his particular relation to his church or covenant people. Hence the employment sometimes of Elohim, sometimes of Jehovah, and sometimes of both together. So, likewise, he presents a comprehensive view of man; now as specific, and now as individual, and hence the double use of "Adam." The rationalistic critic assumes that the inspired writer views subjects as he himself does, bit by bit, and presents them only in a piecemeal manner.

Vol. II., p. 30. The injustice of punishing a person for a sin in which he had no kind of participation gets voice in the passionate utterance of Lucrece, as she sees the face of Helen in the "skilful painting made for Priam's Troy."

> "Show me the strumpet that began this stir,
> That with my nails her beauty I may tear.
> Thy heat of lust, fond Paris, did incur
> This load of wrath that burning Troy doth bear;
> Thy eye kindled the fire that burneth here;

And here in Troy, for trespass of thine eye,
The sire, the son, the dame, and daughter die."

" Why should the private pleasure of some one
    Become the public plague of many mo?
  Let sin, alone committed, light alone
    Upon his head that hath transgressed so,
    Let guiltless souls be freed from guilty woe;
  For one's offence why should so many fall,
  To plague a private sin in general ? "

VOL. II., p. 37.   Owen, like Turrettin, avails himself of
Augustine when necessary, but oscillates between natural
and representative union as he does.   " The first sin in the
world was on many accounts the greatest sin that ever was
in the world.   It was the sin, as it were, of human nature,
wherein there was a conspiracy of all individuals ; ' omnes
eramus unus ille homo' (Aug.); in that one man, or that
one sin, ' we all sinned' (Rom. 5 : 12).   It left not God
one subject, as to moral obedience, on the earth, nor the
least ground for any such to be unto eternity.   When the
angels sinned, the whole race or kind did not prevaricate.
Thousand thousands of them, and ten thousand times ten
thousands continued in their obedience (Dan. 7 : 10)."
(Forgiveness, Works, XIV., 136. Ed. Russell.)   The phraseology of Owen here, shows that the Augustinian doctrine
of the Adamic unity was held hesitatingly by him, with
respect to the point of literal substantial unity.   He quali-
fies the assertion that the first sin was " the sin of human
nature" by the clause, "as it were."   He also speaks of the
angels as a "race " or "kind :" a term which, taken strictly
is not applicable to them.   Witsius (Apostles' Creed,
Dissertation xxvi.) combines natural and representative
union.   "And so it is written: 'The first man Adam,'
the natural and federal head of the rest of mankind, 'was
made a living soul.' "

VOL. II., p. 42.   In his commentary on Gen. 2 : 17,
Paraeus, as quoted by Landis (Original Sin, p. 231), de-

clares that "all the posterity of Adam do communicate in the original offence, not only by participation of a sinful nature, but likewise *in the act of sinning itself* (sed etiam ipso peccandi actu). We all, therefore, when we suffer for his sin, do not suffer simply for the sin of another, but also for our own. And it is said to be imputed to us all not as simply another's, but also as our own. Neither as being innocent, but as companions in the offence, and together guilty with him (non ut simpliciter alienum, sed etiam ut nostrum; nec ut insontibus, sed ut delicti sociis, et una reis)." Owen (Arminianism, ch. vii.) declares that "Scripture is clear that the sin of Adam is the sin of us all, not only by propagation and communication (whereby not his singular [individual] fault, but something of the same nature is devised to us), but also by an imputation of his actual transgression unto us all, his singular [individual] transgression being by this means made ours. The *grounds* of this imputation may be all reduced to his being a common person: 1. As we were then in him and *parts* of him. 2. As he sustained the place of our whole nature in the covenant God made with him." Such a statement as this of Owen agrees with traducianism, not with creationism.

VOL. II., p. 45. The Westminster definition of Adam as a "public person" is so different from that of Christ as a "public person," that it is impossible to maintain, on the ground of it, either that both unions are representative, or that both are natural and substantial. On the contrary, the definition implies that one is natural, and the other representative. Adam, as a "public person," is described as "the root of mankind" (Conf., vi., 3), and one from whom "all mankind descend by ordinary generation" (L C., 22). Christ, as a "public person," is described only as "the head of his church" (L C., 52). Of Adam, it is said that "all mankind were in him" (L C., 92); of Christ it is only said that he is "the head of his members" (L C., 83).

The two "public persons," together with the two unions and the two covenants connected with them, may be thus described: 1. The legal covenant of works being made with Adam as a public person, not for himself only but for his posterity, all mankind originally constituting a common unity and descending from him by ordinary generation, *specifically* and *really* sinned in him and fell with him in the first transgression. 2. The evangelical covenant of grace being made with Christ as a public person, not for himself only but for his elect, all of mankind who are united to him by faith *representatively* and *putatively* suffered with him in his atoning death, and obeyed with him in his perfect obedience. Consequently, the imputation of the sin of Adam to all men is real and meritorious; of the righteousness of Christ to elect men is nominal and gratuitous. The clause "all mankind descending from him by ordinary generation," is not limiting, as if there were some of mankind who do not so descend, and who therefore did not sin in him, but is descriptive. All mankind are a total distinguished by descent from Adam by ordinary generation, and by reason of this descent sinned in and with him when they were all a common specific nature in him. Descent by propagation proves an original unity of the posterity and progenitors, and this unity proves the commission of the " one offence " which made the unity guilty and corrupt.

The Universalism that has infected Calvinistic theology of late originates in the erroneous assumption that Christ is united with the whole human race in the same specific and universal way that Adam was. Hence the assertion that " Christ has redeemed the human race." The Scripture statement is, that he has " redeemed his people " (Luke 1 : 68); and the Westminster statement is, that he has " redeemed his church." The doctrine of a discriminating election of some and preterition of others, which applies to redemption and the representative headship of

Christ, but not to apostasy and the natural headship of Adam, is vehemently opposed by all who make redemption to be as wide as apostasy, and contend that " as all die " without exception " in Adam," so " all shall be made alive " without exception " in Christ." The great difference between the two kinds of " public person " needs to be urged in this reference, so that the natural and universal race-union of Adam and his posterity shall be marked off from the spiritual and individual union of Christ and his people. This is one of the many instances in which the value of accurate dogmatic statements appears. If a certain definition of Christ as a public person is adopted, universal salvation necessarily follows; if it is rejected, it is necessarily excluded.

Another way in which universalism is introduced into Calvinism is, by claiming that the covenant of grace is made with all mankind instead of with a part of it. The only covenant which God has made with all mankind is the legal covenant of which the terms are : " This do and thou shalt live." The terms of the covenant of grace are : " I will put my law in their inward parts, and write it in their hearts; and will be their God, and they shall be my people " (Jer. 31 : 33). This promise is not universal. Accordingly, the Westminster Creed declares that " God doth not leave all men to perish in the estate of sin and misery, . . . but of his mere love and mercy delivereth his *elect* out of it, and bringeth them into an estate of salvation by the second covenant, commonly called the covenant of grace " (L C., 30); and also that : " The covenant of grace was made with Christ as the second Adam, and in him with all the *elect* as his seed " (L C., 31). At the same time all mankind are represented as obtaining a certain kind of benefit from the covenant of grace. This is the *offer* to them of redemption on condition of their own faith and repentance, but not the *effectual application* of redemption by the Holy Spirit in regeneration, which latter is confined to the elect. "The grace of God is manifested in the second covenant, in that he freely provideth and offereth to [all] sinners a mediator, and life and salvation by him; and requiring faith as the condition to interest them in him promiseth and giveth his Holy Spirit to all his *elect*, to work in them that faith with all other saving graces, and to enable them unto all holy obedience" (L C., 32).

According to these statements, the promise in the covenant of grace to the elect is absolute and unconditional, but to the non-elect is relative and conditional. The success of the covenant in the former instance is certain, because the fulfilment on the part of the elect is *secured* by the action of God in overcoming their resistance and inclining and enabling them to keep it. "I will put my law in their inward parts, and write it in their hearts," says God. This inward writing of the law is not dependent upon man's action, but wholly upon God's. But the success of the covenant in the latter instance is uncertain, because its fulfilment on the part of the non-elect is dependent upon *their* action. If they will believe they shall be saved; but God does not promise to subdue their unbelief by "working faith in them, with all other saving graces." No better account of this subject has been given than by Bunyan in his "Come, and Welcome, to Jesus Christ."

"We call that an absolute promise that is made without any condition. That is an absolute promise of God, or of Christ, which maketh over to this or that man any saving spiritual blessing without a condition to be performed on his part for the obtaining thereof. And this Scripture which we are speaking of is such an one. Let the best master of arts on earth show me, if he can, any condition in the text, 'All that the Father giveth me shall come to me,' that depends upon any qualification in us which is not by the same promise to be wrought in us by the Lord Jesus. An absolute promise, therefore, is, as we say, without if or and; that is, it requireth nothing of us that itself may be accomplished. It saith not, they shall if they will; but they shall; not, they shall if they use the means; but they shall. You may say that a will, and the use of means is supposed, though not expressed. But I answer, No, by no means; that is, as a condition of this promise. If they [*i.e.*, a will and means] be at all included in the promise, they are included there as the effect of the absolute promise, not as if it is to be expected that the qualification arise from us. 'Thy people shall be willing in the day of thy power' (Ps. 110:3). This is another absolute promise; but doth this promise suppose a willingness in us as a condition of God's making us willing? Does it mean that they shall be willing, if they are willing; or they shall be willing, if they be willing. This is ridiculous; there is nothing of this supposed. The promise is absolute and certain to us; all that it requireth for its own accomplishment is the mighty power of Christ and his faithfulness to accomplish."

" The difference, therefore, betwixt the absolute and conditional promises is this: 1. They differ in their terms. The absolute promises say, I will, and you shall; the conditional say, I will, if you will; or, Do this, and thou shalt live (Jer. 31:32, 34; Ezek, 34:24-34; Heb. 8:7-12; Jer. 4:1; Ezek. 18:30-32; Matt. 19:21). 2. They differ in their way of communicating good things to men. The absolute promises communicate good things freely, only of grace; the conditional communicate good things only if there be that qualification in us which the promise calls for, not else. 3. The absolute promises engage God, the others engage us; I mean God only, us only. 4. Absolute promises must be fulfilled; conditional may, or may not be fulfilled. The absolute ones must be fulfilled, because of the faithfulness of God; the others may not be, because of the unfaithfulness of men. 5. The absolute promises have, therefore, a sufficiency in themselves to bring about their own fulfilling; the conditional have not so. The absolute promise is therefore a big-bellied promise, because it hath in itself a fulness of all desired things for us, and will, when the time of that promise is come, yield to us mortals that which will verily save us, yea, and make us capable of answering the demands of the conditional promise. Wherefore, though there be a real, yea, an eternal difference in these respects and others, betwixt the conditional and the absolute promise, yet again, in other respects, there is a blessed harmony betwixt them, as may be seen in these particulars. 1. The conditional promise calls for repentance, the absolute gives it (Acts 5 : 30, 31). 2. The conditional promise calls for faith, the absolute promise gives it (Zeph. 3 : 12 ; Rom. 15 : 12). 3. The conditional promise calleth for a new heart, the absolute promise gives it (Ezek. 36). 4. The conditional promise calleth for holy obedience, the absolute promise giveth it, or causeth it (Ezek. 36 : 27). And as they harmoniously agree in this, so again the conditional promise blesseth the man who by the absolute promise is endued with its fruits. As for instance : 1. The absolute promise maketh men upright; and then the conditional follows, saying, ' Blessed are the undefiled in the way, who walk in the law of the Lord ' (Ps. 119 : 1). 2. The absolute promise giveth to this man the fear of the Lord ; and then the conditional followeth, saying, ' Blessed is every one that feareth the Lord ' (Ps. 118 : 1). 3. The absolute promise giveth faith; and then the conditional follows, saying, ' Blessed is he that believeth ' (Zeph. 3 : 12 ; Luke 1 : 45). 4. The absolute promise brings free forgiveness of sins; and then says the conditional, ' Blessed are they whose transgressions are forgiven, and whose sin is covered ' (Rom. 4 : 7, 8). 5. The absolute promise says, That God's elect shall hold out to the end ; then the conditional follows with its blessings, ' He that shall endure to the end, the same shall be saved' (Mark 13 : 13). Thus do the promises gloriously serve one another and us, and this is their harmonious agreement.

In the covenant of saving grace faith is a *means* or *instrument*, not a *condition*. Properly speaking, a condition is something rendered by one party to the other ; for example, in the covenant of works perfect obedience was the condition of life, and this was to be supplied by man. But in the covenant of saving grace faith is not supplied by the believer, but is the gift of God ; by regeneration the believer is inclined and enabled to believe. Faith, therefore, is not a condition of the covenant of saving grace, but a means of its fulfilment. In the covenant of common grace, on the contrary, faith is a condition ; for under this form of grace God demands faith from the sinner and does not give it to him. These remarks apply also to repentance, which in common grace is required of the sinner as something which he is to originate as a condition of salvation, but which in special grace is originated in him by the Holy Spirit, not as a condition to be performed on his part, but as a means or instrument employed by God to accomplish his unconditional promise to the elect, "I will put my laws into their mind, and write them in their hearts."

VOL. II., p. 52. Owen, Arminianism, ch. vii.) thus speaks of the separation of punishment from culpability : "Sin and punishment, though they are sometimes separated by God's *mercy*, pardoning the one and so not inflicting the other, yet never by his *justice*, inflicting the latter when the former is not. Sin imputed by itself alone, without an inherent guilt, was never punished in any but Christ." Augustine (Against Two Letters of the Pelagians, iv., 6) says the same : "But how can the Pelagians say 'that only death passed upon us by Adam's means ?' For if we die because he died, but he died because he sinned, they say that *the punishment passed without the guilt,* and that innocent infants are punished with an unjust penalty by deriving death without the desert of death. This the catholic faith has known of the one and only mediator between God and man, the man Christ Jesus, who condescended to undergo death, that is, the penalty of sin, without sin, for us. As he alone became the Son of man in order that we might through him become sons of God, so he alone, on our behalf, underwent punishment without ill-desert, that we through him might obtain grace without good desert. Because as to us nothing good was due, so to him nothing bad was due. Therefore, commending his love to them to whom he was about to give undeserved life, he was willing to suffer for them an undeserved death. This *special prerogative of the Mediator* the Pelagians endeavor to make void, so that this should no longer be *special in the Lord,* if Adam in such wise suffered a death due to him on account of his guilt as that infants deriving from him no guilt should suffer undeserved death."

VOL. II., p. 53. Augustine gives his view of natural union, and of the relation of Adam's first sin and his subsequent individual transgressions to his posterity in the following extracts :

"Julian then proceeds to ask : 'Why, then, are they whom God created in the devil's power? And he finds an answer to his own question apparently from a phrase of mine. 'Because of sin,' says he, 'not because of nature.' Then framing his answer in reference to mine, he says, 'But as there cannot be offspring without the sexes, so there cannot be sin without the will.' Yes, indeed, such is the truth. For even as 'by one man sin entered into the world, and death by sin, so also has death passed through to all men, for in him all have sinned.' By the evil will of that one man all sinned in him, since all were that one man from whom, therefore, they individually derived original sin" (Marriage and Concupiscence, ii., 15). The unity of Adam and his posterity here affirmed by Augustine is natural, not representative. A constituent can derive nothing from his vicarious representative by propagation; but the posterity of Adam, according to Augustine, derive original sin by this method, which infers an original unity of species or nature. "So soon as the infant, who owes his first birth to others acting under the impulse of natural instincts, has been made partaker of the second birth by others acting under the impulse of spiritual desires, he cannot thenceforward be held under the bond of that [individual] sin in another to which he does not with his own will consent. 'Both the soul of the father is mine,' saith the Lord, 'and the soul of the son is mine; the soul that sinneth, it shall die.' That bond of guilt, which was to be cancelled by the grace of the sacrament of baptism, he derived from Adam for the reason that at the time of Adam's sin he was not yet a soul having a separate life, *i.e.*, another distinct soul respecting which it could be said, 'Both the soul of the father is mine, and soul of the son is mine.' Therefore, now, when a man has a personal, separate existence, being thereby made distinct from his parents, he is not held responsible for that [individual] sin in another which is performed without his consent. In the former case he derived guilt from another, because at the time when the guilt which he derived was incurred he was *one* with the person from whom he derived it, and was *in* him. But one man does not derive guilt from another, when from the fact that each has a separate life belonging to himself the word may apply equally to both, 'The soul that sinneth, it shall die'" (Letter xcviii., 1. To Boniface, A.D. 408).

VOL. II., p. 58. Repentance for Adam's sin is conceivable and possible upon the traducian theory of its origin, but not upon the creationist theory. If the posterity were a specific unity with Adam, and as such participated in the first transgression, repentance for it by any individual who is a part of that unity is virtually repentance for *personal* sin, which presents no difficulty. But if they were not a specific unity with him, and he committed the first transgression as an individual wholly separate from them, and merely as their vicar and representative, then repentance for Adam's sin by Adam's posterity would be repentance for *vicarious* sin, which is impossible.

There is no dispute that the sense of guilt and godly sorrow may accompany the consciousness of innate and inherited depravity in the heart. David gives expression to it in the fifty-first Psalm. He confesses the evil and damnableness of his inborn disposition, and imputes to himself responsibility and guilt for this disposition. In so doing he repents of Adam's sin as *his own* sin, because as an individual he is a propagated part of that one specific nature which "sinned in Adam, and fell with him in his first transgression" (L C., 16). In being conscious of the evil inclination of his will, he is conscious of it as something in the origin of which he was concerned when his individual nature was a part of the common mass in Adam and Eve. This individual nature is a fraction of the specific nature which committed the sin of apostasy from God, which sin is imputable as a whole, and with all its guilt, to each and every one of the individual parts, because the guilt of an act of sin cannot be divided and distributed among the several or many individuals who committed it. The fact that the sense of guilt *does* accompany the sense of inward corruption proves that the individual must have been a sharer in its origin. Otherwise the fact of birth sin, and of inherent depravity would go to *excuse* sin rather than to magnify it. But in the self-consciousness of the regenerate man, it goes to aggravate it. David so represents it. He mentions the fact that he "was shapen in iniquity," and that "in sin did his mother conceive him," in proof not only of the depth of his depravity but of the greatness of its guilt. This is explicable only on the supposition that through his immediate

parents was transmitted that self-determined inclination
of will and sinful disposition of heart which had its responsible origin not in his own father and mother, but in
the first two remote parents from whom he and all other
individuals descend, and in whom they all sinned specifically.

Vol. II., p. 62. Turrettin, in Institutio XVI., iii., 15,
again marks the difference in the kind of union between
Adam and his posterity, and Christ and his people. "Nor
does it follow that if we are constituted unrighteous and
obligated to punishment by the sin propagated from Adam,
we ought, therefore, to be justified by the righteousness inherent in us by the regeneration communicated by Christ,
because the reason (ratio) of each is most diverse. And,
moreover, Paul here (Rom. 5 : 18, 19) instituted a comparison between the first and second Adam, in respect to
the fact [of union], but not in respect to the manner of the
fact" (in re, non in modo rei).

Vol. II., p. 71. Mill commits the same error as Hodge,
in supposing that realism means that the individual contains the whole specific nature instead of being merely a
severed part of it. "If *man*," he says, "was a substance
inhering in each individual man, the essence of man
(whatever that might mean) was naturally supposed to
accompany it; to inhere in John Thompson and Julius
Cæsar, and form the common essence of Thompson and
Julius Cæsar" (Logic, B. I., ch. vi.). When it is said by
the creationist himself that the individual man is a *part*
of the human species, it is not meant, of course, that he
is a part of a nonentity; of something that has only a nominal and fictitious existence. A part of a nonentity would
also be a nonentity; and therefore the denial that the
species is a reality is logically the denial that the individual is such. A fraction of a whole can have no reality
unless the whole has it. The common definition, therefore, of an individual as a portion of the species, implies

18

traducianism, that is, that the species is objectively real, not nominal.

Vol. II. p. 72. The following questions and answers may help to explain the difference between non-individualized human nature and individualized :

1. " Can the specific human nature exist outside of individual persons ? " No ; it must exist either as a whole in the first human pair, or as subdivided parts in the individuals who are constituted out of it by generation. As an entire nature it was created and existed in and with Adam and Eve. As subsequently subdivided and transmitted in parts by propagation, it exists not as at first solely in Adam and Eve, but also in their individual posterity. Either as a whole or as fractional parts it cannot be conceived of as outside of individual persons. Every transmitted part of the specific nature is transmitted in and by particular individuals. 2. " Although the original human nature has been individualized by propagation into innumerable human persons, yet does not each pair, male and female, of these persons contain the whole of the human nature ? Suppose the whole race excepting one pair should now be cut off, or annihilated, would not the human nature be entire in these two ? " No ; no pair of individuals, excepting the first pair of a species, contains the whole nature. *All* the individuals of a race can be propagated only from the *first two* individuals. Should an individual pair be taken at the middle of the series it would be impossible to derive as much population from them as from Adam and Eve. And the reason is, that they do not contain the whole specific nature, but only a portion of it. Should ten pairs of individuals be placed upon one island, and only one pair upon another, more population, the circumstances being the same in both islands, would issue from the ten pairs than from the one ; but neither from ten, nor ten thousand pairs, would so many issue as from Adam and Eve. 3. " After Cain and

Abel were conceived, the specific human nature was in four individuals instead of two ; was there any less of the specific nature in Adam and Eve than there was before any children were conceived ? " Certainly ; a part of the nature is now divided from the primitive whole, and constitutes a separate offspring. This diminishes the original mass in two ways. (*a*) By that fraction of the nature which is formed into the individuals Cain and Abel. (*b*) By that additional fraction of the nature which is taken to be transmitted and propagated by the individuals Cain and Abel. In this way there is a constant diminution of the primitive non-individualized human nature when once its division and individualization begins by conception. The specific human nature will not yield so many individuals from 1882 to the end of the world, as it will have yielded from Adam to the end of the world. Heb. 7 : 9, 10 is cited in proof of the existence of all mankind in Adam, but it is inadequate except in the way of illustration. The tribe of Levi was only a fraction of mankind. Not the entire race, but a small part of it "paid tithes in Abraham." 4. "The non-individualized human nature is a combination of both psychical and physical substance. Is the psychical factor contained in the physical, or the physical in the psychical ? " The meaning of " substance," as defined in Vol. II., pp. 11, 22, 65–67, 79, 84–87, must be remembered. Both psychical and physical substance are *invisibles*. One of them, consequently, is not contained in the other. Mental life or substance is not held in animal life or substance as in a local receptacle of it. Both are co-ordinate but *heterogeneous* principles ; one of them being invisible mind, and the other invisible matter. But as invisibles both co-existed in the primitive non-individualized nature in Adam and Eve, and continue to coexist in every transmitted fraction of it, and produce each its appropriate product ; one, the soul, the other, the body of the individual person. 5. " Why did the entire human nature act in and with the first two individuals, while the transmitted fraction of human nature does not act in and with each of the subsequent millions of individuals? " Because, in the former instance, the entire nature by being *created* in the first two individuals *constitutes a unity* with them, but in the latter instance the fractional part being only *transmitted*, not created, does not constitute a unity with the individual in whom it is. When a specific nature is immediately created in the first pair of individuals, it has had no previous existence, and makes an indispensable part of the newly created unity. But when a part of this nature is separated from the primary mass and is transmitted in and with a subsequent individual in order to be individualized by propagation, it has had a prior existence in the first pair of individuals and a unity with them, and therefore does not constitute a unity with, and a necessary part of, the subsequent individual. The individual in this latter case is complete without it, because he is not a specific individual. He does not require, like Adam and Eve, in order to the completeness of his personality the unification of the specific nature with his individuality. Hence, when the propagated individuals of the human species sin against God, the fraction of human nature in them does not sin in and with them, because it is not *one* with them. It has already sinned in the first transgression in and with Adam, with whom it was one, and is corrupt human nature, but it will not act out its own sinfulness until it is individualized by propagation, and becomes a distinct and separate person by itself. In brief, the total human nature sinned in Adam and Eve because it was a unity with them; but does not sin in their posterity because it is not a unity with them. Only of Adam and Eve can it be said, with St. Paul, "In Adam all die" (1 Cor. 15 : 22); " In whom all sinned " (Rom. 5 : 12) ; and with Augustine, " Omnes eramus unus ille homo."

Augustine asserts the objectivity of human nature as substance or entity as follows : " Man's nature was created at first innocent and without any sin; but that nature of man in which every one is born from Adam now needs the Physician because it is not sound. All good qualities, doubtless, which it still possesses in its make and constitution, namely, life, senses, and intellect, it has from the most high God, its creator. But the flaw which darkens and weakens all those natural excellences so that it has need of illumination and healing, it has not contracted from its blameless Creator, but from that original sin which it committed by free-will. Accordingly, guilty nature has its part in most righteous punishment. For if we are now newly created in Christ we were for all that 'children of wrath even as others.' The entire mass, therefore, incurs penalty; and if the deserved punishment of condemnation were rendered to all, it would without doubt be righteously rendered " (Nature and Grace, ch. 3, 5). The nature is here described as having objective and real existence. " It " was created innocent. " It " needs the healing of the Physician. " It " still possesses life, senses, intellect, will, and other constitutional qualities. "It " committed original sin by free-will. The "entire mass " incurred penalty and deserves punishment. "Because Adam forsook God of his own free-will he experienced the just judgment of God that with his whole race, which being as yet *all placed in him* had sinned with him, he should be condemned. Hence, even if none should be delivered no one could justly blame the judgment of God " (Rebuke and Grace, ch. 28).

Vol. II., p. 78. Pearson (Creed, Art. II.) thus explains the difference between eternal and temporal generation. "In human generation the son is begotten in the same nature with the father, which is performed by derivation, or decision of part of the substance of the parent; but this decision includeth imperfection, because it supposeth a substance divisible, and consequently corporeal; whereas, the essence of God is incorporeal, spiritual, and indivisible, and therefore His nature is really communicated, not by derivation or decision, but by a total and plenary communication. The divine essence being by reason of its simplicity not subject to division, and in respect to its infinity incapable of multiplication, is so communicated as not to be multiplied; insomuch that he which proceedeth by that communication hath not only the same nature, but is also the same God. The Father God, and the Word God; Abraham man, and Isaac man; but Abraham one man, Isaac another man; not so the Father one God, and the Word another, but the Father and the Word both the same God." Pearson, from his creationist position, understands by "human nature" only physical human nature, and does not distinguish with the traducianist between physical and psychical division. By division he means human division of ponderable substance, which, as he says, would imply that the substance is corporeal.

VOL. II., p. 82. The omission of the *justification* of Christ's human nature, while the sanctification of it is asserted, is seen in Owen's account of the subject in his "Communion with God the Father, Son, and Holy Ghost" (Part II., Digression i.). "Christ," he says, "was never federally in Adam, and so not liable to the imputation of Adam's first sin. It is true that sin was imputed to him when he was made sin; thereby he took away the sin of the world. But it was imputed to him in the covenant of the mediator, through his voluntary susception; and not in the covenant of Adam by a legal imputation. Had it been reckoned to him as a descendant from Adam, he had not been a fit high-priest to have offered sacrifices for us, as not being 'separate from sinners' (Heb. 7 : 25). Christ was in Adam in a natural sense from his first creation, in respect of the purpose of God (Luke 3 : 23, 38), yet he was not in him in a law sense until after the fall; so that

as to his own person he had no more to do with the first
sin of Adam than with any personal sin of one whose punishment he voluntarily took upon him. As for the pollution of our nature, it was prevented in him from the instant of conception (Luke 1 : 35). He was 'made of a
woman,' but that portion whereof he was made was sanctified by the Holy Ghost, so that what was born thereof
should be a holy thing." The objections to this view of
the subject, which is common among Calvinistic creation-
ists, are the following : 1. It separates the guilt of sin
from the pollution, and justification from sanctification,
both of which from their nature are inseparable. If, as
Owen concedes, that "portion" of human nature which
was derived from the Virgin was "sanctified by the Holy
Ghost" from the pollution of sin, it necessarily had also
the guilt of sin which required to be expiated in order to
the perfect preparation of the nature for union with the
Logos. Neither Scripture nor reason know of a sin that
is without guilt. Wherever sanctification is required, justification is also. 2. It destroys the unity between that
portion of human nature which the Logos assumed into
union with that remainder which was not so assumed ; in
other words, between Christ's humanity and that of his
people whom he redeemed. The guilt of the first sin was
upon the latter, but not upon the former, according to this
view. But the Scripture describes Christ's human nature,
in its original condition and before it was miraculously prepared for the union with the Logos, as being like that of
fallen man in every respect. It was created holy in Adam,
put upon probation in him, was tempted in him, fell in
him, and came under guilt and condemnation in him, because
it was the "seed of Adam," the "seed of the woman," and
"sinful flesh" in the same way as was the human nature of
David, Abraham, and Adam, whose son Christ is said to
be (Luke 3 : 31, 34, 38). But if, as Owen says, Christ was
in Adam "in a natural sense," but not "in a law sense,"

this could not have been the case, because it is only the law that condemns and charges guilt. St. Paul (Gal. 4 : 4) expressly asserts not only that Christ was "made of a woman," but was "made under the law, to redeem them that were under the law." The implication is that he was "under the law" in the same sense that those whom he redeemed were, and sustained the same relation to it in all respects. 3. This view makes the redemption of the "portion" of human nature which the Logos assumed to be different from the redemption of his people. But Scripture describes it as the same. Christ's humanity was the "first-fruits" of redemption: "Christ the first-fruits, afterward they that are Christ's at his coming" (1 Cor. 15 : 23). Christ's people are redeemed from both the guilt and pollution of Adam's sin; but, according to the view we are criticising, Christ's humanity was redeemed only from the pollution of it.

Instead, therefore, of making Christ's human nature in its original state in the Virgin, as derived from Adam and previous to its miraculous preparation in her for the hypostatical union, to be different from the fallen human nature of Adam and his posterity generally by not being under condemnation but only polluted, and as requiring sanctification, but not justification, it agrees better with Scripture to make it precisely the same in every respect, and then to have it completely justified from guilt and sanctified from pollution. Christ's human nature, before the incarnation, was thus a fractional part of the common fallen human nature, having the same common characteristics with it. As it was in the Virgin mother, it was "sinful flesh" (Rom. 8 : 3). But when it was no longer in the Virgin mother, but was in the God-man, having been made by the miraculous conception the human nature of the Incarnate Word, it was no longer "sinful flesh," but that "holy thing" which Luke (1 : 35) speaks of, and which is described in Heb. 7 : 26 as "holy, harmless, undefiled, and separate from sinners." The difference between Christ's human nature as it was originally in the Virgin mother, and as it subsequently was in him, is marked by St. Paul in Rom. 8 : 3 : "God sent his own Son in the likeness of sinful flesh, and for sin [as an offering for sin, R. V.] condemned sin in the flesh." He does not say that Christ "condemned sin in the *sinful* flesh." The epithet "sinful" in the first clause describes the human nature prior to its assumption ; and the omission of the epithet in the second clause describes it subsequently to this. "Sinful flesh" could not be an offering for sin.

This method of explanation makes the human nature of Christ, after its preparation for assumption by the Logos, to be as *guiltless of Adam's sin* as Owen's explanation does. As the justification of an individual sinner sets him as completely free from guilt and condemnation as if he had never been a sinner at all, so the justification of that "portion" of fallen human nature which the Logos assumed made it as free from the guilt and condemnation of Adam's sin as if it had not fallen and come under condemnation in Adam. And it avoids the serious defect in Owen's explanation, of separating the pollution from the guilt of Adam's sin, and of making the human nature of Christ as it existed in the Virgin mother to be different from that of Adam and his posterity generally, thereby conflicting with Scripture, which represents Christ as "not taking the nature of angels, but the seed of Abraham," and as being "made like unto his brethren in all things " (Heb. 2 : 16, 17).

In Institutio XIII., v. 19, Turrettin gives a similar explanation of the human nature of Christ. "Whatever is born of the flesh is flesh (John 3 : 6), that is, if born according to the order of nature, and in a natural manner, by ordinary generation ; but not if born beyond such order and in a supernatural manner, as was the case with Christ. Hence, although Christ derived origin from sinful Adam, he did not nevertheless derive sin from him, either imputed

or inherent, because he did not descend from him by the
force of the general promise 'Increase and multiply,' but
by virtue of the special promise concerning 'the seed of
the woman.' And although he was in Adam in respect to
nature, he was not in respect to *person*, and moral state or
federal relationship, by which it happens that all the posterity of Adam, Christ excepted, participate in his sin."
The objection to this explanation is this : Christ's "nature" cannot be separated in this manner from his "person," so that what is predicable of the former is not of the
latter ; so that the "nature" might have been in Adam,
but not the "person." The "person" of an individual
man is constituted out of the specific "nature" of man, and
is a fractional part of it, consequently, if the whole was in
Adam the part was also ; and the very same properties
and qualities belong to both. If the "nature" is rational,
immortal, and voluntary, the "person" will be also. If
the "nature" is holy or sinful, the "person" will be so
likewise. Both the intrinsic and the acquired properties
will be alike. The only difference between the "nature"
and the "person" is in the *form*, not in the substance with
its properties and qualities. The "person" of Christ, being a part of the common human nature that was created in
Adam, and which sinned with him in the first transgression,
must have had all the properties and qualities of fallen
human nature. Both the guilt and the pollution of the
first sin attached to it. And therefore, in order to be prepared and fit for union with the Divine nature of the
second trinitarian Person, both the guilt and the pollution
must be completely and perfectly removed.

If the Logos *redeemed* the human nature which he assumed, and in order to assume it, it is evident that the
nature was justified as well as sanctified. Besides the
citations on p. 82 in proof that this was the understanding
of Scripture by the Church, the following from the Formula
Concordiæ (Art. i.) is explicit: "This same human nature

of ours (to wit, his own work, or creation) Christ has redeemed, the same (his own work) he sanctifies, the same he raises from the dead, and with great glory adorns it (to wit, his own work)." See Dogmatic Theology, Vol. II., 297.

Vol. II., p. 83. Owen (Person of Christ. Ed. Russell, XII., 247–249) teaches the divisibility of the common specific nature of man in his explication of the human nature of Christ. "The Scripture abounds in the declaration of the necessity that the satisfaction for sin be made in the nature itself that sinned and is to be saved. 'Christ took not on him the nature of angels. Inasmuch as the children were partakers of flesh and blood, he also himself likewise took part of the same.' The same nature that sinned must work out the reparation and recovery from sin. That *part* of human nature wherein or whereby this work was to be effected, as unto the essence or substance of it, was to be derived from the common root or stock of the same nature in our first parents. It would not suffice hereunto that God should create a man out of the dust of the earth, or out of nothing, of the same nature in general with ourselves. For there would be no cognation or alliance between him and us, so that we should be in any way concerned in what he did and suffered. For this alliance depends solely hereon, 'that God hath of one blood made all nations of men' (Acts 17: 26). Hence it is that the genealogy of Christ is given us in the Gospel not only from Abraham, to declare the faithfulness of God in the promise that he should be of his seed, but from Adam also, to manifest his relation unto the common stock of our nature, and unto all mankind therein."

"This [part of] human nature, wherein the work of our recovery and salvation is to be wrought out, was not to be so derived from the original stock of our kind or race as to bring along with it the same taint of sin, and the same liableness unto guilt upon its own account, as accompany every other individual person in the world. For if this [part of human] nature in him were so defiled as the [part of human] nature is in us before our renovation, it could make no satisfaction for the sin of others."

" To take a little further view hereof, we must consider on what grounds spiritual defilement and guilt do adhere unto our nature, as they are in all our individual persons. And the first of these is, that our entire [specific] nature, as unto our participation of it, was in Adam, as our head and representative. Hence his sin became the sin of us all, and is justly imputed unto us, and charged on us. ' In him we all sinned;' all did so who were in him as their common representative when he sinned. Hereby we became the natural 'children of wrath,' or liable unto the wrath of God, for the common sin of our nature in the natural and legal head or spring of it. And the second ground is, that we derive our [individual part of human] nature from Adam by the way of natural generation. By that means alone is the nature of our first parents as defiled communicated unto us. For by this means do we come to appertain unto the stock as it was degenerate and corrupt. Wherefore that part of our nature [in the person of Christ] wherein and whereby this great work of salvation was to be wrought, must, as unto its essence and substance, be derived from our first parents, yet so as never to have been in Adam as a common representative, nor be derived from him by natural generation. This, as we know, was done in the person of Christ; for his human nature was never in Adam as his representative, nor was he comprised in the [legal] covenant whereon Adam stood. For Christ derived it [his human nature] legally only from and after the first promise, when Adam ceased to be a public person. Nor did it proceed from him [Adam] by natural generation, the only means of the derivation of its depravation and pollution. For it was a ' holy thing' created in the womb of the Virgin by the power of the Most High." [Owen here uses the term " created " not in its strict sense of creation ex nihilo, but of quickening, making alive. He refers to the agency of the Holy Ghost in the conception of the "seed of the woman." He expressly says that "it would not suffice, in the incarnation, that God should create a man out of nothing, for there would be no alliance between the God-man and ourselves."]

In this statement Owen combines traducianism and creationism, natural and representative union, and introduces the following difficulties: 1. This "part" of human nature which the Logos assumed into union with himself was surely in Adam along with all the other parts of the common nature when "all sinned." How could it have been in him and not have been "represented" by him? 2. How could it have been a part of the common human nature and "not be comprised in the legal covenant" which God made with this human nature as it was in Adam? 3. In exempting that "part" of human nature assumed into union by the Logos, as it existed in *Adam* and the *Virgin*, and *prior* to its preparation for this union by the miraculous conception of the Holy Ghost, from "representation" by Adam and participation in the legal covenant, Owen is in conflict with what he says respecting the necessity that Christ's human nature be like that of the race whom he came to save. His individual human nature, being a part of the specific human nature, was "sinful flesh" (Rom. 8: 3), because it "sinned in Adam, and fell with him in the first transgression." But in order to this sining and fall it must not only have been "made of a woman," but "made under the law, to redeem them that were under the law" (Gal. 4: 4), and have been "represented" by Adam, if representation and not natural union be the truth. And because this portion of human nature was in the same fallen and sinful condition with the remainder, it could not be assumed into union as it was, but the miraculous conception by the Holy Ghost was necessary to *fit* it for its union with the second Person of the

Trinity. As Owen himself says (Meditations on the Glory of Christ, Preface), "In this condition, lost, poor, base, yea, cursed, the Lord Christ, the Son of God, found our nature. And hereon, in infinite condescension and compassion, *sanctifying a portion of it* unto himself, he took it to be his own in a holy, ineffable subsistence, in his own Person." In the following passage Owen teaches that the relation of Christ's individual human nature to the specific human nature is like that of any other individual human nature to the specific nature. "The eternal person of the Son of God, or the divine nature in the person of the Son, did, by an ineffable act of his Divine power and love, assume our nature into an individual subsistence in or with himself; that is, to be his own nature, even as the Divine nature is his. This is the infallible foundation of faith, even to them who can comprehend very little of these divine mysteries. They can and do believe that the Son of God did take our nature to be his own; so that whatever was done therein was done by him as it is with every other man. Every man hath human nature appropriated unto himself by an individual subsistence, whereby he becomes to be that man which he is, and not another; or that nature which is common unto all becomes in him [by division and separation of a part] to be peculiarly his own, as if there were none partaker of it but himself. Adam, in his first creation, when all human nature was in him alone, was no more [merely] that individual man which he was, than every man is now the man that he is [merely] by his individual subsistence. [That is to say: Adam was an individual, and also specific as including the whole nature. Each of his posterity is also an individual, and also specific, as partaking of, but not including, the whole nature.] *So the Lord Christ* taking [a part of] that nature which is common unto all into a peculiar subsistence in his own person, it becometh his, and he the man Christ Jesus. This was the [human] mind that was in him. By reason of this assumption of our nature, with his doing and suffering therein, whereby he was found in fashion as a man, the glory of his divine person was veiled, and he made himself of no reputation. It is also to be observed that in the assumption of our nature to be his own nature he did not change it into a thing divine, but preserved it entire in all its essential properties and actings. Hence it really did and suffered, was tried, tempted, and forsaken, as the same nature in any other man might do and be. That nature as it was peculiarly his, and therefore he or his person therein, was exposed unto all the temporary evils which the same nature is subject unto in any other person" (The Glory of Christ. Works, XII., 419).

VOL. II., p. 91. Is the moral agency of the human race in Adam and Eve possible and conceivable? Can a specific human nature, which is subsequently to be transformed by propagation into millions of individuals, act voluntarily and responsibly "in and with" (L C., 22) the first two individuals in whom it was created? Can human nature self-determine to sin, first as a unity and a whole, and then afterward continue this self-determination in every one of the million of parts into which it is subdivided by propagation into separate individuals? It can if the constituent properties are the same in both instances. If the nature as a whole is identical in kind, that is, has the same essential properties of spirituality, rationality, voluntariness, and immortality with its individual parts, what the latter can do the former can. In this case if the individual man can sin the specific man can. There is no dispute that the fractional part of human nature which makes the substance of an individual person of the human species is a spiritual, rational, voluntary, and immortal substance, and is capable of rational and voluntary agency by reason of these properties ; there ought, therefore, to be no denial that the entire human nature as a unity, and prior to its individualization by propagation, is capable of the same kind of agency, because it has the very same qualities. The power of any substance or nature depends upon the kind of properties belonging to it.

Vol. II., p. 96. The statement in the text that "the Arminians reject the doctrine of concreated holiness" needs qualification. Some of the elder Arminians do not. Wesley (Original Sin) opposes Taylor of Norwich, who asserted that "Adam could not be originally created in righteousness and true holiness, because habits of holiness cannot be created without our knowledge, concurrence, or consent." He reasons as follows: "Holiness is love. Cannot God shed abroad this love in any soul without its concurrence? God could create men or angels endued from the very first moment of their existence with whatsoever degree of love he pleased. Your [Taylor's] capital mistake is in defining righteousness as 'the right use and application of our powers.' No; it is the right *state* of our powers. It is the right *disposition* of our soul, the right *temper* of our mind. Take this with you, and you will no more dream that 'God could not create man in righteousness and true holiness.'" Watson (Institutes, Pt. ii., ch. 18) defends Wesley's view, and quotes approvingly Edwards's answer to Taylor on this same point in his treatise on Original Sin. In his Institutes (Vol. II., 77), Watson asserts that "Limborch and some of the later divines of the Arminian school materially departed from the tenets of their master in denying man's natural tendencies to be sinful until they are complied with and approved by the will [in executive volitions]; and affirms a universal pravity of will [inclination] previous to the actual choice" [of means to gratify it].

Vol. II., p. 97. Stillingfleet (Origines I., i., ii.) thus describes the knowledge with which man was created: "If we consider that contemplation of the soul which fixes itself on that infinite Being who was the cause of it, and is properly Θεωρία, it will be found necessary for the soul to be created in a clear and distinct knowledge of him, because of man's immediate obligation to obedience unto him; which must necessarily suppose the knowledge of him whose will must be the rule. For if man were not fully convinced, in the first moment after his creation, of the being of him whom he was to obey, his first work and duty would not have been actual obedience, but a search whether there was any supreme, infinite, and eternal Being or not; and whereon his duty to him was founded, and what might be sufficient declaration of his will and laws, according to which he must regulate his obedience. For man, as he first came from God's hands, was the reflection of God himself on a dark cloud. His knowledge then was more intellectual than discursive, not so much employing his faculties in the operose deductions of reason, but immediately employing them about him who was the fountain of his being and the centre of his happiness. There was not then so vast a difference between the angelical and the human life; the angels and men both fed on the same dainties; all the difference was, they were in the ὑπερῷον, the upper room in heaven, and man in the summer parlor in paradise."

These descriptions of the superior knowledge of man as created, like those of his sinless perfection, which the elder theologians, together with the reformed creeds, often gave, and which are regarded as extravagant by many, apply only to the *specific nature* as it existed in Adam before the fall, not to Adam and Eve after the fall, or to any of the individuals that were propagated out of it. Neither Cain, nor Abel, nor Seth, nor Enoch, nor fallen Adam and Eve possessed the knowledge and holiness belonging to the original nature. No such knowledge and no such sinlessness have characterized any of the generations of mankind, and constitute no part of secular human history. This latter exhibits only the consequences of the apostasy of the specific nature, namely, willing igno-

19

rance of God and alienation from him, the substitution of polytheism and idolatry for monotheism, and all the dreadful development of human depravity in individual and national life. Had the original unity, namely, Adam and his posterity remained as created, this description of man as endowed with an intelligence and character like that of the angels would have been applicable to all the individual persons as well as to the common nature. For this reason the Scripture data respecting the creation of mankind in and with the first pair, and their fall in Eden from their created and ideal position, are of the utmost importance in constructing the theodicy of sin. If they are overlooked or denied it is impossible to justify the penalty of eternal death upon the posterity of Adam, or to make it evident that redemption from the guilt and pollution of original sin by the incarnation and sufferings of incarnate God is real unobliged mercy. Man must have had original holiness and perfection in order to be responsible for subsequent sinfulness and imperfection; and he had these in Adam or not at all.

Vol. II., p. 99. Will in unfallen Adam is thus described by Augustine : " The first man had not that grace by which he should never will to be evil ; but assuredly he had that in which if he willed to abide he would never be evil, and without which also he could not by free-will be good, but which nevertheless by free-will he could forsake. God, therefore, did not will him to be without His grace, which He left in his free-will. Because *free-will is sufficient for evil* [without aid], but is *too little for good* unless it is *aided* by omnipotent good. And if that man had not forsaken that assistance of his free-will, he would always have been good ; but he forsook it, and then was forsaken [of that assistance]. Because such was the nature of the aid that he could forsake it when he would, and that he could continue in it if he would ; but not such that it could be brought about that he [infallibly] would continue. The first is the grace which was given to the first Adam ; but more powerful than this is that in the second Adam. For the first grace is that whereby it is effected that a man may have righteousness if he will ; the second can do more than this, since by it it is effected that he [infallibly] will, and will will so intensely and love with such ardor, that by the will of the Spirit he overcomes the will of the flesh that lusteth in opposition to it " (Rebuke and Grace, ch. 31). In the unfallen Adam there was no "will of the flesh that lusteth in opposition to the Spirit." Had the unfallen will persisted in the perfect holiness in which it was created, that struggle with indwelling sin which is described in Gal. 5 : 16–24, and Rom. 7 : 14–8 : 26, would not have been experienced. The indefectibility that would have resulted would have been only the intensification of Adam's original righteousness to that point where it becomes the non posse peccare, without any of that fight with inward lust which occurs when the regenerate will is enabled to persevere and reach indefectibility after a severe conflict with remaining corruption.

It should be noticed that Augustine in this extract, as often elsewhere, employs the term "grace" to denote that which is given to man by God in creation, in distinction from that which is bestowed in redemption. Unfallen man was not a sinner, and did not need "grace" in the latter sense. But Augustine regards all the endowments of unfallen Adam (his faculties of reason and will, his enlightened understanding and holy heart and inclination) as a gracious bestowment, because the Creator is under no obligation of indebtedness to the creature whom he originates from nonentity. It was a sovereign and unobliged act on the part of God to make man "after his own image in righteousness and true holiness." The creature cannot bring the Creator under an original obligation to him, because this would require him to do a service that he did not owe the Creator, and which he rendered to Him from an independent position—neither of which things characterize the action of a creature. See Luke 17 : 7–10 ; Job 22 : 3 ; 35 : 7 ; Ps. 16 : 2, 3 ; Rom. 11 : 35 ; 1 Cor. 4 : 7 ; 9 : 16, 17.

Vol. II., p. 104. Owen (Holy Spirit, III., iii.) teaches that the freedom of the will consists in its self-motion only, and not in the power to begin another motion contrary to the existing self-motion. "It is will," he says, " and not power [to the contrary] that gives rectitude or obliquity to moral actions." That is to say, it is simple spontaneity or self-determination, and not an ability to do contrary to the existing self-determination that constitutes voluntariness and imparts responsibility to the action of the will. Owen in this place is combating the Pelagian doctrine of freedom.

Vol. II., 107. The possibility of the fall of a holy finite will is explicable by the *finiteness* of its power. If self-motion to good is not omnipotent, but only a certain degree of finite energy, it is plain that it may lapse from holy to sinful self-motion. But when self-motion is almighty, as in the case of God, a change of motion is not conceivable. Omnipotent energy is immutable energy. The infinite is the unchangeable in every particular, because it is the omnipotent ; hence God's infinite self-determination to good is eternal and unalterable, but man's and angel's finite self-determination to good is mutable.

Vol. II., p. 108. Scripture defines freedom as choosing the one particular thing that is *commanded* by God and *refusing* the contrary. "I have set before you life and death : therefore choose life" (Deut. 30 : 19). "Before the child shall know to choose the good and refuse the evil" (Isa. 7 : 16). The Pelagian psychology defines freedom as choosing either the one particular thing commanded by God, or its contrary. In this instance the contrary is not refused but may be chosen ; in which latter case the thing commanded by God is refused. If the will chooses the spiritual good which is commanded, and refuses the contrary spiritual evil, it virtually chooses all varieties of spiritual good, and refuses all varieties of spiritual evil. But if it chooses either spiritual good or spiritual evil, it refuses no variety of the latter. The Scripture's definition of freedom, which is that of Augustine and Calvin, connects freedom with *moral obligation*, in making it to be the spontaneous inclining of the will to what the Divine command *enjoins*, and the spontaneous aversion of the will to what it *forbids*. The Pelagian definition wholly disconnects freedom from moral obligation by making it to be the indifference of the will to both the Divine command and its contrary.

The command of God is to choose *and* refuse, not to choose *or* refuse. The former allows no alternative; the latter does. The former requires only one object or ultimate end, because the choice of good is the rejection of evil; the latter requires two objects, because the choice of good still permits the choice of evil. The former excludes indifference; the latter supposes it. He who chooses good and refuses evil is positively inclined and has moral character. He who chooses either good or evil has no positive inclination to either, and no moral character.

Furthermore, if simultaneous refusal of evil does not accompany the choice of good, the will *dallies* with evil; and dalliance with evil is evil desire itself. Eve's non-resistance and non-rejection of Satan's suggestion to eat of the tree of knowledge implied a wish, more or less strong, for the forbidden knowledge. It is a maxim of the world that "the woman who deliberates is lost." The reason is, that in this deliberation and delay there is toying and playing with the temptation, and no instantaneous rejection of what is proposed. In a yet higher sense the woman in Eden who deliberated respecting Satan's proposition lost herself and her race. That pause and parleying of her mind, instead of resistance and rejection, when temptation was presented, in order to consider and reason about it with Satan, was fatal.

This important feature in the fall of the will, and the origin of sin, did not escape the wonderful insight of John Bunyan. In his Holy War he represents the town of Mansoul first as listening to the falsehoods of Diabolus, and while listening as losing by a shot from the ambush " Mr. *Resistance*, otherwise called Captain Resistance. And a great man in Mansoul this Captain Resistance was ; and a man that the giant Diabolus and his band more feared than they feared the whole town of Mansoul besides." In bringing this about, Diabolus is assisted by "one *Ill-pause*, who was his orator in all difficult matters. When this Ill-pause was making of his speech [in support of the suggestions of Diabolus] to the townsmen, my Lord Innocency, whether by a shot from the camp of the giant Diabolus, or from a sinking qualm that suddenly took him, or rather by the stinking breath of that treacherous villain old Ill-pause (for so I am most apt to think), sank down in the place where he stood, nor could he be brought to life again. Thus these two brave men died ; brave men I call them, for they were the beauty and glory of Mansoul so long as they lived therein ; nor did there now remain any more a noble spirit in Mansoul, they all fell down, and yielded obedience to Diabolus, and became his slaves and vassals as you shall hear. And first they did as Ill-pause had taught them ; they looked, they considered, they were taken with the forbidden fruit, they took thereof and did eat ; and having eaten they became immediately drunken therewith ; so they opened the gate, both Ear-gate and Eye-gate, and let in Diabolus with all his bands." This allegory translated into a philosophy of the human will means that instantaneous resistance and refusal of the contrary must accompany the choice of good, and that the absence of this refusal and resistance, which is implied in the Pelagian indifference and liberty to choose *either* good or evil, is a false definition of human freedom.

The regenerate and sanctified soul offers immediate resistance and refusal to temptation instead of dalliance. Bunyan indicates this in saying that in the fighting by which the town of Mansoul was recaptured by Emmanuel, " Mr. Ill-pause received a grievous wound in the head; some say that his brain-pan was cracked; this I have taken notice of, that he was never after this able to do that mischief to Mansoul as he had done in times past."

The difference between the Augustinian freedom of positive self-determination and the Pelagian freedom of negative indetermination or non-determination, is the same as that between inclination and option. The will may be freely inclined by its self-motion, and yet be unable to reverse its self-motion. It has no option in this case. That is to say, it cannot incline or disincline by a resolution or volition, which is implied in optional power. It is not optional with a miser to make himself generously inclined, and yet his avaricious inclination is voluntary and uncompelled. He is willing in his avarice because he is self-moved in it. It is not optional with a sinner to convert his supreme love of self into supreme love of God, and yet his selfish love is the self-activity of his will. It is necessary in order to responsibility for sin that the will incline freely to sin, and continue so to incline; but not necessary in order to responsibility for sin that it have an optional ability to overcome sin after its voluntary origination. In having power to apostatize, holy Adam had a kind of "power to the contrary," but it differed greatly from the Pelagian " power to the contrary:" 1. In that it was not exerted from a state of indifference, but of positive holiness. 2. In that there was not equal facility to choose good or evil. It was easier for Adam to remain holy than to begin sin. He had an inclination to good and was happy in it.

The Pelagian idea of the will makes its action consist wholly in volitions. The will really has no inclination, because it is constantly *indifferent*. It is indetermined, not self-determined upon this supposition. The volitions occur without any ground or source for them in a permanent disposition or character of the will. But to omit that central action of the will which consists in a steady self-motion to an ultimate end, and resolve all its agency into a series of superficial volitions or choices over which the man has the same optional control that he has over the movement of his muscles, and which have no basis in an inclination or disposition of the faculty, is to omit the most important part of the contents of the will and the most essential element in voluntariness. Employing Kant's phraseology, it is denying will as noumenon, or the real thing itself, and affirming only will as phenomenon, or as it appears to the senses in a series. Or using the category of cause and effect, it is to recognize the effect and overlook the cause. The inclination of the will is the cause of all the volitions exercised by it, and to postulate these latter without the former, is to postulate effects without a cause, a tree without a root.

VOL. II., p. 113. That the holy self-movement of the human will is both the Creator's product and the creature's activity is taught in 1 Chron. 29 : 14. " Who am I, and what is my people, that we should be able to offer so willingly after this sort? for all things come of thee and of thine own have we given thee." The benevolent disposition of the will is a " willing " disposition. It is the spontaneity of the man ; his own personal activity. But that the man is " able " thus to energize is due to the Divine impulse and actuation. God " works in him to will " in this manner. The holy will is compared by our Lord to a vine branch which bears fruit " of itself " (ἀφ᾽ ἑαυτοῦ) ; but in order to do so it must "abide in the vine." The holy will is spontaneous and self-moving, but in order to this the Holy Spirit must be under and behind the self-motion. This important truth, which precludes human egotism and pride, is abundantly taught in Revelation, and from thence has passed into all orthodox theology. Paul like David teaches it. "Work out your own salvation with fear and trembling; for it is God which worketh in you both to will and to do of his good pleasure" (Phil. 2:12, 13). "Not that we are sufficient of ourselves to think anything [holy] as of ourselves; but our sufficiency is of God; who hath made us able ministers of the new testament" (2 Cor. 3:5, 6). "I labored more abundantly than they all; yet not I but the grace of God which was with me" (1 Cor. 15:10). The Son of God teaches it more repeatedly than any of his prophets and apostles. "All that the Father giveth to me shall come to me; and him that cometh to me I will in no wise cast out" (John 6:37). "No man can come to me except the Father which hath sent me draw him" (John 6:44). "No man can come unto me except it were given unto him of my Father" (John 6:65). "I give unto my sheep eternal life. My Father, which gave them me, is greater than all" (John 10:28, 29). "Thou hast given thy Son power over all flesh, that he should give eternal life to as many as thou hast given him" (John 17:2). "I have manifested thy name unto the men which thou gavest me out of the world" (John 17:6). "I pray not for the world, but for them which thou hast given me" (John 17:9). "Holy Father, keep through thine own name those whom thou hast given me" (John 17:11). "Those that thou gavest me I have kept" (John 17:12). "Father, I will that they whom thou hast given me be with me where I am" (John 17:24).

Milton (Par. Lost, iii., 173–181) states the doctrine.

> "Man shall not quite be lost, but saved who will;
> Yet not of will in him, but grace in me,
> Freely vouchsafed; once more I will renew

His lapsed powers, though forfeit and enthralled
By sin to foul exorbitant desires ;
Upheld by me, yet once more he shall stand
On even ground against his mortal foe ;
By me upheld, that he may know how frail
His fallen condition is, and to me owe
All his deliverance, and to none but me."

Vol. II., p. 114. The Pelagian inference that because
the human will can originate sin by solitary self-determination it can originate holiness in the same way, is contained in the common remark that " the sinner is responsible for accepting or rejecting the invitations of the
gospel." He is responsible only for rejecting, not for
accepting them, because the latter act is right and the
former wrong. Responsibility is an idea that is properly
associated only with *sin* and *guilt*. To hold a man responsible implies that he has committed an offence of
some kind. We never say that a person is responsible for
an innocent and virtuous action. Whenever a man's responsibility is inquired into, it is with reference to some
fault with which he is charged. If the sinner voluntarily
rejects the offered mercy of God, he is culpable for so doing, and is therefore amenable to the charge of culpability
and responsible before the divine tribunal because of it.
But if under the operation of the Holy Spirit he accepts
the divine offer of mercy, he is not culpable for so doing
any more than he is meritorious for it, nor is he liable or
responsible to a criminal charge. In the former instance,
in which his voluntary action is sinful, the action is his
alone; in the latter instance, in which his voluntary
action is holy, it is the consequence of God's "working in
him to will." Man is responsible for sin because he is
both the author and the actor of it; but he is not responsible for holiness, because he is only the actor and not
the author. In the above-mentioned statement the term
" free " instead of " responsible " is the proper one. " The

sinner is free in accepting or rejecting the invitations of the gospel." If he accepts them, he does so freely under the actuation of the Holy Spirit. If he rejects them, he does so freely without this actuation and solely by his own self-determination.

Scripture marks the difference between holiness as having God for its author, and sin as having the creature alone for its author, by denominating sin "works of the flesh," and holiness "fruits of the Spirit" (Gal. 5 : 19, 22). Augustine (Grace and Free-Will, ch. 21) says of the use of "wages" for the one, and "gift" for the other : "The apostle says that 'the gift of God is eternal life through Jesus Christ our Lord,' having just said that 'the wages of sin is death.' Deservedly did he call it 'wages,' because everlasting death is awarded as its proper due to diabolical service. Now when it was in his power to say, and rightly to say, 'But the wages [recompense] of righteousness is eternal life,' he yet preferred to say, 'The gift of God is eternal life,' in order that we may hence understand that God does not for any merits of our own, but from his own divine compassion prolong our existence to everlasting life. It is not, however, to be supposed that because he said, 'It is God that worketh in you both to will and to do of his good pleasure,' that free-will is taken away. If this had been his meaning, he would not have said just before, 'Work out your own salvation with fear and trembling.' For when the command is given to 'work,' their free-will is addressed; and when it is added, 'with fear and trembling,' they are warned against boasting of their good deeds as if they were the original authors of them." Man is self-moving and self-determined in *sin* only by reason of God's preserving and upholding agency, not by reason of His inworking and actuating energy; but he is self-moving and self-determined in *holiness* by reason both of God's preserving and actuating power. In the first instance, nothing is requisite but to keep the will in being; the inward nisus and motion to evil being the agency solely of the will itself. In the last instance it is not sufficient merely to sustain the will; it must also be influenced and incited to motion, yet spiritually, not physically. Though actuated by the Holy Spirit, the holy will is nevertheless a self-moving and uncompelled faculty. Holy inclination is the will's right self-motion because of the Divine actuation, or "God's working in the will to will." Sinful inclination is the will's wrong self-motion without Divine actuation. But the motion in both instances is that of mind, not of matter; spiritual, not mechanical; free, not forced motion.

The other view of the will and freedom, namely, that both in holiness and sin the will is merely sustained in being, and by an act of its own alternative choice originates either by its solitary efficiency, is not supported by self-consciousness, which always reports bondage to evil and inability to good, nor by Scripture.

This important difference is sometimes overlooked, and sin seems to be placed in the same relation with holiness to God. The following from Zanchius (Predestination, Introduction, p. 29, Toplady's Trans.) is an instance: "We are hereby taught not only humility before God, but likewise dependence on him. For if we are thoroughly persuaded that of ourselves, and in our own strength, we cannot do good *or evil;* but that being originally created by God, we are incessantly supported, moved, influenced, and directed by him, *this way* or *that*, as he pleases; the natural inference from hence will be, that with simple faith we cast ourselves entirely as on the bosom of his providence." This phraseology is not sufficiently guarded; for taken by itself it teaches that the human will needs Divine help in order to sin, in the same way that it needs it in order to obedience; the truth being, that in the former instance it needs only to be left to itself, while in the latter it requires the positive inworking of the Holy Spirit. But that Zanchius only means, here, that the human will, when sinning, requires to be *upheld* in being, and to have its power of free-will *maintained* by God, is evinced by his statements elsewhere in this treatise: "God as the primary and efficacious cause of all things, is not only the author of those activities done by his elect as *actions*, but also as they are *good* actions; whereas, on the other hand, though he may be said to be the author of all the actions done by the wicked, yet he is not the author of them in a moral sense, as they are *sinful*, but as they are mere *actions* abstractedly from all consideration of the goodness or badness of them" (Introduction, p. 25). "God does not mock his creatures; for if men do not believe his word, nor observe his precepts, the fault is not in him, but in themselves; their unbelief and disobedience are not owing to any ill *infused* into them by God, but to the vitiosity of their depraved nature and the perverseness of their own wills" (Introduction, p. 5). "Augustine, Luther, Bucer, the Scholastic divines, and other learned writers, are not to be blamed for asserting that 'God may in some sense be said to will the existence and commission of sin.' For were this contrary to his determining will of *permission*, either he would not be omnipotent, or sin could have no place in the world; but he is omnipotent, and sin has place in the world, which it could not have, if God had willed otherwise. No one can deny that God *permits* sin; but he neither permits it ignorantly nor unwillingly; therefore knowingly and willingly. Luther maintains this, and Bucer and Augustine. Yet God's voluntary permission of sin lays no man under any forcible or compulsive necessity of committing it; consequently God can by no means be termed the author of sin; to which he is not in the proper sense of the word accessory, but only remotely or negatively so, inasmuch as he could, if he pleased, absolutely prevent it" (Introduction, p. 13). "Since all things are subject to the Divine control, God not only works efficiently in his elect in order that they may will and do that which is pleasing in his sight, but does likewise frequently and powerfully *suffer* the wicked to fill up the measure of their iniquities by committing fresh sins " (Introduction, p. 22). These extracts show that Zanchius means by his statement that " we cannot do good or evil in our own strength," that we are not self-existent and self-sustaining beings.

Vol. II., p. 121. Edwards (Religious Affections, Works, III., 4, 5) defines the moral desires as being the same thing as voluntary inclination, in much the same terms with Augustine. " What are commonly called affections are not essentially different from the will and inclination. In every act of the will whatsoever, the soul either likes or dislikes, is either inclined or disinclined to what is in view. These are not essentially different from those affections of love and hatred ; that liking or inclination of the soul to a thing, if it be in a high degree, and be vigorous and lively, is the very same thing with the affection of love ; and that disliking and disinclining, if in a greater degree, is the very same thing with hatred. As all the exercises of the inclination and will are either in approving and liking, or disapproving and rejecting, so the affections are of two sorts ; they are those by which the soul is carried out to what is in view, cleaving to it, or seeking it; or those by which it is averse from it, and opposes it. Of the former sort are love, desire, hope, joy, gratitude, complacence. Of the latter kind are hatred, fear, anger, grief, and such like."

There are two criticisms to be made upon Edwards's definition : 1. " Approbation " and " disapprobation " of an object are the action of the *conscience* not of the will ; and come under the head of the understanding ; but " liking " and " disliking " are the action of the heart and affections and belong to the will. Edwards here confounds understanding and will, which he has distinguished from each

other elsewhere when he says that "the exercises of the
inclination and will are either approving and liking or
disapproving and rejecting." A man may like what he
disapproves of, and dislike what he approves of. The will
and conscience are different faculties, and in fallen man
are in direct antagonism. 2. It is not necessary that the
"liking" and "disliking," or the moral affections of love
and hatred should "be in a high degree," or "vigorous
and lively," in order to be the inclination of the will. It
is not the degree of a thing that makes the kind, but the
kind itself. If the moral affections are the same thing as
the voluntary inclination, as Edwards affirms, there is no
need of bringing in the intensity or laxity of either in the
definition. Moderate hatred is as really hatred as immod-
erate.

VOL. II., p. 123. When the will is defined as desire, it
is of the highest importance to observe the difference in
kind between sensuous and mental desire. The former
was denominated "animal appetite," and the latter "rational appetite," by the elder Protestant divines. There
is an appetency or craving in both instances, but the one
is in the physical nature, and the other in the spiritual.
The former is involuntary; the latter is voluntary. Eve's
desire for the fruit of the tree of knowledge as "good for
food, and pleasant to the eye," is an example of the first;
her desire for "the knowledge of good and evil," to be
obtained by eating of the fruit, is an example of the last.
The former was innocent; the latter culpable.

This expresses the general relation of involuntary physical appetite to voluntary self-moving desire, or moral
inclination. The appetite for food is physical, organic,
and involuntary; but the desire to satisfy it for the purpose of self-enjoyment is mental and voluntary. The
former is instinctive; the latter is not. The latter is the
gluttonous inclination of the will; its disposition to please
self by means of the physical appetite for food. The

sexual appetite is physical, organic, and involuntary; but the desire to satisfy it for the purpose of self-enjoyment is mental and voluntary. This desire is the voluptuous inclination or self-determination of the will; the wish to please self by the indulgence of sexual appetites instead of pleasing God by obeying his command to deny it. It is not the mere existence of the appetite for food, or of sexual appetite, that evinces the existence of sin in the human soul, but the existence of an inclination in the will to *use* these physical and involuntary appetites for the purpose of personal enjoyment in contradiction to the Divine command forbidding such a use. The sin is in this inclination of the will, or disposition of the heart, to disobey God, not in the mere physical appetite itself. The physical appetite is indeed made inordinate and difficult to control by habitual indulgence; but its nature is not thereby changed. It is still physical and involuntary appetite; not mental, moral, and voluntary inclination.

Mental and moral desire is self-moving and therefore voluntary and responsible, but physical and sensuous desire is the operation of physical law, not of self-determination. The desire for fame or wealth is wholly disconnected from the physical nature, so that it might be experienced by a disembodied spirit. But the desire for food, or alcohol, or the sexual desire, requires a physical nature. These latter are appetites, in distinction from desires; although the older divines sometimes denominated the desires of the mind, in distinction from those of the body, *rational* appetites; the others being animal appetites. St. Paul mentions both in Eph. 2 : 3—"lusts of the flesh, and wills or desires of the mind." Rational or mental desire seeks (appetit) an end, but the end is wholly mental. An animal or physical desire seeks an end, but the end is wholly sensuous. The motion or action in the former instance is that of mind or spirit, and is self-motion, which makes it voluntary and responsible. The motion or action in the latter instance is that of organized vital matter, which moves necessarily by reason of physical properties and in accordance with a physical law to which it is subject. When the body desires food, this is a necessary craving or appetency which never changes. It is not voluntary self-determination which might become the contrary by a revolutionary act of the physical nature. No such revolutionary change is possible within this physical sphere. Man's sensuous and material nature always hungers and always thirsts. But when the rational mind or spirit desires fame, this is a self-moving craving or appetency, which may be changed by grace into its contrary. The ambitious and proud spirit may become a meek and lowly one, and vice versa. This species of desire is not sensuous and physical, occurring by reason of the law of animal and material life, but rational and mental, occurring by the pure self-motion and self-determination of spirit. Mental desires may be lost and restored, and this proves that they are modes of the will. The desire after God and holiness with which man was created was lost in the fall, and is restored in regeneration. It is not so with the involuntary physical desires. The appetites for food, etc., existed after the fall in the same manner as before. The degree of the appetite for food, etc., is increased by the apostasy of the will, and becomes gluttony, but the kind remains the same. There is no revolutionary change into an *aversion* to food, drink, etc. But in the instance of a rational and moral appetite, or mental desire proper, the change is one of kind and not merely of degree. The desire after God and goodness becomes hatred of them. These facts show that the desires of the mind or spirit are voluntary, and those of the body and the material part of man are involuntary. The former are modes of the will ; the latter are modes of instinct and sense. Sensuous desires are merely the operation of physical properties and laws in an individual man or an-

20

imal, and are no more self-moving and voluntary than the operation of the properties of matter and the law of gravitation when a stone falls to the earth. The molecules of inorganic matter in the stone when it falls, and the molecules of organic matter in the man when he craves food, are moved by a physical law that forces their movement. But when the immaterial and spiritual will inclines or determines to an immaterial and moral end, there is no movement of molecules of matter, either inorganic or organic, in accordance with a physical law, but the *self*-motion of spirit as the contrary of matter in all its modes. The doctrine of Plato and of the Greek theism generally, that mind and matter are diverse in kind, and that the motion of the former is self-motion, but that of the latter is not, being instinctive and necessitated by physical properties and laws, is the key to the true doctrine of the will. The self-motion of spirit is free and responsible motion, because it is the product of spirit; and yet, though it be self-motion it may be bondage in reference to the power to *reverse* itself. Evil self-motion left to itself is endless self-motion, for the reasons given in Vol. II., pp. 239–242.

Vol. II., p. 131. He who confines his attention to volitions or choices will not discover the secret of the will any more than he will discover the secret of anything by confining his attention to the effect and overlooking the cause. The defect in many modern treatises on the will arises from regarding the power to choose between two contraries as a complete definition of the voluntary faculty. A choice between two contraries is an effect of an existing bias or inclination of the will as a cause. This bias constitutes the motive to the choice. A comprehensive view of the whole subject of voluntary action requires, therefore, the consideration of both of these modes of the will's action. To study the numerous and constantly changing volitions and choices of the will while neglecting the one single and permanent inclination that prompts and explains them, is to omit the most important part of the problem. It also leads to an erroneous conception of the nature of freedom, because a choice or resolution is indifferent toward its object and may take or reject it with equal facility because of its indifference. There is no inclination or desire for the object in a mere volition. The drunkard does not desire the alcohol by his volition, but only desires to take it as a means of gratifying his inclination or desire for sensual pleasure. If water were as good a means as alcohol for this end, he would choose water. The real will of the man is in the central inclination or self-determination to sensual pleasure, and not in the superficial choice of the means of attaining it. But this inclination is not, like the volition, *indifferent* to the end aimed at by it, namely, sensual pleasure. It is the self-motion of the entire will to this one end, in which it is absorbed with an intense energy and interest that opposes and precludes a contrary self-motion. The person in inclining cannot incline or disincline to the end with the same facility that he can choose or refuse the means. The distinction between inclination and volition is continually being made in common parlance. " I will do it though not inclined," is often said. This means that the speaker wills by a volition, or a choice of means, in a particular instance, to do an act that is contrary to his abiding disposition. By a volition he can decide to have a limb amputated contrary to his desire not to suffer pain. " I am inclined to do it, but will not," is often said. This means that the speaker is in his heart disposed in a certain way, but lacks energy or resolution to execute his inclination by a volition. An example of this is St. Paul's, "The good that I would (θέλω), I do not, but the evil which I would not, (οὐ θέλω), that I do (πράσσω) " (Rom. 7 : 19). By reason of his regeneration and the implanting of the new life he is cen-

trally and steadily inclined to holiness and disinclined to
sin, but in a particular instance, under the stress of a temptation addressed to the *remainders* of his sinful inclination
derived from his fall in Adam, he commits by a volition
or choice, a single sin. His inclination is right, but his
volition is wrong. And, be it observed, the volition in
this instance gets its sinful quality from the *remainders
of sinful inclination*, of which it is the executive, and not
from the *holy inclination*, of which it is not the executive
and with which it conflicts.

The distinction between inclination and volition explains moral ability. A holy angel can tell a lie if he so
desires or inclines to lie ; otherwise, not. Yet as holy
and without the inclination to lie, he could still *speak the
words* of a lie with his vocal organs by the exertion of a
volition that does not agree with his truth-loving disposition. He could formally tell a lie, but not really ; because real lying consists in the *desire* and *inclination* to
deceive. The question is not whether a holy being can
control the muscles and organs of his body, but whether
he can desire and incline to sin. It is possible for a holy
person to fall from God and become a sinful person, and
then he can desire to lie ; but so long as he remains unfallen he cannot so desire. " A good tree cannot bring
forth evil fruit." Before it can do this it must undergo
a radical change and become an evil tree. The same is
true of a sinful person. So long as he is sinful in his disposition and inclination he cannot incline to holiness.
Hence in the creeds inclination and ability are convertible
terms. The Westminster Confession (vii. 3) declares that,
" the Lord promises to give unto all those that are ordained unto life his Holy Spirit, to make them *willing* and
able to believe " (Conf., ix., 4). " When God converts a
sinner he *enables* him freely to *will* and to do that which
is spiritually good " (Conf., xiv., 1). " The elect are *enabled*
to *believe* " (L. C., 59). " Redemption is effectually com-

municated to those who are by the Holy Ghost *enabled* to *believe*" (L. C., 67). "The elect are made *willing* and *able* freely to answer the call" (S. C., 31). "Effectual calling, by renewing the *will*, persuades and *enables* us to embrace Jesus Christ."

Suppose the following propositions to be made by the advocate of "natural ability." 1. I am able to lift a hundred pounds weight, but I am not doing it. 2. I am able to love God supremely, but I am not loving him. In the former instance I must move my muscles by my will. In the latter, I must move my will by my will. In the former instance a volition will move the body and convert the asserted ability into actual lifting. In the latter instance a volition will not move the will and convert the asserted ability into actual loving. In the first instance I do not need to start an *inclination* to lift in order to lift; a mere volition is sufficient to move the muscles that move the limbs. In the latter instance I need to start an inclination to love in order to love, because love is inclination. In the former instance I lift by resolving, not by inclining; in the latter, I love by inclining, not by resolving. There is nothing in lifting, more than in not lifting, that requires feeling or affection. I do not love lifting and hate not-lifting. I am indifferent to both, and would choose one as soon as the other if it would be as good a means to attain my end. But in inclining I am not indifferent but interested. I love the inclining to good or evil, and hate the contrary.

Inclination and volition may be illustrated by the deep Gulf Stream current and the surface waves of the ocean. Both of the former are the movement of the will, as both of the latter are the movement of the ocean. But as the surface undulations have no control over the central current, so the superficial volitions have no control over the inclination.

Augustine marks the difference between inclination and

volition as follows: "There are two things: will [inclination, velle] and ability [volition, posse]. Not every one who has will (vult) has ability (potest); nor every one that has ability has will. For as we sometimes will [desire, volumus] what we are unable to execute (non-possumus), so also we sometimes execute what we do not will [desire, volumus]. Will (velle) is derived from willingness (voluntas), and ability (posse) from ableness (potestas). As the man who inclines [desires, vult] has will (voluntas), so the man who can (potest) has ability (potestatem). But in order that a thing may be done by ability (potestatem), there must be volition (voluntas). [Augustine here uses voluntas to denote volition, though arbitrium would be better. In the previous sentences he has employed it to denote inclination. It is like the indiscriminate use of "will" in Edwards, for example, to denote either inclination or volition]. For no man is said to do a thing with ability, if he did it without any act of will whatever (invitus). Although, if we observe more precisely, even what a man is moved to do against his inclination he nevertheless does by his volition; only he is said to act unwillingly in this instance because he prefers or desires something else. By some unfortunate influence (malo aliquo) he is made to do what he does by a volition, though inclined to avoid the doing of it. But if his inclination is so strong that it overrides such influence, then he resists and does not exert the volition. If, however, contrary to his inclination, he does perform the act by a volition, while it is not performed with a full, free-will [inclination, voluntas] yet it is not performed without will [volition]" (Spirit and Letter, ch. 53). Augustine also describes inclination as desire and affection. "Our will, or love, or pleasure (dilectionem), which is a stronger will [i.e., its deeper movement], is variously affected according as various objects [i.e., ultimate ends] are presented to it, by which we are attracted or repelled" (Trinity, xv., 41).

Vol. II., p. 141. The inclination of the will must originate in *self-motion* and continue to be *self-moving* in order to human freedom, and man's liberty and responsibility must be found in his inclination or nowhere. It cannot be found in the volitions that execute it, because these cannot change the inclination and have no control over it. Hence that definition of freedom which makes it to be merely the acting out of the inclination by volitions is inadequate. Edwards (Remarks on Principles of Morality, Works, II. 182) defines liberty as follows : " Liberty is the power that any one has to do as he pleases, or of conducting in any respect according to his pleasure ; *without considering how his pleasure comes to be as it is.*" That is to say, liberty is the mere power of exerting a volition in accordance with the inclination or " pleasure " of the will, whether the inclination be self-moved or necessitated ab extra. Edwards correctly maintains that the moral connection between a choice or volition and the inclination behind it, is as necessary as the physical connection between cause and effect in the physical world. Liberty or freedom, therefore, cannot be found in this fixed nexus between the inclination and the volition. It must, therefore, be found at a prior point, namely in the inclination or " pleasure " itself, and this requires raising the question " how the pleasure comes to be as it is." For if the inclination or " pleasure " of the will is not voluntary in the sense of self-originated and self-moving, then the volition which follows the inclination, and has not the least control over it, has nothing of freedom in it.

It is for this reason that the *free origin* of man's sinful inclination *in Adam* is a doctrine of the utmost importance. If the fall of human nature in Adam was involuntary, and man's sinful inclination was not and is not self-motion, then the mere volitionary power to act in accordance with this inclination or " pleasure " of the will is no more liberty than is the power of gunpowder to explode if a spark is applied to it.

The allegation is common among opponents of Augustino-Calvinism that original sin and corruption of nature, ascribed to man by this theology, are something not originated by the human will but created and necessitated by God. Watson, who is one of the most candid of Arminians, and has more in common with Calvinism than many of this school, so represents the subject. His argument against unconditional election and preterition depends chiefly upon the assumption that men are arbitrarily predestinated to life or death from a state of inherited depravity which is *wholly involuntary*, and *forced* upon them by the action of God. The following extracts from his Theological Institutes show this: " In whatever light the subject of reprobation be viewed, no *fault*, in any right construction, can be chargeable upon the persons so punished, or, as we may rather say, *destroyed*, since punishment supposes a judicial proceeding which this act shuts out. For either the reprobates are destroyed for a pure reason of sovereignty, *without reference to their sinfulness*, and thus all criminality is left out of the consideration ; or they are destroyed for the sin of Adam, *to which they were not consenting ;* or for personal faults resulting from a corruption of nature which they brought into the world with them, and which God wills not to correct and they have no power to correct themselves " (Institutes, II., 342. McClintock's Ed.). " The doctrine of predestination comes to this, that men are considered in the Divine decree as justly liable to eternal death because they have been placed by some previous decree, or higher branch of the same decree, in circumstances which *necessitate* them to sin. This is not the view which God gives us of his own justice ; and it is contradicted by every notion of justice which has ever obtained among men. Nor is it at all relieved by the subtilty of Zanchius and others, who distinguish between being *necessitated* to sin, and being *forced* to sin ; and argue that because in sinning the repro-

bates follow the motions of their own will they are justly
punishable, though in this they fulfil the predestination
of God. They sin *willingly*, it is said. This is granted;
but could they ever will otherwise? [Augustine answers,
'Yes, in Adam.'] According to this scheme they *will*
from necessity, as well as *act* from necessity" (Institutes,
II., 396, 397). "Upon a close examination of the sub-
lapsarian scheme, it will be found to involve all the leading difficulties of the Calvinistic theory as it is broadly
exhibited by Calvin himself. In both cases reprobation
is grounded on an act of mere will, resting on no reason.
It respects not in either, as its primary cause, the *demerit*
of the creature. Both unite in making sin a *necessary* result
of the circumstances in which God has placed a great part
of mankind which by no effort of theirs can be avoided.
How either of these schemes can escape the charge of
making God the author of sin, which the Synod of Dort
acknowledges to be 'blasphemy,' is inconceivable. For
how does it alter the case of the reprobate whether the
fall of Adam himself was necessitated, or whether he acted
freely? *They*, at least, are necessitated to sin; they come
into the world under a necessitating constitution which is
the result of an act *to which they gave no consent;* and
their case differs in nothing except in circumstances which
do not alter its essential character from that of beings *immediately created* by God with a nature necessarily producing sinful acts" (Institutes, II., 401). "It is manifestly in vain for the Dort Synodists to attempt in the 15th
article to gloss over the doctrine of reprobation by saying that men '*cast themselves* into the common misery by
their *own fault*,' when they only mean that they were cast
into it by Adam, and by *his* fault" (Institutes, II., 405).
"It is most egregiously to trifle with the common-sense of
mankind to call it a righteous procedure in God to punish
capitally, as for a personal offence, those who never could
will or act otherwise, being impelled by an invincible and

incurable natural impulse over which they *never had any control*. Nor is the case at all amended by the quibble that they act willingly, that is, with the consent of the will ; for since the [sinful] will is under a natural and irresistible power to incline only one way, obedience is full as much out of their power by this state of the will, *which they did not bring upon themselves*, as if they were restrained from all obedience to the law of God by an external and irresistible impulse always acting upon them. President Edwards, in his well-known work on the Will, applied the doctrine of philosophical necessity (namely, that the will is swayed by motives; that motives arise from circumstances; that circumstances are ordered by a Power above us, and beyond our control ; and that therefore our volitions necessarily follow an order and chain of events appointed and decreed by infinite wisdom) in aid of Calvinism. But who does not see that this attempt to find a refuge in the doctrine of philosophical necessity affords no shelter to the Calvinian system. For what matters it whether the will is obliged to one class of volitions by the *immediate influence* of God, or by the refusal of his remedial influence, which is the doctrine of the elder Calvinists ; or whether it is obliged to a certain class of volitions by motives that are irresistible in their operation, which result from an arrangement of circumstances ordered by God, and which we cannot control?" (Institutes, II., 439).

We believe that the explanation of original sin and inherited depravity adopted by those Calvinistic schools which deny the natural and substantial union of Adam and his posterity, and which justify the imputation of the first sin to the posterity by vicarious representation and vicarious sinning, gives ground for this assertion of Watson that Calvinism teaches that original sin and inherited depravity are *involuntary* in the posterity; that "they did not bring it upon themselves," and "gave no consent to it ; " and that " their case differs in no essential particular from that of beings immediately created by God with a nature necessarily producing sinful acts." It was this type of Calvinism which Watson had in view, when making the charge of fatalism against Calvinism. But the doctrine of Augustine and the elder Calvinists, of the natural and substantial unity of Adam and his posterity, and the voluntary fall of this entire unity from holiness to sin, and their consequent responsibility for this one act of apostasy, is not liable to this charge. According to this theory the responsible and guilty *origin* of sin and all the retributive suffering that follows it, is to be sought for at the *beginning* of human history, as Moses in Genesis, and Paul in Romans teach, and not later down in the individual choices of individual men. It is possible for the opponent to deny that there was any such natural and specific unity between Adam and his posterity ; in which case he is bound to establish the truth of his denial. But upon the supposition of the truth of the Augustino-Calvinistic theory it is impossible for the opponent to deny that the charge of a created and involuntary depravity in the posterity of Adam is unfounded.

VOL. II., p. 142. According to Kant the categories of the understanding when applied by the understanding to a rational and spiritual faculty like the human will, yield only subjective and relative truth, not objective and absolute. For illustration, bring the will under the category of *causality*. Affirm that it is a true and real cause in the sense that it originates motion and action, and produces effects by free self-determination. When the category of causality is *empirically* applied by the understanding to the will as phenomenon, that is, as choosing means to ends and producing an observable *series* of volitions, no true first cause and real freedom is found. There is only a succession of antecedents and consequents. In this connected chain of phenomena there is no real *be-ginning* of motion. One volition is caused by a preced-ing one, and so backward forever. There is no causation of the kind required, namely, *self*-causation, or *self*-motion. This volitionary movement is ab extra, according to the same law of physical cause and effect which prevails in the physical world. But when the category of causality is applied *intuitively* by the practical reason to the will as noumenon, that is, as inclining or self-moving, the action of the will is not seen as a numerous *series* of movements, but as one *single* and *steady* self-movement; not as a mul-titude of volitions following each other, and dependent upon each other and upon outward circumstances and motives, but as a single and abiding inclination which constitutes the *character*, or *disposition*, of the person him-self. This real and true self-motion is *instantaneous*, not sequacious; "un certain élan libre" (Foullée, La Liberté, 217). As such it is one and indivisible. As such it is timeless; that is, free from successions in time. This does not mean that the person who is thus inclining is not a creature of time, and in time, but that his will in this act of inclining or self-motion does not act *seriatim* according to the common law of physical cause and physical effect, but immediately and instantaneously. According to the law of cause and effect in the physical world the cause and the effect are two distinct things. The motive is the cause, and the volition is the effect. But in the instance of inclining, the cause and the effect are one and the same thing in two aspects. The self-motion is the cause, and the self-motion is also the effect. The self-motion or in-clining is not preceded by something that produces it, such as a motive that is presented by a previous inclination, or by a volition that causes it, but is itself the very first thing from which all motives and volitions issue. There is no character behind the character; no disposition back of the disposition. In this way freedom for the method of the understanding is impossible; but for the method of the practical reason is certain. The understanding proceeds from the phenomena of volitions viewed under the categories of cause and effect, antecedent and consequent, time and place ; the practical reason proceeds from the direct intuition of the inclination as the underlying noumenon of freedom, or the thing in itself, apart from all these categories.

Kant regards the "speculative" reason as reason cognizing by means of the categories of the understanding, which are adapted only to the physical world, not to the moral and spiritual, and as being hampered and limited by them; but the "practical" or "moral" reason as cognizing directly and intuitively without them. The latter is reason in its highest form. Hence Kant maintains that the will and the practical reason are the same thing. This, it is true, was the original and normal relation of the will to the reason as they were created at first, but it is not the actual and present relation. By the fall the human will was thrown into antagonism with the human reason, so that the primary unity and harmony of both have become duality and disharmony. The philosophical in distinction from the theological definition of sin would be : the schism and conflict between will and reason, inclination and conscience. In saying that the will and the practical reason are indentical, Kant means that the will, as *ideal* and *perfect*, is one with the moral law written in the moral reason. He proves it thus : The will is a free faculty. But if it were governed by something other than itself, it would not be free because it would not be *self*-governed. The law that properly controls the will must therefore be in and of the will. But the true and proper law for the will is the reason. Reason, therefore, must be one with the will in such a manner that the will when governed by reason is also *self*-governing and *self*-controlling. Consequently, when the will receives its governing law from something that is not reason, namely, sense and sensual appetite, this is not ideal and true will, and there is no ideal and true freedom. There is self-determination, but not self-government. The will receives its law from that which is not the true and proper self, the reason and conscience. See Kant's Metaphysics of Morals.

It is noteworthy that Milton also indentifies will and reason. God asks respecting the worth of Adam's obedience, in case he had not been left to decide for himself whether he would stand or fall:

> " What pleasure I from such obedience paid,
>   When will and reason (*reason* also is *choice*)
>   Useless and vain, of freedom both despoiled,
>   Made passive both, had served necessity,
>   Not me?" (Par. Lost, iii., 107–111.)

The following extract from Kant's Practical Reason, pp. 269–273, Abbott's Translation, contains his own account of his distinction between will as noumenon and phenomenon; or will in its inward and real nature, and will as it appears in its manifestations. The former, as we have said, is will as a single abiding inclination, which because it is a *unity* having no sequences in it is timeless, or out of relation to time, which always implies a series. The latter is will as a series of choices or volitions, which is in time because it has sequences. Will as phenomenon is a series of antecedents and consequents. Will as noumenon is not a series of antecedents and consequents, but is one steady unbroken volume of self-motion. Respecting a choice or volition, the question What caused it? is proper, because as one of a series of antecedents and consequents it has a cause other than itself, namely preceding volitions, and ultimately the inclination of the will. Respecting the inclination of the will, the question What caused it? is improper, because it has no cause other than itself. It is self-caused, that is, is self-moving. It is not caused either by an antecedent volition or an antecedent inclination. It cannot be explained, as volitions can be, by the method of antecedents and consequents, or of cause and effect. The reasoning of Kant is close, and requires strenuous attention.

"The notion of causality," says Kant, "as *physical necessity*, in opposition to the same notion of causality as *freedom*, concerns only the existence of things so far as they are *determinable in time*, and consequently as phenomena, in opposition to their causality as *things in themselves*. Now if we take the attributes of things in time [*i.e.*, as a series of antecedents and consequents] for attributes of things in themselves [*i.e.*, as single, and without sequences], which is the common error, then it is impossible to reconcile the necessity of the causal relation with freedom ; they are contradictory. For from the former it follows that every event, and consequently every action, that takes place at a certain point of time, is a necessary effect of what existed in time preceding. Now as time past is no longer in my power, it follows that every action of this kind that I perform must be the necessary result of certain antecedents *which are not in my power ;* that is, at the moment in which I am acting in this manner I am not free. Nay, even if I assume that my whole existence is independent of any foreign cause (for instance God), so that the determining principles of my causality, and even of my whole existence, were not outside of myself but *within* me, yet this would not in the least transform that physical necessity into freedom. For at every moment of time I am still under the necessity of being determined to action by that which is *not in my power*, and the series of antecedents and consequents, infinite a parte priori, which I only continue according to a predetermined order, and could never actually begin of myself, would be a continuous physical chain, and therefore my causality of this kind could never be free causality."

" If, then, we would attribute freedom to a being whose existence is determined in time [*i.e.*, by a series of antecedent and consequents, instead of by pure and simple self-motion], we cannot except him from the law of necessity, as to all events in his existence, and consequently as to his actions also; for that would be to hand him over to blind chance. Now as this law of necessary sequence inevitably applies to all the causality of things, so far as their existence is determinable in *time* [*i.e.*, as a series], it follows that if this were the mode in which we had also to conceive of the existence of these things in *themselves* [*i.e.*, as a unity without series], freedom [in the sense of self-motion] must be rejected as a vain and impossible conception. Consequently, if we would still save it, no other way remains but to regard the action of the will so far as it is determinable in time [*i.e.*, is one of a series of antecedents and consequents, like the volitions of the will], and therefore its causality, according to the law of physical necessity, as belonging to *appearance* only [*i.e.*, as merely the phenomenal manifestation], and to attribute freedom to the will as the *thing in itself* [*i.e.*, as the noumenon, or underlying bias, or inclination]. This is certainly inevitable if we would retain both of these contrary concepts [of free inclination and necessary volitions] together; but in application, when we try to explain their combination in one and the same action, great difficulties present themselves which seem to render such a combination impracticable."

" When I say of a man who commits a theft, that by the physical law of causality, or of antecedent and consequent, this deed is a necessary result of the determining causes in preceding time, I say that it was impossible that it could not have happened. How then can the judgment, according to the moral law, make any change and imply that it could have been omitted because the law says that it *ought* to have been omitted; that is, how can a man be called entirely free at the same moment, and with respect to the same action in which he is subject to an inevitable physical necessity? Some try to evade this by saying that the causes that determine his causality are of such a *kind* as to agree with a *comparative* notion of freedom. According to this explanation, that is sometimes called a free effect, the determining physical cause of which lies *within*, in the acting thing itself; *e.g.*, that effect which a projectile produces when it is in free motion, in which case we use the term freedom, because while it is in flight it is not urged by anything *external;* or as we call the motion of a clock a free motion because it moves its hands itself, and therefore does not require to be pushed by external force; so although the volitionary actions of man are necessarily determined by causes which precede them in time, we yet call them free because these causes are *ideas* produced by our own faculties whereby desires are evoked on occasion of circumstances, and hence actions are wrought according to our own pleasure. This is a wretched subterfuge with which some persons still let themselves be put off, and so think they have solved with a petty word-jugglery that difficult problem at the solution of which centuries have labored in vain, and which can therefore scarcely be found so completely on the surface. In fact, in regard to the question about the freedom which must be the foundation of all moral laws and of moral responsibility, it does not matter whether the principles which necessarily determine causality by the physical law of antecedents and consequents reside *within* the subject or *without* him; or in the former case, whether these principles are sensuous and instinctive or are conceived by reason, if, as is admitted by these men themselves, these determining ideas have the ground of their existence in time and in an *antecedent state,* and this again in an antecedent, etc. Then, again, it matters not that these are *internal;* it matters not that they have a psychological and

21

not a mechanical causality, that is, produce actions by means of ideas, and not by bodily movements ; they are still *determining principles* of the causality of a being whose will is determinable in time, and therefore under the necessitation of antecedents in past time, which therefore, when the person has to act, are *no longer in his power*. This may imply psychological freedom (if we choose to apply this term to a merely internal chain of ideas in the mind), but it involves physical necessity and therefore leaves no room for *transcendental, i.e., spiritual freedom*, which must be conceived as independence of everything empirical, and consequently of nature generally, whether it be an object of the internal sense considered in time only, or of the external sense in time and space. Without this freedom in the latter and true sense, which alone is practical a priori, no moral law and no moral responsibility are possible. Just for this reason the necessity of events in time, according to the physical law of causality, may be called the *mechanism* of nature, although we do not mean by this that things which are subject to it must be really material *machines*. We look here only to the necessity of the connection of events in a time-series of antecedents and consequents, as it is developed according to the physical law of cause and effect, whether the subject in which this development takes place is called *automaton materiale* when the mechanical being is moved by matter, or with Leibnitz is called *automaton spirituale* when it is impelled by ideas ; and if the freedom of our will were no other than the latter (say the psychological and comparative, not also transcendental, that is metaphysical and absolute), then it would at bottom be nothing better than the freedom of a turnspit, which when once it is wound up accomplishes its motions of itself."

"Now in order to remove in the supposed case the apparent contradiction between freedom and the mechanism of nature in one and the same action, we must remember what was said in the Critique of the Pure Reason, or in what follows therefrom, namely, that the necessity of nature which cannot coexist with the freedom of the subject or will, appertains only to the attributes of the thing ; that is, subject to time-conditions, consequently only to those of the subject acting as phenomenon [*i.e.*, as exerting volitions and choices] ; that therefore in this respect the determining principles of every action of the same subject reside in what belongs to past time and *is no longer in his power* (in which must be included his own past actions, and the character which these may determine for him in his own eyes as a phenomenon). But the very same subject being, on the other hand, conscious of himself as a thing in himself [in distinction from the manifestation of himself], contemplates his existence also, *in so far as it is not subject to time conditions,* and as determinable only by laws which he gives himself through reason ; and in this his [noumenonal] existence nothing is antecedent to the self-determination [inclination] of his will, but every [volitionary] act, and in general every modification of his being varying according to his internal sense, even the whole series of his existence and experience as a sensible being, is in the consciousness of his supersensible [spiritual] existence nothing but the result, and never the determinant, of his causality as a noumenon. In this view [of the absolute *self*-motion of the will as inclining] the rational being can justly say of every unlawful [volitionary] action which he performs, that he could have left it undone ; although as a phenomenon it is fully determined in the past, and in this respect is infallibly necessary ; for it, with all the past which determines it, belongs to the one single phenomenon of his character which he makes for himself, and in consequence of which he imputes the causality of these phenomenal manifestations of the will to himself as a cause independent of sense."

Kant speaks of a "combination in one and the same action (Handlung) of the freedom of the noumenon with the necessity of the phenomenon. By the "same action" he must mean the action or agency of the same *subject* or *agent*. One and the same action, strictly taken, could not have both of these contrary qualities; but one and the same actor might. The whole aim of Kant's abstruse discussion is to show that one and the same man is free when contemplated in one aspect, and necessitated when viewed in another; that the action of the will when it inclines or self-determines to an ultimate end is absolutely free because depending upon no antecedents, and when it exerts a volition is not free because depending upon something foregoing. It is evident that both of these modes of action cannot be combined in a single act of the will.

Schelling, in his Philosophische Untersuchungen über das Wesen der menschlichen Freiheit, adopts and defends Kant's doctrine of the will as not being within the sphere of physical cause and effect, and with him marks the difference between will as inclination (Wille), and as arbitrary volition (Willkühr). "The ideal philosophy," he says, "was the first to lift the doctrine of freedom into that sphere where alone it is comprehensible. According to this philosophy the intelligible [spiritual] nature of everything, and especially of man, is out of all causal-connection, as well as out of or above all the sequences of time. Hence it [*i.e.*, the inclination of the will] can never be determined by any antecedent, since itself as an absolute unity which must be whole and complete in order that the separate and numerous volitions that manifest it may be possible, is antecedent to everything that is or will be in itself, not only as to time but to nature and conception. We here express the Kantian conception of freedom, not in his exact words but as we believe he must have expressed himself in order to be understood." Schilling then proceeds to combat the doctrine of the indifference of the will.

Respecting this tract of Schelling, Müller (Sin, II., 95, Urwick's Trans.) says that "Schelling was the first to take up the thread of the investigation where Kant had left it, in a work which is unquestionably the most important contribution to modern speculation respecting freedom and evil, and which in profundity and wealth of thought, in nobleness and power of exposition, has seldom been equalled in philosophical literature." It is, however, vitiated by a dualistic view of the nature of the Supreme Being and his relation to good and evil. Schelling maintains that " there are two equally eternal principles, darkness and light, the real and the ideal, the particularizing Self and the universalizing Intellect, both of which are in God, and the union of which is the condition of all life."

Aristotle's distinction between the voluntary and the involuntary is this: "Those things that are done by compulsion, or through ignorance [?] are involuntary; and that is done by compulsion, of which the principle is external, and of such a character that the agent or patient does not at all contribute toward it. That is voluntary, on the contrary, of which the principle is in the agent; and the doing or not doing of the action is in himself also" (Ethics, III., i.). Similarly, Cicero (Somnium Scipionis, sub fine) defines the physical as that which is moved by external impulse, and the spiritual as that which is moved by its own interior self-motion: "Inanimatum est omne quod impulso agitur externo; quod autem anima est, id motu cietur interiore et suo." The "inanimate" here does not mean the lifeless, but that which is destitute of the rational spirit (anima); the "anima" denoting the rational spirit, which is the same thing as the will.

It is important to remember that the fall of the will, while destroying its power to good, does not destroy its self-motion. The will, be it holy or sinful, is immutably

a self-moving faculty.   Satan is as self-determining in disobeying as Gabriel is in obeying.   Respecting this point
Coleridge (Works I., 276, 281, 285) describes the corruption of nature by the fall as "the admission of a nature
into a spiritual essence by its own act," and asserts that
"a nature in a will is inconsistent with freedom" because
there is "no free power in a nature to fulfil a law above
nature," and because a will which has received a nature
into itself "comes under the mechanism of cause and effect."   This abolishes the guiltiness of sin by *transmuting
spirit into nature*, or, as Coleridge uses terms, a voluntary
self-moving essence into an involuntary necessitated substance, or mind into matter.   But the apostasy of the will
still leaves the finite spirit unchanged, as *spirit*.   Original
sin in the will is self-motion still, and not mechanical motion according to the law of cause and effect.   The inability of overcoming it by the will itself arises from the fact
that a volition cannot change an inclination, and not from
the fact, as Coleridge states it, that "spirit" has been transmuted into "nature."   The philosophical use of "nature,"
as the contrary of "spirit," is wholly different from its
theological use as denoting the natural inherited disposition of the will.

Drummond in his Natural Law in the Spiritual
World adopts the same error, and destroys the distinction between the natural and the supernatural, the involuntary and the voluntary.   To assert, as he does, that the
spirit or will of man operates like a law of nature, is the
same as asserting that the human mind operates like
gravity.   The present popularity of this writer has greatly
promoted the anti-supernaturalism of the day.

VOL. II. p. 145.   Carpenter (Physiology, § 666) discrimi-
nates between the voluntary and the volitionary.   "The
term *volitional* was some years since suggested by Dr.
Symonds in an excellent essay on the Connection between
Mind and Muscle, as expressing more emphatically than

voluntary the characteristics of an action proceeding from a distinct choice of the object, and from a determined effort to attain it. The word *voluntary* may perhaps be applied to that wider class of actions in which there is no very distinct choice or conscious effort, but in which the movement flows as it were spontaneously from the antecedent mental state."

VOL. II., p. 146. The neglect of many modern Calvinists to mark the distinction, as the elder did, between inclination and volition, and the adoption of the modern psychology respecting the will, leads to the positions: 1. That self-determination means volitionary action only; and 2. That the state of the will as seen in the disposition or character of the man, in distinction from single acts of the will, is not voluntary agency. The following from Hodge (Theology, III., 52) is an example: "If we take the word voluntary in the sense which implies volition or self-determination, it is evident that faith cannot be defined as voluntary assent. It is not true that in faith as faith there is always, as Aquinas says, an election 'voluntarie declinans in unam partem magis quam in alteram.' To tell a man he can believe if he will is to contradict his consciousness. He tries to believe. He earnestly prays for faith; but he cannot exercise it. It is true, as concerns the sinner in relation to the gospel, that this inability to believe arises from the state of his mind. But *this state of his mind lies below the will.* It cannot be determined or changed by the exercise of any voluntary power. On these grounds the definition of faith, whether as generic or religious, as a voluntary assent to truth, must be considered unsatisfactory." Here what is affirmed is true, but what is denied is erroneous. It is true that "the state of the [sinner's] mind cannot be changed by the exercise of any voluntary power" which he has; but not true that the state of the sinner's mind "lies below the will," and is therefore involuntary. For "the state of the sinner's mind " is the same thing as the state of his will. Mind is often put for will in English usage. The " carnal mind " (φρόνημα τῆς σαρκὸς, Rom. 8 : 6, 7) is the carnal will ; that is, the carnal inclination, or disposition, or character of the will ; the same that Turretin means by " inclinatio pugnans cum lege dei ; " the same that Rivetus means when he defines " concupiscentia " as " inclinatio voluntaria ; " the same that Charnock means by " the sin which is voluntary not by an immediate act of the will [a volition], but by a general or natural inclination ; " the same that Owen means when he declares that " original sin as peccatum originans was voluntary in Adam, and as it is originatum in us, is in our wills habitually [as a habitus or inclination], and not against them ; " and the same that Baxter (Dying Thoughts) means when he says : " As the will is the sinner, so it is the obstinate continuance of a will to sin which is the bondage and the cause of continued sin ; and a continued hell is continued sin, as to the first part at least. Therefore they that continue in hell do continue in a sinning will, and so continue in a love and willingness of so much of hell. So far as God maketh us willing to be delivered from sin, so far we are delivered ; and our initial, imperfect deliverance is the way to more." According to these extracts the " character " is the same thing as the permanent state or disposition of the will. When the character or state of the will is sinful, the *origin* of it must be sought for in the self-determined fall of Adam and his posterity. But when the character or state of the will is holy, the origin of it must be referred to the Holy Spirit in regeneration, who in this case, as he does not in the other, " works in the human will to will." But in both instances the human character is the abiding state and inclination of the human will, and in this use of terms and this psychology, is voluntary. It is the free activity of a rational spirit, not the instinctive and necessitated activity of an animal soul.

Again, it is true that "to tell a man that he can believe if he will, is to contradict his consciousness," but not true "that faith cannot be defined as voluntary." That it is more than a "voluntary *assent* to truth" is certain. It is a voluntary, that is, willing and affectionate *reliance* and *rest* upon Christ's person and work, to which the sinner is "made *willing* and able" in effectual calling (L. C., 67). But after the Holy Spirit has thus made the sinner "willing in the day of his power," it is self-contradictory to say that the faith that results is not voluntary. Whatever is "willing" is certainly voluntary. It is the central and spontaneous movement of the will to Christ as the object of faith. It is true freedom. "If the Son shall make you free, ye shall be free indeed."

Owen (Justification, ch. II.) defines saving faith as voluntary. Speaking of the spurious faith of Agrippa (Acts 26 : 27) he declares that "as it included no act of the will or heart, it was not that faith whereby we are justified." Defining justifying faith he says : " 1. It includeth in it a sincere renunciation of all other ways and means for the attaining of righteousness, life, and salvation. 2. There is in it the will's consent, whereby the soul betakes itself cordially and sincerely as to all its expectation of pardon of sin and righteousness before God, unto the way of salvation proposed in the gospel. This is that which is called 'coming unto Christ,' and 'receiving of him.' 3. There is an acquiescency of the heart in God, as the author and cause of the way of salvation prepared, and as acting in a way of sovereign grace and mercy toward sinners."

Those who adopt the view of the will and of freedom expressed in the above extract from Hodge lay the foundation for the charge often made, that Augustino-Calvinism is fatalism. The volitionary acts of a man unquestionably proceed from the disposition and character of his will, and have the same moral quality with it. But if that

disposition and character itself is not voluntary in the
sense of self-moving, in distinction from moved ab extra
and compelled, the volitions that issue from it are not;
and the disposition or character is certainly not voluntary,
if it "lies below the will" and outside of it. This kind of
fatalistic "determinism" is not chargeable upon the anthropology which is founded upon the elder psychology.
According to this, while the sinful volitions necessarily
agree with the sinful "state of the will," or the sinful
"character," this state of the will or character itself is the
will's self-motion and self-determination : a self-motion
that began in the fall of Adam and his posterity, and
continues by propagated transmission in each and every
individual of them. If the whole unindividualized human
nature in Adam self-determined or inclined to sin, this
self-determination or inclination might be propagated along
with the individual soul, which is a propagated fractional
part of it, and still remain self-determination and inclination. In this way original sin in the individual, though
derived and inherited, is voluntary and responsible agency.

In an article on Regeneration, commonly ascribed to
Hodge (Princeton Essays), there is a better statement of
the extent of the will, and of the voluntariness of its disposition and state. "There is a continual play," it is said,
"upon the double sense of the word 'voluntary.' When
the faculties of the soul are reduced to understanding and
will, it is evident that the latter includes all the affections.
In this sense all liking or disliking, desiring or being
averse to, etc., are voluntary, or acts of the will. But
when we speak of the understanding, will, and affections,
the word 'will' includes much less. It is the power of the
soul to come to a determination [decision] to fix its choice
on some object of desire. In the latter sense will and
desire are not always coincident. A man may desire
money and not will [choose] to make it an object of pur-
suit. When we speak of a volition, of a choice, of a deci-

sion or self-determination of the will, the word 'will' is used in the restricted sense. There are a thousand things capable of ministering to our happiness; riches, honor, sensual pleasure, the service of God; the selection which the soul makes is made by the will in the narrower sense [that is, by a separate volition]. This is a voluntary act in one sense of the term. But in another the *desire* itself which the soul has for these objects, and not merely its particular decision or choice, is a *voluntary* act. For, according to Edwards, 'all choosing, refusing, approving, disapproving, *liking*, *disliking*, directing, commanding, *inclining*, or *being averse*, a *being pleased*, or *displeased* with,' are acts of the will. In this sense all the affections and all the desires are *voluntary* exercises, whether constitutional or not, and not merely the decisions [choices or volitions] to which they lead. Hence self-love, the love of children, the love of society, the desire of esteem, are all voluntary, although springing from native tendencies of the mind." In this use of " voluntary " the writer of this would grant that " faith is voluntary."

In saying, however, that the " constitutional " desires are voluntary, the writer abolishes the distinction commonly made between the two. The " love of children " and the " love of society " are not voluntary, but natural and instinctive. They belong to the fixed constitution of man, and not to his changeable will. Hence they were not reversed by the fall of man. They are not moral and responsible. They do not deserve praise or blame. They exist in the unregenerate as well as the regenerate. See, upon this point, Dogmatic Theology, Vol. II., 119, 120, 214–217.

Vol. II., p. 149. Respecting the freedom of Adam, and the possibility of his remaining holy as created, Stillingfleet (Origines, III., iii.) remarks as follows: " Adam had a power to stand, in that there was no principle of corruption at all in his faculties; but he had a pure and undefiled soul which could not be polluted without its own consent. God cannot be said to be the author of sin, though he did not prevent the fall of man ; because he did not withdraw before his fall any grace or assistance which was necessary for his standing. Had there been, indeed, a necessity of *supernatural* grace to be communicated to man at every moment in order to continue him in his innocency ; and had God before man's fall withdrawn such assistance from him without which it were impossible for him to have stood, it would be very difficult to free God from being the cause of the fall of man. But we are not put to such difficulties for acquitting God from being the author of sin. For if God made man upright, he certainly gave him such a power as might be brought into act without the necessity of any *supervenient* act of grace to elicit that habitual power into particular actions. God would not, certainly, require anything from the creature in his integrity but what he had a power to obey ; and if there were necessary further grace to bring the power into act, then the subtracting of this grace must be by way of *punishment* to man ; which it is hard to conceive for what it should be before man had sinned ; or else God must subtract this grace on purpose that man might fall, which would follow on this supposition, in which case man would be necessitated to fall. But if God did not withdraw any effectual grace from man whereby he must necessarily fall, then though God permitted man to use his liberty, yet he cannot be said to be in any way the author of sin, because man still had a power of standing if he had made a right use of his liberty." Similarly Augustine (Rebuke and Grace, ch. 28) declares that " God made man with free-will, and if he had willed by his own free-will to continue in the state of uprightness and freedom from sin in which he was created, assuredly without any experience of death and of unhappiness he would have received by the merit of that continuance the fulness of blessing with which the

holy angels also are blessed; that is, the impossibility of
falling any more, and the knowledge of this with absolute certainty." This indefectibility, which would have
been the reward of Adam's rejecting the temptation of
Satan and continuing in the holiness in which he was
created, Augustine describes in Rebuke and Grace, ch.
xxxiii. "We must consider with attention in what respect these pairs differ from one another, namely, to be
able not to sin, and not to be able to sin; to be able not
to die, and not to be able to die; to be able not to forsake
good, and not to be able to forsake good. For the first man
was able not to sin, was able not to die, was able not to
forsake good. Are we to say that he who had such a will
could not sin? Or that he to whom it was said, 'If thou
shalt sin thou shalt die by death,' could not die? Or that
he could not forsake good, when by sinning he would forsake this and so die? Therefore the first liberty of the will
was *to be able not to sin*, the last will be much greater, *not to be
able to sin;* the first immortality was to be able not to die, the
last will be much greater, not to be able to die; the first
was the power of perseverance, to be able not to forsake
good, the last will be the felicity of perseverance [*i.e.*,
indefectibility], not to be able to forsake good. But because the last blessings will be preferable and better,
were those first ones, therefore, either no blessings at all
or mere trifling ones?"

VOL. II., p. 151. Anselm (De Libero Arbitrio, ch. i.)
argues as follows respecting the undesirableness of the
power to sin: "Master. To sin is to do something that is injurious and dishonoring, is it not? Disciple. Certainly.
Master. Consequently, that will which is unable to deviate
from the rectitude of not sinning is freer than that will
which is able? Disciple. Nothing seems more rational. Master. Do you think that that which if added diminishes liberty, and subtracted increases it, should be regarded as
a necessary element in liberty? Disciple. I cannot so

think. Master. The power to sin, therefore, which if added to the will diminishes liberty, and if taken away from the will increases liberty, is no part of liberty? Disciple. Nothing is clearer."

According to the Pelagian idea of freedom, as indifference and indetermination involving the power to the contrary, the power to sin is as necessary to liberty as the power to act holily; and writers of this school commonly represent it as one of the excellences and prerogatives of a free moral agent. But if freedom be defined, with Augustine and Anselm, as self-motion pure and simple, it is evident that freedom would not be increased by the addition of a power to sin, because this would be no increase of the self-motion which already exists in self-motion to good. And neither would the self-motion of sin be augmented in the least by the addition to it of the power to be holy. To add a contrary motion to an existing motion is certainly no increase of the existing motion; and if the existing motion is free self-motion, such addition is no addition of freedom.

VOL. II., p. 154. Augustine's explanation of the tree of knowledge is as follows: " Adam and Eve were forbidden to partake of one tree only, which God called the tree of knowledge of good and evil, to signify by this name the consequence of their discovering what good they would experience if they obeyed the prohibition, or what evil if they transgressed it. They are no doubt rightly supposed to have abstained from the forbidden tree previous to the malignant persuasion of the devil, and to have used all which had been allowed them, and therefore among all the others, and before all the others, the tree of life. For what could be more absurd than to suppose that they partook of the fruit of other trees, but not of that which had been equally with others granted to them, and which by its special virtue prevented their animal bodies from undergoing change through the decay of age, and from aging unto death? But they were forbidden, as the test of absolute obedience, the use of a tree which, if it had not been for the prohibition, they might have used without suffering any evil effect whatever; and from this circumstance it may be clearly understood that whatever evil they brought upon themselves, because they made use of it contrary to the prohibition, did not proceed from any noxious or pernicious quality in the fruit of the tree, but wholly from their violated obedience" (Forgiveness and Remission, ii., 35).

Matthew Henry (On Gen. 2 : 8, 9) explains as follows : " The tree of the knowledge of good and evil was so called not because it had any virtue in it to beget or increase useful knowledge, for surely then it would not have been forbidden; but 1. Because there was an express positive revelation of the will of God concerning this tree, so that by it Adam might know moral good and evil. What is good? ' 'Tis good not to eat of this tree.' What is evil? ' 'Tis evil to eat of this tree.' The distinction between all other moral good and evil was written in the heart of man by nature, but this which resulteth from a *positive* law was written upon this tree. 2. Because in the event it proved to give Adam an experimental knowledge of good by the loss of it, and of evil by the sense of it. As the covenant of grace hath in it not only ' Believe and so be saved,' but also, ' Believe not and be damned ' (Mark 16 : 16), so the covenant of innocency had in it not only ' Do this and live,' which was sealed and confirmed by the tree of life, but ' Fail and die,' which Adam was assured of by this other tree; so that in these two trees God set before Adam ' good and evil,' the ' blessing and the curse ' (Deut. 30 : 19). These two trees were as two sacraments or symbols."

Vol. II., p. 158. Augustine (Forgiveness and Baptism, i., 21) thus explains the text, " In the day thou eatest thereof thou shalt surely die." " When Adam sinned then his body lost the grace whereby it used in every part of it to be obedient to the soul. Then there arose in men appetites common to the brutes, which are productive of shame, and which made man ashamed of his own nakedness. Then, also, by a certain disease which was conceived in men from a suddenly infected and pestilential corruption, it was brought about that they lost that stability of life in which they were created, and by reason of the mutations which they experienced in the stages of life the disease issued at last in death. However many were the years they lived in their subsequent life, yet they began to die on the day when they received the law of death, because they kept verging toward old age." Similarly Charnocke (God's Patience) remarks : " So it is to be understood, not of an actual death of the body, but the desert of death, and the necessity of death : ' Thou wilt be obnoxious to death, which will be avoided if thou dost forbear to eat of the forbidden fruit ; thou shalt be a guilty person and so come under a sentence of death, that I may when I please inflict it upon thee.' Death did not come upon Adam that day because his nature was vitiated ; he was then also under an expectation of death, he was obnoxious to it, though that day it was not poured out upon him in the full bitterness and gall of it; as when the apostle saith, ' The body is dead because of sin,' he speaks of the living, and yet tells them the body was dead because of sin ; he means that it was under a sentence, and so a necessity of dying, though not actually dead."

Vol. II. p. 161. Charnocke (Holiness of God, p. 476) describes the ease with which the first sin might have been avoided. " God cannot necessitate sin. Indeed sin cannot be committed by force ; there is no sin but is in some sort voluntary; voluntary in the root or voluntary in the branch ; voluntary by an immediate act [volition] of the will, or voluntary by a general or natural inclination of the will. The plain story of man's apostasy from God dischargeth God from any part in the crime as an encouragement, and excuseth him from any appearance of connivance, when he showed him the tree he had reserved as a mark of his sovereignty, and forbade him to eat of the fruit of it; he backed the prohibition with the threatening of the greatest evil, namely, death ; and in that couched an assurance of the perpetuity of his felicity if he did not rebelliously reach forth his hand to take and 'eat of the fruit.' Though the 'goodness of the fruit for food, and its pleasantness to the eye' (Gen. 3 : 6) might allure him, yet the force of his reason might have quelled the liquorishness of his sense, and the perpetual thinking of and sounding out of the command of God had silenced both Satan and his own appetite. What inward inclination in him to disobey can we suppose there could be from the Creator, when upon the very first offer of the temptation Eve opposes to the tempter the prohibition and threatening of God, and strains it to a higher peg than we find God had delivered it in? For in Gen. 2 : 17 it is, 'You shall not eat of it ;' but she adds (Gen. 3 : 3), 'Neither shall ye touch it,' which was a remark that might have had more influence to restrain her. Had our first parents kept this fixed upon their understandings and thoughts, that God had forbidden any such act as the eating of the fruit, and that he was true to execute the threatening he had uttered, of which veracity of God they could not but have a natural notion, with what ease might they have withstood the devil's attack, and defeated his design! There is no ground for any suspicion of any encouragements, inward impulses, or necessity from God in this affair. A discharge of God from complicity in this first sin will easily imply a freedom of him from all other sins which follow from it. God doth not encourage, or excite, or incline to sin. How can he excite to that which when it is done he will be sure to condemn? How can he be a righteous Judge to sentence a sinner to misery

22

for a crime actuated by a secret inspiration from himself? Iniquity would deserve no reproof from him, if he were in any way positively [and efficiently] the author of it. Were God the author of it in us, what is the reason that our own conscience accuses us for it, and convinces us of it? Conscience, being God's deputy, would not accuse us of it, if the sovereign power by which it acts did incline or force us to it. The apostle Paul execrates such a thought (Rom. 9:14)."

VOL. II., p. 164. The question whether the will or the understanding is the most central, and whether the will follows the understanding, or the converse, is important in determining which is the true ego. Locke (Conduct of the Understanding, in initio) teaches that the will follows the understanding. "The agent determines himself to this or that voluntary action upon some precedent knowledge, or appearance of knowledge, in the understanding. No man ever sets himself about anything but upon some view or other which serves him for a reason for what he does. The will itself, how absolute and uncontrollable soever it may be thought, never fails in its obedience to the dictates of the understanding." This remark is true of the action of the will as choosing the means to an end in volitions, but not as inclining to the ultimate end itself. When a person chooses to steal money he *erroneously* judges with the understanding that money is the chief good. This erroneous judgment of the understanding precedes, and moves him to the volition by which he steals the money. But money appears to be the chief good to the understanding only because the inclination of the will tends to self and the creature as its ultimate end. Did the inclination of the will tend to God and infinite good as its ultimate end, holiness, not money, would be desired as the chief good, and the judgment of the understanding that it is such would follow accordingly. The understanding always judges according to the person's abiding desire or inclination. If this latter is unselfish and right, the judgment is always correct. If it is selfish and wrong, the judgment is always erroneous. A reference to Adam as unfallen and fallen will illustrate this. Unfallen Adam discerned correctly between the greater and the inferior good. He was not deceived into judging the lesser good to be the greater. But fallen Adam was so deceived. How came he to be so? Not by an act of judgment that was *prior* to the change of his inclination and desire. So long as he was unfallen and inclined in his will to God as the chief good, and desired him as such, he did not pass such a false judgment. He judged in accordance with his holy inclination and desire, and his judgment that God is the chief good was true. But when the inclination of his will underwent a revolution, and he came to desire the creature, namely, his wife Eve, instead of the Creator as the chief good, then his judgment followed his inclination, and he esteemed what he desired to be the summum bonum. This demonstrates that the last dictate or judgment of the understanding is according to the will or inclination, and not the will or inclination according to the last judgment of the understanding. Objects appear to the understanding as they agree or disagree with the dominant desire of the heart, or inclination of the will.

The following extract from Charnocke (Goodness of God) is a clear statement of the fact that the will must have a good of some kind, real or seeming, true or false, as its end. "Nothing but a good can be the object of a rational appetite [*i.e.*, the appetency of a rational self-moving soul, in distinction from an instinctive necessitated animal soul]. The will cannot direct its motion to anything under the notion of evil, evil in itself, or evil to it; whatsoever courts it must present itself in the quality of a good in its own nature, or in its present circumstances, to the present state and condition of the desire;

it will not else touch or affect the will. This is the language of that faculty, ' Who will show me any good ? ' Ps. 4 : 6), and good is as inseparably the object of the will's motion, as truth is of the understanding's inquiry. Whatsoever a man would allure another to comply with, he must propose to the person under the notion of some beneficialness in point of honor, profit, or pleasure."

But whether a true or a false good shall be the end aimed at by the will depends upon the state and condition of the will, and not upon the intrinsic quality of the true or the false good. If the will is holy in its inclination, or appetency, the good aimed at by it will be the true good, and the good refused and rejected will be the false good. If the will is sinful in its inclination and desire, the good aimed at will be the false good, and the true will be rejected. The judgment of the understanding respecting the desirableness of the good, in each instance, is not a prior and independent one. It depends upon the existing bias of the will, and follows it. Instead therefore of the maxim that " The will follows the last dictate of the understanding," the truth is, that the last dictate of the understanding follows the will. The understanding will judge that wealth, honor, and pleasure are the good to be sought after, instead of "glory, honor, and immortality," in case the inclination of the will is selfish and carnal and lusts after these. This judgment is a false one, but an actual and real one. It is the judgment of the natural man universally. On the contrary, the understanding will judge that "glory, honor, and immortality" are the summum bonum, if the will is spiritually inclined to them, and this judgment is the true one. It is the judgment of the renewed man.

In this way, it appears that the will, not the understanding, is the most central and profound of the human faculties. It is the ego in its ultimate essence. "For the will is not merely the surface-faculty of single volitions, over which the person has arbitrary control, but also that central and inmost active principle into which all the powers of cognition and feeling are grafted, as into the very core and substance of the personality itself" (Shedd : Literary Essays, 326 ; Theological Essays, 233–235).

This was also Aristotle's view, according to Neander (Grecian and Christian Ethics, Bibliotheca Sacra, Oct., 1853, p. 806). "It is Aristotle's great service to ethics that he has urged the principle that the free determination of the will is the lever of all moral development ; that knowledge is not the first or original element, but the direction [inclination] of the will ; that the judgment does not, as the primal power of the mind, determine the will, but the abiding decision of the will determines the judgment ; that the man by his permanent determination of will forms his character, and this character having become what it is freely, reacts upon the views and judgment of the man."

Jeremy Taylor (Sermon to the University of Dublin) quotes Aristotle's view and endorses it as follows : " Said Aristotle, ' Wickedness corrupts a man's reasoning ; ' it gives him false principles and evil measure of things ; the sweet wine that Ulysses gave to the Cyclops put his eye out ; and a man that hath contracted evil affections and made a league with sin sees only by those measures. A covetous man understands nothing to be good that is not profitable ; and a voluptuous man likes your reasoning well enough if you discourse of 'bonum jucundum,' the pleasures of the sense ; but if you talk to him of the melancholy lectures of the cross, the peace of meekness, and of rest in God, after your long discourse, and his great silence, he cries out, ' What is the matter ? ' He knows not what you mean. Either you must fit his humor or change your discourse. Every man understands by his affections more than by his reason. A man's mind [inclination] must be like your proposition before it can be entertained ; it is a man's mind that gives the emphasis and makes your argument to prevail."

"Do we not see this by daily experience ? Even those things which a good man and an evil man know, they do not know them both alike. A wicked man knows that good is lovely, and sin is of an evil and destructive nature ; and when he is reproved he is convinced ; and when he is observed he is ashamed; and when he is done he is unsatisfied ; and when he pursues his sin he does it in the dark : tell him he shall die, and he sighs deeply, but he knows it as well as you : proceed, and say that after death comes judgment, and the poor man believes and trembles ; he knows that God is angry with him ; and if you tell him that for aught he knows he may be in hell to-morrow, he knows that it is an intolerable truth, but it is also undeniable ; and yet, after all this, he runs to commit his sin with as certain an event and resolution as if he knew no argument against it ; these notices of things terrible and true pass through his understanding as an eagle through the air ; as long as her flight lasted the air was shaken, but there remains no path behind her."

"Now at the same time we see other persons, not so learned it may be, not so much versed in Scripture, yet they say a thing is good and lay hold of it ; they believe glorious things of heaven, and they live accordingly as men that believe themselves ; half a word is enough to make them understand ; a nod is a sufficient reproof ; the crowing of a cock, the singing of a lark, the dawning of the day, and the washing their hands are to them competent memorials of religion and warnings of their duty. What is the reason of this difference ? They both read the same Scriptures, they read and hear the same sermons, they have capable understandings, they both believe what they hear and what they read, and yet the event is vastly different. The reason is that which I am now speaking of ; the one *understands* by one principle, the other by another ; the one understands by nature, and the other by grace ; the one by human learning, and the other by Divine; the one reads the Scriptures without, the other within; the one understands as a son of man, the other as a son of God; the one perceives by the proportions of the world, and the other by the measures of the Spirit; the one understands by reason, and the other by love."

The fact mentioned by St. Paul (1 Tim. 2 : 14), that " Adam was not deceived by Satan " as Eve was, and yet apostatized from God, proves that the first cause of sin is the self-determination of the will, not the misjudgment of the understanding. Says Augustine (City of God, xiv., 11): " For as Aaron was not induced to agree in judgment with the people when they blindly wished him to make an idol, and yet yielded to their constraint ; and as it is not credible that Solomon was so blind as to suppose that idols should be worshipped, but was drawn over to such sacrilege by the blandishments of women ; so we cannot believe that Adam was deceived, and supposed the devil's word to be truth, and therefore trangressed God's law, but that he, by the drawings of kindred, yielded to the woman, the husband to the wife, the one human to the only other human being. The woman accepted as true what the serpent told her, but the man could not bear to be severed from his only companion, even though this involved a partnership in sin. He was not on this account less culpable, but sinned with his eyes open. And so the apostle does not say, ' He did not sin,' but ' He was not deceived.' For he shows that he sinned when he says, ' By one man sin entered into the world,' and immediately after, more distinctly, ' In the likeness of Adam's transgression.' "

Kant (Practical Reason, p. 212, Abbott's Trans.) directs attention to the ambiguity of the expression sub ratione boni. " It may mean : We represent something to ourselves as good, when and because we *desire* it; or we desire something because we *represent* it to ourselves as good, so that either the desire determines the notion of the object as a good, or the notion of the good determines the desire ; so that in the first case sub ratione boni would mean that we will something under the idea of the good ; in the second, in consequence of this idea, which, as determining the will, must precede it."

Vol. II., p. 165. The Formula of Concord (Art. i.) rejects the doctrine that sin is the substance of the soul. "We condemn as a Manichæan error the teaching that original sin is properly, and without any distinction, the very substance, nature, and essence of corrupt man, so that between his corrupt nature after the fall, considered in itself, and original sin, there is no difference at all, and that no distinction can be conceived between them by which original sin can be distinguished from man's nature, even in thought. Dr. Luther, it is true, calls this original evil a sin of nature, personal, essential ; but not as if the nature, person, or essence of man, without any distinction, is itself original sin ; but he speaks after this manner in order that by phrases of this kind the distinction between original sin, which is infixed in human nature, and other sins, which are called actual, may be better understood."

Augustine denies that sin is the substance of the soul, and asserts that it is its agency. "That which we have to say on this subject our author [Pelagius] mentions when concluding this topic he says : ' As we remarked, the passage in which occur the words, The flesh lusteth against the Spirit, must needs have reference not to the substance [of the flesh] but to the works of the flesh.' We, too, allege that this is spoken not of the substance of the flesh but of its works, which proceed from carnal concupiscence—in a word, from sin, concerning which we have this precept : ' Not to let it reign in our mortal body, that we should obey it in the lusts thereof ' " (Nature and Grace, ch. 66). "From the body of this death nothing but God's grace alone delivers us. Not, of course, from the substance of the body, which is good ; but from its carnal offences. It was this that the apostle meant when he said, ' I see another law in my members warring against the law of my mind, and bringing me into captivity to the law of sin which is in my members ' " (Nature and Grace, ch. 62). " There is nothing of what we call evil if there be nothing good. But a good which is wholly without evil is a perfect good. A good, on the other hand, which contains evil is a faulty or imperfect good ; and there can be no evil where there is no good. From all this we arrive at the curious result : that since every being, so far as it is a being, is good, when we say that a faulty being is an evil being we seem to say that what is good is evil, and that nothing but what is good can be evil. Yet there is no escape from this conclusion. When we accurately distinguish we find that it is not because a man is a man that he is an evil, or because he is wicked that he is a good ; but that he is a good because he is a man, and an evil because he is wicked. Whoever, then, says, ' To be a man is an evil,' or ' To be wicked is a good,' falls under the prophetic denunciation : ' Woe unto them that call evil good, and good evil !' For he condemns the work of God, which is the man, and praises the defect of man, which is the wickedness. Therefore every being, even if it be a defective one, in so far as it is a being is good, and in so far as it is defective is evil " (Enchiridion, ch. 13). This means that man as a *substance* is created by God, and as such is good ; man as an *agent* is sinfully self-moving, and as such is evil.

Athanasius, also arguing against the Manichæan hypothesis that sin is a substance and not the misuse or abuse of a creature's will, compares this opinion to that of a person " who were to shut his eyes at noonday, and finding it dark should fancy that darkness is something as real as the light, or that the substance of the light is changed into another substance of a quite contrary nature." (Oration

Against the Gentiles, 7). There is a science of light, namely, optics, but no science of darkness; which evinces the non-substantiality of the latter. Darkness has no properties or qualities that can be examined by instruments, and whose nature can be expressed in the terms of mathematics. It has no theory like that of emission, or of undulation, by which it can be explained. Nothing can be predicated of it of a positive nature. It can be defined only negatively as the absence of light. So, likewise, sin is not a substance, and neither is holiness. But while sin may be defined as the absence of holiness, and darkness as the absence of light, holiness may not be defined as the absence of sin, nor light the absence of darkness. Holiness and light are positive conceptions; sin and darkness are negative.

Vol. II., p. 166. Leighton (Exposition of the Ten Commandments) thus states the relation of the written law to the unwritten: "At first the commandments were written in the heart of man by God's own hand, but as the first tables of stone fell and were broken, so was it with man's heart; by his fall his heart was broken and scattered amongst earthly perishing things that was before whole and entire to his Maker; and so the characters of that law written in it were so shivered and scattered that they could not be perfectly and distinctly read in it; therefore it pleased God to renew that law after this manner by a most solemn delivery with audible voice, and then by writing it on tables of stone. And this is not all, but this same law he doth write anew in the hearts of his children."

Vol. II., p. 171. Edwards (Original Sin, Works, II., 385, Note) makes Adam's sin to be the union of an evil inclining to an end with an evil choice of a means. "Although there was no natural [created] sinful inclination in unfallen Adam, yet an inclination to that sin of eating the forbidden fruit was begotten in him by the delusion and error he was led into, and this inclination to eat the forbidden fruit must precede his actual eating." Strictly speaking, however, the sinful inclination (desire) was not " to eat the forbidden fruit " as fruit, but *to obtain the forbidden knowledge* of good and evil. This *inclination* or desire for the selfish *end* prompted the *choice* of *means* for obtaining it ; that is, the volition by which the fruit was plucked and eaten. Edwards here, as in other places, confounds inclination with volition, and speaks of "an inclination to eat," which properly was only a decision to eat. An inclination is something permanent ; a volition is instantaneous and transient, and is indifferent toward the means it employs. Eve desired the forbidden *knowledge*. This was the main thing with her. She had no desire for the fruit as fruit to satisfy hunger. If she could have obtained the knowledge by any other means she would have chosen it just as readily.

Owen also (Arminianism, Works, V., 123–136. Ed. Russell) describes Adam's sin as the union of inclination and volition ; of an evil desire with an evil act. " In the ninth article of our (English) Church, which is concerning original sin, I observe especially four things : First, That it is an inherent evil, the fault and corruption of the nature of every man. Secondly, That it is a thing not subject or conformable to the law of God ; but hath in itself, even after baptism, the nature of sin. Thirdly, That by it we are averse from God, and inclined to all manner of evil. Fourthly, That it deserveth God's wrath and damnation, all of which are frequently and plainly taught in the word of God. Respecting the first point : It is an inherent sin and pollution of nature, having a proper guilt of its own, making us responsible to the wrath of God, and *not a bare imputation of another's fault to us*, his posterity. David describes it as the being 'shapen in iniquity and conceived in sin.' Neither was this peculiar to him alone ; he had it not from the particular iniquity of his next progenitors, but by an ordinary propagation from the *common parent* of us all. The Scriptures cast an aspersion of guilt, or desert of punishment, on this sinful nature itself; as Eph. 2 : 1–3, 'We are dead in trespasses and sins, being by nature children of wrath.' They fix the original pravity in the heart, will, mind, and understanding (Eph. 4 : 18 ; Rom. 12 : 2 ; Gen. 6 : 5). They place it in the flesh or whole man (Rom. 6 : 6 ; Gal. 5 : 16), so that it is *not a bare imputation of another's fault* but an intrinsical adjacent [associated] corruption of our nature itself, that we call by this name of original sin. In respect of our wills, we are not innocent [but guilty] of the first transgression ; for we all sinned in Adam, as the apostle affirmeth. Now all sin is voluntary, say the Remonstrants, and therefore Adam's transgression was our voluntary sin also, and that in divers respects : First, in that his voluntary act is imputed to us as ours, by reason of the covenant which was made with him in our behalf ; but because this, consisting in an imputation, must be *extrinsical* to us ; therefore, Secondly, we say, that Adam being the root and head of all humankind, and we all branches from that root, all parts of that body of which he was the head, his will may be said to be ours ; we were then all that one man, we were all in him, and had no other will but his ; so that though that [will] be extrinsical unto us considered as particular persons, yet it is intrinsical, as we are all parts of one common nature ; as in him we sinned, so in him we had a will of sinning. So that original sin, though hereditary and natural, is noway *involuntary*, or put into us against our wills. It possesseth our wills and inclines us to voluntary sins. Scripture is clear that the sin of Adam is the sin of us all, not only by propagation and communication (whereby not his singular [individual] fault, but something of the same nature [with it] is derived unto us), but also by an imputation of his actual transgression unto us all, his singular [individual] transgression being by this means made ours. The grounds of this imputation are : 1. That we were then in him and parts of him. 2. That he sustained the place of our whole nature in the covenant God made with him. When divines affirm that by Adam's sin we are guilty of damnation, they do not mean that any are damned for his particular act, but that by his sin and *our sinning in him*, by God's most just ordination we have contracted that exceeding pravity and sinfulness of nature which deserveth the curse of God and eternal damnation. It must be an *inherent uncleanness* that actually excludes out of the kingdom of heaven (Rev. 21 : 27), which uncleanness the apostle shows to be in infants not sanctified by an interest in the covenant." In the same manner with Owen the Formula Concordiæ (Art. I.) prohibits the separation of the first sin from the corruption produced by it. " We reject and condemn that dogma by which it is asserted that original sin is merely the liability and debt arising from another's transgression, transmitted to us apart from any corruption of our nature."

One school of Later-Calvinists, on the contrary, explains the corruption of nature in each individual soul to be the effect of *two sovereign acts of God :* 1. The imputation to it of the vicarious sin of Adam as its representative ; 2. the punitive withholding of divine influences at the instant of its creation ex nihilo, on the ground of this imputation. Hodge, for example (Princeton Essays, I., 146, 149), says : "'According to the common view of immediate imputation, the sin of Adam [as their representative] is imputed to all his posterity as the ground of punishment antecedently to inherent corruption, which in fact *results from the penal withholding of divine influences.* . . . The punishment we suffer for Adam's sin is abandonment on the part of God, the withholding of divine influences ; corruption is *consequent on this abandonment.*" According to this view the corruption of nature is the result not of Adam's agency but of the agency of

God in the two acts above mentioned. It does not naturally and inevitably result from the act of Adam in disobeying the Eden statute. The Elder-Calvinists, on the contrary, holding to the substantial union of Adam and his posterity, explain this corruption of the individual soul as the natural and inseparable consequence of Adam's transgression in Eden, thereby making it to be the culpable and punishable product of Adam and his posterity, as a unity, in their fall from God. Owen is an example in the extract just given: "The Scriptures cast an aspersion of guilt, or desert of punishment on this sinful nature itself; this original pravity in the heart, will, mind, and understanding; so that it is not a bare imputation of another's fault, but an intrinsical adjacent [associated] corruption of our nature itself that we call by this name of original sin. Adam's transgression was our voluntary sin also: First, in that his voluntary act is imputed to us as ours by reason of the covenant which was made with him in our behalf; but because this consisting in an imputation must be *extrinsical* to us therefore, Secondly, we say that Adam being the root and head of all humankind, and we all branches from that root, all parts of that body of which he was the head, his will may be said to be ours; we were all that one man, we were all in him, and had no other will but his; so that though that [will] be extrinsical unto us considered as particular individual persons, yet it is intrinsical as we are all parts of one common nature; as in him we sinned, so in him we had a will of sinning. So that original sin, though hereditary and natural, is in no way *involuntary*, or put into us against our wills. When divines affirm that by Adam's sin we are guilty of damnation, they do not mean that any are damned for his particular act [as an individual representing not including his posterity], but that *by his sin and our sinning in him,* by God's most just ordination *we have contracted that exceeding pravity and sinfulness of nature* which deserveth the curse of God and eternal damnation." It is impossible to make this view of the relation of corruption in the individual to the sin of Adam mean, that "inherent corruption results from the penal withholding of divine influences," and not from Adam's act of transgression.

Vol. II., p. 172. Howe (Vanity of Man as Mortal, sub fine) argues in the same way as Anselm, respecting the simple self-motion and self-origination of the will's inclination or willingness, and the irrationality of seeking any other cause of self-motion than the self. Speaking of the unwillingness of the Christian to die, and his assigning as the reason that he is " unassured of heaven," he says, " It is not so much because we are unassured of heaven, but because we love this world better, and our hearts centre in it as our most desirable good. Therefore we see how unreasonable it is to allege that we are unwilling to change states because we are unassured. The truth is, we are unassured because we are unwilling ; and what then follows ? We are unwilling because we are unwilling. And so we may endlessly dispute round and round, from unwillingness to unwillingness. But is there no way to get out of this unhappy circle ? In order to it, let the case be more fully understood. Either this double unwillingness must be referred to the same thing or to divers, either to itself or to something else. If to the same thing, it is not sense, it signifies nothing. For having to assign a cause of their unwillingness to quit the body, to say it is because they are unwilling is to assign no proper cause. But if they refer the unwillingness to something else than itself, and say that they are unwilling to leave the body because they are unwilling to forsake earth for heaven, this is a proper cause."

A cause, in the proper sense of the term, is something *different* from the effect. But when unwillingness is said to be caused by unwillingness, the so-called cause and effect are not different things but the very same. The

truth is, that when anything is self-caused it is taken out of
the category of cause proper and effect proper, and brought
into that of free-will or self-determination. Hence, to ask
for a cause of sin that is other than the self-inclining of
the will is to make sin like an effect in the natural world ;
in other words, no sin at all.

VOL. II., p. 177. A kind of good in certain respects
can be perceived in an object presented as a temptation to
a holy being, without there being a sinful lust for it. Besides the instance of unfallen Eve and the fruit of the
tree of knowledge as "good for food" and "pleasant to
the eye," that of Christ and his temptation is in point.
When "all the kingdoms of the earth and the glory of
them " were presented to him as an object of temptation,
he could perceive a species of good in earthly power and
dominion without desiring it *ambitiously*, and lusting after
it for the purpose of self-aggrandizement. He could view
it unselfishly as affording its possessor the means of influence and usefulness among mankind, and might desire it
only as such, without longing for it as the means of self-
glorification.

VOL. II., p. 178. Milton represents Adam as perceiving
that the inward desire of Eve for the forbidden knowledge
was lustful, and therefore of the nature of sin.

> " Bold deed hast thou presumed, adventurous Eve,
>   And peril great invoked, who thus hast dared,
>   Had it been only *coveting* to eye
>   That sacred fruit, sacred to abstinence."
>   —Paradise Lost, ix., 920.

VOL. II., p. 182. It is a favorite device of rationalism
to explain Paulinism by Rabbinism. It is contended that
the peculiarities of St. Paul's conception of Christianity
proceed from his training in the Rabbinical theology.
Edersheim (Life of Jesus, I., 165 sq.) refutes this by
showing the essential difference between the Old Testament and the Rabbinical conception of the Messiah and

his redemption. "The general conception which the Rabbis had formed of the Messiah differed totally from what was presented by the Prophet of Nazareth. Thus, what is the fundamental divergence between the two may be said to have existed long before the events which finally divided them. It is the combination of letters which constitutes words, and the same letters may be combined into different words. Similarly, both Rabbinism and what by anticipation we designate Christianity might regard the same predictions as Messianic, and look for their fulfilment; while at the same time the Messianic ideal of the synagogue might be quite other than that to which the faith and the hope of the church have clung."

"The Messiah and his history are not presented in the Old Testament as something separated from, or superadded to, Israel. The history, the institutions, and the predictions of Israel run up into him. He is the typical Israelite, nay, typical Israel itself; alike the crown, the completion, and the representative of Israel. He is *the* Son of God, and *the* Servant of the Lord; but in the highest and only true sense which had given its meaning to all the preparatory development. This organic unity of Israel and the Messiah explains how events, institutions, and predictions which initially were purely Israelitish, could with truth be regarded as finding their full accomplishment in the Messiah. From this point of view the whole Old Testament becomes the perspective in which the figure of the Messiah stands out. And perhaps the most valuable element in Rabbinic commentation on Messianic times is that in which it is so frequently explained that all the miracles and deliverances of Israel's past would be re-enacted, only in a much wider manner, in the days of the Messiah. Thus the whole past was symbolic and typical of the future. It is in this sense that we would understand the two sayings of the Talmud: 'All the prophets prophesied only of the days of the Mes-

23

siah,' and, ' The world was created only for the Messiah.'
In accordance with all this the ancient synagogue found
references to the Messiah in many more passages of the
Old Testament than those verbal predictions to which we
generally appeal. Their number amounts to upward of
456 (75 from the Pentateuch, 243 from the Prophets, and
138 from the Hagiographa), and their Messianic application is supported by more than 558 references to the most
ancient Rabbinic writings. But comparatively few of
these would be termed verbal predictions. Rather would
it seem as if every event were regarded as prophetic, and
every prophecy, whether by fact or by word (prediction),
as a light to cast its sheen on the future, until the picture
of the Messianic age in the far background stood out in
the hundredfold variegated brightness of prophetic events
and prophetic utterances. Of course there was danger
that, amidst these dazzling lights, or in the crowd of figures,
the grand central Personality should not engage the attention it claimed, and so the meaning of the whole be
lost in the contemplation of the details. This danger was
the greater from the absence of any deeper spiritual elements. All that Israel needed : ' Study of the law and
good works,' lay within the reach of everyone ; and all
that Israel hoped for was national restoration. Everything else was but means to these ends ; the Messiah himself only the grand instrument in attaining them. Thus
viewed the picture presented would be of Israel's exaltation, rather than of the salvation of the world. To this
and to the idea of Israel's exclusive spiritual position in
the world must be traced much that otherwise would seem
utterly irrational in the Rabbinic pictures of the latter
days. But in such a picture there would be neither
room nor occasion for a Messiah-Saviour, in the only
sense in which such a heavenly mission could be rational,
or the heart of humanity respond to it. The Rabbinic
ideal of the Messiah was not that of ' a light to lighten

the Gentiles, and the glory of his people Israel'—the satisfaction of the wants of humanity, and the completion of Israel's mission—but quite different even to contrariety. On the other hand, it is equally noteworthy that the purely national elements, which well-nigh formed the sum total of the Rabbinic expectation, scarcely entered into the teaching of Jesus about the kingdom of God. And the more we realize that Jesus did so fundamentally separate himself from all the ideas of his time, the more evidential is it of the fact that he was not the Messiah of Jewish conception, but derived his mission from a source unknown to, or at least ignored by, the leaders of the people."

" But still, as the Rabbinic ideas were at least based on the Old Testament, we need not wonder that they also embodied the chief features of the Messianic history. Accordingly, a careful perusal of their Scripture quotations shows that the main postulates of the New Testament concerning the Messiah are fully supported by Rabbinic statements. Thus, such doctrines as the *pre-mundane existence* of the Messiah ; his *elevation* above Moses, and even above the angels; his *representative* character; his cruel *sufferings* and *derision ;* his *violent death* and that *for* his people; his *work* on behalf of the living and the *dead ;* his *redemption* and restoration of Israel ; the *opposition* of the Gentiles ; their partial *judgment* and *conversion ;* the *prevalence* of his *law ;* the *universal blessings* of the latter days ; and his *kingdom*—can be clearly deduced from unquestioned passages in ancient Rabbinic writings. Only, as we might expect, all is there indistinct, incoherent, unexplained, and from a much lower stand-point. Most painfully is this felt in connection with the one element on which the New Testament most insists. There is, indeed, in Rabbinic writings frequent reference to the sufferings and even the death of the Messiah, and these are brought into connection with our sins—as how could it be otherwise in view of Isaiah liii. and other passages?—and in one most remarkable comment the Messiah is represented as willingly taking upon him all these sufferings, on condition that all Israel—the living, the dead, and those yet unborn—should be saved. But there is only the most indistinct reference to the removal of sin by the Messiah in the sense of vicarious sufferings. In connection with what has been stated one most important point must be kept in view. So far as their opinions can be gathered from their writings the great doctrines of original sin and of the sinfulness of our whole nature were not held by the ancient Rabbis. Of course, it is not meant that they denied the consequences of sin, either as concerned Adam himself or his descendants ; but the final result is far from that seriousness which attaches to the fall in the New Testament, where it is presented as the basis of the need of a Redeemer, who as the Second Adam, restores what the first had lost."

The difference between St. Paul's conception of the Messiah, of the fall and original sin, of vicarious atonement, and of the nature of redemption, and the Rabbinical conception as enunciated by a writer deeply versed in Rabbinical learning is fundamental. Had the apostle not been lifted out of and beyond his early Rabbinical training by the " revelations " and inspiration subsequent to his conversion, of which he repeatedly affirms he was the subject, he never could have made that statement of Christian doctrine which goes under his name, and which, next to the gospels, has exerted more influence than any other part of Scripture in shaping Christianity and Christendom.

Vol. II., p. 187. Graves (Pentateuch, III., iii.) refers the Divine threatening to " visit the sins of the fathers upon the children " to the sufferings in *this* life, which God in an extraordinary manner sometimes inflicted upon violators of the Mosaic statutes and regulations, and not to the retributions of the *future* [eternal] state, which, though well known and taught by Moses, were not presented and employed by him as the sanctions of his legislation. "The only circumstance," he says, "that makes this denunciation appear severe or unjust is the supposition that the sanctions of a future state are understood; which it would certainly be repugnant to the Divine justice to suppose should be distributed according to such a rule as this. But this objection vanishes the moment we are convinced that the punishment here meant relates only to *outward circumstances of prosperity or distress in the present life*. Because if such a direct and visible sanction was necessary in the particular system of providential administration by which God thought fit to govern the Jewish race, it is evident that any inequality as to individuals would be certainly and easily remedied in a future life; so that each should receive his *final* reward exactly according to his true merit in the sight of God, and thus ' the Judge of all the earth do right.' "

"Now it seems undeniable that such an immediate and visible sanction was a necessary part of the Jewish polity, so far as this required a providential distribution of *national* rewards and punishments. These affecting the great mass of the people, and extending through such portions of time as were necessary to give them their full efficacy in forming the national character, could not be confined within the limits of a single generation, or exclude from their operation each private family in succession, as the heads of that family might drop off whose conduct had originally contributed to swell the mass of national guilt, or contribute to the progress of national improvement. This is illustrated in the case of Achan, whose children were involved in the punishment of his violation of the Divine command (Josh. 7 : 24) ; and in the punishment inflicted in consequence of the idolatries of Jeroboam, Baasha, and Ahab, involving their entire posterity."

" But the operation of this sanction was not confined to
the participation of national rewards or punishments;
it certainly affected *individuals* who violated the commands to which it was annexed, even though such violation was confined to themselves and could not therefore
draw down any national chastisement. Let it be recol-
lected that the great crime, the temporal punishment of
which was to extend to the third and fourth generation,
was *idolatry ;* that source of all profaneness and pollution
which under the Jewish polity was not only a violation of
that religious duty for which the children of Israel were
set apart from every nation under heaven, but was besides
the highest crime against the *state,* which acknowledged
Jehovah as supreme sovereign, the sole object of civil allegiance as well as of religious worship. To introduce
idolatry was therefore to subvert the foundation of the
social union and engage in the foulest treason and the
most audacious rebellion. The supreme sovereign therefore denounced against such treason and rebellion not
only condign punishment on the offender himself, but the
extension of this punishment to his family and immediate
descendants; a principle recognized by many of the most
civilized states in which the crime of treason is punished
not only by death but by the confiscation of property and
the taint of blood ; a principle which when carried into
execution by a human tribunal may operate in particular instances with unmerited or excessive severity, but
which in the Jewish theocracy was applied in every instance by unerring justice. ' For the Deity,' as Warburton well observes, ' though he allowed capital punishment
to be inflicted for the crime of lese majesty on the person
of the *offender* by the delegated administration of the law,
yet concerning his *family* or *posterity* he *reserved the inquisition of the crime to himself,* and expressly *forbade* the
magistrate to meddle with it, in the common course of
justice.   The fathers shall not be put to death for the

children, neither shall the children be put to death for the father; every man shall be put to death for his own sin (Deut. 24 : 16). We see the operation of this law in 2 Kings 14 : 5, 6, where we are told that Amaziah, king of Judah, as soon as the kingdom was confirmed in his hand, slew his servants which had slain the king, his father. But the children of the murderers he slew not; according unto that which is written in the book of the law of Moses, wherein the Lord commanded, saying, The fathers shall not be put to death for the children, nor the children be put to death for the fathers; but every man shall be put to death for his own sin. Now God's appropriating to himself the execution of this law would abundantly justify the equity of it, even supposing it had been given as a part of an universal religion; for why was the magistrate forbidden to imitate God's method of punishing but because no power less than omniscient could in all cases keep clear of injustice in such an inquisition?'"

"Maimonides also understands that this visiting of the sins of the fathers upon the children is aimed at idolatry. 'As to that character of God, of visiting the iniquity of the fathers upon the children, know that this relates only to the crime of idolatry; as may be proved from the decalogue, which says, On the third and fourth generation of them who *hate me;* for nobody is said to *hate* God but an idolater; as the law expresses (Deut. 12 : 31), Every abomination to the Lord which he hateth have they done unto their gods. And mention is made of the fourth generation, because no man can hope to see more of his progeny than four generations."

"Thus the principle of visiting the sins of the fathers upon the children unto the third and fourth generations, by extending the *temporal* judgments denounced against the perpetration of idolatry to the immediate posterity of the idolater, is perfectly consistent with Divine justice; because it interferes not with that *final* retribution at which every man shall be rewarded according to his works. That this sanction of the Jewish law was not to be understood as a general principle of the Divine economy under every form of civil society and every degree of religious improvement, but merely as a necessary part of that administration of an extraordinary Providence by which the Jewish law was sanctioned and upheld during the earlier periods of its existence, has been proved by Warburton from a circumstance which infidel writers have laid much stress upon, as an instance of contradiction between different parts of Scripture, when in truth it was only a gradual change in the Divine system, wisely and mercifully adapted to the gradual improvement of the human mind. Toward the conclusion of this extraordinary economy, observes Warburton, when God by the later prophets reveals his purpose to give them a *new dispensation*, in which a future state of rewards and punishments was to be substituted in place of an immediate extraordinary Providence, as the sanction of religion, it is then declared in the most express manner that he will *abrogate* the law of punishing children for the sins of their parents (Jeremiah 31 : 29–33 ; Ezek. 11 : 19–21, ch. 18)."

" In this way, in the Jewish system, a people of gross and carnal minds and short-sighted views, slow to believe anything they could not themselves experience, and therefore almost incapable of being sufficiently influenced by the remote prospect of a future life, and the pure and spiritual blessedness of a celestial existence, were wisely and necessarily placed under a law which was supported by a visible extraordinary Providence, conferring immediate rewards and punishments on the person of the offender; or which laid hold of his most powerful instincts, by denouncing that his crimes would be visited upon his children and his children's children to the third and fourth generation. And this proceeding was a necessary part of that national discipline under which the Jews were placed, and was free from all shadow of injustice. Because when the innocent were afflicted for their parents' crimes, as Warburton has well observed, it was by the deprivation of temporal benefits, in their nature forfeitable. Or should this not so clearly appear, yet we may be sure that God, who reserved to himself the right of visiting the sins of the fathers upon the children, would perfectly rectify any apparent inequality in the course of his providential government over the chosen people in another and a better world, by repaying the innocent who had necessarily suffered here with an eternal and abundant recompense."

That all this class of sufferings which result from the individual sins of immediate ancestors are not penal and retributive, like the suffering that results from the sin of Adam, is also proved by the fact that the *whole* penalty threatened for sin in the legal covenant was physical and spiritual death; and this comes upon every man because of Adam's sin, not because of the sins of secondary ancestors. Furthermore, men are not *twice* punished; once for Adam's sin, and again for their immediate parents' sins. And again, this class of sufferings is not *universal* but extraordinary and special. Penalty proper is common and universal, and falls upon all the posterity of Adam in the same way, and without exception; but the sufferings that befell the family of Korah were uncommon and exceptional, and distinguished them from the rest of the families of Israel. The same is true of the sufferings which have come upon the descendants of Ham, for their father's sin. The descendants of Shem and Japhet have escaped them.

Vol. II., p. 199. Augustine teaches that original sin is guilt in the following extracts: " We understand the apostle to declare that 'judgment' is predicated 'of one offence unto condemnation' entirely on the ground that even if there were in men nothing but original sin, it would be sufficient for their condemnation. For however much heavier will be their condemnation who have added their own sins to the original offence (and it will be the more severe in individual cases, in proportion to the sins of individuals), still, even that sin alone which was originally derived unto men not only excludes from the kingdom of God, which infants are unable to enter (as the Pelagians themselves allow) unless they have received the grace of Christ [in baptism] before they die, but also alienates from salvation and everlasting life, which cannot be anything else than the kingdom of God, to which fellowship with Christ alone introduces us" (Forgiveness and Baptism, i., 15). "The human race lies under a just condemnation, and all men are the children of wrath. Of which wrath the Lord Jesus says: 'He that believeth not the Son shall not see life ; but the wrath of God abideth on him.' He does not say it will come, but it 'abideth on him.' For every man is born with it; whereupon the apostle says : 'We were by nature the children of wrath even as others.' Now as men were lying under this wrath by reason of their original sin, and as this original sin was the more heavy and deadly in proportion to the number and magnitude of the actual sins which were added to it, there was need of a mediator, that is, of a reconciler who by the offering of one sacrifice, of which all the sacrifices of the law and the prophets were types, should take away this wrath " (Enchiridion, ch. 33). "Infants who have not yet done any works of their own, either good or bad, will be condemned on account of original sin alone, if they have not been delivered by the Saviour's grace in the laver of regeneration [i.e., baptism]. As for all others who, in the use of their free-will, have added to original sin sins of their own commission, and who have not been delivered by God's grace from the power of darkness and admitted into the kingdom of Christ, they will receive judgment according to the desert not of original sin only, but also of the acts of their own will " (Letter ccxv. Ad Valentinum).

Vol. II., p. 210. Job (10:15) refers his holiness to God, but his sinfulness to himself as the author. "If I be wicked, woe unto me; and if I be righteous, yet will I not lift up my head." Leighton (Theological Lectures, x.) concisely states the doctrine thus: "If you are sinful and act sinfully, blame yourselves; if you are holy and act holily, praise God."

Vol. II., p. 212. Calvin thus distinguishes original from indwelling sin: "Original sin is the pravity and corruption of our nature which first renders us obnoxious to the wrath of God, and then produces in us the 'works of the flesh.' Two things are to be distinctly observed. First, that our nature being so entirely depraved and vitiated, we are on account of this very corruption considered as convicted and condemned in the sight of God, to whom nothing is acceptable but righteousness, innocence, and purity. And therefore even infants themselves bring their own condemnation into the world with them, who though they have not yet produced the fruits of their iniquity, yet have the seed of it within them; even their whole nature is, as it were, a seed of sin, and therefore cannot but be odious to God. By baptism, believers are certified that this condemnation is removed from them; since the Lord promises us by this sign that a full and entire remission is granted both of the guilt which is to be imputed to us, and of the punishment to be inflicted on account of that guilt. They also receive righteousness such as the people of God may obtain in this life; that is, only by imputation, because the Lord in his mercy accepts them as righteous and innocent."

"The other thing to be remarked is, that this depravity never ceases in us, but is continually producing new fruits —these 'works of the flesh,' which are like the emission of flame and sparks from a furnace, or streams of water from an unfailing spring. For concupiscence never dies, nor is altogether extinguished in men, till by death they are delivered from the body of death. Baptism, indeed, promises us the submersion of our Pharaoh, and the mortification of sin; yet not so that it no longer exists, or gives us no further trouble; but only that it shall never *overcome* us. For so long as we live immured in this prison of the body, the relics of sin will dwell in us; but if we hold fast by faith the promise which God has given us in baptism, they shall not *domineer* or *reign* over us. But let no one deceive himself, let no one indulge himself in his sin, when he hears that sin always dwells in us. These things are not said in order that those who are already too prone to do evil may securely sleep in their sins, but only that those who are tempted by their corrupt propensities may not faint and sink into despondency; but that they may rather reflect that they are yet in the right way, and may consider themselves as having made some progress when they experience their corruption diminishing from day to day, till they shall attain the mark at which they are aiming, even the final destruction of their depravity, which will be accomplished at the close of this mortal life. In the meantime let them not cease to fight manfully, and press forward to complete victory. In all this we say nothing different from what is clearly stated by Paul in the sixth and seventh chapters of the Epistle to the Romans" (Inst., IV., xv., 10–12).

VOL. II., p. 218. Respecting the use of the term "nature" when applied to original sin, the Formula Concordiae (Art. I.) thus defines: " We must carefully observe the various significations of the word 'nature,' the ambiguity of which the Manichæans abusing disguise their error, and lead many simple men into error. For sometimes 'nature' signifies the substance itself of man, as when we say: God created human nature. But sometimes by the word 'nature' is understood the disposition, condition, defect, or vice of a thing implanted and inherent in its nature, as when we say: It is the serpent's nature to strike; man's nature is to sin, and is sin. In this latter signification, the word 'nature' denotes, not the substance itself of man, but something which inheres and is fixed in his nature or substance. As respects the Latin words 'substantia' and 'accidens,' since these are not expressions of Holy Scripture, and moreover are not understood by the common people, we should abstain from them in public assemblies where the unlearned multitude are taught; and in this matter account should be taken of the more simple and untaught. But in schools and among learned men (to whom the signification of these words is known, and who can use them correctly and without abuse, properly discriminating the essence of anything from that which has been added to it from without, and inheres in it by way of accident) they are to be retained in the discussion concerning original sin. For by means of these terms the distinction between the work of God and the work of the devil can be explained with the greatest clearness. For the devil cannot create any substance, but can only by way of accident, and under the permission of God, deprave a substance created by God."

VOL. II. p. 219. Turrettin (X., iv., 39) gives the following account of the distinction between natural and moral inability. "The inability of sinful man is not to be denominated moral simply in distinction from natural, since that is called morally impossible by moral philosophers which arises from custom rather than from nature, and is indeed difficult to be done, but nevertheless is sometimes done, and cannot be reckoned among the things that are absolutely impossible; while the inability of the sinner is innate and insuperable. Neither is it to be denominated natural simply, since that is natural on account of which we are called neither good nor evil, while it is certain that this inability is something vicious and culpable. Nor is it natural in distinction from voluntary, as there is a natural inability in a stone or a brute to speak; since our inability is especially voluntary (maxime voluntaria). Nor is it natural as arising from a lack of natural faculty or power, like the inability of a blind man to see, of a paralytic to walk, of a a dead man to rise from the grave ; because our inability does not exclude but always supposes in man the natural powers of intellect and will."

"It is better, therefore, to denominate the sinner's inability both natural and moral, in different respects. It is *moral*, 1. Objectively, because relating to moral duties. 2. Originally, because it originates from moral corruption spontaneously brought in by the sin of man. 3. Formally, because it is voluntary and culpable, overflowing into the disposition (habitum) of the corrupt will. It is also *natural*, 1. Originally, because it is congenital with us, and by nature ; not as nature was created by God but as nature is corrupted by man ; as we are said by St. Paul to be 'by nature children of wrath,' and by David to be ' shapen in iniquity, and conceived in sin ; ' as poison is natural in a serpent, and rapacity in a wolf. 2. Subjectively, because it infects our whole nature, and causes the deprivation of that power of well-doing which was bestowed upon the first man, and constituted original righteousness. 3. Effectually (Eventualiter), because it is unconquerable and insuperable, not less than the merely natural inability of a blind man to see, or a dead man to rise. For sinful man is no more able to convert himself than a blind man to see, or a dead man to rise from the grave. As therefore this inability is rightly called *moral* and voluntary, to indicate the responsibility and guilt of man, and render him inexcusable, so it is well denominated *natural*, to express the greatness of his corruption and demonstrate the necessity of Divine grace, because, as it is congenital to man, so it is insuperable by him, and he cannot shake it off but by the omnipotent energy of the Holy Spirit."

Vol. II., p. 224. The equivocation and self-contradiction in Edwards's doctrine of " natural ability and inability " are seen by analyzing the following extract from his work on the Will given in "Dogmatic Theology," II., 249 : "If the will [*i.e.*, the inclination] fully complies, and the proposed effect does not prove, according to the laws of nature, to be connected with his [executive] volition, the man is perfectly excused ; he has a natural inability to the thing required. For the will [inclination] itself, as has been observed, is all that can be directly and immediately required by command ; and other things only indirectly as connected with the will. If therefore there be a full compliance of will [inclination], the person has done his duty." Edwards here declares that the person who "has a natural inability to the thing required " because he is prevented by the " laws of nature " from executing his inclination by volitions, has nevertheless "done his duty " by the inward inclining and " complying " of his will. This shows that " natural inability," as Edwards defines it, does not prevent the performance of man's duty to God. If this be so, then " natural inability " is of little consequence. It may exist, and yet the whole duty of man be performed notwithstanding. And on the other hand, if " natural ability " be as Edwards conceives of it, the mere possession of a will apart from its *hostile inclination* towards God, such an ability is not adequate to the performance of the duty of *loving* God supremely. In this case, also, " natural ability " is valueless, because the duty of man cannot be performed by it. This shows that Edwards, in order to meet the exigencies of his argument with his Arminian opponents, employs the term " ability " in a false sense, and not in its true and common signification of real efficient power.

Anselm (Cur Deus Homo, II., xvii.) directs attention to the two meanings of " power," according as reference is had to inclination or to volition. " We found when considering the question whether Christ could lie, that there are two senses of the word 'power' in regard to it : the one referring to his disposition, the other to the outward act; and that though he had the power to lie externally and verbally, he was so disposed (a seipso habuit) that he could not lie inwardly and from inclination." But in this instance there is no equivocal use of "ability," in the sense of quasi-power. The ability of Christ to vocalize the words of a lie was real ability; and his inability to incline to lie was real inability.

VOL. II., p. 226. The question between the advocate of ability and the advocate of inability is, whether sinful man is able to love God supremely because he so wills or inclines under the regenerating operation of the Holy Spirit, or whether he so inclines because of his own inherent power. Is ability the effect of human or of divine power? The advocate of inability contends that ability to love and obey God is the result of *enabling* the fallen will by regenerating it; that ability is the effect of the Divine actuation of the will. The Westminster Confession, which agrees with all the Calvinistic creeds upon this point, represents "enabling" or ability as the result of inclining the will, and inclining as the result of the operation of the Divine Spirit in the will. "Effectual calling is the work of God's almighty power and grace, whereby, by savingly enlightening the minds of his elect, and renewing and powerfully determining their wills, they are made willing and *able* freely to answer his call, and to accept and embrace the grace offered therein " (L. C., 67). Apart from the "powerful determining of the sinful will " in effectual calling, there is no power in the natural man to incline the will from sin to holiness. Edwards asserts this with great energy, both in his doctrinal and controversial writings. In his Reply to Williams (Works, I., 246, 247), for example, he argues that an unconverted person has no right to enter into covenant with God in his own strength, and to promise to keep it by his own inherent power or ability, because he cannot keep his covenant and fulfil his promise. "The promises and oaths of unregenerate men must not only be insincere, but very *presumptuous,* upon these two accounts. 1. Because herein they take an oath to the Most High, which it is ten thousand to one they will break as soon as the words are out of their mouths by continuing still unconverted. To what purpose should ungodly men be encouraged to utter such promises and oaths before the church, for the church's acceptance? How contrary is it to the counsel given by the wise man in Eccl. 5 : 2, 4, 5, 6. 2. When an unconverted man makes such a promise he promises what *he has not to give,* or what *he has not sufficiency for the performance of ;* no sufficiency in himself, nor any sufficiency in any other that he has a claim to, or interest in. There is indeed a sufficiency in God to enable him ; but he has no claim to it. If it be true that an unconverted man who is morally sincere may reasonably, on the encouragement [given by God to all men indiscriminately in the promises of common grace] promise immediately to believe and repent, *though this be not in his own power,* then it will follow [according to Williams's affirmation that 'God will never be worse than his encouragement'] that whenever an unconverted man covenants with such moral sincerity as gives a lawful right to the sacraments [according to Williams and the half-way covenant party], God NEVER will fail of giving him converting grace *that moment* to enable him from thenceforward to believe and repent as he promises."

In his Religious Affections (Works, III., 71), Edwards finds "ability" in "inclination" alone. "This new spiritual sense, and the new dispositions that attend it, are no new faculties but are new principles of nature. By a principle of nature in this place I mean that foundation which is laid in nature, either old [and sinful] or new [and holy], for any particular manner or kind of exercise of the faculties of the soul; or a natural habit or foundation for action *giving a personal ability and disposition* to exert the

24

faculties in exercises of such a certain kind." This implies
that if there be no "foundation for any particular manner
of exercise of the faculties of the soul," that is, no habit,
disposition, or inclination of the will, there is no ability
to exert the faculties. Only a holy disposition is able to
love and obey God; only a sinful disposition is able to
hate and resist him.

VOL. II., p. 230. Calvin and the Reformed theologians
generally assert the "necessity" of sinning in the case of
the fallen will. See the extract from Ursinus (Dogmatic
Theology, II., 222). Edwards does the same as the extract
in Dogmatic Theology, II., 230, shows. But it is not the
necessity of *compulsion* which is the more common signification of the term, but the necessity produced by voluntary
action and the *certainty* which results from a voluntary
state of the will. Edwards (Will, Pt. IV., Sect. iii.) describes it. "Men in their first use of such phrases as
these, 'must, can't, can't help it, can't avoid it, necessary,
unable, impossible, unavoidable, irresistible,' etc., use them
to signify a necessity of *constraint* or *restraint*, a *natural*
necessity or impossibility, or some necessity that *the will
has nothing to do in;* which may be whether men will or
no; and which may be supposed to be just the same, let
men's *inclinations* and *desires* be what they will." Given
an evil inclination, and evil thoughts, purposes, and actions
are necessary in the sense of certain and invariable, but
the evil inclination itself is not necessary in the sense of
compelled. This is self-originated and is the simple self-
motion of the will. Christ teaches this truth when he
says that "a good tree cannot bring forth evil fruit,
neither can a corrupt tree bring forth good fruit" (Matt.
7 : 18). "The fallen will," says Calvin (Inst. II., iii., 5),
is so bound by the slavery of sin that it cannot excite
itself, much less devote itself to anything good; for such
a disposition is the beginning of a conversion to God,
which in the Scriptures is attributed solely to Divine

grace. Thus Jeremiah prays to the Lord to convert or turn him if he would have him turned (Jer. 31 : 18). When I assert that the will being deprived of its liberty [to good] is necessarily drawn or led into evil, I should wonder if anyone considered it as a harsh expression, since it has nothing in it absurd, nor is it unsanctioned by the custom of good men. It offends those who know not how to distinguish between *necessity* (necessitatem) and *compulsion* (coactionem). But if anyone should ask them whether God is not necessarily good (necessario bonus), and whether the devil is not necessarily evil (necessario malus)—what answer will they make? For there is such a close connection between the goodness of God and his deity that his being God is not more necessary than his being good. But the devil is by his [voluntary] fall so alienated from communion with all that is good that he can do nothing but what is evil. But if anyone should yelp (obganniat) that little praise is due to God for his goodness which he is compelled (cogatur) to preserve, shall we not readily reply that his inability to do evil arises from his infinite goodness, and not from the impulse of violence [compulsion]. Therefore if a necessity [infallible certainty] of doing well impairs not the liberty of the Divine will in doing well; if the devil, who cannot but do evil, nevertheless sins *voluntarily*, who then will assert that man sins less voluntarily, because he is under a necessity of sinning [that springs from the state of his will] ? "

In the above extract Calvin speaks of the fallen will's "being deprived of its liberty." He means liberty to *good*, not liberty in the abstract and unqualified sense. For he says that Satan "sins voluntarily." The action of the fallen will is free agency, in the sense of self-motion; but this free action in sin effectually opposes and precludes free action in holiness. One free act prevents another free act. In interpreting the creeds of the Reformation, and the systems of the elder divines, it is important to keep in mind the distinction between liberty and ability (for the two things are inseparable) to good, and liberty and ability to evil. They invariably deny to the fallen will liberty to good, but not liberty to evil, in the sense of enforced self-determination to evil.

Owen (Saints' Perseverance, ch. vi.) explains in the same manner. "God can effectually, and infallibly as to the event, cause his saints to continue trusting in him without the least abridgment of their liberty. If by *necessitated* to continue trusting, not the manner of God's operation with and in them for the compassing of the end proposed, and the efficacy of his grace, whereby he *doth* it, be intended, but only the *certainty* of the issue, rejecting the impropriety of the expression [namely, necessity], the thing itself we affirm to be here promised of God."

Anselm (Cur Deus Homo, II., 5) explains "How although a thing may be necessary God may not do it by a compulsory necessity." He says, "When one does a benefit from a necessity to which he is *unwillingly* subjected, little thanks are due to him, or none at all. But when he *freely* places himself under the necessity of benefiting another, and sustains that necessity without reluctance, then he certainly deserves great thanks for the favor. For this should not be called necessity but grace, inasmuch as he undertook it not with constraint but freely." When God has voluntarily promised a thing, then he is under a necessity of fulfilling his promise; but he was under no necessity to promise. In like manner the sinner has voluntarily fallen from God, and thus came under the necessity of sinning, but was under no necessity of falling from God.

Luther (De Servo Arbitrio, cap. 44) thus distinguishes the two significations of necessity : "We should carefully distinguish between a necessity of infallibility [certainty] and a necessity of coercion ; since both good and evil men, though by their actions they fulfil the decree and appoint-

ment of God, yet are not forcibly constrained to do anything but act willingly."

Edwards, in the following extract, seemingly teaches not
only that the lost are in a helpless and necessitating self-
bondage, but are destitute of liberty and moral agency.
His opponents contended that lost men and angels are still
in a state of trial, because they still had the power to the
contrary. " If," says Edwards, " the damned are in a state
of trial, they must be in a state of liberty and moral agency,
as the advocates of future redemption will own ; and so, according to *their notion of liberty*, must be under no necessity of continuing in their rebellion and wickedness, but
may turn to God in their thorough subjection to his will,
very speedily. And if the devils and damned spirits are
in a state of probation, and have liberty of will, and are
under the last and most extreme means to bring them to
repentance, then it is possible that the greatest part, if not
all of them, may be reclaimed by those extreme means and
brought to repentance before the day of judgment. And
if so, how could it certainly be predicted concerning the
devil, that he 'should be cast into the lake of fire and
brimstone, where the beast and false prophet are, and
should be tormented day and night, forever and ever '?
And how can it be said that when he fell, he was cast down
from heaven, and 'reserved in everlasting chains under
darkness unto the judgment of the great day '? "

In this extract Edwards, *taking the words as they read*,
teaches that the lost are not "in a state of liberty and
moral agency," and that consequently they are under " a
[compulsory] necessity of continuing in their rebellion
and wickedness." But he is using terms in the sense of
his opponents, and adopting "their notion of liberty." By
" liberty and moral agency " they meant power to the contrary, and by " necessity of continuing in wickedness," he
himself does not mean physical necessity but the self-
bondage of the will, which is insuperable by the will. In

denying free moral agency to the sinner, as his *opponents* defined it, he does not deny it as *he himself* defined it, in the sense of "being the immediate agent, or the being that is acting, or in the exercise of the act" (Will, IV., i.). The radical difference between the Augustino-Calvinistic definition of freedom and moral agency on the one side, and the Semi-Pelagian and Arminian on the other, must ever be kept in mind when Edwards and other Calvinists deny "freedom and moral agency" to the fallen will. His intention is to deny that the sinful will can reverse its inclination and become holy by its own energy, but not that the sinful inclination itself is the unforced agency and movement of the will, for which the sinner is responsible. Both Augustine and the elder Calvinists, however, were more careful than Edwards was to avoid such seeming denials of free moral agency to the sinner, because they did not, even for the sake of argument, temporarily adopt their opponents' idea of the will and moral agency, but rigorously stuck to their own idea and definition of it as simple self-determination without power to the contrary. The *self-determination* in sin enabled them to affirm liberty and responsibility in sin ; and the want of power to the contrary enabled them to affirm bondage and inability in sin.

Augustine (Enchiridion, ch. 30) asserts the sinner's freedom in sinning, and denies his freedom to good because of the bondage produced by the sinning. "It was by the evil use of his free-will that man destroyed both it and himself. For as a man who kills himself must of course be alive when he kills himself, but after he has killed himself ceases to live, and cannot restore himself to life, so, when man by his own free-will sinned, then sin being victorious over him the freedom of the will [to good] was lost. 'For of whom a man is overcome, of the same is he brought in bondage.' This is the judgment of the apostle Peter. And as it is certainly true, what kind of liberty, I ask, can the bond-slave possess except when it pleases him to sin ? For he is *freely* in bondage who does with pleasure the will of his master. Accordingly, he who is the servant of sin is free to sin. And hence he will not be free to do right until, being freed from sin, he shall begin to be the servant of righteousness [as St. Paul argues in Rom. 6 : 18-20, 22]. And this is true liberty, for he has pleasure in righteous action ; and it is at the same time a holy bondage, for he is subject to the will of God. But whence comes this liberty to do righteousness, to the man who is in bondage to sin and 'sold under sin,' except he be redeemed by him who has said, 'If the Son shall make you free, ye shall be free indeed' ? And before this redemption is wrought in a man, when he is not yet free to do righteousness, how can he talk of the freedom of his will and his good works, except he be inflated by that foolish pride of boasting which the apostle restrains when he says, 'By grace are ye saved, through faith' ? "

This passage, which might be paralleled with scores like it from Augustine's writings, contains his doctrine of free-will and of freedom. The following are the principal points : 1. Freedom in willing is the actual self-motion or inclining of the will. It excludes indifference, because indifference implies that the will is not yet self-moving and inclining. Freedom is action ; indifference is inaction. 2. A distinguishing characteristic of self-motion and inclination is pleasure. The holy will enjoys obedience ; the sinful will enjoys disobedience. This evinces the freedom of the self-motion of the will ; for were there compulsion there would be no enjoyment. The agent would not be conscious of doing as he pleases. 3. Right self-motion is incompatible with simultaneous wrong self-motion, and the converse. Free action in one direction is inability in respect to the other. Good inclination precludes evil inclination. The servant of sin is free in sinning, but not free to do right, because of his freedom in sin. His bondage to sin is the effect of his self-motion in sin. 4. Freedom to-sin may be affirmed, and freedom to holiness denied. Sinful inclination is as really inclination as holy inclination, but it is false freedom, because it conflicts with the moral law. When, therefore, Augustine and Calvin deny freedom to the sinner, as they often do, they do not deny his self-motion and voluntariness in sin, but his ability to the contrary, or his power to reverse and change his self-motion. (Comp. Shedd: On Romans, 6: 18–20, 22).

VOL. II., p. 241. That "sin is a privation, a defect rather than an effect," may be thus illustrated. Sickness is the mere defect of health; the absence of health. But health is not the mere defect or absence of sickness. Health is the normal and right condition of the body, the positive state having its own positive characteristics. Sickness is the abnormal and wrong condition of the body, which is marked not by a set of positive characteristics antithetic to those of health, but only of negative characteristics which consist in the absence of the positive. For illustration, indigestion is the absence of certain properties that make up digestion, not the presence of certain other properties that make up indigestion. Simply ceasing to digest is indigestion; it is not necessary to introduce some new physical processes in order to indigestion, but merely to stop some old ones. Augustine (Enchiridion, 13, 14) thus explains the subject: "Every being, even if it be a defective one, in so far as it is a being is good, and in so far as it is defective is evil. Good and evil are contraries, but evil cannot exist without good, or in anything that is not good. Good, however, can exist without evil. For a man or an angel can exist without being wicked; but nothing can be wicked except a man or an angel; and so far as he is a man or an angel [that is, a creature of God] he is good; so far as he is wicked he is an evil. Nothing can be corrupted except what is good, for corruption is nothing else but the destruction of good."

Vol. II., p. 251. Sin is idolatry, that is, creature-worship. This is St. Paul's definition, in Rom. 1 : 25 : "Men worshipped and served the creature more than the Creator." All forms and aspects of sin are reducible to this. And this is the inclining of the human will to self as the ultimate end, because self is the particular creature in which selfishness is most interested. All other creatures are subordinate and subservient to this one. This idolatry is both freedom and bondage. "Whosoever [freely] committeth sin is the slave of sin" (John 8 : 34). "Of whom a man is [voluntarily] overcome, of the same is he brought in bondage" (2 Peter 2 : 19). This sin is freedom, because it is the uncompelled self-motion of the will; bondage, because the will is unable to reverse its self-motion. Man is responsible and guilty for this creature-worship, because he originates and perpetuates it by self-determination; and he is helpless and ruined by it, because he cannot overcome and extirpate his central self-determination by his superficial volitions and resolutions.

CHRISTOLOGY

Vol. II., p. 265. God the Son can assume a human nature without thereby incarnating the Trinity, because he assumes a human nature into the unity only of his single person, not into the unity of the three persons. He has the essence only in one mode; and the humanity is united with the essence in this one mode, to the exclusion of the essence in the other two modes of the Father and the Spirit. Only the second trinitarian person is humanized; the first and third are not. It is the simple hypostatical personality, not the complex trinal personality, that "becomes flesh and dwells among us, full of grace and truth." The simple hypostatical person is the Son, or Word; this assumes human nature by the miraculous conception. The complex trinal person is the Trinity or Godhead: this did not assume human nature. Three simple hypostatical persons make one complex trinal person, and three simple hypostatical consciousnesses make one complex self-consciousness. A hypostatical consciousness is not trinal and complex, but single and simple. God the Father's hypostatical consciousness is only the consciousness of being the Father; God the Son's hypostatical consciousness is only the consciousness of being the Son; God the Spirit's hypostatical consciousness is only the consciousness of being the Spirit. There is no complexity of self-beholding, self-cognizing, and self-communing in the hypostatical consciousness. But the self-consciousness of the Triune Godhead is trinal and complex. It results from the whole essence in one mode contemplating the whole essence in another mode, and the whole essence in still another mode perceiving the identity in essence of the other two. There is no trinalizing of a *mode* or *person* of the essence, but only of the essence. No one of the Divine Persons repeats the trinalizing process. The Father does not contemplate himself as Father, and then reunite the duality in the second act. He contemplates himself in the Son. And so with the Son and the Spirit. The Divine Persons see themselves in each other, not in themselves.

VOL. II., p. 269. "The incarnation was not necessary in order that the trinitarian Son of God might be self-conscious." "Self-conscious" here denotes only the hypostatical consciousness of a single Divine Person, not the self-consciousness of the Godhead as triune. No single trinitarian Person can have self-consciousness in this latter sense, because this requires all three distinctions. Self-consciousness in the comprehensive sense is the resultant of the three hypostatical consciousnesses. Still, this hypostatical consciousness may, in a secondary sense, be denominated "self-consciousness," because it is that consciousness which one trinitarian Person has of himself as distinct from the other two. This remark applies also to the statement in Vol. II., p. 306: "This person must be a self-conscious ego," etc.

VOL. II., p. 272. Kidd (Eternal Sonship of Christ, ch. xi.) thus describes the passive relation of Christ's humanity to his divinity, and the fact that the latter is omnipotently controlling in his person. "As the humanity of our Lord was formed for the express purpose of existing in his divinity, it was formed, in an especial manner, to assume the appearances and subjection consonant to the designs of Divinity. It had no will of its own to assume any state ; it could only exist according to the volition of Divinity founded on the Divine constitution. The subjection in its humiliation was therefore of two kinds: A necessary subjection to the Godhead, in whatever condition it existed; and a peculiar subjection indicated by its sufferings in that particular state of humiliation. In relation to God this subjection was a devotion to the Divine will, and a particular devotion to that Divine person in whom it subsisted. This devotion was essential to its very nature, and was communicated in its original conformation. Whilst its actions on earth were really those of humanity, they were those of a humanity whose procedure was in union with a Divine person. They flowed from that person, and were really his; yet they were not the actions of his Divinity, but of his humanity subsisting in his Divine nature. The Son of God could not suffer in his essential Divine nature; yet his assumed human nature was humbled, was 'made a curse for us, for it is written, Cursed is everyone that hangeth on a tree.' But while the Messiah experienced this temporary humiliation, the inherent glory of his [theanthropic] person was not and could not be lost. This humiliation was not natural to him, but was submitted to, that the glory which was natural to a man received into personal union by one of the persons of the Godhead might afterward be exhibited. When therefore the eclipse of the Messiah's human nature was past, it appeared, when he 'ascended up on high,' in that splendor which was peculiar to its exalted state of existence as united with deity."

VOL. II., p. 274, Note. The later Lutheran doctrine of the exinanition of the divine nature differs from the Reformed, in that it is a *preparation* for the union with the human nature, instead of being this union itself. The divine first "empties" itself before it assumes the humanity. According to the Reformed view, the assumption of the humanity is immediate, without any preparation, or kenosis, on the part of the divinity, and the union and incarnation is the kenosis. According to the Lutheran, the Logos "took upon him the form of a servant" before, and in order to, being "made in the likeness of men." According to the Reformed, "taking the form of a servant" was the same thing as being "made in the likeness of men." Hilary, according to Dorner (Person. Christi, I., 1046 sq.) seems to have held this view. According to him the Logos, prior to the incarnation, and in order to it, put off "the form of God" and put on "the form of a servant." This "forma" is the "facies" or countenance; that which appears to a beholder. The Logos emptied himself of the glorious form which belonged to him in the Trinity, and assumed an inglorious form, in order that he might then assume a human nature into union. Hilary supposes that the original resplendent "form of God" could not directly make such an assumption. According to the Reformed view, on the contrary, it could; and there is no need of an exinanition prior to the incarnation.

In Hilary's theory, also, the incarnation is not complete until the exaltation of Christ has occurred; that is, not until the human nature is united with the original resplendent "form of God" as well as with the humbled "form of a servant." But this cannot take place until Christ passes from the estate of humiliation into the heavenly glory. In the Reformed theory the incarnation is complete the instant the human nature is united by the miraculous conception with the Logos in his original resplendent "form of God," which by this union then becomes temporarily "emptied" and humbled, and loses its full resplendence, until at the ascension it is exalted and glorified as at first.

Vol. II., p. 280. Owen (Person of Christ, ch. xix.) compares the influence of the divine nature upon the human, in the complex person of Christ, to that of the soul upon the body, in the case of man's complex person. "As to the way of the communications between the divine and human nature in the personal union between the

Logos and his humanity, we know it not. The glorious immediate emanations of virtue from the divine unto the human nature of Christ, we understand not. Indeed, the actings of natures of different kinds, where both are finite in the same person, one toward the other, is a difficult apprehension. Who knows how directive power and efficacy proceeds from the soul, and is communicated unto the body, unto every the least minute action in every member of it; so as that there is no distance between the direction and the action, or the accomplishment of it; or how, on the other hand, the soul is affected with sorrow or trouble in the moment wherein the body feeleth pain, so as that no distinction can be made between the body's sufferings and the soul's sorrow? How much more is this mutual communication in the same person of divers natures above our comprehension, where one of them is absolutely infinite!"

VOL. II., p. 282. Ursinus (Christian Religion, Q. 48) thus reasons respecting the Lutheran doctrine of the ubiquity of Christ's humanity: "The Ubiquitaries object, 1. In Christ's person the two natures are found in an inseparable union, therefore, wheresoever Christ's deity is, there also must his humanity needs be. Answer: These two natures remain in such sort joined and united that their property remaineth distinct, and neither is turned into the other; which would happen if each nature were infinite and everywhere. Objection 2. Those two natures, whereof one is not where the other is, are sundered, neither remain personally united, but are separated. In Christ are two natures, whereof one, which is his humanity, is not where is the other, which is his deity; therefore the two natures in Christ are not united, but separated. Answer: The major is true, if it be understood of two *equal natures*; that is, either both finite, or both infinite; but false of *unequal natures*, that is, one finite and one infinite. For the finite nature cannot be at once in more places than one; but the infinite nature may be at once both whole *in* the finite nature and whole *without* it. Christ's human nature, which is finite, is but in one place; but his divine nature, which is infinite, is both in Christ's human nature, and without it, and everywhere."

Vol. II., p. 289. Dorner follows Schleiermacher, who (Glaubenslehre, § 97) denies the impersonality of Christ's human nature prior to its assumption by the Logos. Schleiermacher does not recognize the distinction between specific and individual human nature. Human nature, he contends is only individual, and objects that if the human nature of Christ prior to it assumption was impersonal, " it was different from, and inferior to, that of the rest of mankind." The church doctrine on this point he describes as an error of scholasticism. " The position that the human nature of Christ in and for itself is impersonal, or has no [personal] subsistence of its own, but subsists [personally] only through the divine [personality], in this scholastic drapery is very obscure and embarrassing."

In connection with the denial of this tenet, which enters into all the church Christology, Schleiermacher (§ 97) also denies that Christ was born of a virgin. His view is that Christ must have been born in the ordinary manner by the union of both sexes, in order to be a real man like other men; and also that in connection with this ordinary generation there must also have been a creative energy of God, in order to cleanse away the original sin which would naturally accompany it. If Christ's conception in the womb of Mary, he argues, took place without cohabitation with Joseph, this would not preclude sinfulness, because this would naturally issue from his mother, who was sinful. And the creative energy of God could as easily purge away a sinfulness that was derived from both father and mother as that derived from the mother alone. This is true; but the question is not what God could do, but what he did do. And this can be known only from the Gospel account of the subject. This account, given by Matthew and Luke, Schleiermacher declares to be legendary and not historically credible. It is one of the inventions of the Primitive Church. For proof of this we have only his assertion, as is commonly the case when the received manuscript text of the New Testament is declared to be untrustworthy.

Schleiermacher exhibits the same arbitrariness of assertion in declaring that the creeds of the church, both ancient and modern, " are so phrased that they have no dogmatic aim," and do not warrant the deduction of an ecclesiastical doctrine from them. He cites only the ancient Roman and Constantinopolitan creeds, and the modern Augsburg, Helvetic, Gallican, Anglican, and Belgic Confessons, which do not bear out his assertion : each and all being of a very positive dogmatic character. An examination of the individual and conciliar creeds of the Ancient Church will convince any unbiassed mind that the doctrine of the virginal birth of Christ, which constitutes one of the principal articles of the Apostles' Creed, has an ecclesiastical support as strong as any of the doctrines of the Christian faith. The following creeds, to none of which does Schleiermacher allude, contain explicit affirmation of it : Irenæus, Tertullian, Origen, Epiphanius, Basil, Constantinople, Aquileia, Augustine, Maximus Taurinensis, Eusebius Gallicani, Cassian, Chrysologus, Venatius, Alcuin, Etherius. The views of Schleiermacher respecting the virginal birth of Christ have recently been revived by Harnack, whose argument is substantially the same as his. Compare Shedd : Orthodoxy and Heterodoxy, pp. 154–161. Coleridge also (Works, V., 76, 78, 79, 532. Harper's Ed.) takes the same view of the Christopædia in Matthew and Luke's Gospels.

There is no better account of this subject than that given by Charnocke (The Power of God). " 1. Christ was conceived by the Holy Ghost in the womb of the Virgin (Luke 1 : 35): 'The Holy Ghost shall come upon thee, and the power of the Highest shall overshadow thee;' which act is described to be the effect of the infinite power of God. And it describes the supernatural manner of forming the humanity of our Saviour, and signifies not the Divine nature of Christ [namely, the Logos] infusing itself into the womb of the virgin; for the angel refers it to the manner of the operation of the Holy Ghost in the producing the human nature of Christ, and not to the nature assuming that humanity into union with itself. The Holy Ghost, or the third Person in the Trinity, overshadowed the virgin, and by a creative act framed the humanity of Christ, and united it to the Divinity [namely, the Logos]. It is, therefore, expressed by a word of the same import with that used in Gen. 1 : 2. 'The Spirit moved upon the face of the waters,' which signifies a brooding upon the chaos, shadowing it with his wings, as hens sit upon their eggs to form them and hatch them into animals; or else it is an allusion to the 'cloud which covered the tent of the congregation when the glory of the Lord filled the tabernacle' (Ex. 40 : 34). It was not such a creative act as we call immediate, which is a production out of nothing; but a mediate creation, such as God's bringing things into form out of the first [chaotic] matter, which had nothing but an obediential or passive disposition to whatever stamp the powerful wisdom of God should imprint upon it. So the substance of the virgin had no active, but only a passive disposition to this work; the matter of the body was earthly, the substance of the virgin; the forming of it was heavenly, the Holy Ghost working upon that matter. And therefore when it is said that 'she was found with child of the Holy Ghost,' it is to be understood of the efficacy of the Holy Ghost, not of the substance of the Holy Ghost. The matter was natural, but the manner of conceiving was in a supernatural way, above the methods of nature. That

25

part of the flesh of the virgin whereof the human nature of Christ was made, was refined and purified from corruption by the overshadowing of the Holy Ghost. Our Saviour is therefore called ' that holy thing,' though born of the virgin. He was necessarily in some way to descend from Adam. God, indeed, might have created his body out of nothing, or have formed it, as he did Adam's, out of the dust of the ground ; but had he been thus extraordinarily formed, and not propagated from Adam, though he had been a man like one of us, yet he would not have been of kin to us, because it would not have been a nature derived from Adam, the common parent of us all. But now, by this way of producing the humanity of Christ of the substance of the virgin, he is of the same nature that had sinned, and so what he did and suffered may be imputed to us, which, had he been created as Adam was, could not be claimed in a legal and judicial way."

" 2. It was not fitting, however, that he should be propagated and born in the common order of nature of father and mother ; for whatsoever is so born is polluted. ' A clean thing cannot be brought out of an unclean ' (Job 14: 4). And our Saviour had been incapable of being a redeemer had he been tainted with the least spot of our corrupt nature, but would have stood in need of redemption himself. Besides, it had been inconsistent with the holiness of the Divine nature to have assumed a tainted and defiled body [humanity]. He that was the fountain of blessedness to all nations, was not to be subject to the curse of the law for himself, which he would have been had he been conceived in the ordinary way. Again, supposing that Almighty God by his divine power had so perfectly sanctified an earthly father and mother from all original spot, that the human nature might have been transmitted immaculate to him, as well as the Holy Ghost did purge that part of the flesh of the virgin of which the body [humanity] of Christ was made, yet it was not fitting that

that person, who was ' God blessed forever ' as well as man, partaking of our nature, should have a conception in the same manner as ours, but different, and in some measure conformable to the infinite dignity of his person ; which could not have been had not a supernatural power and a Divine Person been concerned as an active principle in it ; besides, such a birth had not been agreeable to the first promise, which calls him ' the Seed of the woman,' not of the man ; and so the veracity of God had suffered some detriment : the Seed of the woman only is set in opposition to the seed of the serpent."

" 3. By this manner of conception the holiness of Christ's human nature is secured, and his fitness for his office is assured to us. It is now a pure and unpolluted humanity that is the temple and tabernacle of the Divinity ; the fulness of the Godhead dwells in him bodily, and dwells in him holily. Though we read of some men sanctified from the womb, it was not a pure and perfect holiness ; it was like the light of fire mixed with smoke, an infused holiness accompanied with a natural taint ; but the holiness of the Redeemer by this conception is like the light of the sun, pure and without spot : the Spirit of holiness supplying the place of a father in a way of creation. His fitness for his office is also assured to us ; for being born of the virgin, one of our nature, but conceived by the Spirit, a Divine Person, the guilt of our sins may be imputed to him, because our nature in him is without the stain of inherent sin ; because, by reason of his supernatural conception, he is capable, as one of kin to us, to bear our curse without being touched by our taint. By this means our sinful nature is assumed without sin in that nature which was assumed by him : flesh he hath, but not sinful flesh (Rom. 8 : 3)." [St. Paul here says that Christ " condemned sin in his flesh," not in his " *sinful* flesh "].

Augustine (Forgiveness and Baptism, ii., 38) thus describes the human nature of Christ as it was first in the virgin mother, and as it was afterward when completely sanctified in the God-man: "The Word, which became flesh, was in the beginning, and was with God (John 1 : 1). But at the same time his participation in our inferior condition, in order to our participation in his higher state, held a kind of medium between the two in his birth in the flesh. We were born in sinful flesh, but he was born in the likeness of sinful flesh ; we were born not only of flesh and blood [human seed], but also of the will of man [human will], and of the will of the flesh [sexual appetite] ; but he was born only of flesh and blood [the seed of the virgin], not of the will of man [human will], nor of the will of the flesh [sexual appetite], but of God. He, therefore, having become man, but still continuing to be God, never had any sin, nor did he assume a flesh of sin though born of a material flesh of sin [*i.e.*, of a flesh which, prior to its miraculous sanctification, was sinful in the virgin mother, because propagated from Adam]. For what he then took of flesh he either cleansed, in order to take it, or cleansed by taking it. His virgin mother, therefore, whose conception of him was not according to the law of sinful flesh, in other words, not by the excitement of carnal concupiscence, he formed in order to choose her [as the mother of the God-man], and chose her in order to be formed from her."

VOL. II., p. 307. The principal difference between the Reformed and the Later-Lutheran Christology lies in the difference between union and transmutation. The former affirms that Jesus Christ is constituted of two divers natures, united together without any change in the properties of either ; the latter, that he is constituted of two diverse natures, one of which when the union takes place, *changes* the other. The Lutheran asserts that the divine nature communicates some of its properties, such as omnipresence, omnipotence, and omniscience to the human nature, thereby expelling the finite properties of confinement to locality, weakness, and ignorance; the Reformed denies this. And this substitution or transmutation of natures for union of natures arose from an erroneous conception of *personality*. The Lutheran assumed that if there is to be only one person there must be only one nature. Hence his conversion of the two natures into a third single one. This was also the erroneous opinion of the ancient monophysitism. If two natures, then two persons; if one nature, then one person. This was the assumption. But a self-conscious person may be simple or complex in his constitution; he may have one nature, or two natures, or three natures. A *trinitarian* person, for example, is constituted of only one nature, namely, the divine. He is wholly spiritual, immaterial, and infinite. The second person in the Godhead, prior to his incarnation, is the divine essence in a particular mode or form of subsistence. He is pure spirit, without body, parts, or passions. A *human* person, again, is constituted of two natures: an immaterial soul and a material body. A man is not, like the unincarnate Son of God, purely and only spirit. He is composed of two substances or natures as diverse as mind and matter. And yet there is only one self, only one self-consciousness, only one person. One and the same man is conscious of the spiritual feelings of his soul, and of the physical sensations of his body. The former issue out of his immaterial nature, the latter out of his material, and both are equally and alike the experience of but one person. Having double natures he has a double form of consciousness or experience, with only a single self-consciousness. In this respect a human person differs from a trinitarian person. The latter can have only one form or mode of consciousness, namely, a spiritual. The former can have two; one spiritual and one sensuous and physical. A divine person has one mode of consciousness and one self-consciousness; a human person has two modes of consciousness and one self-consciousness.

And yet even a human person, like a trinitarian person,

may for a time have self-consciousness or personality with only one nature. When, for example, the human body is separated from the human soul at death, the self-consciousness continues, but only one form of conscious experience is now possible. The soul without the body cannot feel physical sensations. The experience or consciousness of the disembodied state must be wholly mental and spiritual. There can be no sensuous elements in it, because the body with the five senses is temporarily separated from the soul. The man must now get all of his conscious experience through his immaterial nature. There may be, and is, a memory of past sensuous experiences, but no present actual sensation through the bodily senses. Not until the resurrection of the body and its reunion with the soul can both modes of consciousness, the physical and the mental, be experienced again together. This proves that a single self-consciousness, or personality, is possible either with one or with two natures ; only the elements in it will not be so various in one case as in the other.

A *theanthropic* person, again, is yet more complex than a human person. He has three diverse natures, each yielding their diverse experiences or modes of consciousness, and yet only a single self-consciousness. The Lord Jesus Christ is constituted of three substances, distinct and different in kind from each other. He is constituted of one infinite spirit, one finite spirit, and one finite body. The God-man is composed of the divine essence in its filial "form " (Phil. 2 : 6), a rational human soul, and a human body. Why should such a diversity in the components of the one theanthropic person be thought to be incompatible with a single self-consciousness ? If two natures or substances, as different in kind from each other as a man's immaterial spirit and his material body, can constitute only one person and yield a single self-consciousness with its doubleness of experiences or consciousnesses, why is it so difficult as the Later-Lutheran asserts it is, to believe that three

natures or substances as diverse as the divine essence, a
man's spirit, and a man's body, should likewise constitute
only a single person, and yield only a single self-consciousness with its threefoldness of experiences or consciousnesses,
namely, those of the divine essence, of a rational soul, and
of a sensuous body ? If it is not necessary to assume that
spirit is transmuted into body, or body into spirit, in order
to account for a single self-conscious personality in the instance of a man, why is it necessary to assume that the
human nature must be transmuted into the divine in order
that there may be a single self-conscious personality in the
instance of a God-man ? If complexity of natures is not
incompatible with self-consciousness in human psychology,
why is it in theanthropic psychology ? Had more attention been given to the complexity and diversity of natures
found in ordinary human personality, the assumption that
began in Apollinarism, and has run through the whole
kenotic controversy, namely, that personality necessarily
implies simplicity of structure and singleness of nature,
and is incompatible with complexity of structure and
duality and trinality of natures, would have been invali-
dated more readily. If two points are kept in view, namely, that the divine and human natures in Christ's theanthropic person are united but not transmuted, and that the
human nature is assumed into union in its unindividualized
state, there need be no logical difficulty in the construction of Christ's single personality and self-consciousness.
The fathers at Chalcedon did this, and so did leading
schoolmen like Aquinas. The Reformed theologians did
the same ; while some of the Later-Lutheran divines
showed a tendency toward the ancient monophysitism ; a
tendency which in some of their latest speculations has
gone to even a greater extreme than those of Apollinaris
and Eutyches. And finally, if the important distinction
between consciousness and self-consciousness had been
perceived and employed, the conscious experience of the

person at a particular moment, such as a physical sensation
or a mental emotion, which is transient and gives place
to a multitude of similar experiences like it, would not
have been mistaken for the permanent and immutable ego
whose self-consciousness lies under all this stream of consciousnesses or experiences, and combines them into the
unity of a person.

VOL. II., p. 321. The alternation in the self-consciousness of Christ, according as the human and divine natures
advanced or retreated, explains how it was possible for
him to have his desires unrealized and his endeavors
thwarted. The question naturally arises, how Christ could
consistently and sincerely say, "How often would I have
gathered thy children, and ye would not," when as incarnate deity he could have inclined them to come to him?
How could he have wept genuine tears over refusing Jerusalem, when he might, by the irresistible energy of the Holy
Spirit, have overcome the opposition that caused his tears?
The answer is that though he was God incarnate, it was a
part of his humiliation to be "emptied," for most of the
time while here upon earth, of his Divine power—that is,
not to employ it continually and invariably as he did in
his pre-existent state. This exinanition made him like an
ordinary man, who cannot prevail upon men except in the
ordinary way of argument, entreaty, and persuasion, all of
which might fail to move them. Though God incarnate,
yet the nature of his mediatorial office while on earth, as
one of humiliation, prohibited the constant use of his
omnipotence. He was therefore in this low estate subject
to the disappointment and grief which any one of his own
ministers is subject to, when he sees no fruit of his labors,
and grieves over the perversity and obstinacy of men.

VOL. II., p. 323. Ursinus (Christian Religion, Q. 37)
thus explains the communicatio idiomatum, or communication of properties: "The communicating of the properties
is to attribute that to the whole person which is proper

unto one nature; and this is attributed in a concrete term [denoting the person], not in an abstract [denoting the nature]; because the concrete term signifieth the whole person in which are both natures, and, consequently, the properties of that particular nature whereof something is affirmed. But the abstract term signifieth only the nature which is in the whole person, but not the whole person. And therefore it is that nothing hindereth why that which is proper to one nature only may not be affirmed of the whole person, so that this property itself may be in and of the person; but contrariwise of the abstract term, only the properties of that nature designated by it are affirmed unto it. As, for example, of the Godhood [deity], which is the abstract impersonal term, no property of the manhood may be affirmed, but only the properties of the Godhood, because Godhood [deity] signifies not the whole person who has both natures, but only the divine nature itself. But of [incarnate] God, which is the concrete or personal term, the properties not of the Godhood only, but of the manhood also may be affirmed; because incarnate God signifieth not the divine nature merely and only, but the person who hath both the divine nature and the human."

Vol. II., p. 327. Charnocke's (Power of God) account of the hypostatical union of the two natures of Christ in one person is as follows: "1. There is in this redeeming Person a union of two natures. He is God and man in one person. Heb. 1: 8, 9: 'Thy throne, O God, is for ever and ever; God, even thy God, hath anointed thee with the oil of gladness above thy fellows.' The Son is called God, having a throne forever and ever, and the unction speaks him man: the Godhead cannot be anointed, nor hath any fellows. Humanity and Divinity are ascribed to him in Rom. 1: 3, 4: 'He was of the seed of David according to the flesh, and declared to be the son of God by the resurrection from the dead.' The Divinity and humanity are both prophetically joined in Zech. 10 : 10 : 'I will pour out my Spirit;' the pouring forth of the Spirit is an act only of Divine grace and power. 'And they shall look upon me, whom they have pierced;' the same person pours forth the Spirit of God, and is pierced as man. 'The Word was made flesh' (John 1: 14). Word from eternity was made flesh in time; Word and flesh in one person; a great God and a little infant. 2. The terms [factors] of this union were infinitely distant from each other. What greater distance can there be than between the Deity and humanity, between the Creator and a creature? A God of unmixed blessedness is linked personally with a man of perpetual sorrows; infinite purity with a reputed sinner; eternal blessedness with a cursed nature; almightiness with weakness; omniscience with ignorance; immutability with changeableness; incomprehensibleness with comprehensibility ; a holiness incapable of sinning made sin [a sin-offering] ; a person possessed of all the perfections of the Godhead inheriting all the imperfections of the manhood in one person, sin only excepted. 3. This union is strait [strict]. It is not such a union as is between a man and his house he dwells in; nor such a union as is between a man and his garment; nor such a union as one friend hath with another. The straitness [strictness] of this union may be somewhat conceived by the union of fire with iron; fire pierceth through all the parts of iron, it unites itself with every particle, bestows a light, heat, purity upon all of it; you cannot distinguish the iron from the fire, or the fire from the iron, yet they are distinct natures; so the Deity is united to the whole humanity, seasons it, and bestows an excellency upon it, yet the natures still remain distinct. As during that union of fire with iron, the iron is incapable of rust or blackness, so is the humanity as united with the Deity incapable of sin ; and as the operation of fire is attributed to the red-hot iron (as the iron may be said to heat, burn, and the fire may be said to cut and pierce), yet the imperfections of the iron do not affect the fire, so in this mystery those things which belong to the Divinity are ascribed to the humanity, and those things which belong to the humanity are ascribed to the Divinity, in regard to the Person in whom these natures are united. The Divinity of Christ is as really united with the humanity as the soul with the body; so united that the sufferings of the human nature were the sufferings of that 'Person, and the dignity of the Divine was imputed to the human by reason of that unity of both in one Person ; hence the blood of the human nature is said to be the blood of God' (Acts 20 : 28)."

VOL. II., p. 330. Edersheim (Life of Jesus, I., 298) thus explains the impeccability of the God-man : "The passage of Scripture in which Christ's equality with us as regards all temptation is expressed, also emphatically excepts from it this one particular, *sin* (Heb. 4 : 15 ; James 1 : 14); not only in the sense that Christ actually did not sin, nor merely in this, that ' our concupiscence ' had no part in his temptations, but emphatically in this also, that the notion of sin has to be wholly excluded from our thoughts of Christ's temptations."

" To obtain, if we can, a clearer understanding of this subject, two points must be kept in view. Christ's was real, though *unfallen* human nature ; and Christ's human nature was in inseparable *union* with his Divine nature. Now it is clear that human nature, that of Adam before his fall, was created both sinless and peccable. If Christ's human nature was not sinful like ours, but morally like that of Adam before his fall, then must it likewise have been both sinless and in itself peccable. We say, in itself—for there is a great difference between the statement that *human nature*, as Adam and Christ had it, was capable of sinning, and the statement that *Christ* was peccable. From the latter the Christian mind instinctively recoils, even as it is metaphysically impossible to imagine the [infinite and omnipotent] Son of God peccable. Jesus voluntarily took upon himself human nature, with all its infirmities and weaknesses, but without the moral taint of the fall : without sin. It was human nature in itself capable of sinning, but not having sinned. The position of the first Adam was that of being capable of not sinning, not that of being incapable of sinning. The second Adam also had a human nature capable of not sinning, but not incapable of sinning. This explains the possibility of temptation or assault upon him, just as Adam could be tempted before there was any inward consensus [concupiscence] to it. The first Adam would have been ' perfected,' or passed from the capability of not sinning to the incapability of sinning, by obedience. That obedience, or submission to the will of God, was the grand characteristic of Christ's work ; but it was so because he was not only the unsinning, unfallen Man, but also the [infinite and omnipotent] Son of God. With a peccable human nature he himself was impeccable ; not because he obeyed, but being impeccable he so obeyed because his human nature was inseparably *united* with his divine nature. To keep this inseparable union of the two natures out of view would be Nestorianism. To sum up : The second Adam, morally unfallen, though voluntarily subject to all the conditions of our nature, was, with a peccable human nature, absolutely impeccable, as being also the [infinite and omnipotent] Son of God—a peccable nature, yet an impeccable Person : the God-Man ' tempted in regard to all (things) in like manner (as we), without (excepting) sin.' "

Edwards (Will, Pt., III. sec. ii.) argues the impeccability of Christ from the promises made to him, and the operation of the Holy Spirit in him, not from the constitution of his Person. The following are some of the principal points : " It was impossible that the acts of the will of the human soul of Christ should, in any instance, degree, or circumstance, be otherwise than holy, because : 1. God had promised so effectually to preserve and uphold him by his Spirit, under all his temptations, that he could not fail of reaching the end for which he came into the world (Isa. 43 : 1–4 ; 49 : 7–9 ; 50 : 5–9). 2. The same thing is evident from all the promises which God made to the Messiah himself, of his future glory, kingdom, and success in his office and character as a Mediator ; which glory could not have been obtained if his holiness had failed and he had been guilty of sin (Ps. 110 : 4 ; 2 : 7, 8 ; Isa. 52 : 13–15 ; 53 : 10–12). 3. God promised to the Church of God of old to give them a righteous, sinless Saviour, ' in whom all the nations of the earth should be blessed ' (Jer. 23 : 5, 6 ; 33 : 15 ; Isa. 9 : 6, 7 ; Luke 24 : 44 ; Heb. 6 : 17, 18 ; Ps. 89 : 3, 4). 4. God promised the Virgin Mary that her Son should ' save his people from their sins,' and that he ' would give him the throne of his father David, that he should reign over the house of Jacob for ever, and that of his kingdom there should be no end ' (Luke 1 : 45). 5. If it was possible for Christ to have failed of doing the will of his Father, and so to have failed of effectually working out redemption for sinners, then the salvation of all the saints who were saved from the beginning of the world to the death of Christ was not built upon a firm foundation."

VOL. II., p. 331. Calvin (Inst., III., xx., 46) thus dis-criminates between temptation by God and temptation from concupiscence, or inward lust : " The forms of temp-tations are many and various. For the corrupt imag-inations of the mind provoking us to transgressions of the law, whether suggested by our own concupiscence or ex-cited by the devil, are temptations. And these tempta-tions are either from prosperous or adverse events. From prosperous ones, as riches, power, honors, which generally dazzle men's eyes by their glitter, and ensnare them with their blandishments, so that caught with such delusions they forget God. From unpropitious ones, as poverty, reproaches, contempt, afflictions ; overcome by the bitterness of which they fall into despondency, cast away faith and hope, and at length become altogether alienated from God. To both of these kinds of temptations we pray our heavenly Father not to permit us to yield, but rather to sustain us, that, strong in might, we may be able to stand firm against all the assaults of our malignant enemy."

"The temptations of God are widely different from those of Satan. Satan tempts to overthrow, condemn, confound, and destroy. But God, that, by proving his people, he may make a trial of their sincerity, to confirm their strength by exercising it, to mortify, purify, and refine their flesh, which without such restraints would run into the greatest excesses. Besides, Satan attacks persons unarmed and unprepared, to overwhelm the unwary. 'God, with the temptation, always makes a way to escape, that they may be able to bear' whatever he brings upon them (1 Cor. 10 : 13). To some there appears a difficulty in our petition to God that he will not lead us into temptation, whereas, according to James, it is contrary to his nature for him to tempt us (James 1 : 13, 14). But this objection has already been partly answered, because our own lust is properly the cause of all the temptations that seduce and overcome us. Nor does James intend any other than to assert the injustice of transferring to God the tempting concupiscence which we are bound to impute to ourselves because we are conscious of being guilty of it. But notwithstanding this, God may when he sees fit deliver us to Satan, abandon us to a reprobate mind and lustful concupiscence, and in this manner 'lead us into temptation' by a righteous judgment as a punishment of our sinful self-indulgence (Rom. 1 : 24, 26, 28)."

VOL. II., p. 344. There is a difference between trial and seduction, yet both are brought under the term temptation in James 1 : 14. "Every man is tempted when he is drawn away [seduced] of his own lust and enticed." So, also, are they in Gal. 6 : 1. " Considering thyself lest thou also be tempted." The preceding context shows that the term here denotes seduction, or " being overtaken in a fault." Mere trial without seduction is denoted in James 1 : 2, 12. Seduction is temptation with sin, or sinful temptation. Trial is temptation " without sin," or innocent temptation. Ebrard, on Heb. 4 : 15, explains the difference as follows : " Whoever is seduced does not hold a mere passive relation to the seducer, but his own will harmonizes with his ; whoever is tried is purely passive. But it is not merely physical passivity ; headache is not πειρασμός. To get the full meaning of innocent and passive temptation we must mark the difference between nature and spirit, involuntary psychical life and free self-conscious life, innate affections and temperaments and personal character. Our Lord as a real man led a truly human psychical life ; he experienced the feelings of pleasure and pain, of hope, fear, and anxiety as we do. He enjoyed life and recoiled from death. In brief, within the sphere of natural involuntary psychical life he was passively excitable as we are. But duty requires of every man that he rule, and not be ruled by, these instinctive natural affections which are not sinful in themselves. The temperaments illustrate this : That a person is of a sanguine temperament is not sinful ; but if he suffers himself to be carried away through this temperament to anger, this is sin. A phlegmatic temperament is not sinful ; but if it is permitted by the person's will and character to become sloth, this is sin. In this way every innocent temperament involves temptation in the sense of trial, but not in the sense of seduction. The same is true of the natural and instinctive feelings, or affections. That I take pleasure in an undisturbed and comfortable life is not sinful ; but if I am placed by Providence where duty requires me to enter upon a severe experience and a life full of discomfort, and

I refuse, this is sin. I ought to sacrifice my innocent love of comfort to the Divine command." Our Lord's instinctive and sinless recoil from agony and death was a temptation in the sense of a trial to him, but not seduction. It was a temptation "without sin," or *lust* after ease and comfort.

SOTERIOLOGY.

Vol. II., p. 357. Witsius (Apostles' Creed, x., 42–44) thus explains Christ's divesting himself of the mediatorial commission and kingdom, as taught in Cor. 15 : 24–28. "It is certain, 1. That the Divine, essential, and natural kingdom of Christ [as the Second Person of the Trinity] is eternal. 2. That the humanity of Christ will always remain personally united with the Divinity, and will on that account enjoy a glory very far surpassing the glory of all creatures. 3. Christ will always be the Head, that is, by far the most noble member of the church, and as such will be recognized, adored, and praised by the church. 4. The mediatorial kingdom itself will be eternal as to its glorious effects, as well in the Head as in the members. Some of these effects are : In Christ, the effulgence of the Divine majesty shining most brightly in his Person as God-man ; in the elect, complete liberty, the subjugation of all their enemies, the entire abolition of sin, and unutterable joy arising from intimate communion with God. In these respects the kingdom of Christ is eternal, and Paul is so far from opposing these sentiments that, on the contrary, he teaches them at great length."

"But after the day of the last judgment the exercise of Christ's kingly office and the form of his mediatorial kingdom will be widely different from what they now are. 1. The economical government of this kingdom, as now exercised by an ecclesiastical ministry, and by civil authority

26

as conducive to the protection of the church, will then cease, 'when he shall have put down all rule, and all authority, and power.' 2. After the last judgment Christ will render an account to God the Father of his whole mediatorial office, as perfectly accomplished in what relates not only to the purchase, but also to the full application of salvation to the whole church; presenting to him a truly glorious church, not having spot, or wrinkle, or any such thing. To this may be referred the expression, 'He shall deliver up the kingdom,' that is, the church, in her perfect state, 'to God, even the Father.' 3. This account having been rendered, the Godhead itself without the intervention of a Mediator (for which there seems no more occasion, sin being removed) will hold communion immediately with the redeemed, in almost the same manner in which it holds fellowship with the angels; with this difference, however, that the redeemed will through eternity acknowledge themselves indebted to the merits of Christ for this immediate communication of the Deity. This is what is intended by the expression 'that God may be all in all.' 4. There, also, Christ, no longer discharging any part of the mediatorial office, will, with regard to his human nature, be subject unto God, as one of the brethren, possessing manifold and most excellent glory, without any diminution of the glory which he now enjoys. This seems to be intimated by these words, 'And when all things shall be subdued unto him, then shall the Son also himself be subject unto him that put all things under him.' 5. Thus far there 'shall be an end' of the mediatorial kingdom, the exercise of which supposes some imperfection in the church. It is an end of such a nature as brings all things to a state of complete and endless perfection."

Owen (Person of Christ, ch. xix.) says on this subject: " For the discharge of this mediatorial work Christ hath a sovereign power over all things in heaven and earth committed unto him. Herein he doth and must reign. And so absolutely is it vested in him that upon the ceasing of the exercise of it he himself is said to be subject unto God. It is true that the Lord Christ, in his human nature, is always less than, or inferior unto, God, even the Father. In this sense he is in subjection unto him now in heaven. But yet he hath an actual exercise [as Mediator] of divine power, wherein he is absolute and supreme. When this [mediatorial and redeeming power] ceaseth he shall be subject unto the Father in that [human] nature, and only so. Wherefore when this work [of mediation between God and sinners] is perfectly fulfilled and ended, then shall all the mediatory actings of Christ cease forevermore. For God will then have completely finished the whole design of his wisdom and grace [in redemption]. Then will God ' be all in all.' "

Edward Irving (Christ's Kingly Office) remarks to the same effect. " To give up this superinduced power [of Mediator between God and sinful men] and return into the condition of his primeval equality, into the condition of the Son begotten from all eternity, this is, what I understand St. Paul to mean when he saith, ' Then shall the Son also be subject unto him that put all things under him, that God may be all in all ; ' that is, the earth shall no longer be under mediatorial regiment, but under the same direct regiment of God in which the unfallen worlds are. And God—not God and a Mediator, but God in his [tri-] personalities and offices—shall be all in all."

VOL. II., p. 382. The attempt is sometimes made to illustrate vicarious suffering in grace by what is denominated " vicarious suffering in nature." But the analogy is defective. The two things are different in kind, not merely in degree. A mother's suffering for her child is not substitutionary, and has no reference to retributive justice. The following points of difference are evidence : Vicariousness in nature : (a) Is not expiatory, that is, satisfactory of law. (b) Does not release another from the obligation to suffer penalty. (*c*) Is sharing suffering with another. The mother suffers with her child. There are two sufferers. (*d*) Is helping another to bear suffering. The mother assists her child to endure. Vicariousness in grace : (*a*) Is expiatory, that is, satisfactory of law. (*b*) Releases another from the obligation to penal suffering. (*c*) Does not share suffering with another, but endures the whole of it. Christ does not suffer together with the sinner, but " treads the wine-press alone." (*d*) Does not assist the sinner to bear suffering, but suffers in his place. When Christians " bear one another's burdens" such "vicariousness " as this does not release one of them from bearing burdens. It is community and help in enduring a common burden. Neither is suffering *because* of another, as when poverty and disease are inherited by children from their parents, the same as suffering *for* another—that is, in his stead for judicial purposes.

VOL. II., p. 390. Calvin teaches that forgiveness is the non-infliction of penalty upon the transgressor. He says (Inst., III., iv., 30): " What would Christ have done for us if punishment for sins were still inflicted upon us? For when we say that he ' bore all our sins in his own body on the tree, we intend only that he sustained the punishment which was due to our sins. This is more significantly expressed by Isaiah, when he says that the ' chastisement, or correction, of our peace was upon him.' Now what is the correction (correctio) of our peace but the *punishment* due to sins, and which we must have suffered before we could be reconciled to God, if he had not become our substitute ? Thus we see clearly that Christ bore the punishment of sin that he might deliver his people from it. The passages above cited expressly signify that God receives us into favor on this condition, that in forgiving our guilt he remits all the punishment that we had deserved. And whenever David or the other prophets implore the pardon of their sins, they at the same time deprecate the punishment, and to this they are impelled by an apprehension of the divine judgment. Again, when they promise mercy from the Lord, they almost always professedly speak of punishments and the remission of them."

To the same effect Leighton (Lord's Prayer) remarks : " Sin as it is called a debt is taken for the guiltness of sin, which is to owe the suffering of punishment, or an obligement to the curse which the law hath pronounced against sin ; and because this results immediately from sin, therefore sin is often put for the engagement to punishment ; so the apostle's phrase, 1 Cor. 15 : 56, may be taken. So, then, the debt of sin being the tie to punishment which follows upon it, the forgiving of sin can be no other than the acquitting of a man from that curse, setting him free from his debt, or his engagement to suffer."

To a superficial glance the position that forgiveness of sin is the remission to the sinner of its penalty by means of its infliction upon Christ as the sinner's substitute, seems to favor selfishness and a mechanical view of pardon. The person, it is objected, merely desires deliverance from judicial suffering, and when a vicarious satisfaction of justice is offered to him, he coldly accepts it without any real sorrow for his transgression. It is only a mercantile transaction, like that of the exchange and market generally, with no spiritual affection and gratitude toward God the suffering Redeemer. But this objection supposes that the sinner has no true conception of sin as related to law and justice, and no personal interest in the vindication of their claims by penal satisfaction. For if he perceived that the inmost quality of sin is its guilt or desert of penalty, his sorrow over its commission would manifest itself in the desire that it might be punished, and in a willingness to undergo the punishment personally, if this would meet the case. The penalty of sin is the righteous retribution of Infinite Holiness. This is a spiritual evil, and in praying for its remission, or release from obligation to endure it, because it has been endured for him by his Divine Substitute, the penitent sinner has first of all in view the character of God and the nature of justice, and not his own self-interest as shown in a mere wish to escape pain. If he recognizes first of all the punitive demands of righteousness and holiness, and is so desirous that they should be satisfied that he would willingly meet them by his own suffering, if this were possible, this is the highest proof of the sincerity of his sorrow over his disobedience. When the sinner, in the Scripture phrase, "accepts the punishment of his iniquity" (Lev. 26 : 41), he acknowledges its desert of penalty, and then pardon is for him both "the merciful and the just" (Rom. 3 : 26 ; 1 John 1 : 19) release of penalty by means of the vicarious endurance of it by his incarnate and suffering Saviour. This objection to the Old Testament idea of pardon arises from adopting different ideas of sin and justice from those of the Old Testament. If sin is not guilt, or obligation to punishment, and the satisfaction of justice is not inexorably necessary, then mercy is not the vicarious endurance of punishment for the sinner, and pardon is not the remission of penalty.

This subject has obtained from Pearson as clear and concise a statement as can be found in theological literature. It is given in his exposition of the tenth Article of the Apostles' Creed. Well would it have been if all parties and classes in the English Church had adopted respecting the guilt of sin, and its remission by means of Christ's vicarious satisfaction for it, the explanation of the Bishop of Chester, of whom Burnet (History of his Own Times) remarks, that "he was in all respects the greatest divine of his age ; a man of great learning, strong reason, and of a clear judgment. His book on the Creed is among the best that our Church has produced." His explanation is as follows : "The second particular to be considered is the *obligation* of sin, which must be presupposed to the solution or remission of it. Now every sin doth cause a guilt, and every sinner, by being such, becomes a guilty person; *which guilt consisteth in a debt or obligation to suffer a punishment proportionable to the iniquity of the sin.* This obligation to suffer penalty for sin is distinct from the commission of sin. The commission of sin ceaseth with the act, but the obligation to suffer for it never ceaseth. He who but once committed adultery, at that one time sinneth, and at no time after can be said to commit that particular sin; but the guilt, or obligation to suffer punishment for it remaineth on him still, and he may be said forever to be guilty of adultery, because he is forever liable to the wrath of God and obligated to suffer the punishment due to adultery. This obligation to punishment, which remains after the act of sin, is that *reatus peccati* of which the schools, and before them the fathers, spake. The nature of this *reatus* is excellently declared by St. Augustine, when delivering the distinction between actual and original sin. 'In the case of those persons who are born again in Christ, when they receive an entire remission of all their sins, it is necessary, of course, that the guilt [obligation to punishment] also of the still indwelling concupiscence should be remitted, in order that it should not be imputed to them for sin. For even as in the case of those actual sins which cannot be themselves permanent, since they pass away as soon as they are committed, the guilt, or obligation to suffer penalty, yet is permanent, and if not remitted will remain forevermore; so when concupiscence [original sin] is remitted, the guilt, or obligation to suffer penalty, is also taken away. For not to have sin means this, namely, not to be deemed guilty of sin, that is, bound to suffer punishment for it' (Augustine, De Nuptiis, i., 26). This debt, or obligation to punishment, our blessed Saviour thus taught to his disciples: 'Whosoever is angry with his brother without a cause shall be liable (obnoxious, or bound over) to the judgment; and whosoever shall say to his brother,

Raca, shall be liable (obnoxious, or bound over) to the council ; but whosoever shall say, Thou fool, shall be liable (obnoxious, or bound over) to hell fire ' (Matt. 5 : 22). So saith our Saviour again : ' He that shall blaspheme against the Holy Ghost hath never forgiveness, but is in danger of (liable, obnoxious, or bound over to) eternal damnation ' (Mark 3 : 28, 29). From all this it appeareth that after the act of sin is committed and passed by, the guilt, or obligation to suffer the affixed penalty, resulting from that act, remaineth ; that is, the person who committed it continueth still a debtor to the vindictive [retributive] justice of God, and is bound to endure the punishment due unto it."

" What, now, is the *forgiveness* of sin, or in what doth *remission* of sin consist ? The forgiveness containeth in it a reconciliation of an offended God, without which God cannot be conceived to remit, and a satisfaction unto a just God, without which God is not reconciled. The first of these is taught in Rom. 3 : 24, 25, ' We are justified gratuitously by his grace through the redemption that is in Jesus Christ, whom God hath set forth to be a *propitiation* through faith in his blood.' (1 John 2 : 1) : ' We have an advocate with the Father, and he is the *propitiation* for our sins.' (1 John 4 : 10) : ' God loved us, and sent his Son to be the *propitiation* for our sins.' This propitiation amounted to a reconciliation, that is, a kindness after wrath. We must conceive that God was angry with mankind before he determined to give our Saviour ; we cannot imagine that God, who is essentially just, should not abominate iniquity. The first affection, therefore, which we can conceive in him upon the lapse of man, is wrath and indignation. God was most certainly holily angry with mankind before he determined to provide for them a Saviour from this anger. ' God commendeth his love toward us in that while we were yet sinners [and his wrath against sin existed] Christ died for us.' ' When we were without strength, in due time Christ died for the ungodly [with whom justice was displeased].'

' When we were enemies, we were reconciled to God by the death of his Son ' (Rom. 5 : 6, 8, 10). Though it be most true that ' God so loved the world that he gave his only-begotten Son ' (John 3 : 16), yet there is no incongruity in this, that a father should be offended with that son [as a sinner] whom he loveth [as a son] ; and offended with him [in the one relation] at the very time that he loveth him [in the other relation]. Notwithstanding, therefore, that God loved men whom he *created*, yet he was offended with them when they *sinned*, and gave his Son to suffer for their sin in their stead, that through that Son's suffering he might be reconciled to them. This reconciliation [of the holy justice] of God is clearly delivered in the Scriptures as wrought by Christ. ' God hath *reconciled* us to himself by Jesus Christ ' (2 Cor. 5 : 18). ' We were *reconciled* unto God by the death of his Son ' (Rom. 5 : 10). ' By him *reconciling* all things unto himself ' (Col. 1 : 20). In vain is it objected that the Scripture saith our Saviour reconciled man to God, but nowhere teacheth that he reconciled God to man ; for, in the language of Scripture, to ' reconcile a man to God ' means to reconcile God to man ; that is, to cause him who before was angry and offended with a person to be gracious and propitious to him. As the princes of the Philistines spake of David, ' Wherewith should he reconcile himself unto the master? should it not be with the heads of these men ? ' (1 Sam. 29 : 4). Wherewith shall he reconcile Saul, who is highly offended with him ; wherewith shall he make him gracious and favorable, but by betraying these men unto him? As our Saviour adviseth, 'If thou bring thy gift before the altar, and there rememberest that thy brother hath aught against thee, leave there thy gift before the altar, and go thy way, first be reconciled to thy brother ' (Matt. 5 : 23, 24) ; that is, reconcile thy brother to thyself, whom thou hast injured ; render him by thy submission [and compensation] favorable unto thee, who hath something against thee, and is offended at thee.   As the apostle adviseth the wife that 'departeth from her husband to remain unmarried, or to be reconciled to her husband' (1 Cor. 7 : 11), that is, to appease and get the favor of her husband.   In the like manner we are said to be reconciled unto God when God is reconciled, appeased, and become gracious and favorable unto us ; and Christ is said to reconcile us unto God when he hath moved and obtained of God [as holy and sin-hating] to be reconciled unto us; when he hath appeased his holy displeasure and restored us unto his favor."

"Nor is it any wonder God should be thus reconciled to sinners by the death of Christ, who 'while we were yet sinners died for us,' because the punishment which Christ who was our surety endured was a full satisfaction to the justice of God.   'The Son of man came to give his life a ransom for many' (Matt. 20 : 28).   Now a ransom is a price given to redeem such as are in any way in captivity ; anything laid down by way of compensation to take off a bond or obligation, whereby he who before was bound becometh free.   All sinners were obligated to undergo such punishments as are proportionate to their sins, and were by that obligation captivated and in bonds, and Christ did give his life a ransom for them, and that a proper ransom, if that his life were of any price and given as such.   For a ransom is properly something of value given by way of redemption to purchase that which is detained, or given for the releasing of that which is enthralled.   But it is most evident that the life of Christ was laid down as a price ; neither is it more certain that he died than that he bought us : 'Ye are bought with a price' (1 Cor. 6 : 20 ; 7 : 23). It is the 'Lord who bought us' (2 Pet. 2 : 1).   The price which he paid was his blood ; for 'we are not redeemed with corruptible things, as silver and gold, but with the precious blood of Christ' (1 Pet. 18 : 19).   Now as it was the blood of Christ, so it was a price given by way of compensation ; and as that blood was precious, so was it a full and perfect satisfaction. For as the gravity of the offence and iniquity of the sin is augmented and increaseth according to the dignity of the person offended and injured by it, so the value, price, and dignity of that which is given by way of compensation is raised according to the dignity of the person making the satisfaction. God is of infinite majesty against whom we have sinned; and Christ is of the same Divinity, who gave his life a ransom for sinners; for God 'hath purchased his church with his own blood' (Acts 20 : 28). Although therefore God be said to remit our sins, by which we were bound and captivated to his justice, yet he is never said to remit the *price*, without which we had never been ransomed and redeemed; neither can he be said to have remitted it, because he did strictly require and receive it [from his beloved Son, from whom he did not remove the cup of agony]."

" If, then, we consider together, on the side of man the nature and obligation of sin, and on the side of Christ the satisfaction made and the reconciliation wrought, we shall easily perceive how God forgiveth sins, and in what remission of them consisteth. Man being in all conditions [evangelized or unevangelized] under some law [written or unwritten] of God, who hath sovereign power and dominion over him, and therefore owing absolute obedience to that law, whensoever in any way he transgresseth that law, or deviateth from that rule, he becometh thereby a sinner, and contracteth a guilt which is an obligation to endure a punishment proportionable to his offence; and God, who is a Lawgiver and Sovereign, becoming now the party wronged and offended, hath a most just right to punish man as an offender. But Christ, taking upon him the nature of man, and offering himself a sacrifice for man's sin, giveth that unto God, for and instead of the eternal death of man, which is more valuable and acceptable to God than that death could be, and so maketh a sufficient compensation and full satisfaction for the sins of man; which God accepting becometh reconciled unto us, and for the punishment which Christ endured, taketh off our obligation to eternal punishment. Thus man, who violated, by sinning, the law of God, and by that violation offended God, and was thereby obligated to undergo the punishment due unto the sin, and to be inflicted by the wrath of God, is, by the price of the most precious blood of Christ, given and accepted in full compensation and satisfaction for the punishment that was due, restored unto the favor of God, who being thus satisfied, and upon such satisfaction reconciled, is both 'faithful and just' (1 John 1 : 9) [faithful to his promise of mercy, and just to his righteousness and holiness] to take off all obligation to punishment from the sinner; and *in this act consisteth the forgiveness of sins.*"

VOL. II., p. 413. The punishment for suicide, as affixed by Plato (Laws, 873), is remarkably like that of the Christian church. "What shall he suffer who slays him who of all men is said to be nearest and dearest to him? I mean the suicide, who deprives himself by violence of his appointed share of life, not because the law of the state compels him, nor yet under the compulsion of some painful and inevitable fortune which has come upon him, nor because he has had to suffer from irremediable and intolerable shame, but who from indolence or cowardice imposes upon himself an unjust penalty. For him what ceremonies there are to be of purification and burial God knows, and about these the next of kin should inquire of the interpreters and of the laws, and do according to their injunctions. Those who meet their death in this way should be buried alone, and none shall be laid by their side; they shall be buried ingloriously in the borders of the twelve portions of the land, in such places as are uncultivated and nameless, and no column or name shall mark the place of their interment."

Vol. II., p. 418. Calvin teaches that whenever the believer suffers pain from any cause or source whatever, he is not suffering punishment for purposes of law and justice, but corrective chastisement for purposes of self-discipline and spiritual improvement. In his Institutes (III., iv., 31, 32), he says : " Since it highly concerns us to understand the design of those chastisements with which God corrects our sins, and how greatly they differ from the examples of his indignation pursuing the impious and reprobate, I conceive it will not be unseasonable to give a summary account of them. For the sake of perspicuity let us call one *vengeance* or *vindictive judgment*, and the other *chastisement* or *disciplinary judgment*. In vindictive judgment God is to be contemplated as taking vengeance on his enemies, so as to exert his [judicial] wrath against them. We consider it, therefore, strictly speaking, to be the vengeance of God, when the punishment he inflicts is attended with indignation. In disciplinary judgment he is not so severe as to be angry ; nor does he punish in order to destroy or precipitate into perdition. Wherefore it is not properly punishment or vengeance, but correction and admonition. The former is the act of a judge, the latter of a father. For a judge, when he punishes an offender, attends to the crime itself, and inflicts punishment according to the nature and aggravations of it. When a father corrects his child [even] with severity, he does it not to take vengeance or satisfaction of justice, but rather to teach him and render him more cautious for the future. Wherever there is vindictive punishment there is also a manifestation of the [judicial] curse and wrath of God, which he always withholds from believers. Chastisement, on the contrary, is, as the Scriptures teach, both a blessing of God and a testimony of his love."

Vol. II., p. 427. Edwards (Excellency of Christ) thus speaks of the relation of Christ's vicarious sufferings to the Divine justice, and of their being also a manifestation of pity and compassion to the sinner: "Christ never in any act gave so great a manifestation of love to God, and at the same time never so manifested his [compassionate] love toward those who were enemies to God, as in the act of suffering and dying. The blood of Christ that was sweat out and fell in great drops to the ground in his agony, was shed from love to God's enemies and his own. Never did Christ so eminently show his regard to God's honor as in offering up himself a victim to revenging [avenging or retributive] justice to vindicate God's honor; and yet in this, above all, he manifested his [pitying] love to them that dishonored God so as to bring such guilt upon themselves that nothing less than his blood could atone for it. Revenging justice then spent all its force upon him on account of our guilt that was laid upon him; he was not spared at all; and this was the way and means by which Christ stood up for the honor of God's justice. In this the diverse excellences that meet in the person of Christ appeared, namely, his infinite regard for Divine justice, and such compassionate love to those that had exposed themselves to it as induced him thus to yield himself a sacrifice to it."

Vol. II., p. 433. Paley (Sermons on Heb. 9 : 26 and Rom. 6 : 1) thus remarks upon the impossibility of man's meriting heaven, and of his need of obtaining it through the death of Christ: " Souls which are really laboring and endeavoring after salvation, and with sincerity, are every hour made deeply sensible of the deficiency and imperfection of their endeavors. Had they no ground, therefore, for hope, but *merit*, that is to say, could they look for nothing more than they should strictly *deserve*, their prospect would be very unhappy. I see not how they could look for *heaven* at all. They may form a conception of a virtue and obedience which might seem to be entitled to a high reward; but when they come to review their own performances and to compare them with that conception;

when they see how short they have proved of what they ought to have been, and how weak and broken were their best offices ; they will be the first to confess that it is infinitely for their comfort that they have some other resource than their own righteousness. Their acts of piety and devotion toward God are defective in principle, and debased by the mixture of impure motives. They are intermittent, cold, and languid. That heavenly mindedness which ought to be inseparable from religious exercises does not accompany theirs, at least not constantly. Their thankfulness is never what it ought to be, or anything like it. Formality is apt continually to steal upon them in their worship. No man reviews his services toward God but he perceives in them much to be forgiven, much to be excused. That such imperfect services, therefore, should be allowed and accepted, is an act of abounding grace and goodness in God who accepts them ; and we are taught in Scripture that this so-much needed grace and goodness abounds toward us through Jesus Christ, and particularly through his sufferings and death."

" We shall better see the truth of this if we consider well *what salvation is*. It is nothing else than, after this life is ended, being placed in a state of happiness ineffably great, both in degree and duration ; a state, concerning which the following things are said : ' The sufferings of this present time are not worthy to be compared with the glory that shall be revealed.' 'God hath in store for us such things as pass man's understanding.' It is not simply escaping punishment, simply being excused or forgiven, simply a little compensation for the little good we do, but it is infinitely more. Heaven is infinitely greater than the small reward which natural religion leads the moral pagan to expect. What do the Scriptures call it ? ' Glory, honor, immortality, eternal life.' Will anyone contend that salvation in this sense and to this extent ; that heaven, namely, eternal life, glory, honor, immortality ; that a hap-

piness such as there is no way of describing it but by saying that it surpasses human comprehension; will anyone
contend that this is no more than what human virtue
deserves, which in its own proper nature and by its own
merit it is entitled to look forward to and to receive? The
greatest excellence that man ever attained has no such pre-
tensions. The best good action that man ever performed
has no claim to this extent, or anything like it. It is out
of all calculation, and comparison, and proportion, above
and more than any human works can possibly deserve."

"To what, then, are we to ascribe it, that such imperfect
endeavors after holiness should procure, and that they will
in fact procure, to those who sincerely exert them, such an
immense blessing as 'glory, honor, immortality, eternal
life?' The Scriptures attribute it to the free will, the free
gift, the love and mercy of God. This alone is the source,
and fountain, and cause of salvation, the origin from which
it springs, and from which all our hopes of attaining it are
derived. The cause is not in ourselves, nor in anything we
do or can do, but in God, in his good-will and pleasure.
It is in the graciousness of his original offer of mercy.
Therefore, whatever shall have moved and excited and con-
ciliated that good-will and pleasure so as to have procured
that offer to be made, or shall have formed any part or
portion of the motive from which it was made, may most
truly and properly be said to be efficacious in human salvation. And this efficacy is in Scripture attributed to *the
death of Christ*. It is attributed in a variety of ways of
expression, but this is the substance of them all. 'He is a
sacrifice, an offering to God, a propitiation, the precious
sacrifice foreordained, the Lamb slain from the foundation of the world, the Lamb which taketh away the sin of
the world; we are washed in his blood, we are justified by
his blood, we are saved from wrath through him, he has
once suffered for sins the just for the unjust, that he might
bring us to God.' All these terms, and many more that

are used, assert in substance the same thing, namely, the efficacy of the death of Christ in the procuring of human salvation; and human salvation we have seen is 'not simply escaping punishment, but obtaining glory, honor, immortality, and a blessedness such as there is no way of describing it but by saying that it surpasses human comprehension.' "

Edwards (Justification by Faith Alone) teaches the same truth with Paley, but in more technical terms, and in closer connection with systematic theology. "The opponents of the doctrine of the imputation of Christ's active righteousness suppose that there is an absurdity in it. They say that to suppose that God imputes Christ's obedience to us, is to suppose that God is mistaken, and thinks that *we* performed that obedience which Christ performed. But why cannot that righteousness be reckoned to our account, and be accepted for us, without any such absurdity? Why is there any more absurdity in supposing that Christ's obedience of the law is imputed to us, than that his penal satisfaction of the law is imputed? If Christ has suffered the penalty of the law for us and in our stead, then it will follow that his suffering that penalty is imputed to us; that is, is accepted for us, and in our stead, and is reckoned to our account as though we had suffered it. But why may not his obeying the law of God be as rationally reckoned to our account, as his suffering the penalty of the law? Why may not a price to bring into debt [by earning a title to life], be as rationally transferred from one person's account to another, as a price to pay a debt [by atoning for guilt]? There is the very same need of Christ's obeying the law in our stead in order to the reward, as of his suffering the penalty in our stead in order to our escaping the penalty; and the same reason why one should be accepted on our account as the other. One was as requisite to answer the law's demands as the other. The same law that fixes the curse of God as the penalty for not continuing in all things

27

written in the law to do them, has as much fixed the doing these things as the antecedent of living by them. There is, therefore, exactly the same need, from the law, of perfect obedience being fulfilled in order to our obtaining the law's reward, namely, heaven, as there is of death's being suffered in order to our escaping the law's punishment, namely, hell; or the same necessity, by the law, of perfect obedience preceding life, as there is of disobedience being succeeded by death."

VOL. II., p. 441. The *expiation* of sin is distinguishable from the *pardon* of it. The former, conceivably, might take place and the latter not. When Christ died on Calvary, the whole mass, so to speak, of human sin was expiated merely by that death; but the whole mass was not pardoned merely by that death. The claims of law and justice for the sins of the whole world were satisfied by the "offering of the body of Jesus Christ once for all" (Heb. 10: 10); but the sins of every individual man were not forgiven and "blotted out" by this transaction. Still another transaction was requisite in order to this: namely, the work of the Holy Spirit in the heart of the sinner working faith in this expiatory offering, and the declarative act of God saying "Thy sin is forgiven thee." The Son of God, after he had offered one sacrifice for sins forever, "sat down on the right hand of God" (Heb. 10: 12); but if the redeeming work of the Trinity had stopped at this point, not a soul of mankind would have been pardoned and justified, yet the expiatory value of the "one sacrifice" would have been just the same.

VOL. II., p. 445. The standing objection of the Socinian to the vicarious satisfaction of justice, that it presents God in the aspect of implacability and unpaternal severity toward the sinner, falls away when it is considered that *vicarious* satisfaction in distinction from *personal*, is the satisfaction of one Divine attribute by another Divine attribute; of the Divine justice by the Divine mercy. In and by Christ's sufferings and death, God's mercy meets the righteous and

necessary demands of God's justice, and thereby releases the
sinner from his own obligation to do this. Calvin (Inst.
III., xx. 45) directs attention to this feature in redemption.
" Sins are called debts, in the Lord's prayer, because we owe
the penalty of them : a debt we are altogether incapable of
discharging, unless we are released by this remission [through
Christ's satisfaction of justice], which is a pardon flowing
from God's gratuitous mercy when he freely cancels these
debts without any payment from us, *being satisfied by his
own mercy* in Christ, who has once given himself for our
redemption. Those, therefore, who rely on God's being satisfied with their own merits, or the merits of others, and
persuade themselves that remission of sins is purchased by
these satisfactions, have no interest in this gratuitous forgiveness. In this way they do not implore God's mercy, but
appeal to his justice."

VOL. II., p. 470. The Arminians did not carefully distinguish, as the elder Calvinists did, between atonement
and redemption. Barrow, who is Arminian, has four sermons on " The doctrine of Universal Redemption asserted
and explained." He employs the term Saviour in his first
sermon on 1 Tim. 4 : 10, in " the large acceptation of conferring *any kind* of good. Whence God is 'the Saviour of
all men ' as the universal preserver and upholder of all
things, as in the Psalm : ' Thou, Lord, preservest man and
beast' (Ps. 36 : 6). If our Lord be the Saviour of all those
to whom God's truth is declared and his mercy offered ; or
if he be the Saviour of all the members of the visible
church ; particularly, if he be the Saviour of those who
among these, rejecting the overtures and means of grace,
or by disobedience abusing them, shall in the event fail of
being saved, then he is the Saviour of all men." According to this loose use of the term, Christ is the Saviour of
those to whom salvation is offered but not secured by
regenerating grace, and who are eternally lost. Turrettin
(XIV. xiv.) explains " Saviour " in the first part of this text

in the sense of Preserver, quoting Ps. 36 : 6 ; Acts 17 : 28, and citing Chrysostom, Œcumenius, Ambrose, and Aquinas in support of this. This explanation is favored by the phraseology : "We trust in the living God, who is the Saviour of all men, specially of those that believe." The "living God" refers more naturally to the Trinity than to the incarnate second Person ; showing that in the first part of the proposition the apostle has in mind the general providential relations of God to man, and in the second part his special redemptive and actually saving relations. Turrettin would not, with Barrow, denominate Christ " the Saviour of all those to whom God's truth is declared, and his mercy offered, and who by disobedience abusing them fail of being saved."

VOL. II., p. 471. It is surprising that the denial that faith is the effect and not the cause of election and the new birth, should have so much currency, in the face of the numerous and explicit teachings of Scripture. Besides the passages quoted in Vol. II. 471, consider the following description by St. Paul (Eph. 1 : 19, 20) of the Divine omnipotence as exhibited in election to faith and regeneration. "The eyes of your understanding are enlightened, that ye may know what is the exceeding greatness of God's power to us-ward *who believe according to the working of his mighty power* which he wrought in [and by] Christ, when he raised him from the dead and set him at his own right hand in the heavenly places, far above all principality, and authority, and dominion." Again, in his sacerdotal prayer (John 17 : 2), our Lord represents the whole result of his mediatorial work as dependent upon election : "Thou hast given thy Son power over all flesh, that he should give eternal life *to as many as thou hast given him*." He also emphazises the discrimination between the elect and non-elect, by saying (John 17 : 9) : "I pray for them, I pray not for the world, but for them which thou hast *given* me." The Redeemer does not say that he never prayed for the whole sinful world of mankind ; for he did this whenever he uttered the supplication, " Thy kingdom come. Thy will be done on earth, as it is in heaven ; " but on that particular occasion he confines his supplications to a part of the world, namely, the elect.

VOL. II., p. 483. It is important to show that the fault is man's, not God's, when common grace fails of success : 1. Because it evinces that although common grace is not the highest grade of mercy, it is nevertheless a grade of it. It it the exercise of compassion when nothing but justice and retribution are due. Instead of offering pardon, and exerting a certain degree of restraining and softening influence upon the transgressor, which is described in Rom. 2 : 4, God might make no such offer to him, and leave him to the wholly unrestrained workings of his free will. Common grace, in this way, has a real value which is not nullified by anything in its own nature but by the enmity and resistance of the sinful will. But in bringing out this fact, it is important not to nullify the distinction between common and special grace, by combining common grace with the sinner's *co-operation*, whereby common is converted into special and regenerating grace by the sinner's agency. In addition to the remark in the Note on p. 483, the following statement guards the subject still more : Again, to say that common grace would succeed if it were *not resisted* by the sinner, is not the same as saying that common grace would succeed if it were *yielded to* by him. " To give up the contest," is one definition of " yield." Not contesting at all is wholly different from ceasing to contest by yielding. In the former case there is no resistance by the man ; in the latter, there is a resistance which is put a stop to by him. This latter is never done except as the Divine Spirit inclines and enables him.

Owen (Dominion of Sin and Grace, Works, xiv., 411. Ed. Russell) thus describes the sinner's action under common grace, showing both his voluntary resistance of it, and his guilt in frustrating it: "Men who live in sin do voluntarily wrest themselves from under the rule of the law of God, and give themselves up to be slaves unto this tyrant. Could sin lay any just claim to this dominion, had it any title to plead, it were some alleviation of guilt in them that give themselves up to it. But men reject the righteous rule of God's law, and choose this foreign and unjust yoke. Hence it follows that all men have a right in themselves to cast off the rule of sin, and to vindicate themselves into liberty. They may, when they will, plead the right and title of the law of God unto the rule of their souls, to the utter exclusion of all pleas and pretences of sin for its power. They have a right to say unto it, Get thee hence, what have I to do any more with idols? All men, I say, have the right in themselves, because of the natural allegiance they owe to the law of God; but by reason of their own act they have lost the power of themselves to execute this right, and actually to cast off the yoke of sin. This is the work of grace. Sin's dominion is broke only by grace."

"But you will say then, Unto what end serves this right, if they have not the power in themselves to put it in execution? and how can it be charged as an aggravation of their sin that they do not use the right which they have, seeing they have not power so to do? Will you blame a man that hath a right to an estate if he do not recover it when he hath no means so to do?"

"I answer briefly three things. 1. No man living neglects the use of this right to cast off the yoke and dominion of sin because he cannot of himself make use of it, but merely because he will not. [Owen means that the "cannot" has the element of "will not" in it; it is not isolated and abstract inability, but *voluntary* inability.] He doth voluntarily choose to continue under the power of sin, and looks on everything as his enemy that would deliver him. 'The carnal mind is enmity against God, it is not subject unto his law, nor can it be' (Rom. 8 : 7). When the law comes at any time to claim its right and rule over the soul, a man under the power of sin looks on it as an enemy that has come to disturb his peace, and fortifies his mind against it; and when the gospel comes and tenders the way and means for the soul's delivery, offering its aid and assistance to this end, this also is looked on as an enemy, and is rejected, and all its offers, unto that end. See Prov. 1 : 20–25 ; John 3 : 19. This, then, is the condition of everyone that abides under the dominion of sin; he chooses so to do; he continues in that state of sin by an act of his own will; he avows an enmity unto everything which would give him deliverance; and this will be a sore aggravation of his condemnation at the last day."

"2. God may justly require that of any which it is in the power of the grace of the gospel to enable them to perform and comply with; for this is tendered unto them in the preaching of it every day. And although we know not the ways and means of the *effectual* communication of grace unto the souls of men, yet this is certain, that [common] grace is so tendered in the preaching of the gospel that none go without it, none are destitute of its aids and assistances but those alone who by a free act of their own wills do refuse and reject it. This is that which the whole case depends upon, 'You will not come unto me, that you may have life;' and this all unbelievers have, or may have, experience of in themselves. They may know on a due examination of themselves that they do voluntarily refuse the assistance of the [common] grace which is offered for their deliverance; therefore is their destruction of themselves."

"3. There is a time when men lose even the right [to cast off the yoke of sin] also. He who gave up himself to have his ear bored lost all his claim unto future liberty; he was not to go out at the year of jubilee. So there is a time when God *judicially* gives up men to the rule of sin, to abide under it forever; so that they lose all right to liberty. Thus he dealt with many of the idolatrous Gentiles of old (Rom. 1 : 24, 26, 28); and so continues to deal with the like profligate sinners; so he acts toward the generality of the antichristian [infidel] world (2 Thess. 2 : 11, 12), and with many despisers of the gospel (Isa. 6 : 9, 10). When it comes to this, men are cast at law [outlawed], and have lost all right and title unto liberty from the dominion of sin. They may repine sometimes at the service of sin, or the consequences of it, in shame and pain, in the shameful distempers that will pursue many in their uncleanness; yet God having given them up judicially unto sin, they have not so much as a right to put up one prayer or petition for deliverance; nor will they do so, but are bound in the fetters either of presumption and indifference, or of dreadful despair. See their work and ways described in Rom. 2 : 5, 6."

[Though God alone knows whom he has judicially abandoned, and no man has the right to declare a fellow-man to be thus cast away, yet] "The signs or symptoms of the approach of such an irrecoverable condition are: 1. A long continuance in the practice of any known sin. The long-suffering of God for a time waits for repentance (1 Pet. 3 : 20; 2 Pet. 3 : 9). But there is a time when it doth only endure 'vessels of wrath fitted for destruction' (Rom. 9 : 22), which is commonly after long practice of known sin. 2. When convictions have been suppressed and warnings despised. God doth not usually deal thus with men until they have rejected the means of their deliverance. 3. When men contract the guilt of such sins as seem to intrench on the unpardonable sin against the Holy Ghost; such as proud, contemptuous, malicious reproaches of the ways of God, of holiness, of the spirit of Christ and his gospel. 4. A voluntary relinquishment of the means of grace, and conversion unto God, which men have heretofore enjoyed. 5. The resolved choice of wicked, profane, unclean, scoffing society."

The Synod of Dort (Of Divine Predestination) directs attention to the responsibility and guilt of man in frustrating common grace. "The promise of the gospel is that whosoever believeth in Christ crucified shall not perish but have everlasting life. This promise, together with the command to believe, ought to be declared and published to all nations, and to all persons promiscuously and without distinction to whom God out of his good pleasure sends the gospel. And whereas many who are [outwardly] called by the gospel do not repent nor believe in Christ but perish in unbelief, this is not owing to any defect or insufficiency in the sacrifice offered by Christ upon the cross, but is wholly to be imputed to themselves. The death of Christ is of infinite worth and value, abundantly sufficient to expiate the sins of the whole world."

Bates (On Death, ch. vi.) in the same manner describes man's resistance of common grace. "Suppose life be continued, yet sinners that delay repentance can have no rational hopes that they shall sincerely repent in time to come. For, 1. Saving repentance is the gift of God; and is it likely that those who have been insensible to the loud and earnest calls of the Word, inflexible to the gracious methods of God's providence leading them to repentance, should at last obtain converting grace? The gales of the Spirit are very transient, and blow when he pleases; and can it be expected that those who have wilfully and often resisted him should by an exuberant favor receive afterward more powerful grace to overrule their stubborn wills and make them obedient? To expect divine grace, and the powerful workings of the Spirit, after long resisting his holy excitations, is both unreasonable and unrevealed. It is written as with a sunbeam, that God will graciously pardon repenting sinners that reform their lives; but it is nowhere promised that he will give saving repentance to those who securely continue in sin, upon a corrupt confidence that they will repent at last. Our Saviour threat-

ens to him that neglects the improving of grace that is
offered, that 'that which he hath shall be taken away;' yet
men unwilling at present to forsake their sins of pleasure
and profit vainly hope they shall obtain grace hereafter
without any promise from God, and against the tenor of
his threatenings. God has threatened that his Spirit
'shall not always strive with rebellious sinners,' and then
their state is remediless. This may be the case of many
in this life who are insensible of their misery. As con-
sumptive persons decline by degrees, lose their appetite,
color, and strength, till at last they are hopeless, so the
withdrawings of the Spirit are gradual, his motions are
not so strong nor frequent, and upon the continued provo-
cations of the disobedient he finally leaves them under the
most fearful doom. 'He that is filthy, let him be filthy
still; he that is unrighteous, let him be unrighteous still.'
2. Supposing the Holy Spirit be not totally withdrawn,
yet by every day's continuance in sin the heart is more
hardened against the impressions of grace, more averse
from returning to God, and repentance is more difficult
and hazardous. 3. It is uncertain whether God will at
last hear the prayers of such as resist and insult his Spirit
in the common operations of his grace. We are commanded to 'seek the Lord while he may be found, and
call upon him while he is near.' The limitation implies
that if the season be neglected he will hide his face forever. Now in cases of great moment and hazard what
diligence, what caution should be used."

The Westminster Confession (V., vi., 6) sums up the
subject of God's withdrawing common grace after the sinner's resistance and abuse of it as follows : " As for those
wicked and ungodly men whom God as a righteous judge,
for former sins, doth blind and harden (Rom. 1 : 24, 26, 28 ;
11 : 7, 8), from them he not only withholdeth his grace
whereby they might have been enlightened in their understandings, and wrought upon in their hearts (Deut. 29 : 4);

but sometimes also withdraweth the gifts which they had (Matt. 13 : 12) ; and exposeth them to such objects as their corruption makes occasion of sin (2 Kings 8 : 12, 13) ; and withal gives them over to their own lusts, the temptations of the world, and the power of Satan (Ps. 81 : 11, 12 ; 2 Thess. 8 : 15, 32), whereby it comes to pass that they harden themselves even under those means which God useth for the softening of others (Ex. 8 : 15, 32 ; 2 Cor. 2 : 15, 16)."

Vol. II., p. 486. Augustine distinguishes the common from the effectual call in the following passage : " God calls many predestinated children of his to make them members of his only predestinated Son, not with that calling with which they were called who would not come to the marriage, since with that calling were called also the Jews, to whom Christ crucified is an offence, and the Gentiles, to whom Christ crucified is foolishness ; but with that calling he calls the predestinated which the apostle distinguished when he said that he preached Christ, the wisdom of God, and the power of God, to them that were called, Jews as well as Greeks. And it was this calling he meant when he said, 'Not of works, but of him that calleth, it was said unto Rebecca, that the elder shall serve the younger.' Did he say, 'Not of works, but of him that believeth ?' Rather, he actually took this [viz., faith] away from man that he might give the whole to God. Therefore he said, 'But of him that calleth ;' not with any sort of calling whatever, but with that calling wherewith a man is made a believer " (Predestination, ch. 32). " The vessels of mercy were not so called as not to be elected, in respect of which it is said, 'Many are called, but few are elected ;' but because they were called according to God's purpose they are of a certainty also elected by the election of grace, as it is denominated, not of any precedent merits of theirs, because grace is all the merit they have" (Rebuke and Grace, ch. 13). " Whoever are elected are without

doubt also called; but not whoever are called are also
elected.   Those are elected who are called according to
God's purpose, and who are also predestinated and fore-
known " (Rebuke and Grace, ch. 14).

VOL. II., p. 491.   The two uses of "regeneration," in a
wide and narrow sense, by the Reformers and seventeenth-
century divines, are different from those in the Patristic
church, which grew out of the Patristic view of the sacraments.   Augustine, for example, employs the term to denote both the apparently and professedly regenerate, and
the really such.   The former are members of the visible
church, but not of the invisible; the latter belong to the invisible church also.   The former may therefore fall away,
the latter may not.   He remarks as follows in Perseverance, ch. 21: "Of two [professedly] pious (piis) men, why
to one should be given perseverance unto the end, and to
the other it should not be given, is an unsearchable judgment of God.   Yet to believers it ought to be a most certain fact that the former is of the predestinated, the latter
is not.   'For if they had been of us,' says one of the predestinated who had drunk this secret from the breast of
the Lord, 'certainly they would have continued with us.'"
Again, in Rebuke and Grace, ch. 18, he says: "It is
greatly to be wondered at that to some of his own children,
whom he has regenerated in Christ, and to whom he has
given faith, hope, and love, God does not give perseverance
also, when to the children of another [i.e., of Satan] he for-
gives their wickedness, and by the bestowal of his grace
makes them his own children.   Moreover, it is not less
marvellous that some of the children of his friends, that is
of regenerated and good believers, departing this life as infants without baptism, although he certainly might provide
the grace of this laver [of baptism] if he so willed, he yet
alienates from his kingdom into which he introduces their
parents; and some children of his enemies he causes to
come into the hands of Christians, and by means of this

laver introduces into the kingdom from which their parents are aliens. Of both of which things we may exclaim, How unsearchable are the judgments of God."

From the above extracts it will be seen that Augustine held : 1. That baptism is indispensable to regeneration. 2. That there are some non-elect dying infants. 3. That some whom he calls "regenerate" may not persevere. On the first point he differs from Calvin ; on the second he agrees with him ; on the third he seemingly differs, but not really, because he employs "regeneration" in two senses, while Calvin employs it only to denote the really renewed. By the "regenerate" who are not elected and do not persevere, Augustine means those adults who have been baptized and are members of the visible church, but not of the invisible. In his day baptism was denominated "regeneration." By the "regenerate" who are elected and persevere, he means those adults who are members of the invisible church as well as the visible. Employing the term in this double sense, Augustine, unlike Calvin and the Reformed creeds, holds to a genuine "regeneration" that springs from election and predestination, and a spurious "regeneration" that does not. The omission to notice the two uses of the word has led to the assertion, by most Roman Catholic and some Protestant writers, that Augustine's doctrine of election and predestination differs from that of Calvin. Both alike affirm that the truly regenerate are predestinated to perseverance, and never fall away. "Let it not disturb us that to some of his [professed] children God does not give this perseverance. But this is far from being so, however, in the case of those who are predestinated and called according to the promise. For the former, while they live piously [*i.e.*, reputably in church communion] are [popularly] called the children of God ; but because they are afterward to live wickedly [inconsistently with church communion], and to die in wickedness, the foreknowledge of God does not call them God's children."

(Rebuke and Grace, ch. 20). " Some of the children of
perdition, who have not received the gift of perseverance to
the end, begin [apparently] to live in the faith that worketh by love, and live for some time faithfully and righteously, and afterward fall away, and are not taken from
this life before this happens to them. Unless this had
happened to some, men would not have that wholesome
fear [of falling] by which the sin of presumption and self-
security is kept down " (Rebuke and Grace, ch. 40).
Compare also chs. 9, 11, 12, 14, 16. Augustine maintains
that all of the elect and predestinated are the subjects of
true and spiritual regeneration, and never fall away.
"Says St. Paul, ' We know that God worketh all things
for good to them that are called according to his purpose ;
because those whom he foreknew he also did predestinate
to be conformed to the image of his Son. Moreover, whom
he did predestinate, them he also called ; and whom he
called, them he also justified ; and whom he justified,
them he also glorified.' Of these no one perishes, because
all are elected. And they are elected because they were
called according to the purpose : the purpose, however, of
God, not their own " (Rebuke and Grace, ch. 14).

Owen (Preface to Saints' Perseverance), after abundant
citations from Augustine's treatises on the Predestination
and Perseverance of the Saints, in proof that he held that
the elect and predestinated will infallibly persevere, remarks that " there are in Austin and those that agreed
with him sundry expressions commonly urged by the
adversaries of the doctrine of the saints' perseverance,
which grant that many who were ' saints,' ' believing ' and
' regenerate,' fall away and perish forever. The reader
will find them gathered to his hand in Vossius, Grotius,
and Goodwin. The seeming contradiction in Augustine
and his followers—Prosper, Hilary, and Fulgentius—will
easily admit of a reconciliation, if they are allowed to be
interpreters of their own meaning. What weight in those

days was laid upon participation in the sacramental symbols of grace, and what expressions are commonly used concerning those who had obtained that privilege, is known to all. Hence all baptized persons continuing in the profession of the faith and communion of the church they called, counted, and esteemed regenerate and justified, and spake so of them; such as these they affirm might fall away into everlasting destruction; yet what their judgment was concerning their present state, even when they termed them 'regenerate' and 'believers,' in respect to the sacraments and a visible profession of faith, Austin clearly delivers his thoughts, especially in his treatise on Rebuke and Grace. 'They were not,' says he, ch. 20, 'children, even when they were in the profession and name of children. Not because they deliberately simulated righteousness, but because they did not continue in it.' This righteousness he esteemed not to be merely feigned and hypocritical, but rather such as might truly entitle them to the state and condition of the children of God in the sense above expressed. These are the persons which Austin, and those of the same judgment with him, do grant may fall away; such, namely, as upon account of their baptismal entrance into the church, their [outwardly] pious and devout lives, their profession of the faith of the gospel, they called and accounted 'regenerate' believers, whom yet they tell you, upon a thorough search into the nature and causes of holiness, grace, and walking with God, would be found not to be truly and really in that state and condition in which they were esteemed to be; of which they thought this a sufficient proof, that they did not persevere; which evinces that their judgment was that all who are truly, really, and in the sight of God, believers, engrafted into Christ, and adopted into his family, should certainly persevere."

The necessity of baptism by the church, in order to salvation, is the principal point of difference between Augus-

tine and Calvin, and explains the sacramentarianism, together with the double sense of regeneration, which are
found in the system of the former but not in that of the
latter.   The following passages express it : " Take the case
of any infant you please. If he is already in Christ, why
is he baptized ? If, however, he is baptized that he may
be with Christ, it certainly follows that he who is not baptized is not with Christ; and because he is not ' with '
Christ he is ' against' Christ " (Forgiveness and Baptism,
i., 55).   Augustine did not hold the Romish doctrine, that
the mere application of water in the name of the Trinity regenerates the soul.   His view of regeneration was spiritual ;
that it is the effect only of the direct operation of the Holy
Spirit. But he believed that God has *inseparably* connected
the gift of the Spirit to regenerate with the ordinance
of baptism administered to infants within his church.
" From the infant newly born to the old man bent with
age, as there is none shut out from baptism, so there is
none in baptism who does not die to sin.   But [baptized]
infants die only to original sin; those who are older
[when baptized] die also to all the sins which their evil
lives have added to the sin which they inherited from
Adam " (Enchiridion, ch. 43).   " As in a certain manner
the sacrament of Christ's body is Christ's body, and the
sacrament of Christ's blood is Christ's blood, in the same
manner the sacrament of faith is faith.   Now, believing is
nothing else than having faith ; and accordingly, when, on
behalf of an infant as yet incapable of exercising faith, the
answer is given [by his sponsor] that he believes, this answer means that he has faith because of the sacrament of
faith, and that he converts to God because of the sacrament of conversion.   Therefore an infant, although he is
not yet a believer in the sense of having that faith which
includes the consenting will of those who exercise it,
nevertheless becomes a believer through the sacrament of
faith " (Letter xcviii., 9, 10. To Boniface, A.D. 408).   " He

that believeth and is baptized shall be saved ; but he that believeth not shall be damned. Now who is unaware that in the case of infants being baptized is to believe, and not being baptized is not to believe" (Forgiveness and Baptism, i., 40). Augustine, in these passages, defines a sacrament as "that which has some point of real resemblance to the thing of which it is a sacrament." It is a symbol or sign resembling the thing signified. The sponsors answer that "the infant believes," has "some point of resemblance " to actual faith, and this is the " sacrament of faith." His answer, also, that the infant "turns to God," Augustine calls "the sacrament of conversion." In thus making baptism, and the promises of the sponsors, the indispensable condition of the regeneration of the infant by the Holy Spirit, Augustine prepared for the materialistic view of grace formulated at Trent. His own highly spiritual conception of the Holy Spirit's agency in regeneration as *immediate* and *irresistible,* would logically exclude such a necessary dependence on an outward sign and ceremony. Calvin, a thousand years later, saw the inconsistency of the two things, and modified Augustinianism by making salvation depend, as Augustine did, upon the new birth, but not by making, as Augustine did, the new birth to depend upon the baptism of the church. Baptism he held to be the appointed sign and seal of regeneration, and is to be administered whenever it is possible because of the divine command ; but when impossible its omission does not preclude regeneration by the Holy Spirit. Augustine's view leads to the position that salvation outside of the visible church is impossible ; Calvin's view makes salvation outside of it a possibility.

The following extracts from Augustine are of the same tenor with those above cited : " If infants were hurt by no malady of original sin, how is it that they are carried to the Physician Christ for the express purpose of receiving the sacrament of eternal salvation by the pious anxiety of

28

those who run to him? Why rather is it not said to them
by the church: Take hence these innocents; 'they that are
whole need not a physician, but they that are sick;' Christ
'came not to call the righteous but the sinners'? There
never has been heard, there never is heard, there never
will be heard in the church such a fiction concerning
Christ" (Forgiveness and Baptism, i., 23). "Our Lord
himself, wishing to remove from the minds of wrong-be-
lievers that vague and indefinite middle condition which
some would attribute to unbaptized infants, as if by reason
of innocence they were included in eternal life, and yet because of their unbaptized state were not with Christ in his
kingdom, uttered that definite sentence of his which shuts
their mouths: 'He that is not with me is against me'"
(Forgiveness and Baptism, i., 55).

Vol. II., p. 493. Edwards (Works, I., 141) explains the
exhortations, "Make you a new heart," "Be renewed in the
spirit of your minds" as referring to the sanctification of
believers. "It is objected that the apostle sometimes exhorts those that he writes to, to 'put off the old man,'
and 'put on the new man,' and to 'be renewed in the
spirit of their minds,' as exhorting them to seek conversion. I answer, that the meaning is manifestly only this,
that they should mortify the remains of corruption, or of
the old man, and turn more and more from sin unto God.
Then he exhorts the Ephesians to be 'renewed in the
spirit of their mind' (Eph. 4: 22, 23), whom yet he had
before in the same epistle abundantly represented as savingly renewed already."

Vol. II., p. 500. Owen (Holy Spirit, III., v.) describes
the total operation of the Holy Spirit in adult regeneration as twofold. 1. Moral suasion. 2. Internal physical operation. "The Holy Spirit, in the regeneration or
conversion of all that are adult, doth make use of motives, arguments, reasons, and considerations proposed
unto the mind by the preaching and reading of the word,

which are adapted to influence the will and affections. There are none ordinarily converted who are not able to give some account by what considerations they were prevailed upon thereunto. But the *whole* of the work of the Holy Spirit in our conversion doth not consist of this moral suasion. There is also a real *physical work*, whereby he *infuseth a gracious principle of spiritual life* into all that are effectually converted and really regenerated, and without which there is no deliverance from the state of sin and death. That the entire operation of the Holy Spirit in conversion doth not consist in the presentation of motives and arguments, the ensuing reasons do sufficiently evince: 1. If the Holy Spirit worketh no otherwise on men in their regeneration or conversion but by proposing and urging upon them reasons, arguments, and motives, then after his whole work, and notwithstanding it, the will of man remains absolutely *indifferent* whether it will admit them or not; or whether it will convert itself unto God in view of them or not. For the whole of this work consists in proposing *objects* unto the will, with respect to which it is left *undetermined* whether it will choose and close with them or not. And this is what some plead for. For they say that in all men, at least all to whom the gospel is preached, there is such grace present with them that they are able to comply with the word if they please, and so to believe, repent, or do any act of obedience unto God. And if they will, they can refuse and continue in sin. This view ascribes the glory of our regeneration to an act of our own will, and not to the grace of God. It also leaves it absolutely uncertain, notwithstanding the purpose of God and the purchase of Christ, whether any one in the world will be converted. And, finally, it is contrary to many express testimonies of Scripture wherein actual conversion to God is ascribed to his internal operation. 'God worketh in us to will and to do' (Phil. 2:13). The act therefore it-

self of willing, in our conversion, is of God's operation;
and although we ourselves will, yet it is he who causeth
us to will, by working in us to will.   2. Moral persuasion, however advanced or improved, and supposed to be
effectual, yet confers no *new supernatural strength* unto the
soul.   For when the Spirit of God worketh by reasons,
motives, arguments, and objective considerations, and no
otherwise, he is able only to excite and draw out the
strength which we have, delivering the mind and affections from prejudices and other moral impediments ; real
aid and internal spiritual strength neither is nor can be
conferred thereby.   And he who will acknowledge that
there is any such internal spiritual strength communicated
unto us, must also acknowledge that there is another
work of the Spirit of God in us and upon us, than can
be effected by these persuasions."

Owen fortifies his positions by extracts from Augustine's
Anti-Pelagian writings, in which this same distinction is
made in opposition to the views of Cœlestius and Pelagius, who resolved the whole work of the Spirit into
moral suasion.   He also cites from the Semi-Pelagian
fathers and schoolmen, who indeed ascribed more to the
inward operation of the Spirit than did the Pelagians,
but when it came to the question whether the determination of the will to holiness in conversion is wholly or
only partly the effect of Divine grace, affirmed the latter.

VOL. II., p. 502.   The agency of God and man in regeneration is different from that in sanctification.   In the first
instance there is the creative and enlivening energy of the
Holy Spirit in the human spirit.   In such agency there is
no division of the work between the Divine and the human.   Man does not co-operate with God in it.   The entire quickening and creating-anew is the act of God alone.
The proper phraseology for it is, "actuating," "enabling,"
" inclining."   In the second instance, that of sanctification,

there is a *union* of the Divine with the human energy and
a division of the work between the two. The now regenerate will co-operates with the Holy Spirit. It "works
out its salvation with fear and trembling, because God
works also within it to will and to do" (Phil. 2 : 12, 13).
The proper phraseology for this is, "helping," "assisting,"
and "stimulating." When the Holy Spirit actuates and
inclines the human will he does the whole. But when he
helps, excites, and assists it, he does a part. In actuating,
enabling, and inclining, the parties are not co-ordinate,
each working on its own basis, and contributing a Divine
and a human factor to the common result, but one is subordinate and the other controlling. In regeneration God
moves upon the human soul prior, in the order of nature,
and the soul then moves in conversion (not regeneration,
as a consequence. The agency of each, in this instance, is
total and undivided; not partial and shared with the other.
God quickens, actuates, enables, and inclines the human
will without the will's assisting or helping in this because
as ungenerate it sinfully resists ; and the will, as the effect
of this Divine agency, converts, in the acts of faith and
repentance, without God's sharing in this converting activity. As man does not participate and share in the
regenerating and inclining of the will, so God does not
participate and share in the believing and repenting of
the will. God is the sole *author* of regeneration, and man
is the sole *actor* in conversion, namely, in faith and repentance. Thus there is no co-operation between the Divine
and the human in either regeneration or conversion. God
alone regenerates as the cause. There are not two causes
of regeneration, one Divine and one human. Man alone
converts, that is, believes and repents, as the effect of
regeneration. There are not two faiths and repentances ;
one in God and the other in man. But in sanctification
the case is different. Here the growth and increase of
the principle of holiness is an effect of the union and

co-operation of the agency of the Holy Spirit with that of the regenerate will.

The neglect to distinguish between "creating anew," "enabling," "actuating," and "inclining" the human will, and "helping," "assisting," and "stimulating" it, has led to much error. Synergism in regeneration results from overlooking this distinction. What is true of sanctification alone, is transferred to regeneration.

Vol. II., p. 505. If the affections, as in the elder Calvinism, are regarded as modes of the inclination of the will, we may speak also of the expulsive power of a new inclination. The regeneration of the will is the origination *de novo* of a new inclination to God as the ultimate end, and this expels the old inclination, inherited from Adam, to self and the creature. This expulsion, however, leaves some *remainders* of the old inclination, which act like the old inclination in every respect, excepting their degree. They have the same spontaneousness and self-motion, only less strength. They do not *wholly* dominate the man as the old inclination, or " old Adam," as St. Paul calls it, did. And they grow weaker, as the " old Adam " does not in the unregenerate. The regenerate man dies more and more to sin, and lives more and more to holiness. The " new man," or new inclination, is the stronger man within the house, and has bound the " strong man " who still remains in it, and keeps up a conflict that is severe and exhausting, but is a losing battle and a defeat in the end.

Now it is to be observed that in this process of progressive sanctification there is the freedom of *self-determination*, but not of *optional choice*. These remainders of original sin or of sinful inclination are a self-motion that antagonizes the self-motion of the new inclination. One self-determination is opposed to another. The two are " the flesh, which lusteth against the spirit, and are contrary the one to the other, so that ye cannot do the things that ye would" (Gal. 5 : 17). These remainders of sinful self-determination cannot be removed by a power to the contrary inherent in themselves, but must be expelled by the superior energy of the new inclination to holiness. Sin must be driven out by holiness, not convert itself into holiness. This would be the casting out of Satan by Satan, which our Lord asserts to be a contradiction and impossibility. There is no evolution of holiness out of sin, or transmutation of sin into holiness by the exercise of a power of contrary choice.

Vol. II., p. 509. Since regeneration precedes conversion in the order of nature, not of time, it precedes justification in the same order, because faith precedes justification, and faith is one of the acts of conversion. An unbeliever is not justified. "A man is justified by faith, without the deeds of the law" (Rom. 4 : 28). But it does not follow from this that regeneration is the cause or ground of justification, as Dorner asserts in objection to this statement (Christian Doctrine, IV., 206). One thing may be antecedent to another, and yet not the cause of it. Post hoc, non ergo propter hoc. The cause or ground of justification is wholly objective, namely, the sacrifice and satisfaction of Christ. Nothing subjective (and both faith and repentance are subjective acts) enters into the cause or ground of justification. A sinner is not justified, that is, pardoned and accepted as righteous, because he is regenerated. The divine life implanted in regeneration cannot satisfy justice for sin, nor merit eternal life for the sinner ; both of which are requisite in order to justification. But the sinner cannot *appropriate* Christ's objective satisfaction but by the act of faith in it, and he cannot exercise this faith if the Holy Spirit does not incline and enable him to it. And this inclining and enabling is one consequence of the new birth and new life in the soul. " Whosoever believeth is born of God " (1 John 5 : 1).

Vol. II., p. 516. Howe (Redeemer's Tears) thus speaks

of the sinner's agency in respect to regeneration : " Here, perhaps, sinners will inquire, Is there anything, then, to be done by us, whereupon the grace of God may be expected certainly to follow ? To which I answer : 1. That it is certain that nothing can be done by us to *deserve* it, or for the merit of which we may expect it to follow. It were not grace if we had obliged, or brought it under bonds to us, by our deserts. 2. What if nothing can be done by us, upon which it may be *certainly* expected to follow ? Is a certainty of perishing better than a high *probability* of being saved ? 3. Such as live under the gospel have reason to apprehend it *highly probable* that they may obtain that grace which is necessary to their salvation, if they be not wanting to themselves. For, 4. There is generally afforded to such that which is wont to be called common grace. Now, though this grace is not yet certainly saving, yet it tends to that which is so. And none have cause to despair but that, being duly improved and complied with, it may end in it. Let the consciences of men living under the gospel testify in the case. Appeal, sinner, to thine own conscience : Hast thou never felt anything of conviction by the word of God ? Hadst thou never any thought injected of turning to God, of reforming thy life, of making thy peace with God ? Have no desires ever been raised in thee, no fears ? Hast thou never had any tastes and relishes of pleasure (Heb. 6 : 4, 5) in the things of God ? Whence have these come ? What! from thyself, who art not sufficient to think anything as of thyself, *i.e.*, any good or right thought. All must be from that good Spirit that hath been striving with thee ; and might still have been so unto a blessed issue for thy soul, if thou hadst not neglected and disobeyed it."

" And do not go about to excuse thyself by saying that all others have done so too, at one time or another ; and if that therefore be the rule and measure, that they that contend against the strivings and motions of God's Spirit must be finally deserted and given up to perish, who then can be saved ? Think not of pleading so for thy neglecting and despising the grace and spirit of God. It is true that herein the great God shows his *sovereignty ;* when all that enjoy the same advantages for salvation deserve by their slighting them to be forsaken alike, he gives instances and makes examples of just severity and of the victorious power of grace, as seems him good. But our present design is not to justify thy condemnation, but to procure thy salvation ; and therefore to admonish and instruct thee, that though thou are not sure, because some others that have slighted and despised the grace and Spirit of God are, notwithstanding, conquered and saved thereby, it shall therefore fare as well with thee, yet thou hast reason to be confident and hopeful it will be well and happy for thee, if now thou despise and slight them not."

Vol. II., p. 525. In saying that if the unregenerate " suppresses conviction of sin and nullifies common grace, then God may withdraw all grace," conditional preterition does not logically follow. God *may* do this, but it is not *infallibly certain* that he will. He is sovereign to do as he pleases. He does not invariably condition his preterition upon the sinner's action, invariably refusing regenerating grace to all who nullify common grace, and invariably bestowing it upon all who according to the Arminian view do not nullify it. God does not pass by one of two persons in the bestowment of saving grace because of original sin or of actual transgression (Rom. 9 : 11), or of foreseen perseverance in sin, or of foreseen resistance of common grace ; for these are all of them characteristic of both persons alike, and would be a reason for passing by both of them. The Larger Catechism (68) declares that the non-elect " may be, and often are outwardly, called by the ministry of the word, and have some common operations of the Spirit, and *for their wilful neglect and contempt* of the grace offered to them, being *justly left* in their unbelief, do never come to

Jesus Christ." This is a statement of the *possibility*, and *probability*, not of the decreed certainty in the case. As the right use of common grace makes it probable but not infallibly certain that saving grace will follow (see Vol. II., 516–518), so the abuse of common grace makes it probable but not infallibly certain that saving grace will not follow. The Catechism says that the non-elect "*may be*, and often are, justly left because of their neglect of common grace;" but it does not say that they are *always* and *invariably* left because of this neglect. If it did, it would teach conditional preterition.

VOL. II., p. 526. Respecting the encouragement which the sinner has to seek salvation because of the probability, in distinction from the infallible certainty, that the right use of common grace will be followed by saving grace, Howe (Blessedness of the Righteous, ch. xvii.) thus remarks: "Why shouldst thou imagine so sad an issue as that after thine utmost endeavors grace should be withheld and leave thee to perish, because God hath not *bound* himself by promise to thee. What promise have the ravens to be heard when they cry? Experience tells the world that God's unpromised mercies freely flow everywhere. The whole earth is full of his goodness. God promises sinners, indefinitely, pardon and eternal life, for the sake of Christ, on condition that they believe on him. He gives of his good pleasure that grace whereby he *draws* any to Christ, without promise directly made to them. His discovery of his purpose to give such grace, indefinitely, amounts not to a promise claimable by any; for if it be said to be an absolute promise to particular persons, who are they? whose duty is it to believe it made to him? God [in common grace] binds himself to do what he promises [namely, to save on condition of faith]; but hath he anywhere bound himself to do no more? Did he promise thee thy being, or that thou shouldst live to this day? Did he promise thee the bread that sustains thee, or the daily comforts of thy life? Yea, what is nearer the present purpose, did he promise thee a station under the gospel, or that thou shouldst ever hear the name of Christ? If ever his Spirit have in any degree moved upon thy heart and inclined thee at all seriously to consider thy eternal concernments, did he beforehand make thee any promise of that? A promise would give thee a full certainty of the issue, if it were absolute and unconditional; if conditional, as soon as thou performest the condition. But canst thou act upon no lower rate than a foregoing certainty, a preassurance of the event? My friend, consider a little, that it is *hope*, built with those that are rational upon rational probability, with some oftentimes without hope at all, which is the great engine that moves the world, that keeps all sorts of men in action. Doth the husbandman foreknow when he ploughs and sows that the crop will answer his cost and pains? Dost thou foreknow, when thou eatest, it shall refresh thee? when thou takest physic, that it shall recover thy health and save thy life? The Lord knows that in these cases men can be confident and active enough without a promise of infallible success. Wilt thou not, upon the probability and hope thou hast before thee, do as much for thy soul? "

Vol. II., p. 528. Ursinus (Christian Religion, Q. 74) thus replies to the objection that infants should not be baptized because belief is the requisite to baptism, and infants cannot believe : "We deny the proposition which denieth that infants do believe ; for infants of believers regenerated by the Holy Spirit have an inclination to believe, or do believe by inclination ; for faith is in infants potentially and by disposition, albeit faith be not in them actually as in those who are of age and understanding. And as unregenerate infants who are without the church have no actual impiety and wickedness, but an inclination only to wickedness, so godly infants who are in the church have not actual piety and godliness, but an inclination only to godliness; not by nature, indeed, but by the grace of the covenant. Infants have the Holy Ghost and are regenerated by him, as John was filled with the Holy Ghost when as yet he was in the womb; and it was said to Jeremiah, 'Before thou camest out of the womb I sanctified thee.' If infants have the Holy Ghost, then, doubtless, he worketh in them regeneration, good inclinations, new motions, and all other things which are necessary unto salvation; as Peter saith, ' Who can forbid water from them who have received the Holy Ghost as well as we ? ' Wherefore Christ numbered little children amongst believers: ' He that offendeth one of these little ones which believe in me.' Wherefore infants do not profane baptism, as the Anabaptists slander us."

In answer to the objection that if infants are to be baptized, they should also partake of the sacrament of the Lord's supper, Ursinus (Q. 74) replies : " Unto baptism, regeneration by the Holy Ghost and faith, or an inclination to faith and repentance sufficeth ; but in the supper conditions are added and required which hinder the use thereof to be granted unto infants. For in the Scripture it is required : 1. That they who use the sign show forth the death of the Lord. 2. That they try themselves whether they have faith and repentance or no. And seeing the age of infants cannot do these things, it is manifest that infants are for good cause excluded from the supper but not from baptism."

VOL. II., p. 530. The fundamental position of faith as the effect and evidence of regeneration, as the act that unites the soul with Christ, as the instrumental cause of justification, and as the antecedent of repentance, is indicated by our Lord's words to Peter, " Upon this rock I will build my church " (Matt. 16 : 18). That the rock spoken of was the faith, not the person of Peter, was a common explanation of the Fathers. Owen (Person of Christ, Preface) cites the following : " Origen (Tract. in Matt. xvi.)

expressly denies the words to be spoken of Peter. 'If you shall think that the whole church was built on Peter alone, what shall we say of John, and each of the apostles? Shall we dare to say that the gates of hell shall not prevail against Peter alone? Hilary (De Trinitate, ii.) says, 'This is the only immovable foundation; this is the rock of faith confessed by Peter, Thou art the Son of the living God. And Epiphanius (Hær. 39) declares, 'Upon this rock of assured faith (ἐπὶ τῇ πέτρα ταύτῃ τῆς ἀσφαλοῦς πίστεως) I will build my church.' One or two more out of Austin shall close these testimonies. (De verbis Domini, Sermo 13), 'Upon this rock which thou has confessed, upon this rock which thou hast known, saying, Thou art Christ, the Son of the living God, I will build my church: that is, On me myself, the Son of the living God, I will build my church. I will build thee upon myself, and not myself on thee.' And he more fully declareth his mind in Tract. 124 in Ioannem. 'The church in this world is shaken with divers temptations, as with floods and tempests, yet falleth not because it is built on the rock (petra) from which Peter took his name. For the rock is not called petra from Peter, but Peter is so called from petra the rock; as Christ is not so called from Christian, but Christian from Christ. Therefore, said the Lord, Upon this rock will I build my church; because Peter had said, Thou art Christ, the Son of the living God. Upon this rock which thou hast confessed will I build my church. For Christ himself was the rock on which foundation Peter himself was built. For other foundation can no man lay, save that which is laid, which is Jesus Christ.'"

Peter's confession of faith in Christ is the model for all believers, and is represented by Christ as the "rock" upon which his church is built (Matt. 16 : 18). Peter himself so understood the declaration of his Lord. He says, "It is contained in Scripture, Behold I lay in Zion a chief corner-stone, elect, precious, and the stone which the builders disallowed is made the head of the corner " (1 Pet. 2 : 6, 7). Leighton thus expounds this passage : "Jesus Christ is the alone Rock upon which his church is built, not Peter (if we will believe Peter himself, who here teach-eth us that Christ is the chief corner-stone of his church), much less his pretended successors." Nothing can be more incredible than the Romish invention, that Christ is a corner-stone that rests upon the person of one of his dis-ciples as the ledge (πέτρα) or lower foundation.

VOL. II., p. 545. Edwards (Justification by Faith, Works, iv., 104) thus explains the comprehensive nature of justification, and its connection with perseverance of faith. " Although the sinner is actually and finally justified on the first act of faith, yet the perseverance of faith even then comes into consideration as one thing upon which the fit-ness of acceptance to life depends. God, in the act of jus-tification which is passed on a sinner's first believing, has respect to perseverance as being virtually contained in that first act of faith ; and it is looked upon and taken by him that justifies as being as it were a property in that faith that then is. God has respect to the believer's con-tinuance in faith, and he is justified by that, as though it already were, because by divine establishment it shall fol-low ; and it being by divine constitution connected with that first faith as much as if it were a property in it, it is then considered as such, and so justification is not sus-pended ; but were it not for this it would be needful that it should be suspended till the sinner had actually perse-vered in faith."

" And that it is so, that God in that act of final justifica-tion that he passes at the sinner's conversion has respect to perseverance in faith, and future acts of faith as being virtually implied in that first act is further manifest by this, namely, that in a sinner's justification at his conver-sion there is virtually contained a forgiveness as to eternal and deserved punishment not only of all past sins but also of all future infirmities and acts of sin that they shall be guilty of; because that first justification is decisive and final. And yet pardon, in the order of nature, properly follows the crime, and also follows those acts of repentance and faith that respect the crime pardoned, as is manifest both from reason and Scripture. David, in the beginning of Psalm 32, speaks of the forgiveness of sins of his that were doubtless committed long after he was first godly, as being consequent on those sins, and on his repentance and faith with respect to them; and yet this forgiveness is spoken of by the apostle in the 4th of Romans as an instance of justification by faith. Probably the sin David there speaks of is the same that he committed in the matter of Uriah, and so the pardon the same with that release from death or eternal punishment which the prophet Nathan speaks of in 2 Sam. 12 : 13, 'The Lord also hath put away thy sin; thou shalt not die.' Not only does the manifestation of this pardon follow the sin in order of time, but the pardon itself in the order of nature follows David's repentance and faith with respect to this sin; for it is spoken of in the 32d Psalm as depending on it."

"But inasmuch as a sinner in his first justification is forever justified and freed from all obligation to eternal punishment, it hence of necessity follows that future faith and repentance are beheld in that justification as virtually contained in that first faith and repentance; because repentance of those future sins and faith in a Redeemer with respect to them, or, at least the continuance of that habit and principle in the heart that has such an actual repentance and faith in its nature and tendency, is now made sure by God's promise. If remission of sins committed after conversion, in the order of nature, follows that faith and repentance that is after them, then it follows that future sins are respected in the first justification no otherwise than as future faith and repentance are respected in it.

And future faith and repentance are looked upon by him that justifies as virtually implied in the first repentance and faith in the same manner as justification from future sins is virtually implied in the first justification, which is the thing that was to be proved."

Vol. II., p. 550. Concerning the reward promised to works in the instance of the believer, Calvin (Inst., III., xviii., 3), remarks that this rests upon the *evangelical* promise of the gospel, not the *legal* promise of the law. " The grand promise, ' Keep my statutes and judgments; which if a man do he shall live in them' (Lev. 18 : 5), the apostle maintains to be of no value to us if we rest upon it, and that it will be no more beneficial to us than if it had never been given; because it is inapplicable to the holiest of God's servants, who are all far from fulfilling the law, and are encompassed with a multitude of transgressions. But when these are superseded by the evangelical promises which proclaim the gratuitous remission of sins, the consequence is that not only our persons, but also our works, are accepted by God; and not accepted only, but followed by those blessings which were due by the covenant [of works] to the observance of the law. I grant, therefore, that the works of believers are rewarded by those things which the Lord has promised in his law to the followers of righteousness and holiness; but in this recompense it is always necessary to consider the *cause* which conciliates such favor to those works. This we perceive to be threefold: The first is that God averting his eyes from the actions of his servants, which are invariably more deserving of censure than of praise, receives and embraces them in Christ, and by the intervention of faith alone reconciles them to himself without the assistance of works. The second is that in his paternal benignity and indulgence he overlooks the intrinsic unworthiness of these works, and exalts them to such honor that he esteems them of some degree of value. The third cause is that he pardons these works as he receives them, not imputing the imperfection with which they are all so defiled that they might otherwise be accounted rather sins than virtues."

Again, in Inst. III., xviii., 1, he explains the relation of the believer's good works to his justification as follows : " The declaration that God will render to everyone according to his works is easily explained. For that phrase indicates the *order* of events rather than the *cause* of them. It is beyond all doubt that the Lord proceeds to the consummation of our salvation by these gradations of mercy : ' Whom he hath predestinated them he calls; whom he hath called he justifies; and whom he hath justified he finally glorifies' (Rom. 8 : 30). Though he receives his children into eternal life of his mere mercy, yet since he conducts them to the possession of it through a course of good works that he may fulfil his work in them in the order he has appointed, we need not wonder if they are said to be rewarded according to their works, by which they are prepared to receive the crown of immortality. And for this reason they are properly said to ' work out their own salvation,' while, devoting themselves to good works, they aspire to eternal life. Whence it appears that the word *work* is not opposed to grace, but refers to human endeavors; and therefore it does not follow either that believers are the authors of their own salvation, or that salvation proceeds from their works. By their good works they prove themselves to be the genuine children of God, by their resemblance to their heavenly Father in righteousness and holiness."

Augustine's (Grace and Free-Will, ch. 19, 20) explanation is the following : " How is eternal life both a reward for service and a free gift of grace ? This is no small question which must be solved by the Lord's gift. If eternal life is rendered to good works, as the Scripture most openly declares, ' Then he shall reward every man according to his works,' how can eternal life be a matter of

29

grace, seeing that grace is not rendered to works, but is given gratuitously as the apostle himself tells us, 'To him that worketh is the reward not reckoned of grace, but of debt?' This question is not possible of solution, unless we understand that even those good works of ours which are recompensed with eternal life are a part of the grace of God, because of what is said by the Lord Jesus, 'Without me ye can do nothing' (John 15: 5); and by the apostle Paul, 'By grace are ye saved, through faith; and that not of yourselves, it is the gift of God; not of works lest any man should boast.' 'Not of works' is spoken here of the works which you suppose have their origin in yourself alone; but you have to think of works for which God has moulded you. For of these the apostle says, 'We are his workmanship, created in Christ Jesus unto good works.' We are framed, therefore, that is formed and created, 'in the good works which' we have not ourselves prepared, but which 'God hath before ordained that we should walk in them.' It follows, then, dearly beloved, that as your good life is nothing else than God's grace, so the eternal life which is the recompense of a good life is also the grace of God; moreover, the eternal life is given gratuitously, even as the good life is given gratuitously to which the eternal life is given. But that good life to which eternal life is given is solely and simply grace [not reward] ; while this eternal life which is given to it is its [gracious] reward; grace is for grace, as a [relative] remuneration for righteousness, in order that it may be true, because it is true, that God 'shall reward every man according to his works.'"

Ursinus (Christian Religion, Q. 52) thus explains Christ's reference to the works of the believer in the day of judgment: "It is *objected* that unto every man shall be given according to his works: therefore judgment shall be given to all, not according to the gospel, but according to the doctrine of the law. *Answer :* In this sense it shall be

given unto the elect according to their works; not that
their works are merits, but in that they are the effects
of faith. Wherefore, then, unto the elect shall be given
according to their works; that is, they shall be judged
according to the effects of faith; and to be judged according to faith is to be judged according to the gospel.
Now Christ shall rather judge according to works as the
effects of faith, than according to faith as their cause:
1. Because he will have it known to others why he so
judgeth, lest the ungodly and condemned persons might
object that he giveth us eternal life unjustly. He will
prove by our works the fruits of our faith, that our faith
was sincere and true, and therefore we are such as those
to whom life is due according to the promise. Wherefore
he will show them our works and will bring them forth
as testimonies to refute them, that we have in this life
applied unto us Christ's merit. 2. That we may have
comfort in this life, that we shall hereafter, according to
our works, stand at his right hand."

VOL. II., p. 555. That the regenerate can co-operate with
the Holy Spirit, but the unregenerate cannot, is illustrated by the act of prayer. There is no sincere prayer for
a spiritual good except as it is prompted by the Holy
Spirit. The foundation of prayer is a sense of want; of
spiritual poverty and need. "The Spirit helpeth our infirmities; for we know not what we should pray for as we
ought: but the Spirit itself maketh intercession for us with
groanings which cannot be uttered" (Rom. 8 : 26). "I will
pour out upon the house of David, and upon the inhabitants of Jerusalem, the spirit of grace and of supplications"
(Zech. 12 : 10). "Praying always with all prayer and supplication in the Spirit" (Eph. 6 : 18). All desires expressed
in prayer that are prompted solely by unregenerate human
nature, and without the impulse of the Holy Spirit, are
vitiated by selfishness. Man does not precede God, but
God precedes man, in every exercise that is holy and spir-

itual. Consequently, when our Lord says, "Ask and ye shall receive [the Holy Spirit]," he does not mean that the sincere desire and prayer for this blessing arises in the heart prior to any agency of the Holy Spirit upon it; but that the person who feels this desire has already been the subject of the Spirit's influence to this degree, and is to express the desire and so co-operate with the Spirit. In other words, Christ presupposes regeneration as shown in holy and spiritual desires and prayers, when he says, "Ask and ye shall receive; for everyone that [sincerely] asketh receiveth." This line of remark is applicable to all the other means of sanctification. The regenerate co-operates with the Divine Spirit in all struggling with sin, all attendance upon reading and hearing of the word, all confession of sin, all partaking of the Lord's Supper, etc., because the Spirit has gone before him and moved upon his heart. The unregenerate cannot thus co-operate in these acts, because the action of his heart and will is not spiritual, but selfish. His prayers and use of the means of sanctification are prompted by fear, not by love. Consequently the Divine Spirit first regenerates the sinful heart prior to any right co-operating action in it, and then the regenerate heart coworks with the Holy Spirit.

Says Augustine (Grace and Free Will, ch. 33) : "God operates without our assistance, in order that we may will rightly, but when we will rightly he co-operates with us." Says Owen (Sin and Grace, Works, xiv., 459. Ed. Russell) : "The work of first conversion [regeneration] is performed by an immediate act of divine power, without any active co-operation on our part. But this is not the law or rule of the communication or operation of actual grace for the subduing of sin [in the regenerate]. This is given in a way of concurrence with us in the discharge of our duties, and when we are sedulous in them we may be sure we shall not fail of divine assistance."

VOL. II., p. 556. Bates (Of Death, ch. iii.) describes the

completion of sanctification at death. "Death is to a believer an universal remedy against all the evils of this life. It frees him from all injuries and sufferings, and from sin in all its degrees, from all inclinations and temptations to it. He that is dead ceaseth from sin (1 Pet. 4 : 1). Death is the passage from this wilderness to the true Canaan, the rest above. There nothing can disturb the peace or corrupt the purity of the blessed. Beside the privative advantage, the freedom from all the effects of God's displeasure, there is the highest positive good obtained by death ; the spirits of just men are made perfect in heaven. The soul is the glory of man, and grace is the glory of the soul, and both are then in their exaltation. All the faculties of the soul are raised to the highest degrees of natural and divine perfection. In this life grace renews the faculties, but does not elevate them to their highest pitch. It does not make a mean understanding pregnant, nor a frail memory strong, nor a slow tongue eloquent, but sanctifies them as they are. But when the soul is released from this dark body of earth, the understanding is clear and quick, the memory firm, the will and affections ardent and vigorous. And they are enriched with divine light and love and power that makes them fit for the most noble and heavenly operations. The lineaments of God's image on the soul are first drawn here, but at death it receives his last hand. All the celestial colors are added, to give utmost life and lustre to it. Here we are advancing, but by death we arrive at perfection."

Respecting the possibility of complete sanctification in this life, Augustine, in his treatise on Nature and Grace, ch. 49, 70, thus remarks : "Pelagius contends that the point lies in the possibility of a man's not sinning; on which subject it is unnecessary for us to to take ground against him, for in truth I do not much care about expressing a definite opinion on the question whether in the present life there ever have been, or now are, or ever can be, any persons who. have had, or are having, or to have, the love of God so perfectly as to admit of no addition to it; for nothing short of this amounts to a most true, full, and perfect righteousness. For my own part, I am unwilling to dispute the point whether a sinless state is possible in this life." In this treatise, and in another on Man's Perfection in Righteousness, written about the same time (A. D. 415), Augustine does not deny the possibility of sinless perfection in this life; only it is by Divine grace, and not by the natural will as Pelagius asserted. But in his treatise Against Two Letters of the Pelagians (IV., 27) he says: " Let us consider the third point of theirs which is shocking to every member of Christ, that there have been righteous men having absolutely no sin." This treatise was written about 420. In 418 the Council of Carthage condemned the tenet of perfection in this life, in which decision Augustine must have had a leading part. Respecting complete sanctification at death, Augustine (Nature and Grace, ch. 70) says: " Whether there ever has been, or is, or can be, a man living so righteous a life in this world as to have no sin at all, may be an open question among true and pious Christians; but whoever doubts the possibility of this sinless state after the present life is foolish."

Vol. II., p. 560. Augustine (Grace and Free-Will, ch. 18) explains the difference between Paul and James as follows: " Unintelligent persons, with regard to the apostle Paul's statement, 'We conclude that a man is justified by faith without the works of the law,' have thought him to mean that faith suffices to a man even if he lead a bad life, and does no good works. Impossible is it that such a person should be deemed ' a vessel of election ' by that apostle, who, after declaring that ' in Christ Jesus neither circumcision availeth anything, nor uncircumcision,' adds immediately, ' but faith, which worketh by love.' It is such [working] faith which separates God's faithful from unclean demons; for even these ' believe and tremble,' as the apostle James says; but they do not work well. Therefore they have not the faith by which the justified man lives; the faith which works by love in suchwise that God recompenses it according to its works with eternal life. But inasmuch as we have even our good works from God, from whom likewise comes our faith and our love, therefore the same great teacher of the Gentiles has designated ' eternal life ' as his gracious ' gift ' " [as well as his recompense].

The creeds, both Lutheran and Reformed, teach that justifying faith is *working* faith. The Formula Concordiæ (Art. III., viii.) declares that " we are not to imagine any such justifying faith as can exist and abide with a purpose of evil, to wit: of sinning and acting contrary to conscience. But after that man is justified by faith then that true and living faith works by love (Gal. 5 : 6), and good works always follow justifying faith, and are most certainly found together with it, provided only it be a true and living faith. For true faith is never alone, but hath always charity and hope in its train." The Smalcald Articles (xiii.) declare that " hanc fidem, renovationem, et remissionem peccatorum, sequentur bona opera. Dicimus praeterea, ubi non sequuntur bona opera, ibi fidem esse falsam, et non veram."

The Irish Articles, 1615, maintain that justifying faith is working faith, and not faith which does not work, in the following manner: " When we say that we are justified by faith only, we do not mean that the said justifying faith is alone in man without true repentance, hope, charity, and the fear of God, for such a faith is *dead* and cannot justify; neither do we mean that this, our act, to believe in Christ, or this, our faith in Christ, which is within us, doth of itself justify us or deserve our justification unto us, for that were to account ourselves to be justified by the virtue or dignity of something that is within ourselves; but the true understanding and meaning thereof is, that although we hear God's Word and believe it, although we have faith, hope, charity, repentance and the fear of God within us, and add never so many good works thereunto; yet we must renounce the *merit* of all our said virtues, of faith, hope, charity, and all other virtues and good deeds which we have done, or shall do, or can do, as things that be far too weak and imperfect and insufficient to deserve remission of our sins and our justification, and therefore we must trust only in God's mercy and the merits of his most dearly beloved Son, our only Redeemer, Saviour, and Justifier, Jesus Christ. Nevertheless, because faith doth directly send us to Christ for our justification, and that by faith given us by God we embrace the promise of God's mercy and the remission of our sins, which thing none other of our virtues or works doth, therefore the Scripture useth to say that *faith without works*, that *only faith* doth justify us."

The faith which Paul and James both alike mean by justifying faith is not a faith to which works do not naturally belong, but are subjoined to faith from the outside, being produced by another act of the will than that of faith. Works, in their view, are produced by the one single act of faith itself, and thus are an integral element and part of faith itself. The same mental action which produces the faith produces the works. The works are not a separate *addition* to faith, but an *issue* from it. They can no more be separated, even in thought, from faith, than vegetable fruit can be from vegetable life. We do not conceive of grapes as something that can be produced ab extra by another force than that of the vine, and then added to the vital force of the vine, but as the spontaneous, natural, and necessary product of the vine's vitality, and making an integral part of the vine's total action. Our Lord teaches this when He says, "Abide in me, and I in you: as the branch cannot bear fruit of itself [spontaneously] except it abide in the vine, no more can ye except ye abide in me."

Faith and works, then, are two aspects or phases of one and the same principle of divine life in the soul. This one principle, viewed as cause, is faith ; viewed as effect, is works. Just as vegetable vitality and vegetable fruit are two aspects of one and the same principle of physical life. This one principle viewed as cause is the vitality of the vine stock ; viewed as effect is the cluster of grapes. " It is not possible," says Owen (Justification, ch. ii.), " that there should be any exercise of this faith unto justification but where the mind is prepared, disposed, and determined unto universal obedience. And therefore it is denied that any faith, trust, or confidence which may be imagined so as to be absolutely separable from, and have its whole nature consistent with, the absence of all other graces, is that faith which is the especial gift of God, and which in the Gospel is required of us in a way of duty."

The alleged difficulty of harmonizing Paul and James arises, then, from an erroneous view of the relation of good works to living faith. If both of these are regarded as constituting a unity that has two phases or aspects, so that works are faith in *operation*, and faith is works *potentially*, there is no contradiction in saying with Paul that a man is " justified by faith " (Rom. 3 : 28), and with James, that a man is " justified by works " (James 2 : 24). But if faith and good works are not regarded as a unity but as two separable and separate things, one of which can exist without the other, then it is contradictory to say with Paul a man is " justified by faith," and with James that he is " justified by works."

Christlieb (Modern Doubt, p. 530) thus explains the subject : " The difference between Paul and James lies in the language used by each ; inasmuch as what Paul usually designates as ' being saved ' ($\sigma\omega\zeta\epsilon\sigma\vartheta\alpha\iota$, *e.g.*, Eph., 2 : 8) is expressed by James by the word $\delta\iota\kappa\alpha\iota o\hat{\upsilon}\sigma\vartheta\alpha\iota$, which Paul generally applies to the first part of redemption, namely, justification."

After this statement of the inseparability of good works from faith it is important to observe carefully, that the

works which naturally issue from faith are not the cause
or ground of justification any more than the act of faith
itself is.   A man's sins are not remitted, nor does he
acquire a title to eternal life, because of his own merit in
believing, but because of Christ's merits in suffering and
obeying for him; and neither does he obtain these benefits
because of the good works that are inseparable from living
faith.

Vol. II., p. 562.   The Lutheran Formula Concordiæ
(Art. V.) makes the following excellent statement of the
Law and the Gospel as means of grace: 1. "We believe,
teach, and confess that the distinction of the Law and the
Gospel, as a most excellently clear light, is to be retained
with special diligence in the Church of God, in order that
the Word of God, agreeably to the admonition of St. Paul,
may be rightly divided. 2. We believe, teach, and confess
that the Law is properly a doctrine divinely revealed,
which teaches what is just and acceptable to God, and
which also denounces whatever is sinful and contrary to the
divine will. 3. Wherefore, whatever is found in the Holy
Scriptures which convicts of sin, this properly belongs to
the preaching of the Law. 4. The Gospel, on the other
hand, we judge to be properly the doctrine which teaches
what a man ought to believe who has not satisfied the law
of God, and therefore is condemned by the same, to wit:
that it behooves him to believe that Jesus Christ has expiated all his sins, and made satisfaction for them, and has
obtained remission of sins, a righteousness which avails
before God, and eternal life, without the intervention of
any merit of the sinner.   5. But inasmuch as the word
'Gospel' is not always used in Holy Scripture in one and
the same signification, we believe, teach, and confess that
if the term 'Gospel' is understood to denote the whole
doctrine of Christ which he set forth in his ministry, as
also did his apostles (in which signification the word is
used in Mark 1:15, and Acts 20:21), it is rightly said and

taught that the Gospel is a preaching of both repentance and remission of sins. 6. But when the Law and the Gospel are compared together, as in John 1:17, where Moses is described as the teacher of the Law and Christ of the Gospel, we believe, teach, and confess that the Gospel is not a preaching of repentance and convicting of sin, but that it is properly nothing else than a most joyful message and preaching full of consolation, not convicting or terrifying, since it comforts the conscience against the terrors of the Law, and bids it look at the merits of Christ alone, and by a most sweet preaching of the grace and favor of God, obtained through the merits of Christ, lifts it up again. 7. But as respects the revelation of sin, the case stands thus: That veil of Moses of which St. Paul speaks (2 Cor. 3:13-16) is drawn over all men's eyes so long as they hear only the preaching of the Law and nothing of Christ. And so they do not by the Law come to know their sins truly and humbly, but either become hypocrites swelling with an opinion of their own righteousness, like the Pharisees of old, or despair in their sins, as did the traitor Judas. For this cause Christ took it upon himself to explain the Law spiritually (Matt. 5:21-48; Rom. 7:14-24), and in this manner the wrath of God is revealed from heaven against all sinners (Rom. 1:18), in order that by perceiving the true meaning of the Law it may be understood how great is that wrath. And thus, at length, sinners being remanded to the Law, truly and rightly come to know their sins. But such an humble and penitent acknowledgment of sin, Moses alone never could have extorted from them. Although, therefore, this preaching of the passion and death of Christ the Son of God is full of severity and terror, inasmuch as it sets forth the wrath of God against sin, from whence men are at length brought nearer to the Law of God, after the veil of Moses is taken away so that they may exactly perceive how great things God requires from us in his Law, none of which we are able to perform, so that it behooves us to seek the whole of our righteousness in Christ alone. 8. Nevertheless, so long as the passion and death of Christ place before the eyes the wrath of God, and terrify man, so long they are not properly the preaching of the Gospel, but the teaching of the Law and Moses, and are Christ's strange work, through which he proceeds to his proper office, which is to declare the grace of God, to console and vivify. These latter things are the peculiar function of evangelical preaching. We reject, therefore, as a false and perilous dogma the assertion that the Gospel, as distinguished from the Law, is properly a preaching of repentance, rebuking, accusing, and condemning sins, and that it is not solely a preaching of the grace of God, For in this way the Gospel is transformed again into Law, the merit of Christ and the Holy Scriptures are obscured, a true and solid consolation is wrested away from godly souls, and the way is opened to Papal errors and superstitions. 9. We believe that the Law is to be inculcated upon the regenerate also ; that although they who truly believe in Christ, and are sincerely converted to God, are through Christ set free from the curse and constraint of the Law, they are not on that account without Law, inasmuch as the Son of God redeemed them for the very reason that they might meditate on the Law day and night, and continually exercise themselves in the keeping thereof (Ps. 1 : 2 ; 119 : 1 sq.). For not even our first parents, even before the fall, lived wholly without Law, which was certainly at that time graven on their hearts, because the Lord had created them after his own image (Gen. 1 : 26 sq. ; 2 : 16 sq. ; 3 : 3). 10. We therefore believe, teach, and confess that the preaching of the Law should be sedulously urged upon those who truly believe in Christ, are truly converted to God, and are regenerated and justified by faith. For, although they are regenerate and renewed in the spirit of their mind, yet this regeneration and renewal is not absolutely complete, but only begun. And they that believe have continually to struggle with their flesh, that is, with corrupt nature, which inheres in us even till death (Gal. 5 : 17 ; Rom. 7 : 21, 23). And on account of the old Adam, which still remains fixed in the intellect and will of man and in all his powers, there is need that the Law of God should always shine before man, that he may not frame anything in matters of religion under an impulse of self-devised devotion, and may not choose out ways of honoring God not instituted by the Word of God. Also, lest the old Adam should act according to his own bent, but that he may rather be constrained against his own will not only by the admonitions and threats of the Law, but also by chastisements and afflictions, in order that he may render obedience to the Spirit and give himself up captive to the same (1 Cor. 9 : 27 ; Rom. 6 : 12 ; Gal. 6 : 14; Ps. 119 : 1 sq. ; Heb. 12 : 1 ; 13 : 21)."

VOL. II., p. 565. Augustine (In Joannem, Tractatus xxvi., 1. Ed. Migne) expounding the words, " Except ye eat the flesh of the Son of man, and drink his blood, ye have no life in you," says : "Daturus Dominus Spiritum sanctum, dixit se panem qui de cœlo descendit, hortans ut credamus in eum. Credere enim in eum, hoc est manducare panem vivum. Qui credit, manducat : invisibiliter saginatur, quia invisibiliter renascitur." Again (xxvi., 18) he finds a definition of " eating flesh " and " drinking blood," by St. John himself (6 : 56), in the declaration, " He that eateth my flesh, and drinketh my blood, *dwelleth* in me, and I in him." " Hoc est ergo manducare illam escam, et illum bibere potum, in Christo manere, et illum manentem in se habere. Ac per hoc qui non manet in Christo, et in quo non manet Christus, procul dubio nec manducat [spiritualiter] carnem ejus, nec bibit ejus sanguinem [licet carnaliter et visibiliter premat dentibus sacramentum corporis et sanguinis Christi]." The words in brackets are not Augustine's, but the Benedictine editor's.

This view of Augustine, that "believing is eating," and that "eating Christ's flesh and blood" is not to be understood literally, but metaphorically, for trusting in his vicarious atonement, passed into the creeds very widely, and into theological literature.   Zwingle (Expositio Fidei, 1536) declares that " In cœna Domini naturale ac substantiale istud corpus Christi, quo et hic passus est et nunc in cœlis ad dexteram patris sedet, not naturaliter atque per essentiam editur, sed spiritualiter tantum.   *Spiritualiter edere* corpus Christi, nihil aliud quam spiritu ac mente *niti misericordia et bonitate Dei per Christum.*   Sacramentaliter *edere* corpus Christi, cum proprie volumus loqui, est, adjuncto sacremento, *mente et spiritu* corpus Christi *edere.*" The Confession of the Ministers of the Church of Zurich, 1545, as quoted by Hodge (Theology, III., 628) declares that "although the things of which the service of the sacrament is a memorial are not visible or present after a visible or corporal manner, nevertheless believing apprehension and the assurance of faith renders them present, in one sense, to the soul of the believer.   He has truly eaten the bread of Christ who *believes* on Christ, very God and very man, crucified for us, on whom to *believe* is to *eat*, and to *eat* is to *believe.*"   The Heidelberg Catechism, 1563, in answer to the question (76), "What is it to eat of the crucified body and drink the shed blood of Christ?" answers, "It is not only to *embrace with a believing heart* all the sufferings and death of Christ, and thereby to obtain the pardon of sin and life eternal, but also besides that to become more and more united to his sacred body by the Holy Ghost, who dwells both in Christ and in us; so that we, though Christ is in heaven and we on earth, are notwithstanding 'flesh of his flesh and bone of his bone;' and live and are governed forever by one spirit as members of the same body are by one soul."   The Second Helvetic Confession, 1566, describes two kinds of "eating. "   " Manducatio non est unius generis.   Est enim manducatio corporalis, qua cibus in os percipitur ab homine, dentibus atterritur et in ventrem deglutitur. Hoc manducationis genere intellexerunt olim Capernaitæ sibi manducandam carnem Domini, sed refutantur ab ipso, Joann. cap. 6. Est et spiritualis manducatio corporis Christi, non ea quidem, qua existememus cibum mutari in spiritum, sed qua, manente in sua essentia et proprietate corpore et sanguine Domini, ea nobis communicantur spiritualiter, utique non corporali modo, sed spirituali, per Spiritum Sanctum, qui videlicet ea quæ per carnem et sanguinem Domini pro nobis in mortem tradita parata sunt, ipsam inquam *remissionem peccatorum*, liberationem et vitam æternam, *applicat* et *confert* nobis, ita ut Christum in nobis vivat et nos in ipso vivamus. Ex quibus omnibus claret, nos per spiritualem cibum minime intellegere *imaginarium*, nescio quem, cibum, sed ipsum Domini corpus pro nobis traditum, quod percipiatur a fidelibus non corporaliter sed spiritualiter per fidem. In qua se sequimur per omnia doctrinam ipsius Salvatoris Christi Domini, dicentis apud Joann. 6 : 63, ' Caro (nimirum corporaliter manducatio) non prodest quidquam, spiritus est qui vivificat. Verba quæ loquor vobis spiritus et vita sunt.' *Fit autem hic esus et potus spiritualis* etiam *extra Domini cœnam, et quoties aut ubicunque homo in Christum crediderit.* Quo fortassis illud Augustini pertinet : ' Quid paras dentem et ventrem ? Crede et manducasti.' " The Belgic Confession, 1561, declares (Art. 33) that " God has ordained the sacraments in order to seal unto us his promises and to be pledges of his good will and grace toward us, and also to nourish and strengthen our faith ; " and that he " has *added them to the Word of the Gospel* in order the better to represent to our outward senses both that which he *teaches by his written Word*, and that which he works inwardly in our hearts." This view, like that of Calvin, closely associates the sacraments with the written Word, and makes their influence mental and didactic like that of the word, not material and corporeal. The Belgic Confession (Art. 35) thus defines "eating Christ:" "For the support of the spiritual and heavenly life which believers have, God has sent a living bread which descended from heaven, namely, Jesus Christ, which nourishes and strengthens the spiritual life of believers when it is *eaten*, that is to say *when it is applied and received by faith in the mind* (esprit)." It further declares, that "what is eaten and drunk by us is the proper and natural body and the proper blood of Christ [*i.e.*, his real and actual sacrifice for sin]; but the *manner* of our partaking of the same is *not by the mouth, but by the Spirit through faith*." The Thirty-Nine Articles, 1562, teach that "the body of Christ is given, taken, and eaten in the Supper only after a heavenly and spiritual manner; and the means whereby the body of Christ is received and *eaten* in the Supper is *faith*." The Irish Articles, 1615, in almost the same terms say that "the body of Christ is given, taken and eaten in the Lord's Supper only after a heavenly and spiritual manner; and the means whereby the body of Christ is thus received and *eaten* is *faith*." The Westminster Confession, 1647, declares (XXIX., viii., 7) that "worthy partakers of the Supper inwardly by *faith* receive and *feed* upon Christ crucified." In Dogmatics, Vol. II., 565–574, we have presented Zwingli's, Calvin's, and Hooker's doctrine of the Lord's Supper, and shown their agreement with each other, and with the Reformed creeds. They all deny the corporeal and local presence of Christ's body and blood in the bread and wine, together with the literal eating of Christ's flesh and blood by the mouth, and maintain that the words, "This is my body" are metaphorical, and that the believer eats and drinks the flesh and blood of Christ by trusting in his vicarious sacrifice for sin, being enlightened and enabled to this act of faith by the Holy Spirit.

It is noteworthy that Lutheranism, in some of its earlier creed statements, substantially adopted this spiritual view of the Supper, though subsequently departing from it in its development of the doctrine of consubstantiation. Luther's Shorter Catechism, 1529, presents it in the following questions and answers: " What is the use of such eating and drinking? It is shown to us in the words, ' Given and shed for you for the forgiveness of sins ; ' that is to say, through these words, the forgiveness of sins, life and salvation are given to us in the sacrament ; for where there is forgiveness of sins there is also life and salvation. How can corporeal eating and drinking do such great things ? *Eating* and *drinking,* indeed, do not do them, but the *words* which stand here, ' Given and shed for you for the forgiveness of sins.' Which words, besides the corporeal eating and drinking, are the main point in the sacrament ; and he who *believes* these words has that which they say and mean, namely, forgiveness of sins. Who, then, receives this sacrament worthily ? He is truly worthy and well prepared who has *faith* in these words, ' Given and shed for you for the forgiveness of sins.' But he who does not *believe* these words, or doubts, is unworthy and unfit ; for the words ' For you,' require truly believing hearts." In these answers faith in Christ's atonement is declared to be the meaning of eating and drinking his flesh and blood. But the position that Christ's spiritual body is *literally* and *locally present* in and with the material bread and wine, and is literally *eaten by the mouth* when these are eaten, notwithstanding all endeavors to guard and spiritualize it, finally neutralized the earlier affinity with the Reformed doctrine of the Supper, and ended in antagonism and separation. The Saxon Visitation Articles of 1592 mention as a "false and erroneous doctrine of the Calvinists," that "the body of Christ is in the bread and wine as a typified body, which is only signified and prefigured by the bread and wine ; " and that " the body is received by faith alone, which raiseth itself to heaven, and not by the mouth."

30

Vol. II., p. 571. If, as Calvin asserts, "the office of the sacraments is precisely the same as that of the word of God, which is to offer and present Christ to us," and if, as Augustine declares, " a sacrament is a visible word, because it presents the promises of God as in a picture, and places before our eyes an image of them," the question arises, How then does the sacrament of the Supper differ from the other didactic means of grace—such as the preaching and hearing of the word, prayer, and meditation. The answer is, generally, that it consists in teaching the cardinal doctrine of Christ's sacrifice and satisfaction in a *special* and *peculiar* manner. Owen mentions several points of difference. In the seventh of his Sacramental Discourses he remarks : " In the ordinance of the Supper there is a real *exhibition* and *tender* of Christ [as the sacrifice for sin] unto every believing soul. The exhibition and tender of Christ in this ordinance is distinct from the tender of Christ in the promise of the gospel, in that, in the gospel promise, the person of the Father is principally looked upon as proposing and tendering Christ unto us. But in the ordinance of the Supper Christ tenders himself : 'This is my body,' saith he, ' do this in remembrance of me.' He makes an immediate tender of himself [as the oblation for sin] unto a believing soul ; and calls our faith unto a respect to his grace, to his love, to his readiness to unite, and spiritually to incorporate with us. Again, it is a tender of Christ, and an exhibition of Christ, under an especial consideration [or aspect] ; not in general [as in the Scriptures generally], but under this consideration [or aspect], as he is a new and fresh sacrifice in the great work of reconciling, making peace with God, making an end of sin, doing all that was done between God and sinners that they might be at peace." Owen here represents the office of the sacrament of the Supper as the same in *kind* with that of the ministry of the Word. It is didactic of divine truth, like that. But it differs in being confined to a particular truth instead of ranging over the whole field of revelation. And, again, it differs from the ordinary teaching by the Word, in that the instruction is by means of sensuous and visible emblems, and not by articulate language only. Owen mentions a second point of difference in his tenth Sacramental Discourse : " Christ is *present* with us in an especial manner in the sacrament of the Supper. One of the greatest engines that ever the devil made use of to overthrow the faith of the church was by forging such a presence of Christ as is not truly in this ordinance, to drive us off from looking after that presence which is true. It is not a corporeal presence ; there are arguments of sense, reason, and faith that overthrow that. But I will remind you of two texts wherewith it is inconsistent. The first is John 16 : 7, ' It is expedient for you that I go away ; for if I go not away the Comforter will not come unto you.' The corporeal presence of Christ, and the evangelical presence of the Holy Ghost as the Comforter, are inconsistent with each other. But, say the Romish priests, Christ so went away as to his presence, as to come again with his bodily presence [in the sacrament]. No, saith Peter, in Acts 3 : 21, ' The heavens must receive him till the time of the restitution of all things.' We must not, therefore, look for a bodily presence of Christ until the time of the restitution. Christ is [spiritually] present in the sacrament : 1. By representation through sensible emblems. He represents himself as the food of our souls ; and he represents himself as the sacrifice for our sins. There are three ways whereby God represents Christ to the faith of believers : one is by the word of the gospel as written ; the second, by the ministry of the gospel and preaching the word ; and the third is by this sacrament, wherein we represent the Lord's death to the faith of our own souls. 2. By exhibition through emblems. The bread and wine exhibit what they do not themselves contain. The bread doth not contain the body or flesh of Christ; the cup doth not contain the blood of Christ; but they exhibit them. We must not think that the Lord Jesus Christ deludes our souls with empty shows and [fictitious] appearances. It is himself as literally broken and crucified that he exhibits unto us. 3. By obsignation. In the sacrament of the Supper, he seals the covenant. Therefore the cup is called, ' the new covenant in the blood of Christ.' "

In the second of his Sacramental Discourses Owen mentions another characteristic of the sacrament of the Supper, namely, an especial and peculiar *communion* with Christ. This communion, he says, differs from the other forms of communion with the Lord Jesus, in four particulars : " 1. It is commemorative. ' Do this in remembrance of me.' 2. It is professional. It has a peculiar profession attending it : ' Ye show forth the Lord's death till he come.' You make a profession and manifestation of it. 3. It is peculiarly eucharistical. There is a special thanksgiving that ought to attend this ordinance. It is called 'the cup of blessing, or thanksgiving' (εὐλογία). 4. It is a federal ordinance, wherein God confirms the covenant of grace unto us, and wherein he calls upon us to make a recognition of the covenant to God."

VOL. II., p. 574. That baptism is not a means of regeneration but only the sign and seal of it, is evident from its relation to faith. It presupposes faith, and faith presupposes regeneration. Philip said to the eunuch, " If thou believest with all thy heart thou mayest be baptized " (Acts 8 : 37). No faith, no baptism. Christ's command for the church in all time is, " He that [first] believeth, and is baptized [in profession and sign of his faith] shall be saved " (Mark 16 : 16). The apostle Peter (1 Pet. 3 : 21) declares that " Baptism doth save us by the resurrection of Jesus Christ." Not by its own efficacy, therefore, but as the emblem of what has been done by Christ's redemption, whose " resurrection " is one of the constituent factors in it. And in order to preclude the notion that the mere application of water has any spiritual effect like that of regenerating the soul, the apostle explains that baptism does not "save by the putting away of the filth of the flesh," but by "the answer of a good conscience toward God." The "answer of a good conscience" is its pacification through the atonement of Christ for sin, to which baptism has reference. For, as St. Paul says, "As many of us as were baptized with reference to (εἰς) Jesus Christ were baptized with reference to (εἰς) his [atoning] death."

VOL. II., p. 577. Baxter (Directions for Spiritual Peace) thus speaks of the salvation of infants : "Grace is not natural to us, or conveyed by generation. Yet grace is given to our children as well as to us. That it may be so, and is so with some, all will grant who believe that infants may be and are saved ; and that it is so with the infants of believers I have fully proved in my Book of Baptism ; but mark what grace I mean. The grace of remission of original sin, the children of all true believers have at least a high *probability* of, if not a full certainty ; their parent accepting it for himself and them, and dedicating them to Christ, and engaging them in his covenant, so that he takes them for his people, and they take him for their Lord and Saviour. And for the grace of inward renewing of their nature or disposition, it is a secret to us, utterly unknown whether God use to do it in infants or no." According to this, Baxter regarded the election and salvation of infants as individual only. All dying infants are not elected and saved.

VOL. II., p. 581. Mosheim (Commentaries Cent. i., Sect. 5) thus remarks upon "the rite of baptism, by which our Saviour ordained that his followers should be received into the kingdom of heaven, or the new covenant." "My opinion on this subject entirely corresponds with theirs who consider this ceremony as having been adopted by the

Jews long before the time of our Saviour, and used by them in the initiating of strangers who had embraced their religion. The account given in John 1 of the embassy sent by the supreme council of the Jews to John the Baptist, the forerunner of Christ, supports this view. For the rite itself of baptizing with water those who have confessed their sins and promised an amendment of life does not seem to have been regarded by the elders of the Jews as a novelty or as a practice of an unusual kind. The only point on which they require information of John is, from whence he derived his authority to perform this solemn and sacred ceremony. The thing itself occasioned them no surprise, since daily use had rendered it familiar to them : what attracted their attention was that a private individual should take upon him to perform it, contrary to the established usage of the nation."

" An inference of still greater moment may also be drawn from this message sent by the Jewish council to John, which will supply the reason why our Saviour adopted this ancient Jewish practice of baptizing proselytes with water ; for the concluding question put by the messengers evidently implies an expectation in the Jews of that age that the Messiah for whom they looked would baptize men with water. ' If thou be not that Christ, nor Elias, nor that prophet, why baptizest thou then ? ' An opinion, it appears, prevailed amongst the Jews that Elias, whose coming was to precede that of the Messiah, and also the Messiah himself, would initiate their disciples by a ' sacred ablution ; ' and it was necessary, therefore, in order to avoid giving the Jews any pretext for doubt respecting Christ's authority, that both John and himself should accommodate themselves to this popular opinion."

ESCHATOLOGY

Vol. II., p. 600. Tertullian (Apologeticus, 48) represents
Gehenna as the contrary of Paradise. "We Christians are
ridiculed when we preach a punitive Deity, because the
pagan poets and philosophers also teach the same. If we
threaten Gehenna, which is a subterranean storehouse of
secret fire for punishment, we are immediately laughed to
scorn. For this is the heathen river Phlegethon. And if
we mention Paradise, a place of divine felicity destined to
receive the spirits of the holy, separated from the common globe by a wall of fire, the Elysian fields have previously engaged the belief of men. But whence come, I
ask you, these notions of the poets and philosophers so
similar to ours, unless from our mysteries (sacraments)?"

Vol. II., p. 601. Irenæus (Adv. Hær., I., xxvii., 3), like
Origen, mentions as one of the heresies of Marcion, "that
Cain, the Sodomites, the Egyptians, and others like them,
and in fine all the nations who walked in all sorts of
abominations, were saved by the Lord on his descending
into Hades." He also, when enunciating "the faith which
the church has received from the Apostles," makes no
mention of the Descent into Hades (Ad. Hæreses, I., x., 1).
This is conclusive evidence that in the last quarter of the
second century this tenet was not regarded as one of the
cardinal doctrines of Christianity. So well-informed and
influential a bishop would not have omitted it when stating
the creed of the church, had it been as generally accepted

as the doctrines of the trinity incarnation, crucifixion, resurrection, ascension, etc.

Vol. II., p. 604.   Jeremy Taylor (Liberty of Prophe-
sying, sec. i.) acknowledges the spuriousness of the clause
concerning the Descent into Hell.   "For taking out the
article of Christ's descent into Hell, which was not in the
old [Apostles'] creed, as appears in some of the copies I
before referred to in Tertullian, Rufinus, and Irenæus;
and indeed was omitted in all the confessions of the East-
ern churches, in the Church of Rome, and in the Nicene
creed which by adoption came to be the creed of the Catholic Church, all other articles are such as directly constitute the parts and work of our redemption, such as clearly derive the honor to Christ, and enable him with the
capacities of our Saviour and Lord."

Vol. II., p. 605.   Augustine's view of the intermediate
state is somewhat vacillating, although on the whole more
in accord with the Protestant than the Papal doctrine.   In
his letter to Evodius (Letter clxiv.) he makes the following
objection to Christ's preaching to the spirits in prison:
"This is felt by me to be difficult.   If the Lord when he
died preached in hell to spirits in prison, why were those
who continued unbelieving while the ark was a preparing
the only ones counted worthy of this favor, namely, the
Lord's descending into hell?   For in the ages between
the time of Noah and the passion of Christ there died
many thousands of many nations whom he might have
found in hell.   I do not, of course, speak of those who in
that period of time had believed in God, as, for example,
the prophets and patriarchs of Abraham's line, or going
farther back Noah himself and his house, who had been
saved by water, excepting perhaps the one son who afterward was rejected, and, in addition to these, all others
outside of the posterity of Jacob who were believers in
God, such as Job, the citizens of Nineveh, and any others,
whether mentioned in Scripture or existing unknown to

us in the vast human family at any time. I speak only of those many thousands of men who, ignorant of God, and devoted to the worship of devils or of idols, had passed out of this life from the time of Noah to the passion of Christ. How was it that Christ, finding these in hell, did not preach to them, but preached only to those who were unbelieving in the days of Noah when the ark was a preparing? Or if he preached at all, why has Peter mentioned only these, and passed over the innumerable multitude of the others?"

The following extracts exhibit the uncertainty of his mind: "The saying of Scripture that 'the pains of hell were loosed' by the death of Christ, may be understood to refer to himself; meaning that he so far loosed, that is, made ineffectual, the pains of hell that he himself was not held by them, especially since it is added that it was 'impossible for him to be holden of them.' Or if any one, objecting to this interpretation, asks the reason why Christ chose to descend into hell, where those [retributive] pains were which could not possibly hold him in whom the prince and captain of death found nothing which deserved hell-punishment, the words 'the pains of hell were loosed' may be understood as referring not to all but only to some whom he chose to deliver. As to the first man, the father of mankind, it is agreed by almost the entire Church that the Lord loosed him from that prison; although the authority of the canonical Scriptures cannot be cited as speaking expressly in its support, though this seems to be the opinion which is more than any other borne out by the words in the Book of Wisdom (10:1, 2): 'Wisdom preserved the first formed father of the world that was created alone, and brought him out of his fall, and gave him power to rule all things.' Some add to this tradition that the same favor was bestowed on Abel, Seth, Noah and his house, Abraham, Isaac, Jacob, and the other patriarchs and prophets: they also being loosed from those pains at the time when the Lord descended into hell. But for my part, I cannot see how Abraham, into whose bosom the pious beggar in the parable was received, can be understood to have been in these pains. Moreover, *I have not been able to find anywhere in Scripture the term 'hell' [Hades] used in a good sense.* And if this use of the term is nowhere found in the Scriptures, assuredly the 'bosom of Abraham,' that is, the abode of a safe and tranquil rest, is *not to be believed to be a part of hell [Hades].* Nay, from the words of the Master, in which he represents Abraham as saying, 'Between us and you there is a great gulf (chaos) fixed,' it is sufficiently evident that the bosom of that glorious felicity was *not any integral part of hell [Hades].* For what is that great gulf (chaos) but a chasm (hiatus) completely separating those places between which it not only is, but is fixed. Therefore if Scripture, without mentioning hell [Hades] and its pains, had simply said that Christ when he died went to the bosom of Abraham, would any one have dared to say that he 'descended into hell?' But seeing that plain scriptural testimonies make mention of hell and its pains, no reason can be alleged for believing that the Saviour went thither except that he might save some from its pains; but whether he saved all, or only some whom he deemed worthy of this favor, I still query. That he was in hell (apud inferos), and conferred this favor upon [wicked] persons *subjected to these retributive pains,* I do not doubt; but I have not been able to find what benefit he conferred, when he descended into hell, upon those *righteous* persons who were in Abraham's bosom, from whom I do not perceive that he ever withdrew himself, so far as concerns the beatific presence of his divinity. For on the very day that he died he promised that the thief should be with him in paradise at the time when he was himself about to descend to 'loose the pains of hell.' Most certainly, therefore, Christ was simultaneously in paradise and the bosom of Abraham in his beatific wisdom, and in hell [Hades] *in his condemning power ;* for since the Godhead is confined by no limits, where is it not present? At the same time, however, so far as regarded his created nature, in assuming which he became man while still continuing to be God ; that is to say, so far as regarded his human soul ; he was in hell—as is plainly declared by the words of Scripture, ' Thou wilt not leave my soul in hell ' " (Letter clxiv., 2, 5, 6–8, to Evodius, A.D. 414). It is to be noticed that in these extracts Augustine uses the word "hell," to denote the abode of the lost alone. He does not understand it to mean a non-penal underworld containing both the evil and the good. " Abraham's bosom," he says, is not within it ; and the inhabitants of it, like " the pious beggar," do not suffer the pains of punitive torment. " Hell," for him, here means only the place of penal retribution ; as it does also in the Septuagint, Vulgate, Luther's, and James's versions. At the same time it is to be observed that in other places Augustine employs " hell " to denote the abode of the saints redeemed under the *old* dispensation. He describes them as being in " hell," and delivered therefrom by Christ's descent for that purpose, and asserts that those redeemed under the new dispensation do not go to " hell " and are not so delivered. " If it does not seem irrational to believe that the ancient saints who believed in Christ and his then future coming were kept in places far removed indeed from the torments of the wicked, yet in ' hell ' (apud inferos), until Christ's blood and his descent into these places delivered them, then, certainly, good Christians, redeemed by that price already paid, are wholly ignorant of ' hell ' (inferos nesciunt) while they wait for the resurrection of their bodies and the reception of their eternal reward " (De Civitate, xx., 15). In saying that the Old Testament saints were in " hell," before the descent of Christ to deliver them, Augustine conflicts with his assertion in his letter to Evodius, that he " has not been able to find anywhere in Scripture the term 'hell' used in a good sense"—that is, to denote the place where the good dwell. The explanation is, that the eschatology of the Church was in an unsettled state, and on the way to the doctrine of purgatory, and Augustine sometimes clung to the earlier doctrine of the Apostolic age, which, like Scripture, knows nothing of the Descensus, and sometimes followed the current of his time.

The following extracts from Augustine respecting Christ's "preaching to the spirits in prison," and the possibility that those who die unbelieving may believe and repent in the middle state, agree with the doctrine of Calvin and the Reformers. "If we accept the opinion that men who did not believe while they were in life can in hell (apud inferos) believe in Christ, who can endure the contradictions both of reason and faith which must follow? In the first place, if this were true, we should have no reason for mourning over those [as hopelessly lost] who have departed from the body without the grace of faith, and there would be no ground for being solicitous and urgent that men should accept the grace of God before they die, lest they should suffer eternal death. If, secondly, it be alleged that in hell those only believe to no purpose and in vain who refused to accept here on earth the gospel preached to them, but that believing will profit those who never despised a gospel which they never had it in their power to hear, another still more absurd consequence is involved, namely, that the gospel ought not to be preached at all here upon earth, since all men shall certainly die, and in order to get any benefit from believing the gospel in hell must not have incurred the guilt of rejecting it here on earth" (Letter clxiv., ch. 13. To Evodius). The opinion that men are not damnable for original sin and actual transgression, but only for rejecting the offer of mercy, has been revived by the present advocates of salvation in the middle state. The

objection which Augustine here makes to it is the same
which the advocate of modern missions makes, namely,
that it takes away the principal motive for preaching the
gospel to men in this life as the only " day of salvation."
" Consider, I pray you, whether what the apostle Peter says
concerning spirits shut up in prison who were unbelieving
in the days of Noah, may not have been written without
any reference to hell, but rather to the typical nature of
those times as related to the present time. For that transaction had been typical of future events, so that those who
do not believe the gospel in our age, when the church is
being built up in all nations, may be understood to be
like those who did not believe in that age while the ark
was preparing ; also, that those who have believed and
are saved by baptism may be compared to those who at
that time, being in the ark, were saved by water ; wherefore he says, ' So baptism by a like figure saves you.' Let
us therefore interpret the rest of the statements concerning them that believed not, so as to harmonize with the
analogy of the figure, and refuse to entertain the thought
that the gospel was once preached, or is even to this hour
being preached, in hell, in order to make men believe and
be delivered from its pains, as if a church had been established there as well as on earth " (Letter clxiv., ch. 15).
" Those who have inferred from the words, ' He preached
to the spirits in prison,' that Peter held the opinion that
Christ preached to disembodied souls in hell, seem to me
to have been led to this view by imagining that the term
' spirits ' could not be used to designate souls which were
at the time of the preaching still in the bodies of men,
and which, being shut up in the darkness of ignorance,
were, so to speak, ' in prison '—a prison such as that from
which the Psalmist sought deliverance in the prayer,
' Bring my soul out of prison, that I may praise thy
name.' Instances in which ' soul ' and ' spirit ' denote
living persons on earth are, Rom. 13 : 1 ; 1 John 4 : 1, 3 "

(Letter clxiv., 16). " Let it not be regarded as an objection to the interpretation that the apostle Peter says that Christ himself preached to the spirits shut up in the prison of sin, who were unbelieving in the days of Noah, that Christ had not yet come. Though he had not come bodily, yet from the beginning of the human race he came often to this earth, whether to rebuke the wicked, as Cain, and before that, Adam and his wife, when they sinned ; or to comfort the good, or to admonish them ; so that some should believe to their salvation, and others should refuse to believe to their condemnation ; coming not in the flesh but in the spirit, speaking by suitable manifestations of himself to such persons and in such manner as seemed good to him " (Letter clxiv., 17). " There cannot be any middle life between holiness and sin, nor any middle judicial sentence between reward and punishment " (On Free-Will, iii., 66). Augustine is explicit respecting the finality and endlessness of the punishment of the unregenerate dead, but respecting the temporary chastisement of the regenerate dead in the middle state, and prayers for their deliverance, he was involved in the errors of his time, and makes some statements which are justly cited by Roman Catholic theologians in support of the doctrine of purgatory. Concerning the first point, he says : " When the Judge of quick and dead has said, Depart from me, ye cursed, into the eternal fire which is prepared for the devil and his angels, and, these shall go away into the eternal punishment, it were excessively presumptuous to say that the punishment of any of those whom God has said shall go away into eternal punishment shall not be eternal, and so bring either despair or doubt upon the corresponding promise of life eternal " (City of God, xxi., 24). Respecting the second points, the following extracts exhibit his views : " The church prays for the wicked as long as they live, but she does not pray for the *unbelieving* and *godless* who are dead. For some of the dead, indeed, the prayer

of the church or of pious individuals is heard; but it is
for those who, having been *regenerated* in Christ, did not
spend their life so wickedly that they can be judged unworthy of such compassion, nor so well that they can be
considered to have no need of it.   As, also, after the resurrection there will be some of the [regenerate] dead to
whom, after they have endured the pains proper to the
spirits of the dead, mercy shall be accorded, and acquittal
from the punishment of the eternal fire.   For were there
not some whose sins, though not remitted in this life, shall
be remitted in that which is to come, it could not be truly
said, ' They shall not be forgiven, neither in this world,
neither in that which is to come' " (City of God, xxi., 24,
A.D. 413–426).   " Temporary punishments are suffered by
some in this life only, by others after death, by others
both now and then; but all of them before that last and
strictest judgment " (City of God, xxi., 13).   " It is a matter that may be inquired into, and either ascertained or
left doubtful, whether some believers shall pass through a
kind of purgatorial fire, and, in proportion as they have
loved with more or less devotion the goods that perish, be
less or more quickly delivered from it " (Enchiridion, ch.
69, A.D. 425).   " It cannot be denied that the souls of the
[regenerate] dead are benefited by the piety of their living friends, who offer the sacrifice of the Mediator, or give
alms in the church on their behalf " (Enchiridion, ch.
110).

VOL. II., p. 617.   Tholuck thus evinces the heavenly
blessedness of the Old Testament saints, from the Old
Testament :   " The Psalms show that the Old Testament
saints stood to God, in the relation of love, to a much
greater extent than some suppose.   Who can be untouched
on hearing the words of David at the beginning of the
Psalm of thanksgiving which he sang toward the close of
his life :   ' I will love thee, O Lord, my strength ' (Ps. 18 :
1).   ' Thou art my Lord, I have no good beyond thee ' (Ps.

16 : 2). No Christian could describe in sweeter language the
peace of reconciliation than we find it done in Psalms 16,
23, 26, 27, 71, 73, 103. How happy must have been their
communion with God who say, ' How excellent is thy lov-
ing-kindness, O God! therefore the children of men put
their trust under the shadow of thy wings ; they are abundantly satisfied with the fatness of thy house, and thou
makest them drink of the river of thy pleasures' (Ps. 36 :
8, 9). 'Blessed is the man whom thou choosest and
causest to approach unto thee, that he may dwell in
thy courts ; he shall be satisfied with the goodness of
thy house, even of thy holy temple' (Ps. 65 : 5). 'Thy
loving - kindness is better than life. When I remember thee upon my bed, and meditate on thee in the
night watches ' (Ps. 63 : 4, 7). It is always a mark of a
strong and healthy divine life when the traces of God are
recognized in surrounding nature. Do classical songs celebrate the traces of God in nature? The Psalms do this
eminently. Compare Psalms 8, 18, 19, 29, 104, 107, 147.
The Old Testament saints were remarkable for the depth
and sincerity of their worship of God. ' There is no attribute,' says Herder, ' no perfection of God left unex-
pressed in the simplest and most powerful manner in the
Psalms and the Prophets.' In fact we can hardly realize
how much energy and freshness the Christian belief in
and worship of God would lose, were the lofty utterances
of the Psalms concerning the Divine excellence and glory
withdrawn from the Christian Church. See Psalms 33,
47, 65, 86, 90, 91, 97, 103, 104, 139. The Old Testament
saints did not merely fear the Divine law, but loved it.
The law is described as their delight, as sweeter than
honey and the honeycomb ; as the riches, the peculiar
portion and possession of the righteous, as the song in
the house of his pilgrimage (Ps. 19 : 8–11 ; 119 : 54–57 ;
103 : 11). Is it possible to find an instance of more thorough absorption of the human will in the law of God than

this ? ' I delight to do thy will, O my God ; yea thy law is within my heart ' (Ps. 40 : 9). We are therefore entitled to say that morality of the purest kind, as the effect of filial love and reverence of God, formed part of the obedience of the Old Testament saints. The depth of their convictions of sin on the one hand, and their fervent sense of the Divine mercy and of intimacy and communion with God on the other, constituted a religious experience not exceeded by anything of the kind in the patristic, mediæval, and modern Church " (On the Psalms, Introduction, iv.).

Baxter (Dying Thoughts : Appendix) thus argues in proof that the Old Testament saints at death went to paradise or heaven : " Sure it is not true that the souls of the fathers, before Christ's coming, did not enter into heaven, but lay in some inferior limbus. For Moses and Elijah came from heaven ; their shining glory showed that, and their discourse with Christ, and the voice and glory that went with them. And it is not to be thought that they were separated from the rest of the souls of the faithful, and, with Enoch, were in heaven by themselves alone, and the rest elsewhere. Though it is said that God's house hath many mansions, and there are various degrees of glory, yet the blessed are all fellow-citizens of one society, and children of one family of God. And they that came from east and west shall sit down with Abraham, Isaac, and Jacob, in the kingdom of God ; and Lazarus is in Abraham's bosom, and the believing thief with Christ in Paradise."

VOL. II., p. 627. Calvin (Institutes, II., xvi., 8–10) says that " though it appears from the writings of the fathers that the article concerning the ' descent into hell ' was not always in common use in the churches, yet in discussing a system of doctrine it is necessary to introduce it as containing a mystery highly useful. Indeed there are some of the fathers who do not omit it. Hence we may conject-

31

ure that it was inserted a little after the days of the apostles, and was not immediately but gradually received in the churches. It was explained in different senses. Some are of opinion that the clause contains nothing new, but is only a repetition in other words of what had been said respecting Christ's burial ; because the word here rendered 'hell' is frequently used in the Scriptures to signify the *grave*. I admit the truth of this observation respecting the meaning of the word, that it is frequently to be understood of the 'grave ;' but their opinion is opposed by two reasons, which induce me to dissent from them. For what carelessness it would betray, after a plain fact had been stated in the most explicit manner, to assert it a second time in an obscure statement calculated rather to perplex than to elucidate it. When two phrases expressive of the same thing are connected together, the latter ought to be an explanation of the former. But what an explanation would this be if one were to express it thus : ' When Christ is said to have been buried, the meaning is, that he descended into hell ! ' Besides, again, it is not probable that such a superfluous tautology could have found its way into this compendium in which the principal articles of faith are expressed with the utmost possible brevity. Others explain the clause to mean that Christ descended to the souls of the fathers who had died under the Old Testament dispensation, for the purpose of announcing to them the accomplishment of redemption, and liberating them from the prison in which they were confined. To this purpose they pervert the passages, Ps. 107 : 16, and Zechariah 9 : 11. I freely confess, indeed, that Christ illuminated the souls of the Old Testament saints by the power of his Spirit, so that they might know that the grace which they had only tasted by hope was then exhibited to the whole world. And probably to this we may accommodate that passage in Peter, where he says that Christ ' went and preached unto the spirits who were keeping watch as in a tower.' This is generally rendered, 'the spirits in prison,' but I conceive improperly. The context also gives us to understand that the faithful who had died before that time were partakers of the same grace with us. For the apostle amplifies the efficacy of the death of Christ from this consideration, that it penetrated even to the dead. 'For this cause was the gospel preached also to them that are dead, that they might be judged according to men in the flesh, but live according to God in the spirit' (1 Pet. 4 : 6)."

"But laying aside all consideration of the Creed, we have to seek for a more certain explanation of the descent of Christ into hell; and we find one in the Divine word replete with singular consolation to the believer. If Christ had merely died a corporeal death, no end would have been accomplished by it. It was requisite, also, that he should feel the severity of the Divine retribution in order to appease the wrath of God, and satisfy his justice. Hence it was necessary for him to contend with the powers of hell and the horror of eternal death. We have already stated from the prophet that 'the punishment of our peace was upon him,' that 'he was wounded for our transgressions and bruised for our iniquities;' the meaning of which is, that he was made a substitute and surety for transgressors, and even treated as a criminal himself, and bore all the punishments which would have been inflicted upon them; only with this exception, that 'it was not possible that he should be [forever] holden of the pains of death' (Acts 2 : 24). Therefore it is no wonder if he be said to have descended into hell, since he suffered that death which the righteous wrath of God inflicts on transgressors. It is an inadequate objection to say that by this explanation the order of things is perverted, because it makes that subsequent to his burial which really preceded it. For those sufferings of Christ which were visible to men [in the Garden and on the Cross] are very properly followed by that invisible and mysterious infliction which he suffered from the hand of God; in order to assure us that not only the body of Christ was given as the price of our redemption, but that there was another and more excellent ransom, since he suffered in his soul a dreadful agony [equal to that] of a person condemned and irretrievably lost." [Christ's estate of humiliation and suffering did not end at his crucifixion but his resurrection. During the interval between these, he was, therefore, still suffering, " the just for the unjust."]

Selden (Table-Talk) thus explains the term "hell" in the article on the Descent: " There are two texts for Christ's descending into hell, the one Ps. 16 : 10 ; the other Acts 2 : 27, 31. The Bible that was in use when the Thirty-Nine Articles were made has 'hell;' but the Bible that was in Queen Elizabeth's time, when the Articles were confirmed, reads it 'grave;' and so it continued till the new translation in King James's time, when it is 'hell' again. By this we may gather that the Church of England declined, as much as they could, the Article concerning the Descent; otherwise they never would have altered the Bible."

" This may be the interpretation of the clause, ' He descended into hell.' He may be dead and buried, then his soul ascended into heaven. Afterward he descended again into hell, that is, into the grave, to fetch his body and to rise again. To understand by 'hell' the grave is no tautology, because the Creed first tells what Christ suffered, ' He was crucified, dead, and buried ;' then it tells us what he did, 'He descended into hell, the third day he rose again, he ascended,' etc. " Whitby explains like Selden. See Dogmatic Theology, II. 607.

VOL. II., p. 645. Neither the phrase "second resurrection" nor the phrase "first death" are found in Scripture. They are inferences from the phrases, " first resurrection " and "second death," which are found there; the former in Rev. 20 : 5, 6 ; the latter in Rev. 2 : 11 ; 20 : 6, 14 ;

21 : 8. The inferred " first death " and the inferred " second resurrection " are both of them physical. The " first death " is destroyed by the resurrection of the body (1 Cor. 15 : 26, 54, 55 ; 1 Tim. 1 : 10 ; Heb. 2 : 14) ; the " second death " is indestructible (Rev. 20 : 14, 10). The " second resurrection " is that of the body ; and the " first resurrection " is that of the soul in regeneration. One death and one resurrection are directly taught, and one death and one resurrection indirectly taught in Scripture. One of each is physical, and one of each is spiritual. But the order is different in each class. The first death is physical, and the second is spiritual ; the first resurrection is spiritual, and the second physical.

Leighton (On 1 Pet. 22) explains the phrase " newborn babes " as denoting the new birth, and says that " this new birth is the same that St. John calls the first resurrection, and pronounces them blessed that partake of it. ' Blessed are they that have part in the first resurrection, the second death shall have no power over them ' (Rev. 20 : 6). This new life put us out of danger and fear of that eternal death. ' We are passed from death to life,' says St. John (1 John, 3 : 14), speaking of those that are born again."

VOL. II., p. 648. Howe (Blessedness of the Righteous, ch. ix.) notices the fact that Pythagoras, Plato, and the New-Platonists not only held the soul to be of a different substance from the body, and capable of existing and acting without it, but also " that we are borne down by the body to the earth, and are continually recalled by it from the contemplation of higher things, and that the body must therefore be relinquished as much as possible even here, and altogether in another life, that free and unencumbered we may discern truth and love goodness." He then proceeds to argue in support of the diversity of nature between soul and body, and the independence of the former, as follows : " If it be possible enough to form an unexceptionable notion of a spiritual being distinct and separable from any corporeal substance (which the learned Dr. More hath sufficiently demonstrated in his treatise on the Immortality of the Soul) with its proper attributes and powers peculiar to itself, what can reasonably withhold me from asserting that, being separated from the body, it may as well operate alone (I mean exert such operations as are proper to such a spiritual being) as exist alone? What we find it here, in fact, in its present state, acting only with dependence on a body, will no more infer that it can act no otherwise, than its present existence in a body will that it can never exist out of it; neither of which inferences amounts to more than the trifling exploded argument a non esse ad non posse, that because a thing is not it cannot be, and would make as good sense as to say, such an one walks in his clothes, therefore out of them he cannot move a foot. Yea, and the very use itself which the soul now makes of corporeal organs and instruments, plainly evidences that it doth exert some action of its own wherein they assist it not. For it supposes *an operation upon them* antecedent to *any operation by them*. Nothing [material] can be my instrument which is not first the subject of my [mental] action; as when I use a pen I act upon it in order to my action by it; that is, I impress a motion upon it, in order whereunto I use not the pen or any other such material instrument; and though I cannot produce the designed effect, that is, leave such characters so and so figured, without it, my hand can yet, without it, perform its own action, proper to itself, and produce many nobler effects. When therefore the soul makes use of a bodily organ, its action upon it must needs at last be without the ministry of any organ, unless you multiply to it body upon body ad infinitum. And if possibly it perform not some meaner and grosser pieces of drudgery when out of the body, wherein it made use of its help and service when in the body, that is no more a disparagement or diminution than it is to the magistrate that law and decency permit him not to apprehend or execute a malefactor with his own hand. It may yet perform those operations which are proper to itself; that is, such as are more noble and excellent, and immediately conducive to its own felicity. Which sort of actions, as cogitation and dilection [thinking and loving], though because being done in the body there is conjunct with them an agitation of the spirits in the brain and heart [in modern phrase, a molecular motion of their particles], it yet seems to me more reasonable that as to these agitations the spirits [molecular motions] are rather subjects than instruments; that the whole essence of these mental acts of thinking and loving is antecedent to the motion of the bodily spirits [molecular motion]; [this is illustrated by the priority of the mental feeling of shame to the bodily flush that accompanies it. The feeling is antecedent to the blush, or molecular motion, and causes it; not the blush antecedent to the feeling and its cause]; and that this bodily motion is certainly but only incidentally consequent upon the thinking and loving merely by reason of the present but soluble union the soul hath with the body. The purity and refinedness of these bodily spirits [molecular motions] doth only remove what would hinder such mental acts as thinking and loving, rather than contribute positively thereunto. And so little is the alliance between a thought and any bodily or material thing, even those very finest spirits themselves, that I dare say that whoever sets himself closely and strictly to consider and debate the matter with his own faculties, will find it much more easily apprehensible how the acts of intellection and volition may be performed without these corporeal spirits than by them."

"As therefore the doctrine of the soul's activity out of its earthly body hath favor and friendship enough from philosophers, so I doubt not but that upon the most strict and ready disquisition it would be as much befriended by philosophy itself. In the meantime it deserves to be considered with some regret that this doctrine should find the generality of learned pagans more forward advocates than some learned and worthy advocates of the Christian faith ; which is only imputable to the undue measure and excess of an otherwise just zeal in these latter for the resurrection of the body, so far transporting them that they became willing to let go one truth that they might hold another the faster, and to ransom this at the too dear and unnecessary expense of the former ; accounting they could never make sure enough the resurrection of the body without making the soul's dependence on it so absolute and necessary that it should be able to do nothing but sleep in the meanwhile. Whereas it seems a great deal more inconceivable how such a being as the soul is, once quit of the entanglements and encumbrances of the body, should sleep at all, than how it should act without the body."

In a similar manner Baxter (Dying Thoughts) argues for the independence of the soul upon matter. " Why should my want of formal conceptions of the future state of separated souls, and my strangeness to the manner of their subsistence and operations induce me to doubt of those general points which are evident, and beyond all rational doubting ? That souls are substances, and not annihilated, and essentially the same when they forsake the body as before, I doubt not. Otherwise, neither the Christian's resurrection nor the Pythagorean's transmigration were a possible thing. For if the soul cease to be, it cannot pass into another body, nor can it re-enter into this. If God raise this body, then it must be by another soul. For the same soul to be annihilated and yet to begin again to be, is a contradiction ; for the second beginning would be by creation, which maketh a new soul and not the same that was before. It is the invisible things that are excellent, active, operative, and permanent. The visible things are of themselves but lifeless dross. It is the *unseen* part of plants and flowers which causeth all their growth and beauty, their fruit and sweetness. Passive matter is but moved up and down by the invisible active powers, as chessmen are moved from place to place by the game-ster's hands. What a loathsome corpse were the world without the invisible spirits and natures that animate, actuate, or move it. To doubt of the being or continua-tion of the most excellent, spiritual parts of creation, when we live in a world that is actuated by them, and where everything demonstrates them, as their effects, is more foolish than to doubt of the being of those gross materials which we see."

In support of the independence of the soul of the body, Plato in the Phædo (64, 65) remarks that "the philoso-pher is entirely concerned with the soul, and not with the body ; and would like, as far as he can, be quit of the body and turn to the soul." And this for the reason that "thought is best when the mind is gathered into herself and none of these bodily things trouble her; neither sounds, nor sights, nor pain, nor any pleasure ; when she has as little as possible to do with the body, and has no bodily sense or feeling, but is aspiring after true being. The philosopher despises the body; his soul runs away from the body, and desires to be alone and by herself."

The doctrine of the immortality of the soul is even more deeply intrenched in the human constitution than that of the Divine existence, for it is sometimes held when the latter is overlooked or even speculatively denied. The belief in the continued existence of their ancestors is found in the most degraded tribes, and exerts more influence upon them than their belief in their fetishes. The wor-ship of ancestors has a more prominent place in Confucian-ism than the worship of the Deity. When the idea of God has become extremely dim in the savage, he still confi-dently believes that the souls of his ancestors are existing

and wandering in another life. Such is the position of
this truth in natural religion. And it is woven through
and through the fabric of revealed religion. " Life and
immortality are brought into sunlight by the gospel"
(φωτίσαντος ζωὴν καὶ ἀφθαρσίαν διὰ τοῦ εὐαγγελίου, 2 Tim.
1 : 10).

But irrepressible and universal as it is, the doctrine of
man's immortality is an astonishing one, and difficult to
entertain. For it means that every frail finite man is to
be as long-enduring as the infinite and eternal God; that
there will no more be an end to the existence of the man
who died to-day than there will be of the Deity who made
him. God is denominated "The Ancient of Days." But
every immortal spirit that ever dwelt in a human body will
also be an " ancient of days." The little infant consigned
to the grave yesterday will one day be millions and bill-
ions of years old ; will one day have an antiquity with
which the vastness of the geological ages is nothing. For
this is what immortality means and involves. We find it
difficult to entertain the idea of an earthly life like that of
Adam and Seth, continuing for nearly a thousand years—
a period longer than from Romulus to Augustus Cæsar ;
than from Constantine to Charlemagne ; than from Alfred
to Victoria. But what is this in comparison with endless
duration ? The entire six thousand years of human history, which seem so long to the historical student and are
crowded with an immensity of incident, are only a mote in
the sunbeam, a drop in the ocean, compared with the biography of an immortal. Yes, man *must* exist. He has no
option. Necessity is laid upon him. He cannot extin-
guish himself. He cannot cease to be.

Vol. II., p. 650. The passage Job 19 : 25–27 is referred
to the resurrection of the body by the Septuagint, Vulgate,
Targum (partly), Clemens Romanus, Origen, Cyril Jerusalem, Ephraem, Epiphanius, Jerome, Augustine, Schoolmen, Luther's Version, English Version, Reformed Creeds,

Cocceius, Schultens, Michaelis, Rosenmüller, Pearson, Owen, J. P. Smith, Lee, Wordsworth. See Lange on Job, 19, pp. 460–465. Eichhorn, Knapp, Hoffman, Noyes explain מִבְּשָׂרִי, "from out of my flesh," or "in my flesh." Conant explains, "without my flesh."

VOL. II., p. 652. Augustine (Faith and Creed, ch. x.) adopts dichometry in the constitution of man. "There are three things of which man consists, namely, spirit, soul, and body; which again are spoken of as two, because frequently the soul is named along with the spirit; for a certain rational part of the same, of which beasts are destitute, is called spirit: the principal part in us is the spirit; next, the life whereby we are united with the body is called the soul; finally, the body itself, as it is visible, is the last part in us."

VOL. II., p. 653. Augustine (Enchiridion, 91–93) thus distinguishes between the resurrection body of the redeemed and the lost. "The bodies of the saints shall rise again free from every defect and blemish, as from all corruption, weight, and impediment. For their ease of movement shall be as complete as their happiness. Whence their bodies have been called *spiritual*, though undoubtedly they shall be bodies, and not spirits. For just as now the body is called *animate*, though it is a body, and not a soul [anima], so then the body shall be called spiritual, though it shall be a body, not a spirit (1 Cor. 15:44). Hence, as far as regards the corruption which now weighs down the soul, and the vices which urge 'the flesh to lust against the spirit,' it shall not then be flesh, but body; for these are bodies which are called celestial. Wherefore it is said, 'Flesh and blood cannot inherit the kingdom of God;' and as if in explanation of this, 'neither doth corruption inherit incorruption.' What the apostle first called 'flesh and blood' he afterward calls 'corruption;' and what he first called 'the kingdom of God,' he afterward calls 'incorruption.' But as far as regards the substance,

even then it shall be flesh. For even after the resurrection the body of Christ was called flesh (Luke 24 : 39).
The apostle, however, says : 'It is sown a natural body ; it
is raised a spiritual body ;' because so perfect shall then
be the harmony between flesh and spirit, the spirit keeping
alive the subjugated flesh without any need of nourishment, that no part of our nature shall be in discord with
another ; but as we shall be free from enemies without, so
we shall not have ourselves for enemies within."

"But as for those who, out of the mass of perdition
caused by the first man's sin, are not redeemed through
the one Mediator between God and man, they too shall
rise again, each with his own body, but only to be punished
with the devil and his angels. Now, whether they shall
rise again with all their diseases and deformities of body,
bringing with them the diseased and deformed limbs
which they had here, it would be labor lost to inquire.
For we need not weary ourselves in speculating about their
appearance, which is a matter of uncertainty, when their
eternal damnation is a matter of certainty. Nor need we
inquire in what sense their body shall be incorruptible, if
it be susceptible of pain ; or in what sense corruptible, if it
be free from the possibility of death. For there is no true
life except where there is happiness in life, and no true
incorruption except where health is unbroken by any pain.
When, however, the unhappy are not permitted to die,
then, if I may so say, death itself dies not; and where pain
without intermission afflicts the soul, and never comes
to an end, corruption itself is not ended. This is called
in Holy Scripture 'the second death' (Rev. 2 : 11). And
neither the first death, which takes place when the soul is
compelled to leave the body, nor the second death, which
takes place when the soul is not permitted to leave the
suffering body, would have been inflicted on man had no
one sinned. And, of course, the mildest punishment of all
will fall upon those who have added no actual transgres-

sions to the original sin they brought with them ; and as
for the rest, who have added such actual transgressions,
the punishment of each will be the more tolerable in the
next world, according as his iniquity has been less in this
world."

VOL. II., p. 654. In order to personal identity there
must be a rational soul. The animal, because it has only
an animal soul destitute of reason, cannot have the consciousness of personality and personal identity. A man
or angel is conscious that his soul is the same entity to-
day that it was yesterday or ten years ago. Sameness of
mental substance in every particular is requisite in order
to personal identity. The very same identical soul, with
identically the same properties, without loss or alteration of
any of them that exist in old age existed in infancy and
childhood. Again, in order to the personal identity of a
man there must be a material body, because man as a person is a union of soul and body. Though the soul is the
principal part of a man, it is not the whole of him. Hence
in the intermediate or disembodied state, though the most
important part of the person exists, yet a perfectly complete person is lacking. This is the reason for the resurrection of the body. The body, however, does not require
to be *so strictly the same in every particular* as the soul
does. Some of its properties may be different ; but none
of the properties of the soul may be. There is only one
kind of mental substance, but there is more than one kind
of material substance. Consequently the body can be
changed from a "natural" to a "spiritual" body, and still
be recognized as the same body. The body of "flesh and
blood" of this life may become the "spiritual body" of the
next life, and in union with the rational soul constitute the
same person. This spiritual body can have form, limbs,
lineaments, and all the appearance of a human body, and
yet not all of the very same particles, no more, no less,
and no different, go to the making of it. All those prop-

erties which in this life required food for their support, for
example, may be exchanged for properties that do not require it.　On the side, therefore, of the body, there is not
so strict an identity of substance and properties as there is
on the side of the soul.

The recognition of one disembodied spirit by another is
more difficult of explanation than the recognition of one
embodied spirit by another.　Dives and Lazarus were both
of them destitute of bodies, yet they knew one another.
How does the human spirit recognize and know itself?
Not by means of the body which it inhabits, but directly.
A man is not assisted in knowing himself by calling to
mind the features of his own face, and the characteristics
of his own body.　His knowledge of himself is independent of these latter, being the immediate consciousness of
himself; that is, of his spirit.　Similarly, his knowledge of
the *mind* or *spirit* of another man is not the result of his
sensuous perception of the man's bodily form and features,
but of his mental and spiritual traits; and the knowledge
of these does not depend upon the knowledge of the physical traits.　He is not helped to the knowledge that another person is learned or benevolent because he is tall or
short in stature.

VOL. II., p. 657.　Hodge (Theology, III. 775–779), remarks upon bodily identity as follows: " In the church
it has often been assumed that sameness of substance is
essential to the identity between our present and future
bodies.　This idea has been pressed sometimes to the
utmost extreme.　Augustine seems to have thought that
all the matter which at any period entered into the organism of our present bodies would in some way be restored
in the resurrection.　Thomas Aquinas was more moderate.
He taught that only those particles which entered into
the composition of the body at death would enter into the
composition of the resurrection body.　Others assume
that it is not necessary to the identity contended for that

all the particles of the body at death should be included in the resurrection body. It is enough that the new body should be formed exclusively out of particles belonging to the present body. But as the body after the resurrection is to be refined and ethereal, a tenth, a hundredth, or a ten-thousandth portion of these particles would suffice."

" Identity in living organisms is higher and more inscrutable than in works of art. The acorn and the oak are the same ; but in what sense ? Not in substance, not in form. The infant and the man are the same through all the stages of life—boyhood, manhood, and old age ; the substance of the body, however, is in a state of perpetual change. It is said this change is complete every seven years. Hence if a man live to be seventy years old, the substance of the body, during this period, has been entirely changed ten times. Here, then, is an identity independent of sameness of substance. Our future bodies, therefore, may be the same as those we now have, although not a particle that was in the one should be in the other. It may readily be admitted by those who adhere to the generally received doctrine that man consists of soul and body (and not of spirit, soul, and body) ; that the soul, besides its rational, voluntary, and moral faculties, has in it what may be called a principle of animal life. That is, that it has not only faculties which fit it for the higher exercises of a rational creature capable of fellowship with God, but also faculties which fit it for living in organic union with a material body. It may also be admitted that the soul, in this aspect, is the animating principle of the body, that by which all its functions are carried on. And it may further be admitted that the soul, in this aspect, is that which gives identity to the human body through all the changes of substance to which it is here subjected. And, finally, it may be admitted, such being the case, that the body which the soul is to have at the resurrection is as really and truly identical with that which it had on earth, as the body of the man of mature life is the same which he had when he was an infant. All this may pass for what it is worth. What stands sure is what the Bible teaches, that our heavenly bodies are in some high, true, and real sense, to be of the same nature as those which we now have. There are two negative statements in the Bible on this subject which imply a great deal. One is, that in the resurrection men 'neither marry nor are given in marriage, but are as the angels of God.' The other is, that 'flesh and blood cannot inherit the kingdom of God.' Three things are implied in these passages. 1. That the bodies of men must be specially suited to the state of existence in which they are to live and act. 2. That our present bodies, consisting as they do of flesh and blood, are not adapted to our future state of being. 3. That everything in the organization of our bodies designed to meet our present necessities will cease with the life that now is. If blood be no longer our life, we shall have no need of organs of respiration and nutrition. The following particulars, however, may be inferred with more or less confidence from what the Bible has revealed on this subject. 1. That our bodies after the resurrection will retain the human form. 2. That the future body will be a glorified likeness of what it was on earth. 3. That we shall not only recognize our friends in heaven, but also know, without introduction, prophets, apostles, confessors, and martyrs of whom we have heard while here on earth."

Perowne (Immortality, Lecture IV.) argues that bodily identity consists wholly in the sameness of the organizing principle. " We maintain that the same body which has been laid in the grave may be raised at the last day, even though not one single material particle which went to constitute the one body shall be found in the other. For what is it that is necessary to the identity of the body? The identity of the body does not depend on the identity

of the material particles of which it is composed. These
are in a state of perpetual flux. The body of our childhood is not the body of our youth, nor the body of our
youth that of our manhood, nor the body of our manhood
that of our old age. Every particle is changed, and yet it
is the same body; the person to whom it belongs still
continues the same person. If you insist upon it that
every particle of matter of which my body is built must be
brought together to form my new resurrection body, then
I ask, What body during this present life is my true body?
Is it the body of my childhood, or of my youth, or of my
old age? The body in which I die is no more truly mine,
than the body with which I came into the world. Both
are mine, both are in some sense the same body, and
yet they have not a single material particle in common.
What possible reason is there then for contending that
the body which is laid in the grave must be brought together again, particle for particle, at the resurrection,
when it is no more essentially a part of myself than my
body at any other stage of my existence? The only thing
of which we need to be assured is, that *the principle of
identity* which governs the formation of the body in this
life shall govern its formation at the resurrection. In the
ever-flowing torrent of our life, as wave after wave passes
through our bodily frame, bringing with it growth and
variety in the structure, there is some principle, or law, or
specific form, call it what you will, which remains ever
the same. The organism is essentially one, despite the
changes of size, of form, of inward constitution. This
holds true in every region of nature where there is life;
of the acorn which becomes an oak; of the worm which
changes to a chrysalis, and then to a butterfly. Is it not
the same with man? Is not the human embryo the same
individual when it becomes child, youth, old man? And
yet does there remain in the oak, in the butterfly, in the
man, a single one of the ponderable molecules which ex-

32

isted in the germ, the egg, the embryo? And still, we repeat, it is the same vegetable, the same insect, the same man."

" What then is this thing which remains ever the same in the vegetable in all its developments, in the insect in all its metamorphoses, in the human body in every phase of its existence? What is this which never perishes, is never destroyed in all the changes and fluctuations of the material organism? It escapes all our investigations ; we see it only in its manifestations in the phenomena of life. But that it is a reality all observation goes to show ; and if through all the changes of the body during this life this principle continues in all its force, why may it not survive the shock of death? Why may not this 'specific form,' as Gregory of Nyssa terms it, remain united to the soul, as he conjectured, and as other thinkers like Leibnitz have supposed, after its separation from the body, and thus become at length the [Providential] agent in the resurrection, by reconstituting, though in a new and transfigured condition, the body which was dissolved at death? Why may not the same body which was sown in corruption be raised in incorruption, and that which was sown a natural body be raised a spiritual body? There is, at least, nothing improbable in such a supposition ; there is everything in the analogies of nature to confirm it ; and when revelation is silent we may be thankful for such glimpses of probability as come to us in aid of our faith."

Respecting the nature of the resurrection body, Augustine (Letter xcv., 7, 8. Ad Paulinum, A.D. 408) thus remarks : " As to the resurrection of the body, and the future offices of its members in the incorruptible and immortal state, it is to be held most firmly as a true doctrine of Holy Scripture that these visible and earthly bodies which are now called ' natural ' (animalia, 1 Cor. 15 : 44), shall, in the resurrection of the just, be spiritual bodies.

At the same time I do not know how the quality of a spiritual body can be comprehended and described by us, seeing that it lies beyond the range of our experience. There shall be, assuredly, in such bodies no corruption, and therefore they shall not require the perishable nourishment which is now necessary ; yet though unnecessary, it will not be impossible for them at their pleasure to take and consume food ; otherwise it would not have been taken by our Lord after his resurrection, who has given us such an example of the resurrection of the body that the apostle argues from it, 'If the dead rise not, then is not Christ raised.' But he, when he appeared to his disciples, having all his members, and using them according to their functions, also pointed out to them the places where his wounds had been, respecting which I have always supposed that they were the scars and not the wounds themselves, and that they were there not of necessity but according to his free exercise of power. He gave at that time the clearest evidence of the ease with which he exercised this power, both by showing himself in ' another form ' to the two disciples, and by his appearing not as a spirit, but in his true body, although the doors were shut (Mark 16 : 12, 14 ; Luke 24 : 15–43 ; John 20 : 14–29)." Again (Letter cxlviii. 16. Ad Fortunatianum, A.D. 413) he says : " As to the spiritual body which we shall have in the resurrection, how great a change for the better it is to undergo—whether it shall then become pure spirit, so that the whole man shall then be a spirit, or shall (as I rather think, but yet do not confidently maintain) become a spiritual body in such a way as to be called spiritual because of a certain wonderful facility in its movements, but at the same time to retain its material substance, which cannot live and feel by itself but only through the spirit which uses it, as our present body is animated and used by the soul inhabiting it ; and whether, if the properties of the body then immortal and incor-

ruptible shall remain unchanged, it shall then in some degree aid the spirit to see visible, *i.e.*, material things, as at
present we are unable to see anything of this kind except
through the eyes of the body, or whether our spirit shall
then be able to know material things directly without the
instrumentality of the body (for God himself does not
know these things through bodily senses)—on these and
many other things that perplex us, I confess that I have
not yet read anything which I regard as sufficiently settled
to deserve to be taught to men."

Vol. II., p. 660. Bates (On Death, ch. ii.) thus speaks
of the private judgment at death : "Death is fearful in
the apprehension of conscience, as it is the most sensible
mark of God's wrath which is heavier than death, and a
summons to give an account of all things done in this life,
to the righteous Judge of the world. 'It is appointed to all
men once to die, and afterward the judgment' (Heb. 9 :
27). The penal fear is more wounding to the spirit than
the natural and physical. When the awakened sinner
presently expects the citation to appear before the tribunal above, where no excuses, no supplications, no privileges
avail, where the cause of eternal life and death must be
decided, and the awards of justice be immediately executed, O the convulsions and agonies of conscience in that
hour ! This made a heathen, a governor of a province, to
tremble before a poor prisoner. When Paul 'reasoned of
righteousness, temperance, and judgment to come, Felix
trembled' (Acts 24 : 25)." Again Bates (Eternal Judgment,
ch. v.) remarks that "The day of death is equivalent to
the day of judgment; for immediately after it there is a
final decision of men's states forever. But the distinction
that is made between men at death is private and particular, and not sufficient for the honor of God's government ;
hence at the last day all men that have lived in the several
successions of ages shall appear, and justice have a solemn
process and triumph before angels and men."

The private judgment is taught in the lines of Toplady's hymn :

> " When mine eyelids close in death,
> When I rise to worlds unknown,
> See thee on thy judgment throne,
> Rock of ages ! cleft for me,
> Let me hide myself in thee."

The Scriptures teach it, in declaring that at death Judas "went to his own place " (Acts 1 : 25), and knew that he did ; and also that Dives " died and was buried, and in hell he lifted up his eyes being in torments " (Luke 16 : 22, 23).

Leighton (Exposition of the Apostles' Creed) describes the private judgment : " It is certainly most congruous, that there shall be a solemn judicial proceeding on entering and placing man in the after-state. And that this be done not only in each particular apart, but most conspicuously in all together, so that the justice and mercy of God may not only be accomplished, but acknowledged and magnified, and that not only severally in the individual persons of men and angels, but universally, jointly, and manifestly in the view of all, as upon one theatre. Each ungodly man shall not only read, whether he will or no, the justice of God in himself, and his own condemnation, which all of them shall do before that time to their souls' *particular* judgment ; but they shall then see the same justice in all the rest of the condemned world."

Pearson (Creed, Art. vii.) connects the private with the general judgment. " It is necessary that we should believe that an account must be given of all our actions ; and not only so, but that this account will be exacted according to the rule of God's revealed will, that ' God shall judge the secrets of men by Jesus Christ, according to the gospel' (Rom. 2 : 16). There is in every man not only a power to reflect, but a necessary reflection upon his actions ; not only a voluntary remembrance, but also an irresistible judgment of his own conversation. Now if there were no other judge besides our own souls, we should be regardless of our own sentence, and wholly unconcerned in our own condemnations. But if we were persuaded that these reflections of conscience are to be so many witnesses before the tribunal of heaven, and that we are to carry in our own hearts a testimony either to absolve or condemn us, we must infallibly watch over that unquiet inmate, and endeavor above all things for a good conscience."

Vol. II., p. 663. The Belgic Confession (Art. xxxvii.) says that in the last day, "the books, that is to say the conscience, shall be opened, and the dead be judged according to what they shall have done." Bates (Eternal Judgment, ch. iv.) declares that, "the conscience of every man shall be opened by the omniscience of God, and give an accusing or excusing testimony of all things (Rom. 2 : 15, 16). For these acts of conscience, in the present life, have a final respect to God's tribunal; and though the accounts are so vast there shall be an exact agreement between the books of God's omniscience and of conscience in the day of judgment. Now, indeed, the conscience of man, though never so inquisitive and diligent in examining and revising his ways, is unable to take a just account of his sins. As one that would tell the first-appearing stars in the evening, before he can reckon them others appear and confound his memory with their number, so when conscience is seriously intent in reflecting upon itself, before it can reckon up the sins committed against one command, innumerable others appear. This made the Psalmist, upon the survey of his actions, break forth in amazement and perplexity: ' Mine iniquities are more than the hairs of my head, therefore my heart fails me' (Ps. 40 : 12). But it will be one of the miracles of that day to enlarge the view of conscience to all their sins. Now, the records of conscience are often obliterated, and the sins written therein are forgotten; but then they shall appear in so clear an impression that the wicked shall be inexcusable to themselves, and conscience subscribes their condemnation. This information of conscience, at the last, will make the sinner speechless; for the book of accounts with Divine justice was always in God's own keeping, and whatever is recorded there was written with his own hand."

"Other witnesses, also, will appear to finish the process of that day. 1. Satan will then bring in a bloody charge against the wicked. This is intimated in that fearful imprecation, 'Let Satan stand at his right hand; when he is judged let him be condemned' (Ps. 109 : 6, 7). He is now an active watchful spirit whose diligence is equal to his malice, and by violent temptations draws men to sin. But then he will be their most bitter accuser, not from zeal for justice but pure malignity. 2. The wicked themselves will accuse one another. Then all that have been jointly engaged in the commission of sin will impeach each other. The inferior instruments will accuse their directors for their pernicious counsel, and the directors will accuse the instruments for their wicked compliance. 3. All the holy servants of God, who by their instructions, counsels, admonitions, examples, have endeavored to make the world better, will give a heavy testimony against them. Indeed, the very presence of the saints will upbraid the wicked for their resisting all the warning melting entreaties, all the grave and serious reproofs, all the tender, earnest expostulations, that were ineffectual by the hardness of their hearts."

VOL. II., p. 668. Augustine thus states his view of endless punishment : " The Church justly abominates the opinion of Origen, that even they whom the Lord says are to be punished with everlasting punishment, and also the devil himself and his angels, after a time, however protracted, will be purged and released from their penalties, and shall then cleave to the saints who reign with God in blessedness " (Proceedings of Pelagius, ch. 10). "Eter-

nal punishment seems hard and unjust to human perceptions, because in the weakness of our mortal condition
there is wanting that highest wisdom by which it can be
perceived how great a wickedness *was committed in that
first transgression.* The more enjoyment man found in
God, the greater was his wickedness in abandoning God;
and he who destroyed in himself a good that might have
been eternal, become deserving of eternal evil. Hence
the whole mass of the human race is condemned; for he
who at first gave entrance to sin has been punished with
all his posterity *who were in him as in a root,* so that no
one is exempt from this just and deserved punishment unless delivered by mercy and undeserved grace. And the
human race is so apportioned that in some is displayed
the efficacy of merciful grace, in the rest the efficacy of just
retribution. For both could not be displayed in all; for
if all had remained under the punishment of just condemnation there would have been seen in no one the mercy
of redeeming grace; and on the other hand, if all had
been transferred from darkness to light, the strict justice
of retribution would have been manifested in none. But
many more are left under punishment than are delivered
from it, in order that it may thus be shown what was due
to all. And had it been inflicted on all, no one could
justly have found fault with the justice of him who taketh
vengeance; whereas, in the deliverance of so many from
that just award, there is cause to render the most hearty
thanks to the gratuitous bounty of him who delivers"
(City of God, xxi., 12). An analysis of the doctrine contained in these extracts respecting eternal retribution,
gives the following particulars: 1. Original sin is the
self-determination of the human species in Adam, and is
punishable for the same reason that any wrong self-determination is. Sinful inclination originated in this manner is as voluntary and unforced agency as any volition
prompted by it. The whole human race, consequently,

responsibly ruined themselves in Adam's fall, and made themselves justly liable to eternal death. Actual transgression is not the primary, but the secondary reason for future punishment. It adds to original sin and increases the degree of the penalty, but is not the first ground for it. The principal Scripture for this is Rom. 5 : 12–19. 2. Salvation from eternal death is undeserved, because guilt has no desert but that of penalty ; it cannot therefore be claimed as due by any man, and it is bestowed without obligation on the part of God, and upon whomsoever he chooses. 3. When bestowed, it manifests his attribute of mercy, and that in its highest form of self-sacrifice in the vicarious sufferings and death of his Son ; and when not bestowed, it manifests his justice. It will be seen from this analysis that the self-produced and responsible fall of the human race in Adam is the key to Augustine's doctrine of endless retribution. If it be denied, or disproved, universalism is the logical consequence. For if original sin and sinful inclination are necessitated and guiltless, so are the actual transgressions that issue from it. The stream has the same qualities with the fountain. 4. The number of the saved is less than that of the lost. Modern Calvinists have departed from Augustine in affirming the converse, by teaching the regeneration of all who die in infancy.

Vol. II., p. 673. The agnostic position which Dorner takes respecting the doctrine of endless punishment, in saying that it "remains veiled in mystery," though formally negative and non-committal is really as positive as direct denial and attack. Agnosticism, generally, is a crafty way of casting doubt upon truth, and of rejecting it. If a person says that there may or may not be a God, but that no one knows certainly, this has the same practical effect as avowed atheism. It tends to destroy the belief in a deity and the fear of him. So also, if a person says that there may or may not be salvation after death, this has the same general influence as positive universalism. It contributes to weaken the conviction that men will be endlessly punished for the deeds done in the body. If I say to a person: "The Bible is reticent upon the subject of the future life. It does not positively teach that probation ends for all mankind at death. It may or it may not; no one knows certainly," I relieve him in a great measure from the fear of hell. For he will regard the assertion that there possibly may be a future probation as equivalent to the assertion of the probability of such a probation. If a thing is possible, it may be actual; and when the thing possible is strongly desired, and its contrary is greatly dreaded, the possibility will be construed into actuality. It will be of little use for the agnostic in eschatology to put in a caveat, and attempt to *warn* the sinner. If he reminds him that we do not certainly know that there is salvation after death, the reply will be, that neither do we certainly know that there will not be. A theorist of this class writes as follows : " What resources may be available in other worlds, only the great arbiter can know. Hence modern theology emphasizes with solemn appeal the need of instant surrender of the heart to God. Delay is dangerous, and it may be fatal." " And it may not be fatal," is the agnostic sinner's reply, which takes all the force out of this so-called " solemn appeal and warning."

This agnostic method of sapping the doctrine of endless retribution is not only wanting in frank and open dealing in an argument, but is chargeable with falsifying Divine revelation. To say that the Bible " veils the subject of endless punishment in mystery," and that it is "reticent upon the subject of the future life," in the face of such an eschatology as the Son of God presents in the twenty-fifth chapter of Matthew, to say nothing of the great mass of similar teaching in other parts of the Divine word, is an assumption and assurance that is contradicted by the well-nigh unanimous verdict of all readers and students of Scripture in all time.

VOL. II., p. 676. In Christ's account of the day of judgment he describes himself as dividing mankind into two classes, saying to one, " Come, ye blessed," and to the other, "Depart, ye cursed." This language naturally implies that these two classes are to exist always and forever. It makes the impression of finality, and has been so understood by the immense majority of readers. But if the penalty of sin is only remedial and temporary, there is ultimately only one class. All men are finally blest of God. Upon this supposition the transactions of the judgment-day are a mere unmeaning show. The day of doom, instead of being a solemn administration of Divine justice, having a final and irrevocable character, as our Lord represents, is only a spectacle like a scene in a play. A temporary curse is pronounced from the throne of judgment upon some men that is afterward followed by an eternal blessing upon them. This view destroys the moral sincerity and veracity of the Son of God. It is inconceivable that he who is and styles himself the Truth should engage in such a false and deluding transaction before the assembled universe, and that to any of mankind who he foreknows will finally be his friends and enter eternal joy, he will speak the words : " Ye serpents, ye generation of vipers, how can ye escape the damnation of hell." It is incredible that the righteous Judge of the universe will at one time say to some of mankind : " Depart from me, ye cursed, into everlasting fire, prepared for the devil and his angels," and at a subsequent time say to this very same class, " Come, ye blessed of my Father, inherit the kingdom prepared for you from the foundation of the world."

VOL. II., p. 681. Respecting the use of figures in describing the misery of hell, Paley (Sermon xxxi.) states the case with great plainness and power. " I admit that it is

very difficult to handle the dreadful subject of the punishment of hell properly; and one cause amongst others of
the difficulty is, that it is not for one poor sinner to denounce such appalling terrors, such tremendous consequences against another. Damnation is a word which lies
not in the mouth of man, who is a worm, toward any of
his fellow-creatures whatsoever; yet it is absolutely necessary that the threatenings of Almighty God be known and
published. Therefore, we begin by observing that the
accounts which the Scriptures contain of the punishment
of hell are, for the most part, delivered in figurative or
metaphorical terms; that is to say, in terms which represent things of which we have no notion by a comparison
with things with which we have a notion. Therefore take
notice what those figures and metaphors are. They are
of the most dreadful kind which words can express; and
be they understood how they may, ever so figuratively, it
is plain that they convey, and were intended to convey,
ideas of horrible torment. They are such as these : ' Being cast into hell, where the worm dieth not, and where
the fire is not quenched.' It is 'burning the chaff with
unquenchable fire.' It is 'going into fire everlasting,
which is prepared for the devil and his angels.' It is ' being cast with all the members into hell, where the worm
dieth not, and the fire is not quenched.' These are heart-
appalling expressions; and were undoubtedly intended by
the person who used them, who was no other than our
Lord Jesus Christ himself, to describe terrible endurings,
positive, actual pains of the most horrible kinds. I have
said that the punishment of hell is thus represented to us
in figurative speech. I now say that from the nature of
things it could not have been represented to us in any
other. It is of the very nature of pain that it cannot be
known but by being felt. It is impossible to give to anyone an exact conception of it without his actually tasting
it. Experience alone teaches its acuteness and intensity.

For which reason, when it was necessary that the punishment of hell should be set forth in Scripture for our warning, and set forth to terrify us from our sins, it could only be done as it has been done by comparing it with sufferings of which we can form conception, and making use of terms drawn from these sufferings. When words less figurative and more direct, but at the same time more general are adopted, they are not less strong otherwise than as they are more general. ' Indignation and wrath, tribulation and anguish, upon every soul of man that doeth evil.' These are St. Paul's words. It is a short sentence, but enough to make the stoutest heart tremble ; for though it unfold no particulars, it clearly designates positive torment.''

VOL. II., p. 683. Olshausen on Matt. 12 : 32, thus interprets : '' To explain this passage as meaning that although the sin against the Holy Ghost shall not be forgiven in this æon nor the next æon, it shall be afterward, plainly contradicts the intention of the speaker. For the proposition, ' it shall not be forgiven,' is the direct contrary of the proposition, ' it shall be forgiven,' and the adjunct, ' neither in this æon, neither in the æon to come,' is certainly intended to *strengthen*, not to weaken, the affirmation of non-forgiveness. Matthew does not conceive of the $\alpha i \grave{\omega} \nu$ $\mu \acute{\epsilon} \lambda \lambda \omega \nu$ as only a fractional part of future duration which is to be followed by other fractions indefinitely, but as constituting, in connection with $\alpha i \grave{\omega} \nu$ $o \check{\upsilon} \tau o \varsigma$, the whole of duration.'' Consequently, if a sin is not forgiven in either æon, it is never forgiven. This same reasoning applies to that other interpretation of this passage which makes it teach that all sins excepting that against the Holy Ghost shall be forgiven in the world to come, if they have not been forgiven in this world. To hold out the hope of forgiveness in the next world is to destroy the force and effect of the threat to punish sin which is made in this world ; and it cannot be supposed that God would thus weaken and undo all his punitive legislation and menace here in time.

VOL. II., p. 685. Anselm (Proslagion, xxi.) describes the rhetorical plural as the equivalent of the literal singular. "For as an age of time contains all things pertaining to time, so Thine eternity contains even ages of time themselves. Thine eternity is called an age (αἰὼν) on account of its indivisible immensity."

VOL. II., p. 696. Another explanation of those texts which seem to teach that the dead are unconscious, is given by Edwards (God's End in Creation, ch. II., sec. iv.). "There are several scriptures which lead us to suppose that the great thing God seeks of the moral world, and the end to be aimed at by moral agents, is the manifestation or making known of the Divine perfections. This seems implied in that argument God's people sometimes made use of, in deprecating a state of death and destruction ; that in such a state they cannot proclaim the glorious excellency of God. 'Shall thy loving-tenderness be declared in the grave, or thy faithfulness in destruction? Shall thy wonders be known in the dark, and thy righteousness in the land of forgetfulness?' (Ps. 88 : 18, 19 ; 30: 9). The argument seems to be this : Why should we perish? And how shall thine end, for which thou hast made us, be obtained in a state of destruction in which thy glory cannot be declared? 'The grave cannot praise thee, death cannot celebrate thee. The living, the living, he shall praise thee, as I do this day ; the father to the children shall make known thy truth' (Isa. 38 : 18, 19)."

Canon Cook (Bible Commentary), in his introduction to the Psalms, § 17, and in his interpretation of them, gives the following view of the "Notices of the Future State" contained in this part of Scripture : "Respecting the feelings and hopes of the Psalmist touching a future state, it is clear, on the one hand, that no formal revela-

tion of a future state of retribution had as yet been vouch-
safed to the Israelites. It is indeed certain, our Lord's
authority makes it certain, that this truth was *implicitly*
contained in God's manifestation of himself as the God of
Abraham and the fathers ; and also that the patriarchs
of old looked upon life here but as a pilgrimage (Heb.
11 : 13). David himself (Ps. 39 : 12) prays, 'Hear my
prayer, O Lord, and hold not thy peace at my tears :
for I am a stranger with thee, and a sojourner, as all
my fathers were.' The stranger is one who is merely
a guest for a season, the sojourner one who lives as a
client under the protection of a prince or noble : neither
has any right or settled footing in the land. An image which is at once humbling, and suggestive of a sure
hope. The earth is not the home of man. Compare
Lev. 25 : 23 ; 1 Chron. 29 : 15 ; Ps. 119 : 19. Still we cannot reasonably doubt that to the generality of the people,
the grave, or the unknown Sheol, of which the grave is the
entrance, bounded the region of hope and fear [as it does
to the generality of mankind to-day]. It has been shown
in the introduction and notes to Job that the writer of
that book at least felt that attempts to vindicate the
righteousness of God would be futile, were the problem of
the future state left unsolved ; and that in the agony of the
death-struggle, when all other hope was finally abandoned, the conviction sprang up that God would manifest himself in some unknown way as the Redeemer.
But the hope was after all vague and suggestive ; little
more than a preparation for a future disclosure of the
truth."

" It would be easy to settle the question were we to decide it by reference to the numerous passages in which the
state of the departed is represented as one of darkness,
where there is no ' remembrance of God,' where ' he is not
praised,' neither loved nor dreaded. On looking at these
passages carefully, we may indeed find reason to conclude

that they speak of the condition of those who are the objects of divine punishment, and that they express the fears of one who regards himself as having incurred the divine displeasure. Such, for example, is Ps. 6 : 5. David here speaks of those who die, not saved; see verse 4. For such there is no opportunity to celebrate the mercy of God, or to give him thanks. David knew that life is the season for serving God, and this knowledge sufficed for practical purposes until the life and immortality dimly anticipated by the patriarchs were brought to light by Christ. Again, Ps. 16 : 8–11 (quoted by St. Peter in Acts 2 : 31, and by St. Paul in Acts 13 : 35, in proof of the resurrection), contains one of the very clearest and strongest declarations of belief in a blessed futurity which can be adduced from the Old Testament. As such it is recognized by ancient and modern interpreters, none speaking out more clearly than Ewald, who says : 'It goes beyond other words of David, nor is anything corresponding to it found in later Hebrew writers.' There is but one adequate explanation of such a fact, namely, that the Spirit of Christ which was in David as a prophet (1 Pet. 1 : 11 ; Acts 2 : 30) moved and controlled his utterances, so that while they expressed fully his own yearnings, they 'signified beforehand the glory that should follow' in the resurrection of Christ."

"But even in those psalms which contain such declarations as make the impression of a final triumph of death, and the cessation of consciousness, we are struck by the expression of feelings which are wholly incompatible with the certainty of annihilation: in none are there more lively, joyous expressions of trust and hope ; see especially the last half of Ps. 146, and 13 : 3 contrasted with 13 : 5. Nor are these expressions to be explained as referring to the anticipation of a temporary deliverance from death, or to the postponement of a general and inevitable doom. The Psalmists speak of thanks to be offered to the Lord

God forever (30 : 12 ; 61 : 8 ; 145 : 1, 21) ; of an eternal portion in heaven (16 : 11 ; 17 : 15) ; and of the end of the upright as peace (37 : 37). In the very depth of humiliation and hopelessness, so far as this life is concerned, God is called upon as helper, deliverer and redeemer ; as 'the Lord my salvation' (38 : 22 ; 88 : 1). The general judgment is regarded as a day when the wicked shall not stand in the congregation of the righteous (1 : 5), as the morning of the eternal day when the upright shall have dominion over the wicked (49 : 14), when the righteous shall see the light, while the man who is 'in honor and understandeth not is like the beasts that perish' (49 : 20). Taking such statements in their combination and mutual bearings, as explaining, developing, and illustrating each other, it is strange that any should fail to recognize throughout the psalms a state of feelings and convictions which speak of a deep, though it may be half-conscious faith in the perpetuity of the soul, the light, the glory (16 : 9), the spiritual principle of God's rational creatures. The soul will see 'light in God's light' (36 : 9) ; 'God will be its portion for ever' (73 : 26). Touching the great bulk of the Davidic psalms, indeed of the whole psalter, there are throughout indications, more or less distinct, sometimes faint, sometimes singularly bright and strong, of an undercurrent of feeling in harmony with those undying and irrepressible aspirations which God has implanted in souls bearing his impress, and capable of union with him ; a union which excludes the possibility of annihilation."

Upon this general subject, Baxter (Dying Thoughts, Introduction) remarks as follows : " I have often marvelled to find David in the Psalms, and other saints before Christ's coming, to have expressed so great a sense of the things of this present life, and to have said so little of another ; to have made so great a matter of prosperity, dominions, and victories on the one hand, and of enemies, success, and persecution on the other. But I consider that it was not

33

for mere personal, carnal interest, but for the church of God, and for his honor, word, and worship. And they knew that if things go well with us on earth, they will be sure to go well in heaven. If the militant church prosper in holiness, there is no doubt but it will triumph in glory. God will be sure to do his part in receiving souls if they be here prepared for his receipt. And Satan doth much of his damning work by men; so that if we escape their temptations we escape much of our danger. If idolaters prospered, Israel was tempted to idolatry. The Greek church is almost swallowed up by Turkish prosperity and dominion. Most follow the powerful and prosperous side. And therefore for God's cause, and for heavenly, everlasting interest, our own state, but much more the church's, must be greatly regarded here on earth. Indeed, if earth be desired only for earth, and prosperity loved but for the present welfare of the flesh, it is the certain mark of damning carnality and an earthly mind. But to desire peace, and prosperity, and power to be in the hands of wise and faithful men, for the sake of souls and the increase of the church, and the honor of God, that his name may be hallowed, his kingdom come, his will be done on earth as it is in heaven, this is to be the chief of our prayers to God."

VOL. II., p. 709. Augustine's view of pagan virtue is thus expressed: "You allude in your letter to the fact that Xenocrates converted Polemo from a dissipated to a sober life, though the latter was not only habitually intemperate, but was actually intoxicated at the time. Now although this was, as you truthfully apprehend, not a case of conversion to God, but of emancipation from a particular form of self-indulgence, I would not ascribe even this amount of improvement wrought in him to the power of man, but to the power of God. For even in the body all excellent things, such as beauty, vigor, health, and the like, are the work of God, to whom nature owes its creation and preservation; how much more certain, then, must it be, that none but God can impart excellent quality to the soul. If, therefore, Polemo, when he exchanged a life of dissipation for a life of sobriety, had so understood whence the gift came, that renouncing the superstitions of the heathen he had rendered worship to the Divine Giver, he would then have become not only temperate, but truly wise and savingly religious; which would have secured to him not merely the practice of virtue in this life, but also immortal blessedness in the life to come" (Letter cxliv., 2). "If we say that all without exception who were found in hell were delivered therefrom by Christ when he descended thither, who would not rejoice if this could be proved? Especially would men rejoice for the sake of some who are known to us by their literary labors—poets, philosophers, and orators—who have held up to contempt the false gods of the nations, and have even occasionally confessed the one true God, although along with the rest they observed superstitious rites, and also for the sake of many more of whom we have no literary remains, but respecting whom we have learned from the writings of these others that their lives were to a certain extent praiseworthy, so that with the exception of idolatry and serving the creature rather than the Creator, they may be held up as models of frugality, self-sacrifice, chastity, sobriety, braving death in their country's defence, and keeping faith not only with their fellow-citizens but also their enemies. All these things, indeed, when they are not performed in true humility to the glory of God, but in pride and for the sake of human praise and glory, become morally worthless and unprofitable; nevertheless, as indications of a certain temper of mind, they please us so much that we would desire that those in whom they exist should either by special favor or along with all mankind without exception be freed from the pains of hell, were it not that the verdict of human sensibility is different from that of the perfect holiness and justice of God." (Letter clxiv., 4. To Evodius.)

Vol. II., p. 713. Müller (Sin, II., 281) thus describes the sinful selfishness of childhood. "We meet with this *natural egoism* in childhood generally, not indeed always in the form of violent passion and self-will, but sometimes under the garb of prevailing passivity and natural softness of disposition and tractableness of character; even in these cases none but a very superficial observer can fail to trace the selfish principle, though modified in its manifestations by natural temperament. An unbiassed observation of childhood, when once the moral consciousness is awakened, will satisfy anyone that in the most tender-hearted and affectionate child there is a tendency to indulge hostile feelings against anything that hinders it in the attainment of its own wishes and desires, and that it is wont thoughtlessly to give way to this impulse provided it be not held in check by other influences, by blood relationship, or judicious tutelage. Even in the best-dispositioned children we may discover, in greater or less degree, an element of hatred usually aroused by wounded self-love, and an element of falsehood which in disputes with its playmates, or in answer to its parents or teachers, wilfully sacrifices truth for the sake of self. Experience indeed shows that this self-seeking on the child's part chiefly appears in the gratification of particular affections and in sensuous pleasures, so that these seem to be the excitants tempting it to wrong-doing, and the outward material of its sins; but can this circumstance justify our reducing the principle of selfishness to the excessive strength of particular affections? By no means; on the contrary, the predominance of particular affections and sensuous desires to which experience thus witnesses arises from a radical disturbance in that other sphere of life which is actuated by the perverted will. Experience, moreover, unequivocally testifies that as human development advances, selfishness shows itself equally in the spiritual nature, and sometimes with such strength as to ignore and suppress the calls of the sensuous nature, and of particular affections. The theory of sensuousness or of particular affections is quite insufficient to explain these phenomena."

VOL. II., p. 714. Owen (Arminianism, Ch. vii.) teaches the salvation of some infants outside of the covenant and the church. " In this inquiry respecting the desert of original sin, the question is not, *What shall be the certain lot of those that depart this life under the guilt of this sin only?* but what this hereditary and native corruption doth *deserve* in all those in whom it is? For as St. Paul saith, 'We judge not them that are without,' especially *infants* (1 Cor. 5 : 13). But for the *demerit* of this corruption before the justice of God, our Saviour expressly affirmeth that unless a man be born again 'he cannot enter the kingdom of heaven;' and let them that can, distinguish between a not going to heaven, and a going to hell: a third receptacle for souls in Scripture we find not. St. Paul also tells us, that 'by nature we are children of wrath;' even originally and actually we are guilty of, and obnoxious unto, that wrath which is accompanied with fiery indignation that shall consume the adversaries. Again, we are assured that no unclean thing shall enter into heaven (Rev. 21); with which hell-deserving uncleanness children are polluted, and, therefore, unless it be purged by the blood of Christ, they have no interest in everlasting happiness. By this means sin is come upon all to condemnation, and *yet we do not peremptorily censure to hell all infants departing this world without the laver of regeneration* [*i.e.*, baptism], the ordinary means of waiving the punishment due to this pollution. This is the question de facto which we before rejected: yea, and *two* ways there are whereby God saveth such infants, snatching them like brands from the fire: First, by interesting them into the covenant, if their immediate or remote parents have been believers;

he is a God of them and of their seed, extending his mercy unto a thousand generations of them that fear him.   Secondly, by his grace of election which is most free and *not tied to any conditions ;* by which I make no doubt that God taketh many infants unto himself in Christ, *whose parents never knew, or had been despisers of, the gospel.*   And this is the doctrine of our [English] Church, agreeable to the Scripture affirming the desert of original sin to be God's wrath and damnation."

Matthew Henry (On 2 Sam. 12 : 15–25) remarks respecting infant salvation :   "Nathan had told David that the child should certainly die, yet while it is within the reach of prayer he earnestly intercedes with God for it, chiefly, we may suppose, that its soul might be safe and happy in another world, and that his own sin might not come against the child, and that it might not fare the worse for that in the future state.   The child died when it was seven days old, and therefore not circumcised, which David might perhaps interpret as a further token of God's displeasure, that it died before it was brought under the seal of the covenant.   Yet he doth not therefore doubt of its being happy, for the benefits of the covenant do not depend upon the seals.   Godly parents have great reason to hope concerning their children that die in infancy, that it is well with their souls in the other world ; for the promise is ' to us and our seed,' which shall be performed to those who do not put a bar in their own door, as infants do not."

Vol. II., p. 719.   Graves (Pentateuch II., iii.) remarks upon "The striking difference that exists between the Mosaic penal code, and that of most modern states.   No injury affecting property was punished by death.   Restitution was required, or an additional fine imposed suited to the nature of the offence ; or at the utmost, if the offender was too poor to make restitution, or pay the regulated fine, he might be sold as a slave, still, however, within the pale of the Jewish nation.   But this slavery could not exceed seven years, as the Sabbatic year would terminate it. It must be acknowledged that the Jewish law adjusted its punishments more suitably to the real degree of moral depravity of the different species of crime, than modern codes which permit some of the most atrocious instances of moral turpitude to pass with trivial punishments, or none at all, while they punish even slight invasions of property with ignominious death. If in England the crimes of adultery, obstinate disobedience to parents, and perjury when intended to destroy the innocent man's life, cannot now be capitally punished, because penal laws so extremely rigorous would not be executed, and therefore would be ineffectual, while we daily see our scaffolds loaded with criminals prosecuted and condemned for violations of property, will the conclusion be favorable to modern manners? Can we avoid suspecting that our hearts are more anxious for money than for virtue; and that such lenity proves we slight the crimes to which we are thus indulgent, notwithstanding the religion we profess, rather than that we act from pure mercy to the criminal?" In the Levitical economy, no sacrifice was appointed for the crime of murder. "Ye shall take no satisfaction (כֹּפֶר) for the life of a murderer which is guilty of death; but he shall surely be put to death" (Num. 35 : 31).

Vol. II., p. 734. The spontaneous impulse to invoke the holy and just retribution of God upon diabolical wickedness, when it is persisted in and not repented of, finds expression in the imprecatory psalms; only purified by impersonal judicial feeling from the personal and selfish emotion which exasperates the natural man. Those who would exclude the imprecatory psalms from both the liturgical and the didactic services of the church utterly misconceive their nature. They suppose them to be the expression of the revengeful anger of the individual on account of some injury done to himself by sin, instead of being *the judicial displeasure of the conscience* at sin as the

violation of the divine law and the dishonor of God. " Do
not I hate them, O Lord, that hate thee? I hate them
with perfect hatred; I count them mine enemies " (Ps.
139 : 21, 22). In this instance, David hates the hater of
God, not the hater of himself. The person spoken of is
not David's enemy, but God's enemy; by reason of his
own love and reverence for God he so identifies himself
with God that he "counts" God's enemy as his own
enemy, and his invocation of the Divine retribution thereby obtains the dispassionateness and righteousness of
God's own action (Ps. 119 : 52, 53.) The following extract
from Tholuck (On the Psalms, Introduction IV., iii.)
places the subject in a clear and true light. " The attitude
of the Psalmists towards their enemies has always formed
an objection to their morality. Instead of the mild voice
of placability and compassion, we hear, it is said, the tu-
mult of revenge, and prayers for the condemnation of their
foes. Augustine felt this difficulty, and endeavored to remove it by saying that the reference is not to the *wishes* of
the Psalmists, but only to *predictions* of God's retributions
suspended over confirmed sinners. 'In verbis quidem
figura optantis apparet, sed intelligitur præscientia nunti-
antis' (Sermo xxii.). The opinion is considerably current
that love to enemies is enjoined as a duty only in the
New Testament. But the erroneousness of this is evident
from Ex. 23 : 4, 5 ; Lev. 19 : 18 ; Job 31 : 29 ; Prov. 24 : 17,
18, 29 ; 25 : 21, 22. In order to form a right estimate of
the imprecatory psalms, we must consider *the end contemplated by punishment.* One view is that with God, and
also with the truly righteous man, punishment springs
from benevolence and love, and contemplates the improvement of man. But what is to be done if you have to do
with an impenitent and incorrigible sinner? By his impenitence he is persisting in sin, justifying his sin, and
reaffirming it. No one, certainly, would maintain that
this concentration of sin into hardness and insensibility

is a reason why it should not suffer the intrinsic desert of sin. That there is no prospect and probability of improvement in this case is no reason why the criminal should be dismissed without any infliction. Improvement as the end does not exhaust the purpose of penalty. Philosophy agrees with Christianity that the first and principal purpose of punishment is *retribution;* that is, that the happiness of the individual criminal be wholly sacrificed to the higher demands of justice as expressed in the law of God and the State. Hence to demand, not from selfish and personal motives but from a sense of the holiness of God and his law, that the hardened sinner be punished in order to vindicate the authority of both, is as little to be regarded as evidencing moral imperfection, as to desire that those who are susceptible of improvement should be reformed by means of painful correctives. If, therefore, it can be shown that the imprecations and prayers for the Divine retribution do not flow from the vindictive disposition, the personal irritability, and passion of the Psalmist, but from the conscientious and unselfish motives relating to God and law just now alluded to, the objection to the imprecatory psalms is removed. These supplications would then correspond to the desire of a good monarch, or a just judge, to discover the guilty that justice might be administered. David the king gives expression to this desire in many instances. 'I will walk within my house with a perfect heart. I will set no wicked thing before mine eyes; I hate the work of them that turn aside; it shall not cleave to me. A froward heart shall depart from me; I will not know a wicked person. Whoso privily slandereth his neighbor, him will I cut off; him that hath a high look and a proud heart will not I suffer. He that worketh deceit shall not dwell within my house; he that telleth lies shall not tarry in my sight. I will early destroy all the wicked of the land; that I may cut off all wicked doers from the city of the Lord' (Ps. 101). It is not injury and dishonor to himself personally to which he refers in this language, but dishonor to God. He disavows personal and selfish revenge. ' If I have rewarded evil unto him that was at peace with me (yea, I have delivered him that without cause is mine enemy), let the enemy pursue my soul and take it; yea, let him tread down my life upon the earth' (Ps. 7 : 5, 6). Having sinned, he invokes punitive infliction upon himself. ' Let the righteous [God] smite me, it shall be a kindness; and let him reprove me, it shall be an excellent oil' (Ps. 141 : 5)."

" The Psalmists frequently mention reasons like the following for their prayers for the punishment of sinners : that the holiness of God and his righteous government of the world should be acknowledged; that the faith of the pious should be strengthened; that the haughtiness of the ungodly should be brought within bounds ; that they should know that God is the righteous judge of the world, and that the fulfilment of his promises to maintain right and justice should not fail.   See Ps. 5 : 11, 12 ; 9 : 20, 21 ; 12: 9 ; 22 : 23–32 ; 28 : 4, 5 ; 35 : 24 ; 40 : 17 ; 59 : 14 ; 109: 27 ; 142 : 8.   The invocation of the Divine judgments upon the heathen, such as Ps. 79 : 6, ' Pour out thy wrath upon the heathen that have not known thee; and upon the kingdoms that have not called upon thy name,' is the expression of a desire that the true religion may prevail in the earth.   The victory of the heathen over Israel threatened the destruction of it.   Moreover, it should be observed that aversion towards a nation as a whole, on account of its enmity to Jehovah, does not exclude sympathy and kindness towards the individuals of it viewed merely as human beings.   An instance of this kind occurs in 2 Kings 6 : 22.   From this point of view, even Lessing once advocated the so-called vindictive psalms."

" In the New Testament the same expression of desire for righteous retribution upon the incorrigibly wicked appears.   In terms not less severe than those in the Psalms,

Christ announces judgment to the 'cursed' (Matt. 25 : 41), and sentences the hypocritical and selfish Pharisees to 'the damnation of hell' (Matt. 23 : 33). Peter in the name of God smote Ananias and Sapphira with instantaneous death, for their blasphemy of the Holy Ghost; and his words to both of them contain not the slightest trace of personal and selfish anger. He said to Simon the sorcerer, in holy indignation, 'Thy money perish with thee,' yet added, 'Repent therefore of this thy wickedness.' Did not Paul strike Elymas the sorcerer with blindness, and call him a 'child of the devil'? Did he not solemnly 'deliver unto Satan for the destruction of the flesh' the wicked Corinthian who had married his step-mother, and say, 'Alexander the coppersmith did me much evil; the Lord reward him according to his works'? Such is the general nature of the imprecations in the Psalms, even if we should concede that in a few instances, like Ps. 137 : 8, 9, there may have been some blending of the unhallowed flame of personal passion with the holy fire."

In his comment upon Ps. 5 : 10, Tholuck thus explains: "'Make them [consciously] guilty' means, 'May Divine justice cause them to *feel* their guilt by the failure of their enterprises, and make them perceive that they did not only oppose man but God.' The Lord said (Deut. 32: 35), 'To me belongeth vengeance and recompense.' That declaration caused David to refrain from taking vengeance into his own hands and to refer it to God, as he said to Saul, 'The Lord judge between me and thee, and the Lord avenge me of thee; but mine hand shall not be upon thee' (1 Sam. 24:12). In this psalm, he supplicates vengeance at the hands of God, not for his personal gratification, but mainly because the cause of oppressed innocence is always that of God, and because the Divine glory is sullied when wickedness triumphs. Proud men have not the remotest idea that God sets so great a value upon poor mortals that he should consider his eternal majesty injured when they

are injured. They no more think that their blows will
strike heaven than they do when they tread the dust or
mud under foot. But the Divine wisdom now and then
furnishes the most palpable evidence how precious are to
him those 'little ones,' as Christ calls them. With this
correspond the words of the prophet, 'He that toucheth
you, toucheth the apple of his eye' (Zech. 2 : 8). As still
another ground for the supplicated manifestation of God's
punitive justice, the Psalmist adduces the eternal praise
and gratitude of the entire company of the godly which
should be paid to him for this manifestation. 'I remembered thy judgments of old, O Lord, and have comforted
myself' (Ps. 119 : 52). For God is not like an unfeeling
idol, unheedful of the sacrifices of praise which man his
creature offers to him, but he is like a father who rejoices
in the honor and love which his children bear to him.
David, here and elsewhere, so completely regards all the
pious as one component whole, where if 'one member be
honored all the members rejoice with it' (1 Cor. 12 : 26),
that he considers his own deliverance as their common
interest ; for are not benefits conferred on individuals
pledges to the rest ? "

It must always be remembered that when the Psalmist
invokes the retribution of God upon the enemies of God,
he supposes their impenitence and persistence in enmity.
And what other feeling than the desire that obstinate and
persevering hostility to God and his government should
be punished is proper ? David never calls down the
judicial vengeance of heaven upon the humble and penitent man who confesses his sin and endeavors to forsake
it. This shows that his feeling is not revengeful and selfish ; for when mere revenge exists, no discrimination is
made between penitence and impenitence. The cry for
mercy is disregarded by the malignant and exasperated
man, and he wreaks his anger upon the object of it, without regard to the state of mind which may be in the one

who has injured him. When David says, "Mine eye also shall see my desire upon mine enemies, and mine ears also shall hear my desire of the wicked that shall rise up against me" (Ps. 92:11), he assumes that there is no relenting on their part, and no intention to change their course of conduct. And that "mine enemies" means God's enemies is proved by the preceding context : "For, lo, thine enemies, O Lord, for, lo, thine enemies shall perish; all the workers of iniquity shall be scattered" (Ps. 92 : 9).

Butler (On Human Nature, Sermon vi.) evinces the ethical nature of dispassionate resentment against hardened and obstinate wickedness. "The indignation raised by cruelty and injustice, and the desire to have it punished which persons even when not affected by it feel, is by no means malice. No ; it is resentment against vice and wickedness, it is one of the common bonds by which society is held together, a fellow-feeling which each individual has in behalf of the whole species, as well as of himself ; and it does not appear that this, generally speaking, is at all too excessive among mankind. It is not natural but moral evil, it is not suffering but injury, which raises that anger or resentment of which we are speaking. The natural object of it is not one who appears to the suffering person to have been only the innocent occasion of his pain or loss, but one who has been in a moral sense injurious to himself or others."

VOL. II., p. 746. The existence of a comparatively small kingdom of evil within the vast holy and blessed universe of God is plainly taught in the Apocalypse. 1. It is denominated "the bottomless pit." "The fifth angel sounded, and to him was given the key of the bottomless pit. And he opened the bottomless pit; and there arose a smoke out of the pit, as the smoke of a great furnace. And there came out of the smoke locusts upon the earth ; and unto them was given power as the scorpions of earth have power. And it was commanded them that they should hurt only those men which have not the seal of God in their foreheads. And their torment was as the torment of a scorpion when he striketh a man " (Rev. 9 : 1–5). 2. Satan, or the Devil, is the prince and head of this kingdom. " They had a king over them, which is the angel of the bottomless pit, whose name in the Hebrew tongue is Abaddon, but in the Greek tongue hath his name Apollyon " (Rev. 9 : 11). " And the great dragon was cast out, that old serpent the Devil, and Satan, which deceiveth the whole world ; he was cast out into the earth, and his angels were cast out with him " (Rev. 12 : 9). 3. The members of the kingdom of evil are characterized by willing, wilful, and intense hatred of God and holiness, and by an impenitent and blaspheming spirit. " They worshipped the beast, saying, Who is like unto the beast ? who is able to make war with him ? And the beast opened his mouth in blasphemy against God, to blaspheme his name, and his tabernacle, and them that dwell in heaven. And they blasphemed the God of heaven because of their pains, and repented not of their deeds " (Rev. 13 : 4, 6 ; 16 : 11). 4. The misery of the kingdom of evil is awful and endless. " The smoke of their torment ascendeth up forever and ever ; and they have no rest day nor night, who worship the beast and his image, and whosoever receiveth the mark of his name. The beast and the false prophet shall be tormented day and night forever and ever " (Rev. 14 : 11 ; 20 : 10).

Vol. II., p. 749. The Bohemian Confession (Art. iv.) enunciates the often-forgotten truth, that the torments of hell, like sin itself, originate in the finite will, not in the Infinite ; in man, not in God. " Ut enim Deus non est causa peccati, ita non est [causa] pœnæ." The author of sin is the real author of hell. Says Augustine (Trinity, IV., xii.), " The judge inflicts punishment on the guilty ; yet it is not *the justice of the judge*, but *the desert of the crime*, which is the cause of punishment."

Vol. II., p. 751. The boundlessness of the Divine mercy, of which Dante speaks, supposes penitence for sin, and penitence necessarily begins with the acknowledgment of justice, because mercy exists and is known only as the *antithesis* of justice. If there were no justice in God, there could be no mercy in him; for mercy is releasing from justice. Here is the fatal defect in spurious penitence. The sinner does not begin at the beginning, by bending the knee before the Holy One. Justice must first be recognized in order to any experience of mercy. Whoever denies the justice of God and recalcitrates at it will be eternally kept in *contact* and *conflict* with it, and never know anything of the Divine compassion. He will find it an iron wall through which he cannot break. God, for him, will be a perfectly just and righteously punitive being, and nothing more. But whoever humbly recognizes justice by confessing sin and guilt will find that the Supreme Being is infinitely and tenderly pitiful, and will forgive and eradicate the deepest sin. For the mercy has been manifested at the cost to the Eternal Trinity of a self-sacrifice to satisfy justice of which neither man nor angel has any conception, and which was necessitated by the *inexorable* nature of law and retribution. To deny, therefore, or combat this inexorableness makes the manifestation of pity and mercy on the part of God an utter impossibility.

Accordingly, in all the Biblical descriptions of the lost, the absence of sorrow for sin as related to justice, and the hatred of justice itself, are invariable elements. Satan and his angels, together with condemned men, are utterly and malignantly impenitent. "The fourth angel poured out his vial upon the sun; and power was given unto him to scorch men with fire. And men were scorched with great heat, and blasphemed the name of God who hath power over these plagues; and *they repented not* to give him glory. And the fifth angel poured out his vial upon the seat of the beast; and his kingdom was full of darkness; and they gnawed their tongues for pain, and blasphemed the God of heaven because of their pains and their sores, and *repented not* of their deeds " (Rev. 16 : 8–11). Lost men " despise the goodness, and forbearance, and long-suffering of God, that lead to *repentance*," and "in proportion to (*κατὰ*) their *hardness and impenitent heart*, treasure up wrath against the day of wrath" (Rom. 2 : 4, 5).